Pro WCF 4

Practical Microsoft SOA Implementation
SECOND EDITION

Nishith Pathak

Apress®

Pro WCF 4: Practical Microsoft SOA Implementation, Second Edition

ISBN-13 (pbk): 978-1-4302-3368-8

ISBN-13 (electronic): 978-1-4302-3368-5

Printed and bound in the United States of America 9 8 7 6 5 4 3 2 1

President and Publisher: Paul Manning
Lead Editor: Mark Beckner
Development Editor: Jonathan Hassell
Technical Reviewer: Henry Li
Editorial Board: Steve Anglin, Mark Beckner, Ewan Buckingham, Gary Cornell, Jonathan Gennick, Jonathan Hassell, Michelle Lowman, Matthew Moodie, Jeff Olson, Jeffrey Pepper, Frank Pohlmann, Douglas Pundick, Ben Renow-Clarke, Dominic Shakeshaft, Matt Wade, Tom Welsh
Coordinating Editor: Adam Heath
Copy Editor: Damon Larson
Compositor: MacPS, LLC.
Indexer: BIM Indexing and Proofreading Services
Artist: April Milne
Cover Designer: Anna Ishchenko

Distributed to the book trade worldwide by Springer Science+Business Media, LLC., 233 Spring Street, 6th Floor, New York, NY 10013. Phone 1-800-SPRINGER, fax (201) 348-4505, e-mail orders-ny@springer-sbm.com, or visit www.springeronline.com.

For information on translations, please e-mail rights@apress.com, or visit www.apress.com.

Apress and friends of ED books may be purchased in bulk for academic, corporate, or promotional use. eBook versions and licenses are also available for most titles. For more information, reference our Special Bulk Sales–eBook Licensing web page at www.apress.com/info/bulksales.

The source code for this book is available to readers at www.apress.com. You will need to answer questions pertaining to this book in order to successfully download the code.

To my grandfather Late Mahesh Chandra Pathak for his blessings and moral values. To my parents, Pankaj and Bina Pathak, for their immense support and for teaching me to do what I believe in. You are really Most Valuable Parents (MVPs) of this world. To my lovely sister, Tanwi—your smiling face gives me a lot of strength and inspiration to do better each day. To my Guruji JP Kukreti, who has been there for me countless times and is always someone who provides me with comfort, understanding, spiritual beliefs, and lots of motivation. Guruji, this book would not have been possible without your blessings and inspirations. I also appreciate the help, support, and encouragement of my friends. Lastly, I thank God for blessing me with such wonderful people in my life.

Contents at a Glance

Contents

About the Author

 **Nishith Pathak** is a Microsoft Most Valuable Professional (MVP), reviewer, published Apress author, speaker, and Microsoft purist who has been working on the .NET platform since its early beta days. Nishith was born, raised, and educated in a town called Kotdwara in Uttarakhand, India. His expertise lies in architecting and delivering enterprise solutions to Fortune 100 companies spanning the globe. He is a contributing author and an avid technical reviewer for multiple electronic and print publications. Over the years, he has also been involved in providing consultancy and training services to corporations. Nishith is also a frequent speaker, and conducts webcasts for Microsoft India and user groups on various upcoming technologies.

Nishith lives in Delhi, India. He is a member of various advisor groups for Microsoft. Currently, he is focused on key areas of the Microsoft platform, specifically cloud computing, building rich Internet applications, and helping companies architect solutions based on service-oriented architecture. Beyond that, as time permits, he spends time with his friends and amuses them with his interests in palmistry and astrology. You can contact him at nispathak@hotmail.com and visit his blog at http://dotnetpathak.blogspot.com.

About the Technical Reviewer

 **Henry Li** has a strong background in laser physics and optics, and studied computer science in college in China. He is a technical consultant specializing in enterprise application integration and distributed systems solutions. Henry has many years of professional consultant experience with large-scale enterprise organizations as well as small businesses. He has worked with numerous large-scale middleware infrastructures, front-end and back-end architectures, and implementations based upon Microsoft .NET and BizTalk technology. He has served clients such as diversity enterprise organizations, government agencies, semiconductor manufactures, and industry equipment facility manufactures. He is also author of the book *Introducting Windows Azure* (Apress, 2010).

Acknowledgments

First and foremost, thanks to all of the people at Apress who put their sincere efforts into publishing this book. Mark Beckner and Adam Heath deserve special thanks. I remember exchanging a lot of e-mails with Mark before really taking on this project. Thanks to Adam for doing a fabulous job of project management and constantly pushing me to do my best. Thanks also go to Jonathan Hassell, who reviewed the book and made extensive suggestions. I would like to thank Henry Li for his tech review. Damon Larson saved me from a series of embarrassing errors and omissions. I am really amazed with your efficient copyediting work. It was a pleasure working with you. I would not hesitate to say that you are all extremely talented people. Each of you helped this book immensely, and I'm looking forward to working with everyone on the next one. Last but not least, thanks to my family and friends, and the people of Kotdwara, Uttarakhand, India for being so kind and supportive, and making my dreams come true.

—Nishith Pathak

Introduction

This book is a complete guide to Windows Communication Foundation (WCF) from a service-oriented architecture (SOA) perspective. With each new version of the .NET Framework, Microsoft has improved many key areas of WCF. In .NET 4.0, Microsoft has given developers a better experience and enabled them to become more productive. The book not only provides deep insight into the new WCF functionality that ships with .NET 4.0—such as service discovery, routing services, and simplified configuration—but also provides extensive examples to make it easier to put the new concepts into practice. You'll learn how to move your current offerings to WCF, and how to integrate those applications with WCF 4.0. This book offers genuine insight into solving real enterprise problems using WCF and .NET 4.0. This books covers the following:

- The new features of WCF with .NET 4.0

- The WCF programming model

- Implementing WS-Discovery and routing services in WCF

- How queue management and reliable messaging work in WCF

- Implementing transaction support in WCF

- How to make WCF services interoperable with other SOA offerings

- Best practices for using WCF effectively

- Developing WCF applications with Visual Studio 2010

It will also address the business drivers that dictate the need for these WCF features, as well as the industry best practices for applying them.

Who This Book Is For

The release of .NET 4.0 brought a wide range of new functionality to WCF. Developers and architects with experience using WCF 3.5 or earlier who want to be able to apply this new functionality to their applications will benefit greatly from the discussions and code samples in this book. This book is also a great resource for application developers and architects new to SOA and/or the core concepts of WCF.

An Overview of This Book

This book specifically targets WCF in .NET 4.0. The text that you hold in your hands is a massive retelling of this book's first printing to account for all of the major changes that are found in .NET 4.0. Not only will you find brand-new chapters, you will find that many of the previous chapters have been expanded in great detail. This book divided into three parts, each of which contains related chapters. The following sections describe each part. The book also has one appendix, where you'll find a description of the sample application used throughout this book.

Part 1: Introducing Windows Communication Foundation

This part of the book explains the business motives and pain points of the various distributed technologies developed by Microsoft. It explains how you can address these issues using WCF. Once you understand some of these basic concepts of WCF, including the business and technological factors, you can appreciate its simplicity and flexibility. Chapter 1 covers the service standards and introduces WCF. Chapter 2 explains the new features of WCF that ship with .NET 4.0. Chapter 3 discusses the unified programming model of WCF and how WCF provides the best tools for creating secure, interoperable web services.

Part 2: Programming with WCF

This part covers the technical features of WCF in detail. You'll concentrate on the programming aspects of WCF with the assistance of a fictitious stock market application. Chapter 4 guides you through installing and creating WCF services. Chapter 5 covers creating services, and the various hosting options available in WCF services. Chapter 6 discusses how to manage WCF services to obtain the best return on investment for your application.

Part 3: Advanced Topics in WCF

Real-world SOA applications will have many demanding features to implement. These complex real-world web service implementations will address security issues (both client and service), reliable messaging, transactions, COM+ integration, data integration issues, and peer-to-peer communications. In Chapters 7 through 12, you will concentrate on these topics. In addition, you'll investigate the WCF interoperability options available to seamlessly communicate with non-Microsoft platforms in Chapter 13.

Prerequisites

To get the most out of this book, you should install WCF and the .NET Framework 4.0. I recommend using Microsoft Visual Studio 2010 as the development environment to experiment with the code samples, which you can find in the Source Code section of the Apress web site (www.apress.com).

Obtaining Updates for This Book

As you read through this text, you may find the occasional grammatical or code error (although I sure hope not). If this is the case my sincere apologies. Being human, I am sure that a glitch or two may be present, regardless of my best efforts. If this is the case, you can obtain the current errata list from the Apress web site (located once again on the home page for this book), as well as information on how to notify me of any errors you might find.

Contacting the Author

If you have any questions regarding this book's source code, are in need of clarification for a given example, or simply wish to offer your thoughts regarding WCF and .NET 4.0, feel free to drop me a line at nispathak@hotmail.com. I will do my best to get back to you in a timely fashion; however, like yourself, I get busy from time to time.

Thanks for buying this text. I hope you enjoy reading it and putting your newfound knowledge to good use.

PART I

Introducing Windows Communication Foundation

Part 1 of this book introduces web service standards and the fundamental components of service-oriented architecture (SOA). Once you have an understanding of some of these concepts, you can appreciate the simplicity and flexibility of Windows Communication Foundation (WCF). This part also discusses how SOA principles are applied in WCF. Chapter 1 covers the reasons SOA is needed, and provides a brief introduction to WCF. Chapter 2 looks at some of the key new features of WCF that were released with .NET 4.0. This is followed by a discussion of the WCF programming model in Chapter 3.

■ ■ ■

WCF and SOA Basics

In today's world, implementing distributed systems that provide business value in a reliable fashion presents many challenges. We take many features for granted when developing nondistributed systems—features that can become issues when working with disparate distributed systems. Although some of these challenges are obvious (such as a loss of connectivity leading to data being lost or corrupted), for other aspects—such as tightly coupled systems—the dependencies between various system components make it cost prohibitive to make changes to meet the demands of the business. Business processes are quite often supported by systems that run on different platforms and technologies both within and outside of the organization. Service-oriented architecture (SOA) is a mechanism that enables organizations to facilitate communication between systems running on multiple platforms.

During the past decade, a lot of research has been done in the field of distributed computing. Microsoft and other leading vendors have come up with various distributed technologies. Each of these technologies reduces the convolution of building rich applications and lowers development costs. The latest from Microsoft is Windows Communication Foundation (WCF), which provides a uniform way of developing distributed applications by providing a service-oriented programming model.

WCF (formerly known as Indigo) handles the communication infrastructure of .NET 3.x and later, which allows you to create a diverse range of applications through its simplified model. Based on the notion of services, WCF contains the best features of today's distributed technology stack for developing the connected systems. This chapter not only introduces the fundamental concepts of SOA, but also provides a brief discussion of WCF and its features. After completing this chapter, you will have learned about the following:

- What SOA means, and what makes it the preferred approach to designing complex heterogeneous IT systems

- The four tenets of SOA

- Existing distributed technologies and their pitfalls

- The key architectural concepts and features that underpin WCF

- How WCF unifies existing distributed technologies

Understanding SOA

It is not practical to build monolithic systems in current multinational enterprises. These systems often take many years to implement and usually address a narrow set of objectives. Today a business needs to be agile and adapt processes quickly, and SOA is a design principle that can help address this business need. Although any kind of implementation can be an SOA implementation, unfortunately many implementations using web services are marketed as SOA implementations when they are not.

In reality, SOA is a collection of *well-defined services*. A *service* is an autonomous (business) system that accepts one or more requests and returns one or more responses via a set of published and well-defined interfaces. Each of these individual services can be modified independently of other services to help respond to the ever-evolving market conditions of a business.

Unlike traditional, tightly coupled architectures, SOA implements a set of loosely coupled services that collectively achieve the desired results; in addition, since the underlying implementation details are hidden from the consumer, changes to the implementation won't affect the service, as long as the contract does not change. This allows systems based on SOA to respond more quickly and cost-effectively for the business.

Although some of these aspects might be similar to component-based development (which is based on strict interfaces), the key difference is that SOA provides an approach based on open standards and generic messages that aren't specific to any platform or programming language. As a result, you can achieve a high degree of loose coupling and interoperability across platforms and technologies.

■**Note** Although SOA might seem abstract, it marks a significant shift from procedural and object-oriented languages to a more loosely coupled set of autonomous tasks. SOA is more than a collection of services. It's a methodology encompassing policies, procedures, and best practices that allow the services to be provided and consumed effectively. SOA is not a product that can be bought off the shelf; however, many vendors have products that can form the basis of an SOA implementation.

It is important that the services don't get reduced to a set of interfaces, since they are the keys to communication between the provider and the consumer of the service. In a traditional client-server world, the provider will be a server and the consumer will be a client. When factoring in services, try to model the flow and process on recognized business events and existing business processes. You also need to answer a few questions to ensure a clean design for services:

- What services do you need?
- What services are available to consume?
- What services will operate together?
- What substitute services are available?
- What dependencies exist between various services and other applications?
- Does the application have components that qualify it for being a service?

Service orientation, as described earlier, is about services and messages. Figure 1–1 shows an example of how service providers and consumers can coexist with a repository to form an SOA implementation. Service *providers* are components that execute some business logic based on predetermined inputs and outputs, and expose this functionality through an SOA implementation. A *consumer*, on the other hand, is a set of components interested in using one or more of the services offered by the providers. A *repository* contains a description of the services, where the providers register their services and consumers find what services are provided.

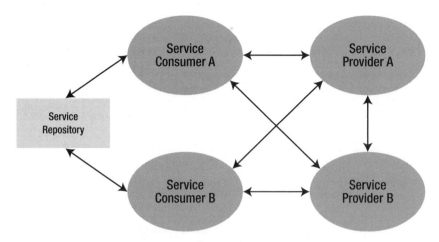

Figure 1–1. *How SOA components interact with each other*

What Is a Service?

The term *service* has been used to describe everything from web services (discussed later in the chapter) to business processes. You should use services to represent the functions of the business and explicitly define the boundaries of what the business does, which essentially will define what the service can and cannot do. The key is that it is not a technology-driven approach, but rather a business-driven approach.

■**Note** The term *loose coupling* refers to situations in which any two entities reduce the assumptions they make about each other when they try to exchange information. Contrary to this, tight coupling increases the range of assumptions made between two entities (such as when the communication protocol becomes more complex), as well as the efficiency of their communication. However, the two entities also become less tolerant to changes in, say, interruptions in the communication, because they are tightly bound (or coupled) to each other. Local method invocation is an excellent example of tight coupling, because it requires many assumptions to be made between the called and calling routines, since both need to be in the same process, use the same language, pass the same number of parameters in the agreed data formats, and so on.

Service orientation is a business-driven modeling strategy that defines business functionality in terms of loosely coupled autonomous business systems (or services) that exchange information based on messages. The term *services* is used in many contexts, but in the context of service orientation, a service is based on four fundamental tenets. We'll discuss these four tenets, originally proposed by the WCF team at Microsoft, in the following sections.

Tenet 1: Boundaries Are Explicit

Crossing boundaries is an expensive operation because it can constitute various elements, such as data marshaling, security, physical location, and so on. Some of the design principles to keep in mind vis-à-vis the first tenet are as follows:

- *Know your boundaries*: A well-defined and published public interface is the main entry point into the service, and all interactions occur using that.

- *Services should be easy to consume*: It should be easy for other developers to consume the service. Also, the service interface should allow the ability to evolve over time without breaking existing consumers of the service.

- *Avoid remote procedure call (RPC) interfaces*: Instead, use explicit messages.

- *Keep the service surface area small*: Provide fewer public interfaces, make sure they accept a well-defined message, and make them respond likewise with a well-defined message. As the number of public interfaces grows, it becomes increasingly difficult to consume and maintain the service.

- *Don't expose implementation details*: These should be kept internal in order to avoid tight coupling between the consumer and the service.

Tenet 2: Services Are Autonomous

Services are self-contained and act independently in all aspects—deploying, versioning, and so on. Any assumptions made to the contrary about the service boundaries will most likely cause the boundaries to change themselves. Services need to be isolated and decoupled to accomplish the goal of making them autonomous.

The design principles to keep in mind for the second tenet are as follows:

- Service versioning and deployment are independent of the system in which they are deployed.

- Contracts, once published, should not be changed.

- Adopt a pessimistic approach, and isolate services from failure.

■**Note** *Business Process Execution Language (BPEL)* is a business process language that is based on XML and built using web service standards. You can use BPEL to define and manage a long-running business process. BPEL is an orchestration language and is used for abstracting the "collaboration and sequencing" logic from various web services into a formal process definition that is based on XML, Web Services Description Language (WSDL), and XML Schema. BPEL is also known as BPEL4WS or WSBPEL.

Tenet 3: Services Share the Schema and Contract, Not the Class

Services interacts using policies, schemas, and behaviors instead of classes, which have traditionally provided most of this functionality. The service contract should contain the message formats (defined using an XML schema), message exchange patterns (MEPs, which are defined in WSDL), any WS-Policy requirements, and any BPEL that may be required. The biggest challenge you face is the stability of the service, once it has been published, which can become difficult to change without impacting any of the consumers.

The design principles to keep in mind for the third tenet are as follows:

- Service contracts constituting data, WSDL, and the policy do not change, and remain stable.

- Contracts should be as explicit as possible; this will ensure that there is no confusion over the intent and use of the service. Additional contracts should be defined for newer versions of the server in the future.

- If breaking service contracts is inescapable, then version the services, because this minimizes the ripple effect to existing consumers of the service.

- Do not expose internal data representation publicly; the public data scheme should be absolute.

Tenet 4: Service Compatibility Is Based on Policy

At times you will not be able to express all the requirements of service interaction via WSDL alone; this is when you can use policies. Policy expressions essentially separate the structural and semantic compatibilities. In other words, they separate what is communicated from how/to whom a message is communicated. A policy assertion identifies a behavior of a policy entity and provides domain-specific semantics. When designing a service, you need to ensure that policy assertions are as explicit as possible regarding service expectations and semantic compatibilities.

The four tenets of service orientation provide you with a set of fundamental principles when you are designing services. When defining a service, it is always easier to work with well-defined requirements, because that allows for a well-defined scope and purpose of a service. This enables a service to encapsulate distinct functionality with a clear-cut context. Sadly, more often than not, requirements are not well defined, which poses more of a problem. It is difficult to define the service that accurately represents its capabilities because one cannot relate the service operations by some logical context.

When defining services from scratch, it is helpful to categorize them according to the set of existing business service models already established within the organization. Because these models already establish some of the context and purpose within their boundaries, new services are easier to design.

In addition, the naming of the service should also influence the naming of the individual operations within the service. As stated earlier, a well-named service will already establish a clear context for and meaning of the service, and the individual operations should be rationalized so as not to be confusing or contradict the service. Also, because the context is established, you should use clear and concise naming standards for your operations. For example, a service that performs stock operations would have an operation named GetQuote, as opposed to GetStockQuote, because the stock context has already been established. Similarly, if you can reuse the service, then avoid naming the operations after some particular task; rather, try to keep the naming as generic as possible.

Naming conventions might not seem important at first, but as your service inventory in the organization grows, so will the potential to reuse and leverage the existing service to achieve integration within the various groups and systems. The effort required to establish a consistent naming convention within an organization pays off quickly. A consistent set of services that cleanly establishes the level of clarity between the services enables easier interoperability and reuse.

Unfortunately, no magic bullet can help you standardize at the right level of granularity that will enable service orientation. But the key point to remember is that the service should achieve the right balance to facilitate both current and upcoming data requirements, in essence meeting the business's need to be more agile and responsive to market conditions.

COMPONENTS VS. SERVICES: ARE THEY THE SAME?

It is natural to be confused about the terms *component* and *service*, and what they mean. A *component* is a piece of compiled code that can be assembled with other components to build applications. Components can also be easily reused within the same application or across different applications. This helps reduce the cost of developing and maintaining the application once the components mature within an organization. Components are usually associated with the object-oriented programming (OOP) paradigm.

A *service* is implemented by one or more components, and is a higher-level aggregation. Component reuse seems to work well in homogeneous environments; service orientation fills the gap by establishing reuse in heterogeneous environments by aggregating one or more components into a service and making them accessible through messages using open standards. These service definitions are deployed with the service, and they govern the communication from the consumers of the service via various contracts and policies, among other things.

SOA also assists in promoting reuse in the enterprise. Services can provide a significant benefit because you can achieve reuse at many levels of abstraction, as compared to traditional methods (e.g., object orientation provides only objects as the primary reuse mechanism). SOA can offer reuse at multiple levels, including code, services, and functionality. This feature enhances flexibility in the design of enterprise applications.

WCF makes it easier for developers to create services that adhere to the principle of service orientation. For example, on the inside communication, you can use object-oriented technology to implement one or more components that constitute a service. The outside communication with the service is based on messages. In the end, both of these technologies are complementary to each other and collectively provide the overall SOA architecture.

A Brief History of the Microsoft Distributed Stack

Microsoft developed the *Component Object Model (COM)* to enable applications to interact with each other and to promote reusability. COM is a set of specifications that, when followed, allows software components to communicate with each other. Although COM provides the ability to reuse the components locally, it was not designed to work well with remote components.

Few specifications and extensions have been made that were based on COM and that interacted with remote components. However, the need for remote method invocations grew substantially. To address this concern, Microsoft developed the *Distributed Component Object Model (DCOM)*. DCOM is a proprietary wire protocol standard from Microsoft that extends COM, so it works in distributed environments. DCOM provides an opportunity to distribute your component across different locations according to the application requirements. In addition, DCOM provides basic infrastructure support, such as reliability, security, location independence, and efficient communication between COM objects that reside across processes and machines.

Though COM and DCOM are able to provide reusability and a distributed platform, they suffer from problems of versioning, reference counting, and so on. To remedy this, Microsoft introduced .NET, the result of a vision to be more connected than ever. Microsoft wanted to deliver software as a "service" and also resolve issues related to COM/DCOM. The release of .NET was seen as the biggest revolution on the Microsoft platform after the introduction of Windows.

.NET Remoting was introduced to provide a way to create distributed applications in .NET. (Today, developers have additional options for creating distributed applications, including XML web services and service components). Essentially, .NET Remoting takes a lot of lessons from DCOM. It replaces DCOM as the preferred technology for building distributed applications. It addresses problems that have wounded distributed applications for many years (i.e., interoperability support, extensibility support, efficient lifetime management, custom hosts, and an easy configuration process). .NET Remoting delivers on the promises of easily distributed computing by providing a simple, extensible programming model, without compromising flexibility, scalability, and robustness. It comes with a default implementation of components, including channels and protocols, but all of them are pluggable and can be replaced with better options without much code modification.

Prior to .NET, processes were used to isolate applications from each other. Each process had its own virtual address space, and the code that ran in one process could not access the code or data of another process. In .NET, one process can now run multiple applications in a separate application domain and thereby avoid cross-process communication in many scenarios. In normal situations, an object cannot access the data outside its application domain. Anything that crosses an application domain is marshaled by the .NET runtime. Not only does .NET Remoting enable communication between application domains, but it can also be extended across processes, machines, and networks. It is flexible with regard to the channels and formatters it can use, and it offers a wide variety of options for maintaining state.

Though .NET Remoting provides great performance and flexibility, it too suffers from some vital pitfalls. .NET Remoting works best when using assemblies that are developed using .NET. .NET Remoting works fairly well if one organization has control over both ends of the wire. Therefore, it works well in an intranet, where you have complete control of deployment, versioning, and testing; but it doesn't work as well over the Internet.

.NET Remoting is proprietary to .NET and works seamlessly to exchange data between two .NET applications. It is deeply rooted in the Common Language Runtime (CLR) and relies on the CLR to obtain metadata. This metadata means that the client must understand .NET in order to communicate with endpoints exposed by .NET Remoting.

Asynchronous-based communication requires a custom messaging infrastructure. Fortunately, many middleware systems, such as IBM's MQSeries and Microsoft Message Queuing (MSMQ), provide built-in, powerful capabilities to address these issues. (These packaged software products provide transactional support, guaranteed delivery, and security.)

Message queues are stores that hold application-specific messages. Applications can read, send, store, and delete the messages in queues. MSMQ is a set of objects that allows you to perform message queueing in Windows. You can use this technology to collect a series of messages, send them to the server for processing, and receive the results when they are finished. MSMQ essentially provides the infrastructure for developing highly available business-critical applications. System.Messaging is the .NET layer on top of MSMQ. It gives you the ability to build queued applications through .NET.

One of the limitations of MSMQ concerns the way it handles corrupted messages. A message is referred to as "corrupted" when the message cannot get processed after several attempts. These corrupted message(s) block other messages in the queue. Since MSMQ does not support the handling of corrupted message(s), developers used to write a lot of code to deal with them. Few features of MSMQ are tightly integrated with Active Directory. Another issue with MSMQ is that developers need to write MSMQ-specific plumbing code in client and service code, especially while writing complex listener code to listen to these queues.

Every distributed component requires some basic services to work in a multiuser environment. In the early days of COM, developers spent a large amount of time creating an infrastructure to handle large numbers of transactions, provide queuing infrastructure, and so on, for running the components.

COM+ (also known as *Component Services*) provides an infrastructure that applications use to access services and capabilities beyond the scope of the developers who are actually building those applications. It also supports multitier architecture by providing the surrogate process for hosting the business objects. In many ways, COM+ is a combination of COM, DCOM, Microsoft Transaction Server (MTS), and MSMQ in a single product. This application infrastructure includes services such as transactions, resource management, security, and synchronization. By providing these services, it enables you to concentrate on building serviced components rather than worrying about the infrastructure required to run these business components. COM+ was initially used to provide an infrastructure for COM components, but this does not mean it cannot be used from .NET. .NET components can also utilize COM+ services through the attributes and classes residing in the System.EnterpriseServices namespace. .NET Enterprise Services, which is the .NET layer on top of COM+, provides the necessary service infrastructure to .NET assemblies. The classes in .NET that can be hosted by the COM+ application and can use COM+ services are called *serviced components*. Any class in .NET that derives directly or indirectly from the System.EnterpriseServices.ServicedComponent class is called a *serviced component class*.

Enterprise Services is a component-oriented technology. It is used inside the service boundary and implements the complex business logic contained in transactions that span multiple objects and resources. However, Enterprise Services applications are tightly coupled with the application infrastructure. Microsoft has always regarded Enterprise Services as the core technology for providing the infrastructure, but it also suffers heavily from interoperability issues.

Why Are Web Services the Preferred Option?

Unfortunately, with an existing distributed technology stack, you'll often find a number of limitations, especially with interoperability between platforms. For example, if you try to deploy a COM+ application to converse across a firewall, smart routers, or organizational boundaries, you'll often find some significant differences. Most of the earlier distributed component technologies were not built to deal with firewalls and intelligent routers. For instance, if you build an application using Microsoft Enterprise Services (a set of classes provided by Microsoft to be leveraged in enterprise applications), how do you utilize the application from a Java client? Considering that most enterprises work on different technologies and platforms, interoperability is a major issue. Generally, companies used to buy some complex software and invest a lot of money in building a bridge between the existing components to make them distributed. Other complexities and difficulties arose when these custom solutions needed to be extended further. Web services solve these problems by relying on open standards and protocols that are widely accepted.

Web services are not just another way of creating distributed applications. The distinguishing characteristic of web services, compared to other distributed technologies, is that rather than relying on proprietary standards or protocols, they rely on open web standards (such as SOAP, HTTP, and XML). These open standards are widely recognized and accepted across the industry. Web services have changed how distributed applications are created. The Internet has created a demand for a loosely coupled and interoperable distributed technology. Specifically, prior to web services, most of the distributed technologies relied on the object-oriented paradigm, but the Web has created a need for distributed components that are autonomous and platform independent.

■**Note** Simply put, SOAP is a lightweight communication protocol for web services based on XML. It is used to exchange structured and typed information between systems. SOAP allows you to invoke methods on remote machines without knowing specific details of the platform or software running on those machines. XML is used to represent the data, while the data is structured according to the SOAP schema. The only thing both the consumer and provider need to agree on is this common schema, defined by SOAP. Overall, SOAP keeps things as simple as possible and provides minimum functionality. SOAP used to stand for "Simple Object Access Protocol," but the W3C dropped that name when the focus shifted from object access to object interoperability via a generalized XML messaging format as part of SOAP 1.2.

XML web services are designed with interoperability in mind, and are easily callable from non-Windows platforms. It is common to confuse web services with .NET Remoting. Web services and .NET Remoting are related, but web services have a more simplified programming model than .NET Remoting. In other words, .NET Remoting and web services look similar from a high-level architecture level, but they differ in the way they work. For example, they both have different ways of serializing data into messages. .NET Remoting supports RPC-based communication by default, and web services support message-based communication by default. Web services rely on XML Schema for data types, and .NET Remoting relies on the CLR. You can use .NET Remoting to build web services, but the WSDL generated by .NET Remoting is not widely adopted and might be ignored by some clients. Though you can use either for creating components, .NET Remoting is suitable for creating components to be used by your own application running in the .NET environment, and XML web services create components that can be accessible to any application connected via the Internet.

Through web services, Microsoft wants to achieve the best of both worlds—web development and component-based development. Web services were the first step toward service orientation, which is a set of guiding principles for developing loosely coupled distributed applications. SOA is a vision of services that have well-defined interfaces. These loosely coupled interfaces communicate through messages described by the XML Schema Definition (XSD) and through the message patterns described by WSDL. This provides for a great base architecture for building distributed applications. Since a web service and its clients are independent of each other, they need to adhere only to the XSD and WSDL document standards in order to communicate.

The next Microsoft offering to address SOA is WCF. We'll now discuss how WCF complements web services and enhances their value.

What Does WCF Solve?

WCF is not just another way of creating a distributed solution—it also provides a number of benefits compared to its predecessors. If you look at the background of WCF, you'll find that work on WCF started with the release of .NET. Microsoft unveiled this technology at the 2003 Microsoft Product Developers Conference in Los Angeles, California. In other words, it has taken years to build and come to market. WCF addresses lots of issues; Figure 1–2 shows the three main design goals of WCF.

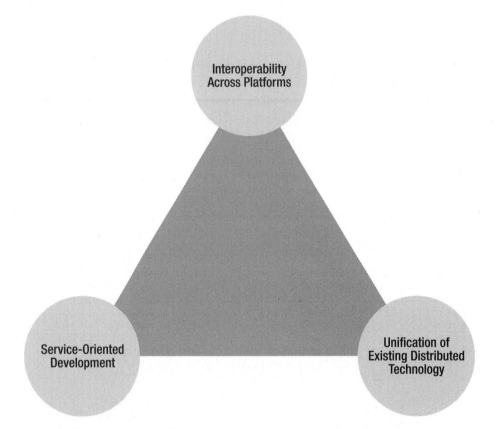

Figure 1-2. Design goals of WCF

The following subsections describe these three design goals in detail.

Unification of Existing Technologies

The current world of enterprise computing has many distributed technologies, each of which has a notion to perform a specific task and have a distinct role in the space. Apart from that, these distributed technologies are based on different programming models. For example, if you are building an application that communicates over HTTP, you will be required to change your programming model if you want to switch to using TCP. If you are used to building XML web services today, you don't have the ability to support transactions with message queuing enabled without changing your programming model. This has created problems for developers, who have to keep learning different APIs for different ways of building distributed components.

The constant fight since the 1990s between distributed technologies has led to a debate about which technology is best suited for developing distributed applications in the long term. One of the interesting questions is, Why not have just one technology that can be used in all situations? WCF is Microsoft's solution to distributed application development for enterprise applications. It avoids confusion by taking all the capabilities of the existing distributed systems' technology stacks and enables you to use one clean and simple API. In other words, WCF brings the entire existing distributed stack under one roof. All you need to do as a developer is reference the System.ServiceModel assembly and import its namespace.

As shown in Figure 1–3, WCF subsumes the best of all the distributed technologies. WCF brings together the efficiency of ASMX, the ability to adopt transactions with Enterprise Services using only attributes, the extensibility and flexibility of .NET Remoting, the supremacy of MSMQ for building queued applications, and WSE's interoperability through WS-*. Microsoft took all these capabilities and built a single, steady infrastructure in the form of WCF.

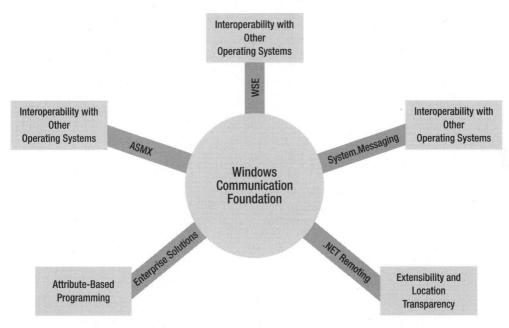

Figure 1–3. Unification of distributed technologies

Interoperability Across Platforms

Most of the big software companies are developing software using proprietary protocols that are tightly coupled with a specific platform. This software succumbs to the problem of not being interoperable with other software running on different platforms. When you look at any large enterprise in particular, you often notice a number of disparate systems built and bought over periods of time. Often these systems are incompatible with one another. The ability to link the systems becomes a crucial need for a large number of organizations. In addition, newly developed applications need to interoperate with the existing platforms, and the business needs to support applications written in different programming languages with different technologies. Also, companies need seamless interoperability across the organization between purchased software from different software vendors.

Interoperability was a major issue for all the major software vendors, and they all wanted to use a widely accepted and adopted suite of protocols. To solve this issue, industry leaders such as Microsoft, IBM, BEA, and Sun formed the *Web Services Interoperability (WS-I)* organization, which has developed a suite of specifications that, if adopted, allows software to seamlessly communicate with other software running on different platforms.

Some of the great features of the WS-I specifications are that they are simple, small, modular, and easy to implement. You are free to choose which specification you need to implement. For example, implementing WS-Security does not mandate that you implement transaction specifications, and it is broken down into several layers (e.g., there is a specification for sending a digital signature in a SOAP message, and a different specification for sending a simple username and password in SOAP). The core architecture of a web service specification is WSDL. Therefore, WCF speaks the language of the latest web service suite of protocols for achieving seamless interoperability across platforms.

Figure 1–4 shows that the WCF native messaging protocol is SOAP, which as an open standard provides the opportunity for WCF services to interact with different technologies running on different platforms and non-Windows operating systems. Since services are based on open standards, other applications can use them without requiring that these clients possess detailed knowledge about a service's underlying implementation. This is exciting for software architects, because they can know that their WCF application that runs on a Windows 2003 or Vista web server can do reliable messaging with a Java application running on an IBM mainframe. The technical world will not speak in different languages anymore, and with WCF, diverse and heterogeneous systems can coexist peacefully.

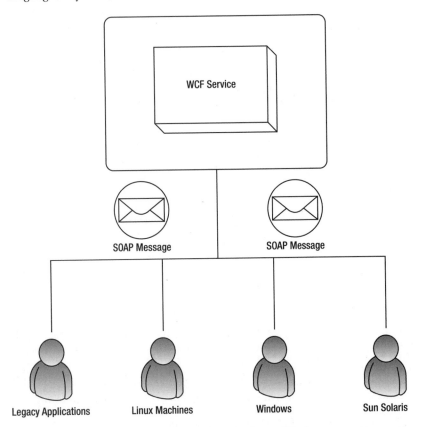

Figure 1–4. Interoperability with Windows and non-Windows operating systems

Not only can WCF interact with its counterparts from other vendors, but it can also exist peacefully with predecessors including COM+ and Enterprise Services. For developers, this drastically reduces the amount of infrastructure code required to achieve heterogeneous interoperability.

WCF As a Service-Oriented Development Tool

WCF is the first programming model built from the ground up to provide explicit service-oriented application development and future-ready business orientation. Service orientation is not a technology, but a design concept. Service orientation uses the best practices for building today's distributed applications. Purists and gurus of distributed applications consider service orientation to be the design guideline for overcoming some of the complication in designing loosely coupled applications. Service orientation is not a new concept—it has been around for some years. Some projects have tried to implement the concept of service orientation by tweaking existing distributed technologies; these projects have always demanded a framework that has built-in support for service orientation. Although existing distributed technologies can offer the groundwork for interoperability and integration, a new platform was required—a new infrastructure that makes it much easier to build these distributed technologies.

Although it may seem surprising, one of the most intriguing parts of designing a service is deciding how it should expose its functionality to the outside world. The level of granularity of the service quite often is one of the most heated topics of debate within an organization. If the service is "finely grained," then the focus is on exchanging small amounts of data to complete a specific task. This is usually associated with the more traditional RPC communication style. Any additional tasks, if required, are invoked similarly. Since message-based service invocations are expensive, finely grained approaches aren't practical in most situations because the overhead of transmitting and processing many individual messages isn't acceptable. On the other hand, coarse-grained services expose more functionality within the same service invocation, combining many small tasks. This relates to fewer messages transmitted with more data, as opposed to many messages with less data. In other words, coarse-grained services are less chatty, which results in less overhead on both ends of the service, allowing it to scale better.

When designing services, you need to think beyond basic object-oriented design principles and use the four tenets of service orientation discussed previously in this chapter as the guiding principles. Figure 1–5 shows the four tenets of service orientation. One of the challenges in developing WCF is shifting developers' mindsets away from building distributed systems in terms of objects and components, and toward building distributed systems as services. WCF offers that foundation for service-oriented applications built on Windows; it will be basic to the SOA efforts of many organizations.

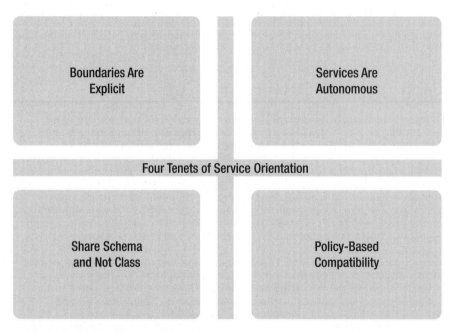

Figure 1–5. Four tenets of service orientation

Until now you have probably been creating applications using an OOP model. Service-oriented architecture (SOA) presents a fundamental shift in dealing with the difficulties of building distributed systems. The following are some of the key differences between object-oriented and service-oriented programming:

- Technology and business are changing rapidly, and companies are constantly investing in application development. For years, developers and organizations have struggled to build software based on object-oriented paradigms that adapt as fast as businesses change. Design needs to be flexible and time tested. Services of WCF are built in an autonomous way, and by following key principles of SOA, they promise less maintenance cost, allow for change, and are interoperable across platforms.

- Most object-oriented applications target homogeneous environments, and no simple and flexible way exists in object orientation to work in heterogeneous environments, because it is tightly coupled with the platform being built. An SOA application targets both heterogeneous and homogeneous environments.

- Object-oriented developers share interfaces and classes that give them a comfortable way to program. However, the programming practices are much simpler if the schema is shared, rather than the objects. A schema is defined in the XML Schema language, and contracts are defined in WSDL. An SOA application (WCF) allows you to share schemas, not objects.

- In object-oriented architecture, either behaviors are implicitly remote or everything is distributed by default. For instance, take a look at the following interface:

```
public interface Ihello
{
string Hello(string name);
}
```

This interface can be accessed remotely without any restrictions. Classes are also not left behind, and an access specifier determines the behavior of the class. Classes have the default access specifier. This default and implicit behavior of object orientation proves to be an issue in developing complex applications where thousands of objects interact with each other. In WCF, the behavior is explicitly defined remotely by decorating the class with the appropriate attributes. Nothing is visible outside your code, unless you want that facet of your code to be publicly exposed to a service-oriented interface. The concepts of "public" and "private" are pointless when identifying methods on a service contract. With WCF, you will need to start writing applications explicitly as being remote. Similarly to the [WebMethods] attributes of web services, you can decorate methods with the OperationContract attribute. Chapter 4 covers more about OperationContract and how to create a service.

- OOP gives a tight coupling with the underlying platform, and services are free to act independently. A service and its clients are independent of each other, and as long as they agree upon the interface, it hardly matters whether they are written in different languages, are using different runtime environments, or are being executed on different operating systems.

- Most distributed object technologies have the goal of making remote objects look as much as possible like local objects. Microsoft and other companies have gone to extraordinary lengths to ensure that a call to a remote component is as easy as a call to the local component. However, a call to a remote component involves a lot of work behind the scenes, and is abstracted from the programmer. (For example, Visual Basic 6.0 uses COM in an abstracted manner. How many Visual Basic developers are aware of COM?) Although this approach simplifies development in some ways by providing rapid application development, it also hides the important differences between local and remote objects. Contrary to this, services avoid this problem by making interactions between services and their clients more explicit.

- Most of the technology based on object orientation provides a way to encapsulate code in classes, which requires an explicit compilation in case of any changes. Service orientation, on the other hand, supports policy-based compatibility, through which code that needs to be changed frequently can be put in a configuration-based file. This policy-based configuration can be changed when required. Services encapsulate behavior and information in a way that is immeasurably more flexible and reusable than objects.

Exploring Features in WCF

To a distributed object veteran, WCF might look like yet another distributed technology. WCF has taken a lot of features from the existing distributed stack, but also extends the existing features and defines new boundaries. We'll now discuss some of the new features in WCF.

Developer Productivity

WCF increases a developer's productivity by simplifying the development of service-oriented applications. Previously, developers were forced to learn different APIs for building distributed components. It cannot be denied that developers who are good at building service components might not be as efficient at building remote components using .NET Remoting. Creating custom solutions that require the functionality of two or more distributed technologies has always raised butterflies in the bellies of developers and architects.

WCF has a simple, unified programming model that offers the potential to create applications with diverse requirements. WCF is built from the ground up to support the features of service orientation. One of the best aspects of WCF is that developers using existing technologies will find their favorite features in it, and all developers will benefit from the consistent architecture. The WCF support of the declarative and imperative programming model will make you write less code, which offers the likelihood of fewer errors. Applications that required hundreds to thousands of lines of code prior to WCF can now be created with just a few lines.

Attribute-Based Development

WCF is a message-plumbing engine and has a simple, clear, and flexible programming model that sits at the top of the message engine. The programming model provides different ways to leverage the message engine. You can use the classes to directly write code that's similar to other distributed applications developed in other technologies, such as DCOM. You also get the opportunity to use configuration files that can be changed at runtime. WCF also supports an attribute-based programming model. One of the main intentions of SOA is to separate the application code from the messaging infrastructure. The developer specifies infrastructure requirements declaratively by decorating the service class with custom attributes, but does not actually write any infrastructure code.

In simple terms, you can think of an attribute as a simple string or annotation. Attributes are just declarative tags that, when applied to classes, methods, properties, and so on, provide viable information about behavior to the CLR, and provide the way to add metadata to the runtime. You can view metadata through any of the metadata-reading tools (e.g., ILDASM). Attributes have been part of .NET since its beta releases, but the power of attributes has never been explored in the enterprise world. In WCF, attributes are central to the programming model and are treated as first-class citizens. This attribute-based model is not a new concept in WCF, but it has its roots in Enterprise Services and web services. Microsoft used the attribute-based programming model in MTS. If you have created a web service using .NET, you are already familiar with the [WebMethods] attribute. WCF has extended the immense support of declarative programming in the message engine. So, whenever you need transactional support or some security, you just need to decorate the service class with the specific attributes, and the messaging engine will provide you with the necessary infrastructure to achieve your desired result. This offers a real advantage to developers, who can now concentrate on the real logic and then decorate the class and methods with the appropriate attribute to get the necessary infrastructure.

Attribute-based programming is simply the best way to get things done with the WCF engine, but you should also not forget the power of the object model of WCF. Depending on your application requirements, you can fulfill different application needs through minor configuration file changes. You can use an extensible API programming model for instances where you need finer-grained control.

Actually, most of the attributes in WCF are shortcuts for imperative tasks you can do via APIs. Which method you use depends on your requirements.

Coexisting with Existing Technology

With .NET, Microsoft espouses a vision of how the Internet can make businesses more efficient and deliver services to consumers. WCF takes all the capabilities of the existing technology stacks without relying upon any of them. WCF is a new investment and relies on the classes that are available in the .NET Framework 3.0 or later. All your existing investments will run side by side with WCF. Applications built with these earlier technologies will continue to work unchanged on systems with WCF installed. WCF also provides you with an opportunity to communicate with, or even replace, existing Windows communications APIs and technologies, including ASMX, ASP.NET web services, Web Services Enhancements (WSE), Enterprise Services, System.Messaging, and .NET Remoting.

■**Note** WCF has been coded with Managed C#, so that existing technology will be able to coexist with WCF, because WCF is just another managed-code implementation. The development of WCF started in parallel with .NET 1.x and .NET 2.0, and it is therefore being smoothly integrated into the existing technologies in the space. We cover coexistence in later chapters in more detail.

Hosting Services

A class implementing a WCF service is typically compiled into a library, and thus it needs a process to host the services. If you look at earlier distributed technologies, you will find that most of the distributed technologies are bound with only one hosting environment. For example, ASMX web services can be hosted only with HttpRuntime on IIS. A COM+ application requires component services as the hosting environment. .NET Remoting is a bit more flexible, with channels and transports being used. This limits the variety of clients that can access your component.

WCF has been made with a vision to allow endpoints to be available for any kind of scenario. A WCF component can be hosted in any kind of environment in .NET 3.0 or later, be it a console application, a Windows application, or IIS. In fact, it hardly matters whether the WCF client knows which environment is hosting its services. (Not only does the WCF client provide you with a variety of hosting environments, but it also supports various activation models.) A service hosted in IIS offers a lot of benefits, including automatic object activation and periodic recycling. Additionally, it comes with a tight coupling with HTTP. However, WCF gives you the freedom to self-host a WCF service. (Chapter 5 details the hosting options.) This is the reason that WCF services are called *services* as opposed to *web services*. The terminology has changed because you can host services without a web server. Earlier, web services used a default transport protocol, such as HTTP. WCF provides different transport mechanisms, including TCP, Custom, UDP, and MSMQ.

■**Note** The ability to host services in normal EXEs requires the code to activate and run the services. These services are generally also called *self-hosting* services. Self-hosting services give you the flexibility to use transports other than HTTP with service development today. Chapter 5 describes hosting environments in more detail.

Migration/Integration with Existing Technology

WCF has raised the curiosity level of developers working with existing distributed technologies, largely because existing applications are likely to be impacted by WCF in the near future. Many companies have made significant investments in applications built on ASMX, WSE, and System.EnterpriseServices. Here are some important questions when thinking about working with WCF:

- Will new applications developed using WCF work with your existing applications? For example, will your new WCF-transacted application work with your existing transaction application built on System.Transactions?

- Will you be able to upgrade your existing applications with WCF?

Fortunately, the answers to these questions are yes and yes! In truth, existing distributed applications cannot be migrated to WCF in a single day, but Microsoft has created a durable surface for WCF to interoperate with existing investments. The WCF team consists of the same developers who built the System.Messaging, System.EnterpriseServices, WSE, ASMX, and .NET Remoting technologies. Also, WCF can use WS-* or HTTP bindings to communicate with ASMX pages, as shown in Figure 1–6. In other words, integration with existing systems was on the minds of the WCF team from the beginning.

Microsoft has implemented a set of capabilities within the WCF product suite to enable you to interact with and reuse COM+ applications without having to fundamentally change your programming experience. Therefore, if you have COM+ applications, WCF lets you essentially write code that can access existing WCF applications as if they were COM+ applications. Also, a command-line tool called COMSVCConfig.exe (discussed in Chapter 10) lets an existing COM+ application spit out a WCF stub to interoperate with COM+ applications. The stub brokers call back and forth between the stub and COM+ applications. MSMQ also integrates well with WCF. If you have an existing MSMQ application and use it to send messages back and forth between systems using queues, then WCF offers an msmqIntegrationBinding binding that allows communication with existing MSMQ applications. If you want to use a WCF application to utilize MSMQ on the wire, this binding is available to you, so your applications can communicate with MSMQ applications openly.

A WCF application not only interoperates with applications running on other platforms, but also integrates with other distributed programming models that Microsoft has come up with over the past ten years. Previously, Microsoft had been providing the upgrade path through the use of wizards. While wizards were meant to provide an easy way to perform complex tasks, they are truly only good in labs, and should only be used for upgrading sample and testing applications. Using wizards to upgrade complex applications is ill advised. This time around, Microsoft, having learned from past experiences, is using a more practical approach—providing whitepapers, guidance, samples, demos, and examples illustrating how to port applications from ASMX, Enterprise Services, .NET Remoting, WSE, and MSMQ to WCF and other technologies. These examples also address many of the concerns you'll have when going through the porting process.

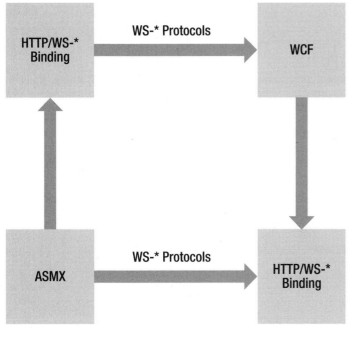

Figure 1–6. ASMX-to-WCF connectivity

■**Note** You can find more information about integration between WCF and MSMQ in Chapter 8.

One Service, Multiple Endpoints

If you look at the current distributed technology stack, you will find that services are tightly coupled with the transport, channels, URLs, and features that the stack provides. Service development is greatly affected by the transport you use. After defining the service, you have to specify some vital information, including what this service can do, how can it be accessed, and where it is available. These three are encapsulated in endpoints. An *endpoint* contains information about the path through which the service is available. One service can have multiple endpoints, which makes it flexible and interoperable for any application requirement. Each of these endpoints can differ with regard to address, binding requirements, and the contract being implemented.

WCF provides a unique way to create services, independent of the transport being used. Figure 1–7 shows that the same service can be exposed with two different endpoints. The endpoints in this figure have different binding requirements. For example, endpoint 1 and endpoint 2 run on different transport protocols, one supporting the transaction and the other supporting the reliability and security. In the future, if you need to have another client that has different binding requirements, all you need to do is create another endpoint in the configuration file. This enables you to serve the needs of two or more clients requiring the same business logic encapsulated in the service with different technical capabilities.

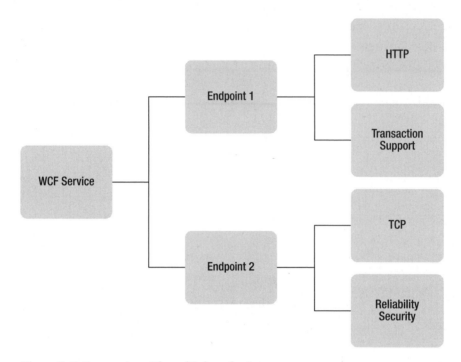

Figure 1–7. *One service with multiple endpoints*

Integration Technologies

In addition to extending the functionality of the .NET Framework and Visual Studio, you can use WCF with BizTalk Server to provide both brokered and unbrokered application-to-application communication. BizTalk Server and WCF are complementary to each other. BizTalk Server provides business process orchestration, message transformation, business activity monitoring, and more through designers and visual tools. WCF provides a unified framework for building secure and reliable transacted services. BizTalk Server is a key technology in (and is responsible for orchestrating) WCF services. In future versions of BizTalk Server, the orchestration process will use a workflow foundation. BizTalk Server provides a WCF adapter that enables WFC services to be incorporated into business process orchestration. In future versions of BizTalk Server, the integration between these technologies will be even more seamless, with WCF providing the core messaging and web service capabilities of BizTalk Server, and with WCF integrated into the native protocol of BizTalk Server.

How Do You Unify All These Technologies?

Most of these distributed technologies are based on the same concept. However, all of them provide specific services that are unique to the product (e.g., if you want to do queuing, you need to use MSMQ or System.Messaging; if you want to do transactions, you need to use System.EnterpriseServices; if you want to do security, you need to use WSE). As a programmer, you are constantly forced to switch between these programming models.

Therefore, we need one distributed technology to gather the capabilities of the existing stack and provide a solution with a simple and flexible programming model. WCF does a great job of providing a unified programming model wherein you can compose all these different functionalities into your application without having to do a lot of context switching. Going forward, you just have to learn one programming model—WCF. If you want queuing, you just add an attribute to your WCF service contract that makes it queued. If you want to secure the communication with your WCF service, you just add the appropriate security attributes for authentication and privacy. If you are after transaction support, you just add the transaction attribute. This new programming paradigm should help you concentrate more on the business logic.

WCF provides a single programming model to leverage the features of any distributed technology in the stack, as shown in Figure 1–8. Though WCF takes the best features of all the distributed technology in the stack, the team developing WCF has not chosen to extend any of the existing distributed technologies; instead, the whole infrastructure has been revamped to support the predecessors and use the classes available in the .NET Framework 3.0. Developers can now select the features they need to incorporate into the component (i.e., developers can choose to implement security and reliability without requiring the transaction support).

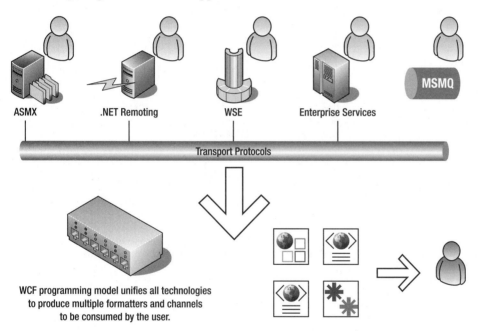

Figure 1–8. *Unification of existing technologies*

Programming bugs are common in development environments. During testing, you can trap runtime errors by debugging the code. But finding bugs in the product environment is not as easy. You need the appropriate tools to help in instrumentation and monitoring the health of an application. *Tracing* describes the process of receiving informative messages about the execution of a web application. In ASP.NET, tracing takes place through the methods available in the Trace class residing in the Systems.Diagnostics namespace. WCF extends the tracing capabilities of ASP.NET with lots of new features. WCF also allows for end-to-end tracing through a trace viewer called svcTraceViewer.exe, and also allows for message logging in the XML files.

■**Note** Chapter 6 covers tracing in more detail.

WCF also allows for *queue management*, which is similar to the queued components of COM+, and extends the API of MSMQ. With the queue management features of WCF, developers no longer need to write complex plumbing code for sending and receiving queues in an application. WCF comes with `NetProfileMsmqBinding` and other custom bindings to interact with queues. It also resolves the ability to handle corrupted messages, which was a nightmare for many MSMQ developers. As opposed to MSMQ, the queue management of WCF also supports application-to-application security, and does not require Active Directory. WCF supports queue management through bindings, and you can decide the appropriate binding depending on the consuming application's requirements.

■**Note** For more information about queue management, please refer to Chapter 8.

Writing a WCF application is similar to writing other types of applications; you don't need to be concerned with the protocols or transport being used. Service endpoints that are the combination of address, binding, and contract (commonly known as the ABCs of WCF) can be specified in the configuration file, which is separate from the service being developed. Endpoints are not a new concept; they were defined earlier in WSDL, but WCF extends this extensible model to other technologies such as Enterprise Services, thus giving a consistent model to its predecessors.

■**Note** Chapters 2 and 3 cover the ABCs of WCF in more detail.

Services can now have multiple endpoints. These endpoints can be defined in either the code or the configuration file. By using configuration files, WCF can facilitate changes to bindings without impacting the code.

Summary

This chapter introduced the concepts of services and SOA. It also described the governing principles for services in terms of four tenets. It is important to understand that, at the end of the day, SOA is not about how to invoke objects remotely or how to write services; it is all about how to send messages from one application to another in a loosely coupled fashion. Web services provide just one of the many ways to send messages between disparate systems. Adopting an SOA approach is important to an enterprise in that it provides the business agility and IT flexibility needed to be able to succeed in today's marketplace.

This chapter also introduced the new features of WCF, the challenges it helps to resolve, and the unification of various distributed technologies.

The next chapter will introduce the new features of WCF in .NET 4.0 that have made WCF more developer-friendly and easier to use. It will also illustrate how WCF addresses SOA concepts to promote WCF as a practical SOA implementation from Microsoft.

CHAPTER 2

■ ■ ■

What's New in WCF 4

Reusability is the key to success in a distributed environment. Most of the architecture focuses on the way to maximize the components' usage in an easy and efficient manner. Most components are built on an object-oriented paradigm that also provides reuse in terms of encapsulating the state (data) and behavior (function) in a container called a *class*. In Chapter 1, we discussed flaws in object-oriented architecture that mandate the need of loosely coupled SOA. Services compose a distributed system that can be loosely coupled to achieve a particular business goal. These services can later be composed differently to achieve a different business goal. Today, more and more work is being distributed, and the code that we write to coordinate that work is getting complex. This not only brings complexity in writing complex services, but requires a lot of management and makes tracking services more difficult.

As discussed in Chapter 1, WCF combines and extends the connectivity features found in the .NET Framework 1.0, 1.1, and 2.0. These include technologies such as ASP.NET web services (ASMX), .NET Remoting, Enterprise Services, Web Services Enhancements (WSE), and the System.Messaging namespace. WCF is meant to provide an easier-to-understand and unified programming model compared to the previous set of technologies. It provides a layer that developers can use to connect two applications or components together through messaging. It should make you more productive when creating connected system applications. In addition, it provides superior ways to extend the programming model if the existing rich functionality doesn't fulfill your requirements.

With each new version of the .NET Framework beginning with 3.0, Microsoft has attempted to resolve some of the key areas of WCF. In .NET 4.0, Microsoft has attempted to give developers a better experience and become more productive. One of the important lessons learned from the previous versions is that WCF needs to be feature-rich, but at the same time flexible, so that we can easily build WCF services that will satisfy almost any need. Considerable enhancements have been made to the framework and lots of supports and standards have been added.

In this chapter, you'll learn about the following:

- How simplified configuration has made developers' lives easy

- About the key architectural changes made in WCF in .NET 4.0

- About the new WCF features introduced in .NET 4.0

Introducing the ABCs of WCF

Before diving into the new features of WCF in .NET 4.0, it is important to become familiar with some of the basics of WCF. We'll first cover the ABCs of WCF. As mentioned in Chapter 1, "ABC" stands for "address, binding, and contract":

- The *address* specifies where the messages can be sent (or where the service lives).

- The *binding* describes how to send the messages.

- The *contract* describes what the messages should contain.

Obviously, clients need to know the ABCs of a service to be able to use it. Usually you can refer to these three items as the *endpoint* of a service as defined in WCF. An endpoint acts as a gateway to the outside world. Web Services Description Language (WSDL) is meant to describe service endpoints in a standardized way. A WSDL file describes what a service can do, how a service can be accessed, and where the service can be found.

■**Note** We will be going into more detail about endpoints in Chapter 3.

The WCF stack maps almost on a one-to-one basis to all the SOA principles (as shown in Figure 2–1, which covers both concrete and abstract implementations). WCF simplifies the development of connected systems because it unifies a wide range of distributed systems in a composite and extensible architecture. This architecture can span various transport layers, security systems, messaging patterns, network topologies, and hosting models.

■**Note** Chapter 3 will explain certain aspects of the WCF stack shown in Figure 2–1, including the service contract, the message contract, and the data contract.

Building an application in terms of services, not components, also provides enormous benefits in terms of code, service, and functionality reuse, as well as the ability to glue together dynamic, agile business applications and services. WCF makes it easy for developers to create services that adhere to the principle of service orientation.

If you are an object orientation person, you may find a few things to be restrictive in SOA. The SOA world is a world of messages, not objects. Only a few key features (such as the ability to pass an object reference) are not available in WCF. Actually, the paradigm has shifted now from object-oriented to service-oriented, and it makes more sense to pass messages between services instead of objects.

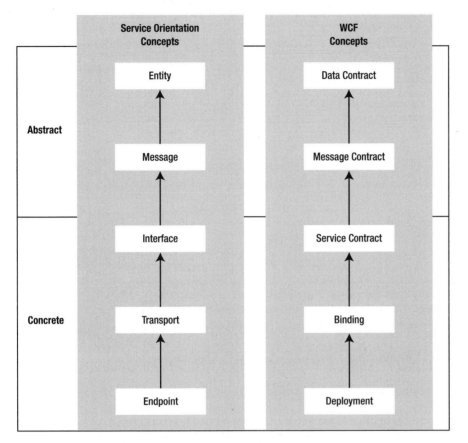

Figure 2–1. WCF and service orientation mapping

Standard Endpoints

Endpoints are a combination of an address, a binding, and a contract. For some scenarios, you always end up using a specific combination of an address, a binding, and a contract. For example, in the case of a MEX endpoint, you always need to specify IMetadataExchange for the service contract, and you're most likely to choose HTTP as the transport protocol. So instead of forcing you to always specify this manually, .NET 4.0 provides a standard endpoint definition for metadata exchange that satisfies these requirements—MEXEndpoint. Similarly, .NET 4.0 ships with several other "preconfigured" standard endpoints (discussed later in this chapter) that satisfy most-frequent-usage scenarios. You can simply reuse them as-is. To illustrate this, we'll create a simple WCF service demo.

First, open Visual Studio 2010, click File ➤ New ➤ Project, select WCF Service Library, and apply the service name, as shown in Figure 2–2.

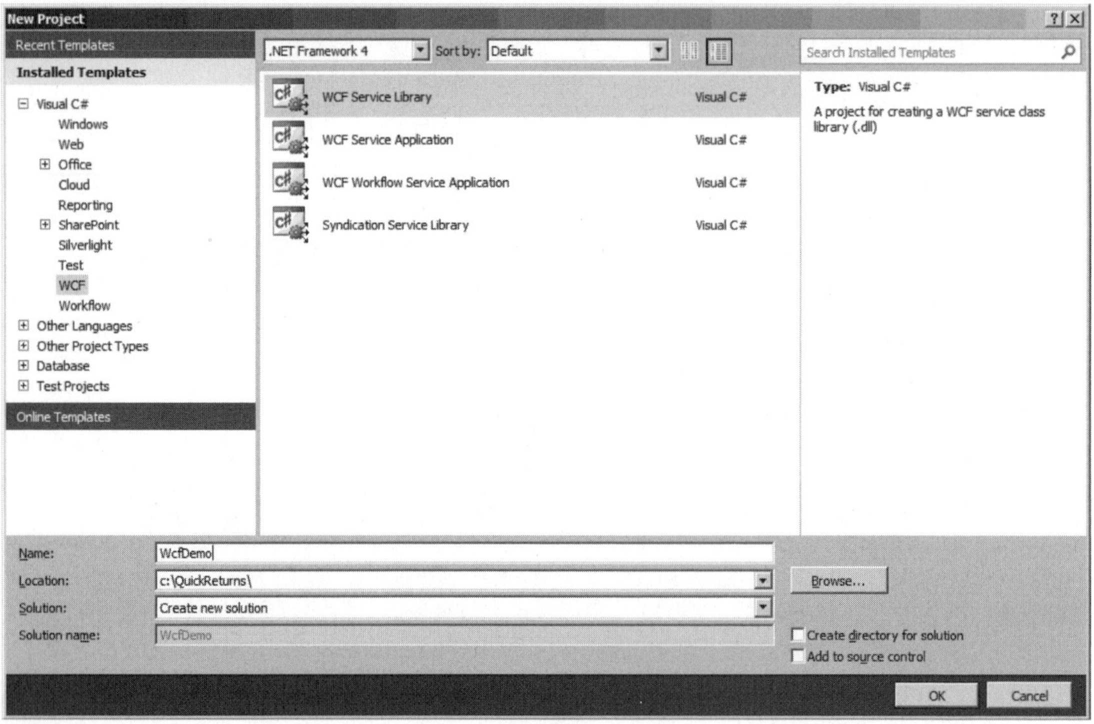

Figure 2–2. Creating new applications with Visual Studio 2010

Click OK. Open the `App.config` file and remove the `System.ServiceModel` section. By removing this section, you are removing all the endpoints that have been created by default by the Visual Studio template. Your `App.config` should now contain just what appears in Listing 2–1.

Listing 2–1. Code of the App.config File

```
<?xml version="1.0" encoding="utf-8" ?>
<configuration>
   <system.web>
   <compilation debug="true" />
   </system.web>
   </configuration>
```

WCF ships with the WCF Configuration Editor for viewing a configuration file. If you right-click your `App.config` file for the first time in Visual Studio 2010, you will not find the option of editing the configuration file in the WCF Configuration Editor. This requires additional steps: click WCF Configuration Editor in the Tools menu, and then right-click `App.config`. You will find the option Edit WCF Configuration, as shown in Figure 2–3.

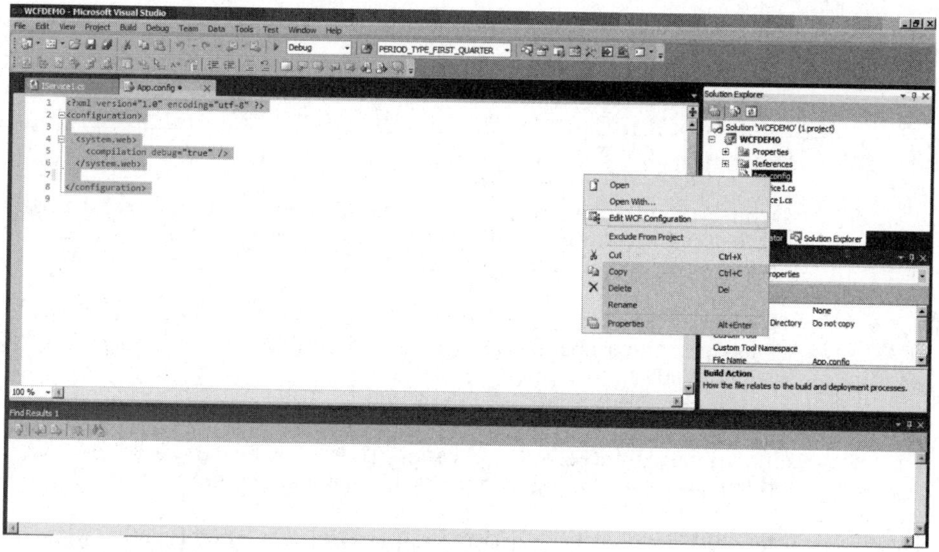

Figure 2–3. The Edit WCF Configuration option

Click Edit WCF Configuration. This will open the App.config file in the WCF Configuration Editor. Navigate to Standard Endpoint Extensions, as shown in Figure 2–4.

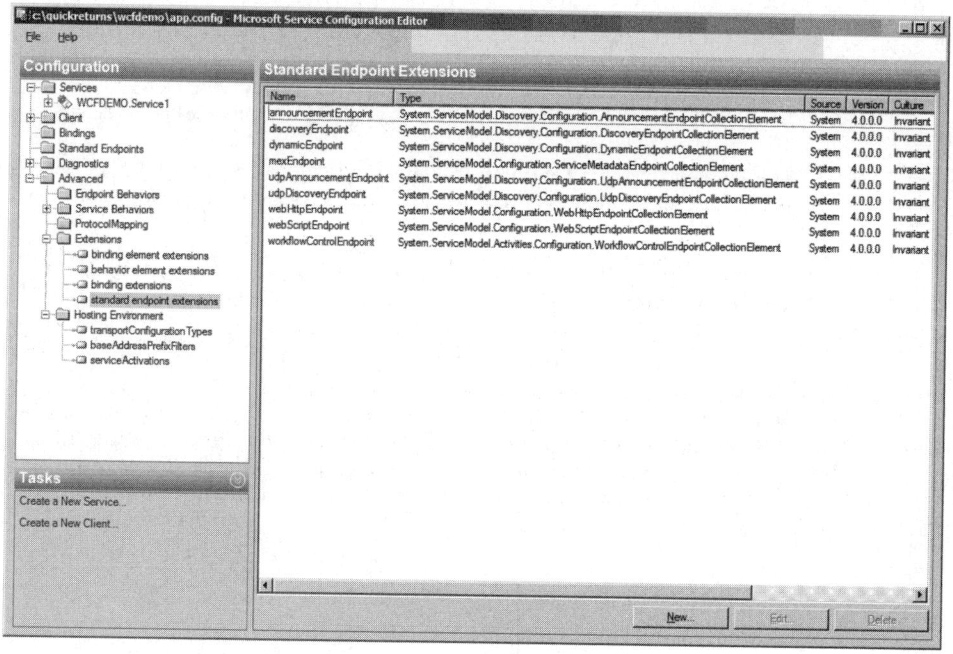

Figure 2–4. Standard endpoints from machine.config

You will see all the default standard endpoints that ship with .NET 4.0. Table 2–1 describes each of these endpoints.

Table 2–1. New Endpoints in WCF 4.0

Standard Endpoint	Description
MEXEndpoint	Defines a standard endpoint for MEX, configured with IMetadataExchange for the service contract, mexHttpBinding as the default binding (you can change this), and an empty address.
AnnouncementEndpoint	Used by services to send announcement messages, especially for discovery of services. The user still needs to specify the address and binding when using this standard endpoint.
DiscoveryEndpoint	Used by services to send discovery messages that deal with discovery operations within a client application. The user needs to specify the address and the binding when using this standard endpoint.
UdpDiscoveryEndpoint	Derived from DiscoveryEndpoint, this standard endpoint is preconfigured for discovery operations over a multicast address using UDP binding.
UdpAnnouncementEndpoint	Derived from AnnouncementEndpoint, this endpoint is used by services to send announcement messages over a UDP binding over a multicast address.
DynamicEndpoint	Uses WS-Discovery to find the endpoint address dynamically at runtime.
WebHttpEndpoint	Has a WebHttpBinding binding that automatically adds the WebHttpBehavior behavior. This is mainly used to expose REST services.
WebScriptEndpoint	Has a WebHttpBinding binding that automatically adds the WebScriptEnablingBehavior behavior. This is used to expose Ajax services.
WorkflowControlEndpoint	Enables you to call control operations (creating, suspending, terminating, etc.) on workflow instances.

These standard endpoint definitions cater to some of the most common scenarios of WCF. Since these endpoints are specified in the machine.config file, they are available to use in your applications by default. You do not need to specify the address, binding, and contract when using standard endpoints. You refer to standard endpoints by name using the kind attribute, as shown in Listing 2–2. However, there are some standard endpoints that require you to explicitly specify contract and binding details as well (as mentioned in Table 2–1).

Listing 2–2. The kind Attribute in an Endpoint

```
<system.serviceModel>
  <services>
    <service name="TradeService">
      <endpoint kind=" webHttpEndpoint" contract="ITradeService />
    </service>
  </services>
</system.serviceModel>
```

There are often times when you would like to tweak these standard endpoints a little bit. You can do this by making changes using the standardEndpoints section, and then referencing it in the endpoint section using the endpointConfiguration attribute, as shown in Listing 2–3.

Listing 2–3. Changes Made in the standardEndpoints Section of the App.config File

```
<system.serviceModel>
  <services>
    <service name="TradeService">
      <endpoint kind=" webHttpEndpoint" contract="ITradeService"
endpointConfiguration="TradeConfig"/>
    </service>
  </services>
  <standardEndpoints>
      <webHttpEndpoint>
      <standardEndpoint name="TradeConfig"  transferMode="Buffered"/>
      </webHttpEndpoint>
  </standardEndpoints>
</system.serviceModel>
```

Simplified Configuration

Microsoft built WCF as a universal programming model to communicate with other distributed systems. You can write code for one service and consume this code in multiple ways over the wire. The WCF programming model provides tremendous flexibility by exposing service and channel configuration options to the developer. One of the main intentions of SOA is to separate the application code from the messaging infrastructure. The developer specifies infrastructure requirements declaratively by decorating the service class with custom attributes or putting them in a configuration file, but does not actually write any infrastructure code. This model was fantastic, but it also led to confusion among developers, who ended up with tons of options for configuring services. Those veterans of WCF on .NET 3.x will probably agree that WCF services are very easy to develop, but somewhat difficult to configure. My experience with working on WCF showed me that the costliest and most time-consuming aspects of building distributed applications using WCF involve configuration. Even a simple console application required developers to be acquainted with service model concepts.

Two other goals that Microsoft's team had in mind while developing WCF were providing developers using existing technologies with their favorite features, and allowing developers to benefit from the consistent architecture. In WCF 3.x, hosting the WCF service required us to explicitly state specific endpoints and behavior in the configuration file. This became a source of confusion for the developers who came from the ASMX world, who were more familiar with default configurations. In ASMX, you don't need to configure endpoints to consume the web service. You just need to create a service and decorate your methods with the WebMethod attribute, and a default configuration will be created that allows the web service consumer to consume the service without delay.

Microsoft wanted to make it possible to configure a WCF service like an ASMX web service. WCF 4.0 has helped developers by providing default configurations for hosting a WCF service. It is now possible to host services free of any configurations. These default configurations can be broadly classified at three levels:

- Default endpoints

- Default bindings

- Default behavior

Each of these default configurations makes the application look cleaner and allows developers to get rid of some of the underpinnings of WCF by providing abstraction. However, it is also important to understand how each of these default settings works behind the framework to better utilize WCF.

Now let's take a deeper look at each of these default settings.

■**Note** Though this chapter discusses new features introduced in WCF 4.0, you will often be redirected to later chapters for more detail.

Default Endpoints

You should always include at least one service endpoint through which the outside world can be communicated with. The .NET Framework 3.x gives an error when WCF services are deployed without any endpoint. In WCF 3.x, in order to expose a service to the outside world, you needed to specify endpoints imperatively or through configuration. In .NET 4.0, you don't have to explicitly specify endpoints or bindings, but the framework will give you some defaults. You can now build a configurationless WCF service and consume it across the wire.

Let's look at an example of hosting our TradeService class in .NET 3.x code and .NET 4.0, as shown in Table 2–2. TradeService is a service exposed by our imaginary company, QuickReturns Ltd. (The TradeService class will be discussed further in Chapter 3.)

Table 2–2. ServiceHost Instantiation Based on Imperative Calls

Code in .NET 3.x	Code in .NET 4.0
``using System;

using System.ServiceModel;
using ExchangeService as
QuickReturns.StockTrading.ExchangeService;
using ExchangeService.Contracts;

namespace ExchangeService.Hosts
{
    class Program
    {
        static void Main(string[] args)
        {
            Uri address = new Uri
("http://localhost:8080/QuickReturns/Exchange"
);
Type serviceType = typeof(TradeService);
basicHttpBinding binding = new
basicHttpBinding();
 ServiceHost host = new
ServiceHost(serviceType);

host.AddServiceEndpoint(typeof(ITradeService),
binding, address);
 host.Open();
 Console.WriteLine("Service started: Press
Return to exit");
 Console.ReadLine();
        }   } }``` | ```using System;

using System.ServiceModel;
using ExchangeService as
QuickReturns.StockTrading.ExchangeService;
using ExchangeService.Contracts;

namespace ExchangeService.Hosts
{
    class Program
    {
        static void Main(string[] args)
        {
            Uri address = new Uri
("http://localhost:8080/QuickReturns/Exchange"
);
ServiceHost host = new
ServiceHost(typeof(TradeService);
host.Open();
 Console.WriteLine("Service started: Press
Return to exit");
 Console.ReadLine();
        }
    }
}``` |

Both of these code samples give the same result as hosting the TradeService using basicHttpBinding. If you look at the .NET 4.0 code, you will find that no endpoints have been specified. In .NET 4.0, the framework provides default endpoints if no endpoints have been specified. This is made possible by the addition of the AddDefaultEndpoints method in the ServiceHostBaseClass. Table 2–3 gives the specifications for AddDefaultEndpoints.

Table 2–3. AddDefaultEndpoints Specifications

Address Section	Description
Class name	System.ServiceModel.ServiceHostBase
Input parameter	None
Return type	Read-only collection of default endpoints
Signature	Public virtual ReadOnlyCollection<ServiceEndpoint> AddDefaultEndpoints();

The AddDefaultEndpoints method adds the default service endpoints for all base addresses in each contract found in the service host with the default binding. Note that this method is implicitly called by the framework only when the service has not been configured with any endpoints. If you configure the service with at least one endpoint explicitly, you will no longer see any of these default endpoints. However, you can always call AddDefaultEndpoints if you would still like to add the set of default endpoints for each base address.

Default Bindings

As mentioned, an endpoint comprises three pieces of information: an address, a binding, and a contract. The address is the location that the application hosting the service uses to advertise the service. The binding element specifies items such as the transport mechanism used to access the service and the protocol to use, among others. For each service contract that the service implements, WCF 4.0 by default provides one endpoint per base address that is currently configured within the host. This is good, but these endpoints also take default bindings with them. This means that there must be some mapping that the framework uses to know which binding to use for each different base address that's configured. You can see an example of this with the ProtocolMapping section in machine.config file, shown in Figure 2–5.

Open the App.config file defined earlier in this chapter in the WCF Configuration Editor. Go to the ProtocolMapping section, and you will find four schemes associated with the specific binding.

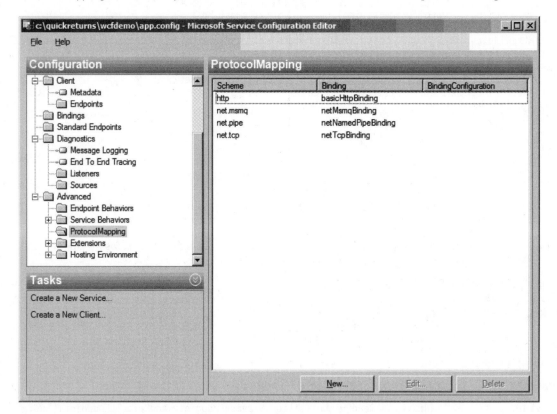

Figure 2–5. ProtocolMapping section in the Microsoft Service Configuration Editior

You can also see this protocol mapping defined by opening the machine.config file; this is shown in Listing 2–4.

Listing 2–4. The ProtocolMapping Section in machine.config

```
<system.serviceModel>
<protocolMapping>
     <clear />
     <add scheme="http" binding="basicHttpBinding" bindingConfiguration="" />
     <add scheme="net.tcp" binding="netTcpBinding" bindingConfiguration="" />
     <add scheme="net.pipe" binding="netNamedPipeBinding" bindingConfiguration="" />
     <add scheme="net.msmq" binding="netMsmqBinding" bindingConfiguration="" />
</protocolMapping>
</system.serviceModel>
```

This protocolMapping uses the basicHttpBinding whenever the scheme is http, and the netTcpBinding when the scheme is net.tcp. Since this mapping is set in a machine.config file, it is applicable, by default, to all the WCF applications developed on the machine. This default binding is inferred from the protocol scheme of the baseAddress.

Note machine.config contains the machine-level configuration settings. Any settings mentioned in machine.config are applied to all the .NET applications by default. If any of your settings are required to be overridden by your application, you can override them by using the application configuration file (web.config for web applications).

The extensibility of WCF gives an opportunity to override this protocol mapping at the machine or application level. Listing 2–5 shows how to override the protocol mapping by adding the protocolMapping section in the App.config file.

Listing 2–5. Modifying the protocolMapping Section in App.config

```
<protocolMapping>
     <remove scheme="http" />
     <add binding="wsHttpBinding" scheme ="http"/>
</protocolMapping>
```

Adding this snippet to an application's App.config file will make all the http baseaddress URIs exposed in the application host follow wsHttpBinding. You can also customize wsHttpBinding to encode messages as Mtom by using the following configuration, which applies to all the http basesaddress URIs exposed by this application, as shown in Listing 2–6.

Listing 2–6. Customizing wsHttpBinding

```
<protocolMapping>
     <remove scheme="http" />
     <add binding="wsHttpBinding" scheme ="http" bindingconfiguration ="myBindingConfig"/>
</protocolMapping>
<bindings>
     <wsHttpBinding>
```

```
        <binding name=myBindingConfig messageEncoding ="Mtom" />
      </wsHttpBinding>
    </bindings>
```

In .NET 3.x, there is no concept of a default binding configuration. Each of the binding sections requires the name attribute to be associated with each of the endpoints that require that configuration.

In Listing 2–7, there is no name attribute attached to the bindings section. This means that we have configured wsHttpBinding for no security, and that this is the default binding configuration for wsHttpBinding. This default configuration for bindings is also one of the new enhancements in .NET 4.0. Any endpoint that uses wsHttpBinding in this application configuration file will use the preceding configuration of No Security by default. In cases where there is a binding configuration that needs to be applied to only some services of the application, you can specify the binding name and apply it to those specific services, as in .NET 3.x.

Listing 2–7. Default Binding in WCF 4.0

```
<bindings>
    <wsHttpBinding>
      <binding>
        <security mode="None"></security>
      </binding>
    </wsHttpBinding>
</bindings>
```

Default Behavior

Consider a scenario in which each of the WCF services has to expose WSDL. In .NET 3.x, in order to view WSDL, we needed to add a serviceBehavior and set the httpGetEnabled property to true, as shown in Listing 2–8.

Listing 2–8. Default Behavior

```
    <serviceBehaviors>
      <behavior name="httpbehavior">
        <serviceMetadata httpGetEnabled="True"/>
        </behavior>
    </serviceBehaviors>
  </behaviors>
```

Once this was done, we needed to apply this behavior to each service, as follows:

```
<service name="QuickReturns.demoservice" behaviorConfiguration=" httpbehavior ">
```

This was subject to errors if the same behavior needed to be applied to many services. Often developers made mistakes by not specifying the behavior configuration for their respective services. In WCF 4.0, you can define a behavior without giving a name to it, as shown in Listing 2–9.

Listing 2–9. A Behavior Without a Name in WCF 4.0

```
<behaviors>
    <serviceBehaviors>
      <behavior name="">
        <serviceMetadata httpGetEnabled="True"/>
      </behavior>
```

```
      </serviceBehaviors>
</behaviors>
```

This behavior will then become the default behavior for all the services exposed by that application. If you set this setting in machine.config, then each service developed and deployed on the machine will be able to get WSDL over HTTP. In case there is a service behavior that needs to be applied to only certain services of the application, you can still specify the behavior name and apply that to the specific services, as in .NET 3.x.

Fileless Activation

.NET 4.0 also offers support for fileless activation inside of IIS and Windows Activation Services (WAS), which removes the need for an SVC file altogether. You can now describe virtual service activation endpoints that map to your service types in web.config. This makes it possible to activate WCF services without the need for SVC files, thereby creating a fileless activation. In order to do this, all you need to do is to go into your config file and add relative addresses that you want to be able to activate, as shown in Listing 2–10.

Listing 2–10. Fileless Activation

```
<serviceActivations>
        <clear />
<add relativeAddress="/hello.svc" service="HelloService" />
<add relativeAddress="/hello" service="HelloService" />
 </serviceActivations>
</serviceHostingEnvironment>
```

Service Discovery

As mentioned, services provide functionality over the Internet using standard protocols. In a typical scenario, there exists at least a service provider that publishes a service and a service consumer that uses that service. As described in Chapter 1, in order for a consumer to use a service, providers usually supplement a web service endpoint with an interface description using WSDL. Optionally, a provider can explicitly register a service with a web services registry such as UDDI. However, for smaller networks, centralized registries such as UDDI might not be suitable. Consider another scenario, wherein services used by client applications change their locations. One way to deal with this situation is to inform your clients about the new updated location of the service. This is fine if you only have a few clients to notify, but this might not be realistic if you have tens of thousands of clients consuming your service.

Service discovery helps address these issues by providing a standard way for clients to discover services. There have been different ways of accomplishing service discovery over the years. WS-Discovery is one of the standards that have been in the web service community for a long time. This is a standard protocol that is defined by an industry group such as BEA Systems or Microsoft to standardize and formalize the discovery of a service on the wire. Instead of knowing exactly where the service is located at runtime, a client can send out a pro-request and discover a service that might be around. It's a kind of replacement for UDDI for smaller networks, and contains more capabilities for discovering the service.

Note The Organization for the Advancement of Structured Information Standards (OASIS) also approved WS-Discovery in mid-2009. .NET 4.0 is not the first Microsoft product to implement WS-Discovery. In fact, there are a lot of places within Windows that implement WS-Discovery. Windows Vista uses the WS-Discovery mechanism to locate people when a user clicks "People near me." WS-Discovery can be used by a printer to announce its presence on a network. The specifications for WS-Discovery are available at `http://specs.xmlsoap.org/ws/2005/04/discovery/ws-discovery.pdf`.

The concept of WS-Discovery defines the SOAP-based protocol that helps discover the location endpoints of the service at runtime. The client application uses this protocol to probe the service endpoints, and then uses this endpoint address to call the WCF service. WS-Discovery supports two modes to discover the service:

- Ad hoc mode

- Managed mode

These modes are based on different means of transmission: unicast and multicast. It is important to understand these two transmissions.

Unicast transmission is the process of sending of messages to a single network destination identified by a unique address. It is a one-to-one connection between a service provider and its consumer. In Figure 2–6, the message sent by sender A to consumer D is unicast. In *multicast transmission* , data is sent simultaneously in a single transmission to interested destinations only. In the figure, the message sent from sender A to consumers C, D, and G is an example of a multicast transmission.

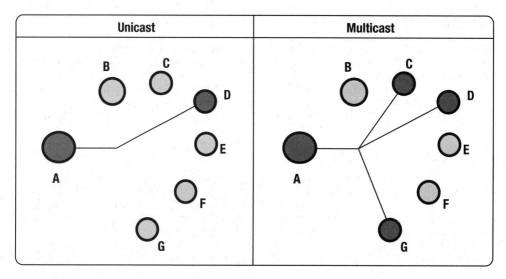

Figure 2–6. Unicast and multicast transmission

In ad hoc mode, a client can probe for a service by sending multicast messages. Services that match the probe can respond back to the client in unicast fashion. Optionally, a service can send multicast messages when it joins or leaves the network. The following are some characteristics of ad hoc clients:

- An ad hoc client is responsible for listening for any multicast message that a service can send.

- An ad hoc client sends a multicast Probe message to locate a service.

- An ad hoc client can find a service by sending a Resolve message in a multicast fashion, in case service endpoints are changed.

The following are some characteristics of ad hoc services:

- An ad hoc service can optionally send a multicast message when it joins the network.

- An ad hoc service that matches Probe message criteria can respond back to a ProbeMatch message in a unicast transmission.

- An ad hoc service can accept and respond to any unicast Probe messages.

- An ad hoc service can respond back to a client with a ResolveMatch message in a unicast transmission that matches the Resolve message criteria.

- An ad hoc service can send a multicast message when leaving a network.

Microsoft has also been successful in abstracting WS standards for application developers. Application developers can now invest time in building services rather than worrying about the underlying implementation that has been abstracted by the framework. Let's take a look at ad hoc mode used with the TradeService service mentioned earlier. Since there is no change in the service contract or implementation used to enable service discovery, we just need to tweak the process that hosts the service to enable service discovery. Listing 2–11 instantiates TradeService in a specific service host with imperative endpoints, and also enables it for service discovery.

Listing 2–11. ServiceHost Instantiation and Enabling for Service Discovery

```
using System;
using System.ServiceModel;
using QuickReturns.StockTrading.ExchangeService;
using QuickReturns.StockTrading.ExchangeService.Contracts;
using System.ServiceModel.Discovery;

namespace QuickReturns.StockTrading.ExchangeService.Hosts
{
    class Program
    {
        static void Main(string[] args)
        {
        Uri address = new Uri
        ("http://localhost:8080/QuickReturns/Exchange");

        ServiceHost host = new ServiceHost(typeof(TradeService);

        ServiceDiscoveryBehavior discoveryBehavior= new ServiceDiscoveryBehavior();
```

```
        host.Description.Behaviors.Add(discoveryBehavior);

        host.Open();
        host.AddServiceEndpoint(new UdpDiscoveryEndpoint());
                    discoveryBehavior.AnnouncementEndpoints.Add(new
    UdpAnnouncementEndpoint());

            Console.WriteLine("Service started: Press Return to exit");

            Console.ReadLine();
                    }
        }
}
```

If you look at the preceding bold code, you will find that there are two steps for making a service discoverable:

1. First, you tell the WCF runtime that your service supports the WS-Discovery protocol. This is done by adding the ServiceDescriptionBehavior in the service behavior's collection. The ServiceDescriptionBehavior can be added imperatively, as mentioned in the preceding listing, or in the configuration file, as shown here:

```
<serviceBehaviors>
    <behavior name="servicebehavior">
    <serviceDiscovery />
    </behavior>
</serviceBehaviors>
```

2. Second, you make your service listen to the WS-Discovery messages. This is done by adding a UdpDiscoveryEndpoint, either imperatively or in the config file. This step makes your service ready to receive and interpret WS-Discovery messages from different clients on the network. Optionally, your service can send a multicast message on the network. This is achieved by adding a new UdpAnnoucement endpoint to the list of service endpoints mentioned in the preceding example.

At the client end, you just need to create an instance of discoveryClient by passing a new endpoint as udpDiscoveryEndpoint. Once done, you can call the DiscoveryClient.find method and pass the find criteria. The following method snippet looks for any service type that implements ITradeService.

```
DiscoveryClient discoveryClient = new DiscoveryClient(new UdpDiscoveryEndpoint());
Findresponse findresponse = discoveryClient.find(new FindCriteria(typeOf(ITradeService)));
```

The Findresponse object has an endpoints collection that stores all the endpoints that implement ITradeService. Once we get any one endpoint in the Findresponse collection, we can call any method of ITradeService like a normal proxy method.

In managed mode, a client and service do not interact directly; they instead have a discovery proxy between them. A managed mode service sends an announcement to the discovery proxy when it joins or leaves the network. A client can probe for a service by sending a unicast message to a discovery proxy. The discovery proxy responds back to the client in a unicast fashion with the list of services that match the criteria.

The following are some characteristics of managed mode clients:

- A managed mode client is responsible for listening to any unicast message that a discovery proxy can send.

- A managed mode client sends a unicast Probe message to a discovery proxy to locate the service.

- A managed mode client can find services by sending a Resolve message in a unicast fashion, in case service endpoints are changed.

The following are some characteristics of discovery proxies:

- A discovery proxy keeps track of all the managed mode service endpoints.

- A discovery proxy is responsible for listening for any unicast message that a managed client or managed proxy can send.

- A discovery proxy responds back with a ProbeMatch message to the client in a unicast message.

- A discovery proxy is responsible for sending a ResolveMatch response for any unicast Resolve request.

The following are some characteristics of managed mode services:

- A managed mode service can optionally send a unicast message to a discovery proxy when it joins a network.

- A managed mode service can accept and respond to any unicast Probe messages.

- A managed mode service can send a multicast message when leaving a network.

Support of Visual Studio

A technology can only be successful if it has the required tools and designers to develop the components. Since the introduction of Visual Basic, Microsoft has always tried to simplify development by utilizing Visual Studio and the integrated development environment (IDE). WCF applications can be created with Visual Studio 2005 or later.

Figure 2–7 shows templates, IntelliSense in the configuration file, and the familiar IDE for creating WCF services in Visual Studio 2010. Developers who are already familiar with the Visual Studio IDE can leverage it to create connected service-oriented systems. You don't need to learn a new language to create service-oriented applications. Languages such as C# and Visual Basic .NET, plus all the other CLR-compatible languages, have been extended to use the capabilities of the classes of WCF. Chapter 4 discusses the Visual Studio IDE and how WCF utilizes the IDE.

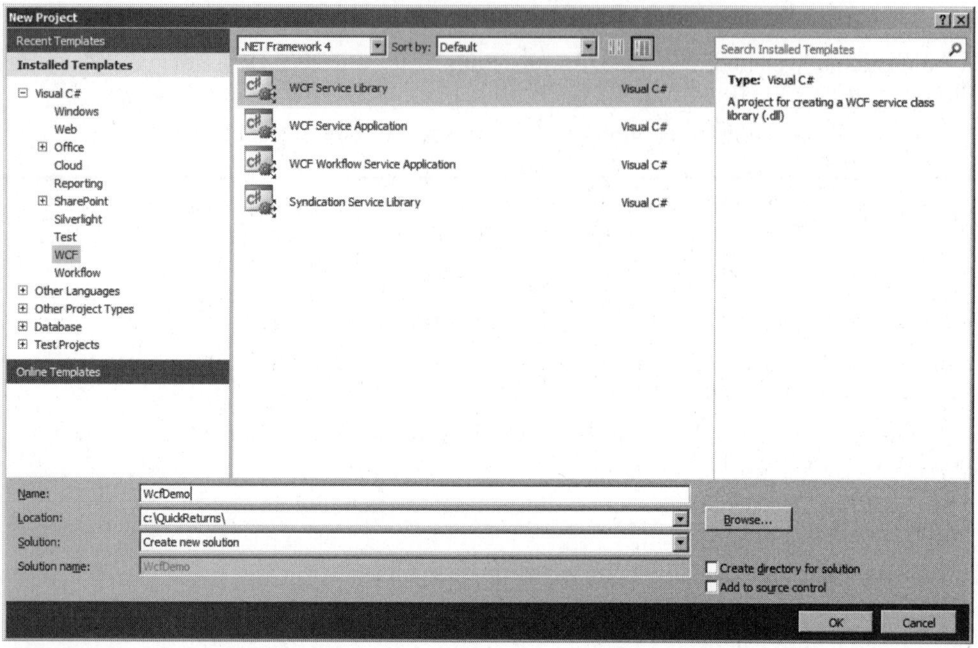

Figure 2–7. Creating a WCF service in Visual Studio .NET 2010

The following list describes the four default WCF templates that come with Visual Studio 2010 (also shown in Figure 2–7):

- *WCF Service Library*: This template is used for creating a WCF service. Use this project if you want a separate project for hosting a WCF service and another project for creating a WCF service library.

- *WCF Service Application*: This template allows you to create WCF services that are being hosted by a local web server. This template not only comes with a default WCF service, but also has the SVC file associated with it so that users can browse the WCF service by navigating to the URL.

- *WCF Workflow Service Application*: This template allows you to create a WCF workflow service. A WCF workflow service provides a way to integrate WCF and Workflow Foundation (WF). We will be discussing workflow services later in this chapter and in upcoming chapters.

- *Syndication Service Library*: This template allows you to create a syndication service that can be exposed as a WCF service.

Routing Service

In .NET 3.x, Microsoft has done remarkable work providing a framework that can set up a WCF service, its clients, and the communication pattern between them. Oftentimes, in a practical scenario, there is a need to have a router or middle agent between the client and services to do some service prioritization, message transformation, or content-based routing; or to perform some logic before reaching out to the service. This has been a common requirement for building a scalable, large, connected system application. In .NET 4.0, WCF provides this middle agent—it's called a *routing service*. Consider a scenario in which a service supports a protocol (let's say TCP) that is not supported by the client. The client would like to communicate using another protocol (say HTTP). In WCF 3.x, you would create an additional service between the client and the service that can do protocol bridging, as shown in Figure 2–8.

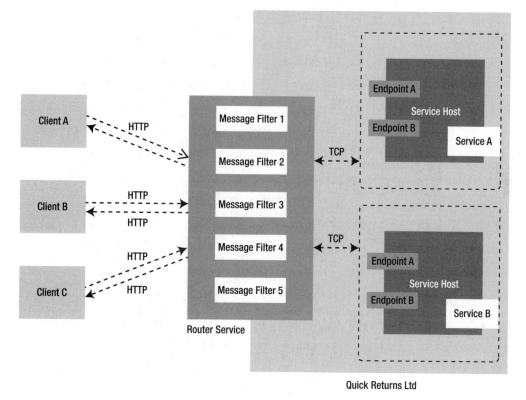

Figure 2–8. RoutingService doing protocol bridging

As shown in Figure 2–8, RoutingService can be of enormous help with protocol bridging. It can let you offer an endpoint over plain, basic HTTP, which is widely accessible and helps interoperability. Clients can talk to this RoutingService endpoint over plain HTTP, and RoutingService can talk with back-end internal services using netTcpBinding. This improves performance as well as interoperability with a wide variety of clients. All the clients interact with RoutingService using basicHTTPbinding, and RoutingService talks with internal services using netTcpBinding.

Another scenario in which a routing service can be of great help is when doing content-based routing. As shown in Figure 2–9, the routing service inspects the SOAP headers and routes the request to the appropriate service based on the existence of a userToken in the SOAP header. Although this was possible in .NET 3.x, it led to multiple endpoints being exposed to the outside world, with each endpoint responding to pockets of clients. In reality, there is a lot of overhead with publicly exposed endpoints. Having a routing service (as shown in Figure 2–9) enables you to have only one endpoint exposed to the outside world, and the routing service does the heavy lifting of taking the message, figuring out the value of the message, and sending it to the appropriate service(s). This avoids management of these costly endpoints by just exposing one endpoint publicly. The routing service also supports the concept of trusted *subsystems*, meaning that when a call comes in, it is validated, authenticated, and passed internally to the systems that need it. RoutingService has additional benefits as well—for example, you don't have to perform security configuration and management on every single endpoint, as these have already been handled by the routing service before it's sent to the back-end services, as shown in Figure 2–9.

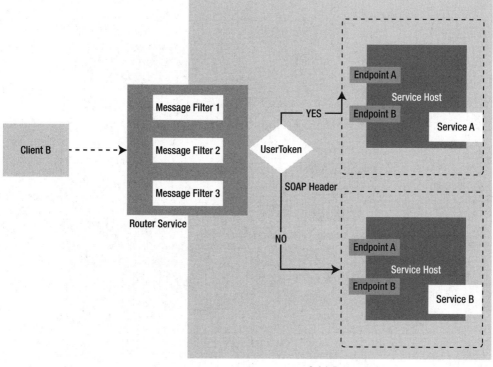

Figure 2–9. RoutingService in content-based routing

Another area in which RoutingService can really help is with error handling. Let's take a classic example, where RoutingService sends a request to an endpoint that is not available. A typical implementation would just send a Fault message back to the client.

As shown in Figure 2–10, with RoutingService you can opt for trying a bunch of alternatives before actually sending a Fault message back to the client. Developers often complain that service-oriented applications have the drawback of complexity along with benefit of scalability, which poses a lot of problems for the client. RoutingService can take this complexity away.

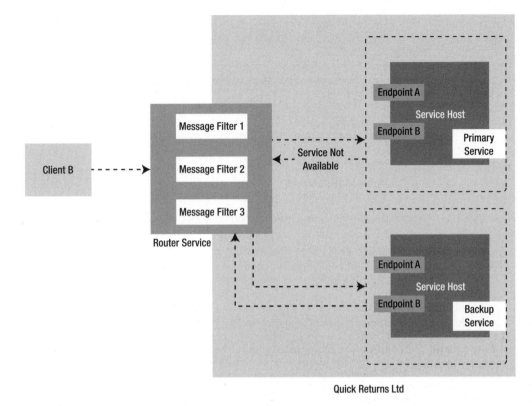

Figure 2–10. RoutingService using alternate services to handle errors

---

■**Note** RoutingService in no way replaces a load balancer. It just acts as an intermediary agent that takes the message in, applies the necessary logic, and redirects this to the intended internal service for its perusal. For network load balancing, we would still require a load balancer to be placed in front of the routing service. In future versions, you may expect to find a load balancer service that can do the task of load balancing, or maybe some built-in features within the routing service.

Until now, if we had to do routing using WCF, we would have needed to build our own router, which would involve a lot of effort. With RoutingService, WCF 4.0 has a router built into the framework. WCF 4.0 offers a built-in class called RoutingService. This class in essence is just a WCF service that resides in the System.ServiceModel.Routing namespace. This namespace contains the classes described in Table 2–4.

Table 2–4. Classes in the System.ServiceModel.Routing Namespace

Classes	Description
RoutingService	Defines a routing service class that routes messages between endpoints based on filter criteria
RoutingBehavior	Defines the routing behavior used to configure the destination endpoints, filters, and filtering options to be used during routing
RoutingExtension	Provides runtime access to the routing service to allow dynamic modification of the routing configuration
RoutingConfiguration	Defines the configuration information used by the RoutingExtension class
SoapProcessingBehavior	Defines the client endpoint behavior used to marshal messages between different binding types and message versions

Now let's take a look at the implementation of RoutingService. First we need to host the routing service and specify the endpoints on which the routing service is accessible. You can host the RoutingService instances in your application like a traditional WCF service, and you can configure these either by code or by configuration file. For our example, let's host the routing service in IIS using wsHttpBinding, as shown in the following snippet from the config file:

```
<service name="System.ServiceModel.Routing.RoutingService"
behaviorConfiguration="QuickReturnRoutedBehavior">
  <endpoint
address=" http://localhost:8080/QuickReturnsRouters/"
 binding="wsHttpBinding"                name="MyRoutingEndpoint"
contract="System.ServiceModel.Routing.IRequestReplyRouter"/>
    </service>
```

Have a look at the contract name in the preceding snippet. It is IrequestReplyRouter, which is one of the service contracts that RoutingService implements. Table 2–5 shows all the service contracts that RoutingService implements. Each of these service contracts is implemented in RoutingService to support multiple messaging patterns. While configuring the RoutingService, you need to specify one of these interfaces in the contract.

Table 2–5. Interface Implemented by the System.ServiceModel.Routing.RoutingService Class

Classes	Description
IDuplexSessionRouter	Defines interfaces required to process messages from duplex session channels
IRequestReplyRouter	Defines interfaces required to process messages from request-reply channels
ISimplexDatagramRouter	Defines interfaces required to process messages from simplex datagrams
ISimplexSessionRouter	Defines interfaces required to process messages from simplex session channels

The second step to initiating the routing service is to include it in the service behavior. So, apart from specifying the endpoint of the routing service, the preceding snippet also specifies the use of behaviorConfiguration as a QuickReturnRoutedBehavior that is defined in the application configuration file, as follows:

```
<behaviors>
    <serviceBehaviors>
      <behavior name=" QuickReturnRoutedBehavior ">
        <serviceMetadata httpGetEnabled="True"/>
        <serviceDebug includeExceptionDetailInFaults="True"/>
        <routing routingTableName="ServiceRouterTable"/>
      </behavior>
    </serviceBehaviors>
</behaviors>
```

In order to host a routing service, you need to add a routing behavior, as shown in the preceding snippet, by specifying the routingTableName, which is a filter table you would use with RoutingServiceInstance.

When a message comes into the routing service, RoutingService needs to know where it should route it. Another step is to configure destination endpoints to which the routing service may redirect the request, as shown in the following snippet. For this example, I would like RoutingService to redirect to the WCF service exchangeService (which we will create in Chapter 5).

```
<client>
    <endpoint
    name="ExchangeService" binding="wsHttpBinding"
    address=" http://localhost:8080/QuickReturns/Exchange.svc"
    contract="*">
    </endpoint>
</client>
```

This RoutingService class has a built-in filtering mechanism that lets you specify filtering criteria based on what you would like to route to the appropriate endpoint. The routing service will then do the filtering based on the input set in the App.config file, and will route the request to the appropriate service. This is implemented using message filters and message filter tables. *Message filter tables* can be considered a big reservoir of message filters. *Message filters* are sets of rules that are configured using a message filter table. Once these rules are satisfied by RoutingService, it then routes the message to the endpoint associated with these message filters. So, a message comes in, the framework sends it to a message filter table, and the message is propagated to all of those. All the matched responses are collected and then sent to appropriate endpoint(s). In Listing 2–12, we used MatchAll as the message filter type that will route all the services.

Listing 2–12. MatchAll Message Filter

```
<routing>
    <!--Filter For Detecting Messages Headers to redirect-->
    <filters>
      <filter name="MyFilter_1" filterType="MatchAll"/>
    </filters>
    <!--Define Routing Table, This will Map the service with Filter-->
    <routingTables>
      <table name="ServiceRouterTable">
        <entries>
          <add filterName="MyFilter_1" endpointName=" ExchangeService "/>
        </entries>
      </table>
    </routingTables>
</routing>
```

Notice that the name of the routing table is configured as ServiceRouterTable, which was specified while setting up the routing behavior. Also, the endpoint name has been configured as ExchangeService, which we created subsequently. Apart from the preceding message filter, there are several message filters available out of the box. One of them, Action, routes a SOAP action of a particular message. Another message filter, Address, routes based on the address. Another one is the XPATH message filter table. XPATH is a language for traversing XML data. A SOAP message is an XML message, and XPATH message filters let you extract a specific element out of SOAP messages, and decide the further action based on the value. All of these message filters are described in more detail in Chapter 11. The .NET Framework also provides an opportunity for developers to create custom message filters as well.

The last step is to point to the routing service on the client side, not the actual service. RoutingService will do the magic of routing to the actual service based on the filtering criteria.

Improved REST Support

The Web has exhibited exponential growth over the years, and can be considered a large distributed system. The early stages of Web were all about static content linked together to provide useful information. Over time, the Web has evolved a lot. Right now, we have a content-driven Web that is growing more and more every day. The richness of the client is increasing rapidly. Today, we live in a world where the browser doesn't just render content; it has become more of an application container. You can install applications like Silverlight, Flash, or a JavaScript engine inside this container. One of the specific features of the Web is its loyalty to HTTP. HTTP is the baseline application protocol of the Web. It provides a set of operations in the form of GET, PUT, or POST, and also a standard set of responses known as *status codes*.

Representational State Transfer (REST) is a simple way of building services. It has been widely used for a long time. REST is not a specification, but an architectural style used for building distributed, hypermedia-driven applications. It involves building data-oriented services by defining resources that implement interfaces that are uniform, and that can be located/identified by a URI. It has now been accepted by Microsoft and other industry titans for developing services.

■**Note** The term *REST* was coined by Roy Fieldings, an American-born computer scientist and one of the principal authors of the HTTP specification (RFC 2616). He didn't invent the principle of REST, but he was the first person to identify the characteristics and architectural underpinnings of the Web that makes it so successful and phenomenally scalable. His doctoral thesis, in which he first describes the term *REST*, is available at www.ics.uci.edu/~fielding/pubs/dissertation/top.htm.

When we talk about building RESTful APIs, we are actually talking about using HTTP in the manner in which it was intended to be used. REST enables the use of HTTP GET, POST, and PUT operations, so you don't have to use SOAP. Most of us who use SOAP and WS-* realize that it's a bit complicated to build and develop services around it. There are lots of pros and cons to using REST vs. SOAP, and comparing those is outside the scope of this chapter. However, it's important to understand that there are lots of scenarios where REST makes sense, and lots of others where SOAP makes sense.

Since the inception of the .NET Framework, Microsoft has been investing a lot in SOAP. There has been a radical shift in the Microsoft approach in the past few years toward using REST. The usefulness of REST has now been acknowledged by Microsoft. In .NET 3.0 and earlier, there was no REST support, and one needed to write a lot of extension elements in order to have REST on WCF. In .NET 3.5, Microsoft added some initial support for REST, and made it possible to build REST-style services using WCF. The support of REST in .NET 3.5 was widely adopted by the community and thereby resulted in improved REST support in .NET 4.0. Now, in .NET 4.0, Microsoft has made REST a first-class way of building services.

Most of the classes for the REST programming model reside in the `System.ServiceModel.Web` namespace. The `WebServiceHost` class has been modified to support the REST programming model and is now used to host REST services. If a user has not created an explicit endpoint at his base address, the `WebServiceHost` class automatically creates a default endpoint using `WebHttpBinding`.

In order to host the REST service, you need to use the `WebServiceHost` class (not the `ServiceHost` class). All the REST API methods reside in the `System.ServiceModel.Web` namespace. When you configure a `WebServiceHost` instance to host a service, it automatically configures your service with the `WebHttpBehavior` and adds a default HTTP endpoint configured with the `WebHttpBinding`. The `WebHttpBehavior` is used to modify the WCF dispatching layer to use a RESTful-based context to route messages. One of the biggest problems with using REST is that you can't use WSDL or proxy generation. One of the supports that has been introduced in WCF 4.0 is the automatic help page, which describes the RESTful service. In addition, it disables the HTTP help page when it creates this default endpoint. Set the `HelpEnabled` property to `true` in the `WebHttpBehavior` to enable the HTTP help page. Listing 2–13 shows how to enable this property for the `TradeService` class.

Listing 2–13. Enabling the HelpEnabled Property for the TradeService Class

```
<startup><supportedRuntime version="v4.0" sku=".NETFramework,Version=v4.0"/></startup>
   <system.serviceModel>
      <serviceHostingEnvironment aspNetCompatibilityEnabled="true" />
      <services>
        <service name="RESTSERVICE.TradeService">
<endpoint address="" behaviorConfiguration="TradeServiceBehavior"
binding="webHttpBinding" contract="RESTSERVICE.ITradeService">
        </endpoint>
      </service>
    </services>
    <behaviors>
      <endpointBehaviors>
```

```
            <behavior name="TradeServiceBehavior">
              <webHttp helpEnabled="true" />
            </behavior>
          </endpointBehaviors>
        </behaviors>
      </system.serviceModel>
```

Now you can view the help page by adding /help to the end of the REST service URL. This help page provides the following:

- A description of each operation annotated with [WebGet] or [WebInvoke]

- A URI template

- A supported HTTP operation and message format

For each request/response, the help page also provides an XML schema and a corresponding sample XML instance that consumers can use to integrate with the service. REST's greatest benefit is that it's based on HTTP caching, and Microsoft has provided a lot of features in .NET 4.0 that enable HTTP caching support over the wire, which in turn enables the services to be more scalable. The [AspNetCacheProfile] attribute enables you to use the ASP.NET caching profile along with your GET-based operations. The [AspNetCacheProfile] attribute will point to the ASP.NET cache profile section in web.config, where the details about how the response should be cached are specified. The [AspNetCacheProfile] attribute makes it much easier to take advantage of HTTP caching. Listing 2–14 shows how to apply the [AspNetCacheProfile] attribute to a service operation. In this case, the cache profile named CacheforTradeService will be used for the TradeSecurity operation.

Listing 2–14. Using the [AspNetCacheProfile] Attribute

```
[ServiceContract]
public interface ITradeService
    {

        [AspNetCacheProfile("CacheforTradeService")]
        [OperationContract]
        [WebGet]
        decimal TradeSecurity(string ticker, int quantity);
    }



<configuration>
    <system.web>
      <compilation debug="true" targetFramework="4.0" />
      <caching>
  <outputCache enableOutputCache="true"/>
        <outputCacheSettings>
          <outputCacheProfiles>
 <add name=" CacheforTradeService " duration="120" varyByParam="ticker" varyByHeader="Accept"
/>
          </outputCacheProfiles>
        </outputCacheSettings>
      </caching>
    </system.web>

</configuration>
```

The duration is specified in seconds, so a value of 120 indicates that the response should be cached for 2 minutes. The `varyByParam` attribute specifies that requests with different values for the `ticker` URI query string parameter should be considered to be different requests, and should be cached separately. Likewise, the `varyByHeader` attribute specifies that requests with different `Accept` header values should be considered different requests.

Workflow Services

Workflow is a long-running, declarative, visual programming medium that can abstract details of an application. WCF is standard model for distributed applications and provides a service-oriented, contract message–based programming model. Both of these technologies are complementary to each other. Workflow provides a very natural way to build and consume services. So, after .NET 3.0, when Microsoft released the first version of WF and WCF together, developers and architects started using them together and found them complementary. One of the features of WF is that it provides you with a long-running, durable application. When WF and WCF are integrated, WF can benefit from the service orientation features of WCF and interact via messages. Many people have successfully built workflows and exposed them as WCF services. Workflow services provide integration between the two products. with the help of workflow services, you can

- Expose a WCF service as a workflow

- Consume a WCF service inside workflow

One of Microsoft's basic design goals for workflow services was to avoid a radical design change in WF and WCF. Microsoft wanted workflow services to be built on top of the existing WF and WCF programming model. NET 4.0 builds upon prior investments in WCF and WF to enable developers to create connected and declarative applications. Workflow services were introduced as a part of .NET 3.x. In .NET 4.0, more features have been added to them, making them more intuitive for developers.

WCF services can now be completely XAML-based. If you create a workflow service using a Visual Studio 2010 template, you will get a default file called `Service1.xamlx`, as shown in Figure 2–11. Notice that the service has been represented in a standard workflow designer. This file contains the service definition, and the implementation is simply a XAML-based workflow.

In .NET 3.5, only two WCF-related activities were supported:

- Send

- Receive

The Send activity is used to invoke an operation, and the Receive activity is used to implement an operation. In a normal scenario, you will have a Send activity on the client side and a Receive activity on the service side. In .NET 4.0, Microsoft has extended the activities to support two more:

- SendAndReceiveReply

- ReceiveAndSendReply

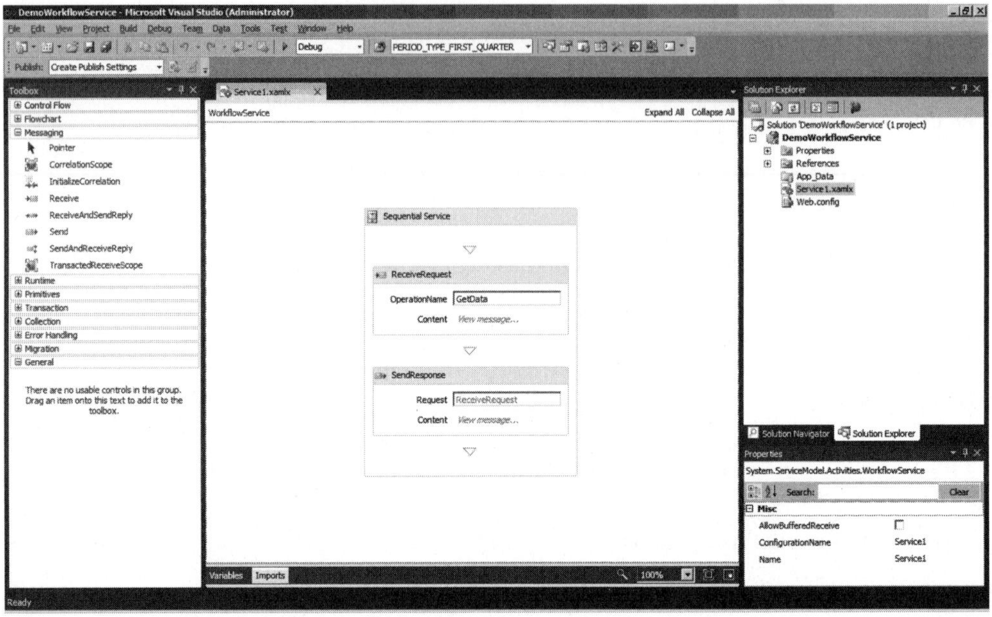

Figure 2–11. Workflow services in Visual Studio 2010

SendAndReceiveReply sends a SOAP message and waits for the reply. ReceiveAndSendReply receives a SOAP message and sends a reply to the sender. You can now enable "Add Service reference" while in the workflow environment. This will help to get all the types and activities that are needed to complete the workflow. Visual Studio 2010 will create a separate custom activity for each operation found in the WSDL document. NET 4.0 also ships with a standard endpoint called WorkflowControlEndpoint, which enables you to call control operations on workflow instances. WorkflowServiceHost has been redesigned in the .NET 4.0 programming model, and now resides in the System.ServiceModel.Activities assembly. .NET 4.0 now supports content-based correlation as well. Correlation helps in resolving the correlation issues that may arise when multiple workflow instances are waiting for the same event. CorrelationHandle does this by associating the incoming message with the right workflow instance. This is done by using the workflow variable type CorrelationHandle. All the activity that needs to participate in the same correlation should have a value of CorrelationHandle in the CorrelatesWith property.

Workflow services should be used if the services are doing a lot of asynchronous work, such as calling a database or another service. Workflow pushes the complexity of coordinating the asynchronous code into the framework. This enables you to maintain a much simpler service. If you have services that perform parallel work, consider using workflow services, as it is very easy to express the parallel tasks in workflow. Figure 2–12 shows the Workflow service application template in Visual Studio 2010.

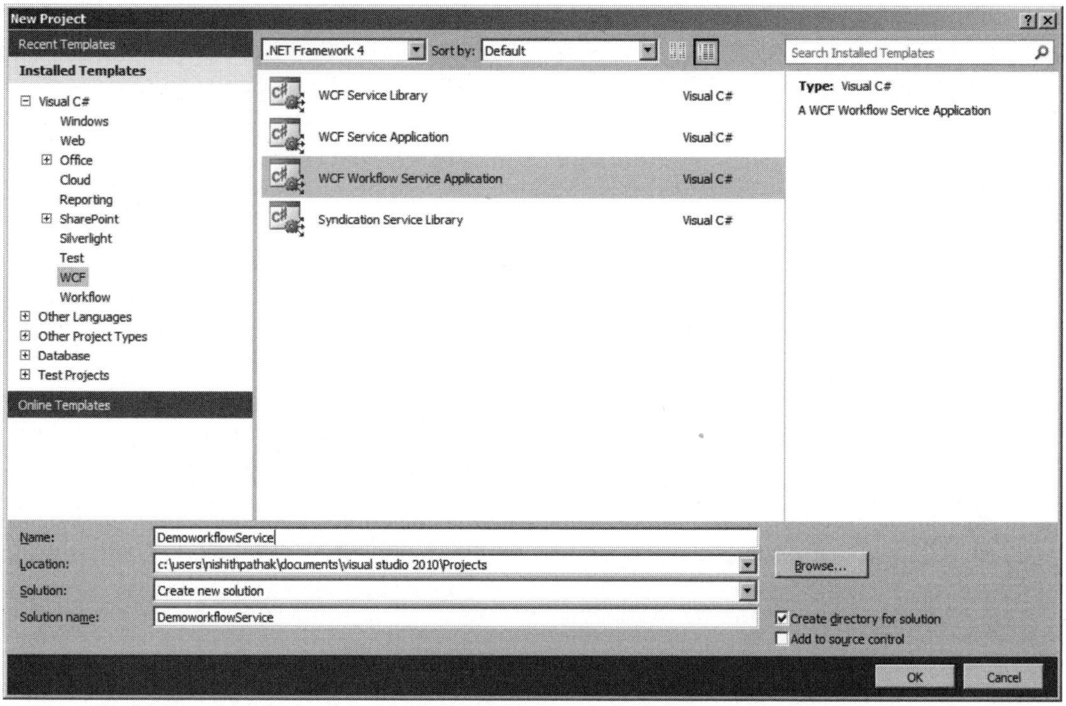

Figure 2–12. Workflow services using a Visual Studio 2010 template

If you would like to ensure the message order before responding to a message, then you can express this logic in workflow quite naturally. You might also consider also using workflow services if your services are executed in sequence, or are expected to be long-running and need to be persisted.

Summary

.NET 4.0 provides an interesting new landscape for WCF, and makes it a lot easier to use. There are lots of default configurations that are easy to override, and in many scenarios it's easy to define the default settings in the `machine.config` file. WS-Discovery is one of the best features provided in WCF 4.0. Using this mechanism, a client application can dynamically discover endpoint addresses and make a call to a WCF service. WCF 4.0's `RoutingService` is in my opinion the best feature provided by .NET 4.0. It reduces the complication and time for developing routings using code.

WCF provides a number of benefits that will make developers more productive, reduce the number of bugs, speed up application development, and simplify deployment. WCF helps achieve all those challenges using a unified programming model that provides for a unified message style based on open standards and optimized for binary communication where applicable. WCF's unified programming model also provides for building secure, reliable, and interoperable applications. With that said, IT managers are understandably wary of using WCF, since it's a relatively new technology that has a moderately steep learning curve. However, for most organizations, the benefits will far outweigh the negatives; and with WCF, you'll see great productivity gains in future development projects.

In Chapter 3 we'll explain the unified programming model, and further explore the productivity you will gain from using WCF.

CHAPTER 3

■ ■ ■

Exploring the WCF Programming Model

Building connected systems on the Microsoft platform usually means using multiple technologies and as many different programming models. WCF comes with a unified programming model that makes your life as a developer much easier. Some of the benefits are as follows:

- Built-in support for a broad set of web service protocols

- Implicit use of service-oriented development principles

- A single API for building connected systems

The heart of WCF lives inside the System.ServiceModel namespace and the messaging system underneath it. This chapter won't go into the details of all the classes in the namespaces. (We will go through most of them throughout the next chapters.) This chapter will give you a basic understanding of the programming model, and should give you a starting point to understand the more complex concepts of WCF.

To illustrate how to use WCF, we will present a case study of a fictitious company called QuickReturns Ltd. QuickReturns Ltd. is a stock-trading company that needs a connected system to trade stock on a stock exchange. Typical actors in these types of systems are market makers and asset managers. *Asset managers* are individuals who provide portfolio management and issue stock trades through a market. Asset managers make decisions about what securities to buy or sell in order to establish a portfolio that meets a client's needs. *Market makers* provide execution activities on a set of stocks listed on an exchange. They provide liquidity needs for investors. They clear and settle transactions through a depository. The appendix of this book describes the QuickReturns Ltd. case study. In this chapter, we will define the initial set of contracts and services that the QuickReturns Ltd. system offers.

After completing this chapter

- You'll be familiar with the core architecture of WCF.

- You'll be familiar with all the terms that are used in WCF.

- You'll understand the unified programming model of WCF.

- You'll be able to start developing your first WCF-enabled application.

- You'll know the areas of WCF that can be extended.

Introducing the Technical Architecture

Though you can install and use WCF with .NET 3.0, you'll want to use it with .NET 4.0 so that you can leverage all the new features that are supported (see Chapter 2 again for details on these features). To be able to use WCF with Visual Studio 2010 and .NET 4.0, you have to install one of the following operating systems:

- Windows XP SP3 or later

- Windows Server 2003 SP2 or later

- Windows Vista SP1

- Windows 7

- Windows Server 2008 (not supported in the Server Core role)

You'll also need a development environment to develop connected system applications with WCF. The development environment for WCF can be Visual Studio 2005 or above. However, since this book covers Visual Studio 2010 features, we recommend using Visual Studio 2010.

■**Note** The Windows Software Development Kit (SDK) comes with a lot of sample code you can use to learn WCF and the other frameworks that are part of the .NET Framework 4.0. You can get the latest version at the .NET Framework Developer Center, at http://msdn.microsoft.com/hi-in/netframework/default.aspx. Finally, refer to http://msdn.microsoft.com/en-us/netframework/default.aspx for additional news, samples, and resources.

Introducing the Programming Approach

You can accomplish your development goals with WCF 4 through any of the following approaches:

- Using the object model programmatically.

- Using configuration files.

- Using declarative programming (attributes).

You will use all these approaches in most of your applications, and it is a great benefit for developers to be able to choose their preference. In most of your applications, you'll want to avoid hard-coding anything so that your apps can remain flexible for other developers. Hence, it is important to make your application configurable.The object model is the richest model, in which you can basically accomplish anything you like. The WCF configuration model is built on top of the object model.

You also have to make sure you know the order of precedence in WCF (since you can override one model with another). The order in which settings are applied is as follows:

1. Attributes are applied.

2. The configuration is applied.

3. The code runs.

In the following sections, we will show how to accomplish the same goals in different ways.

WCF Programming Model

In this section, we'll address clients, services, endpoints, and behaviors on the service model side. Together, the address, binding, and contract are commonly referred to as an *endpoint*. Figure 3–1 illustrates all the components for consuming WCF services using the programming model and using and extending the messaging layer. In addition, you can see how the service model manipulates the messaging layer and which terms fit where.

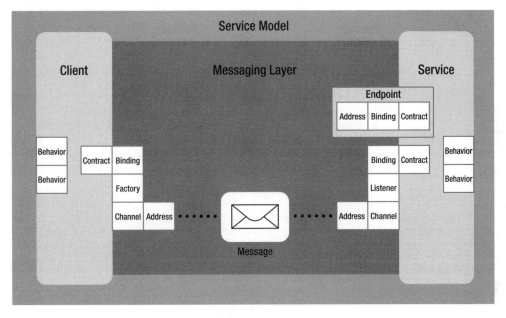

Figure 3–1. The WCF programming model

On the client side, there is only one endpoint. Think of the client as a piece inside your program that is able to communicate with a service—not your entire application. This is commonly referred to as a *proxy* for that service. Of course, it is possible to have your client connect to multiple services by using multiple proxies with different endpoints (i.e., connected to different services). The client side can have a specific behavior to perform local configuration, such as concurrency, instancing, throttling, error handling, transaction control, security, and so on. (We will be discussing these in Chapters 6 through 10.)

The service side can have multiple endpoints. A service just sits around and waits for messages to come in on its endpoints. The service side has the same behaviors as the client side with regard to local configuration and operations.

You will learn more about behaviors, factories, listeners, and channels later in this chapter. Now we'll cover addresses, bindings, and contracts (commonly knows as the ABCs of WCF) in much greater detail.

Addresses

Addressing a service is essential to being able to use a service. You need to have the address of a service to be able to send it a message. Addresses in WCF are URLs that define the protocol used, the machine where the service is running, and the path to the service. The port number is an optional field in the URL and depends on the protocol used. Table 3–1 lists the addressing specifications.

Table 3–1. Addressing Specifications

Address Section	Description
Transport scheme	This defines the transport protocol (or scheme).
Machine name	This specifies the fully qualified domain name of the machine.
Port	This is an optional field and is specified as :port. Port 80 is the default for HTTP addresses.
Path	This is the specific path to the service. You can define paths as names of directories by using a forward slash. For example, /Stock/GetQuote is the path in the following address: http://localhost:8080/Stock/GetQuote.

So, the format of a service address is as follows:

```
scheme://<machinename>[:port]/path1/path2
```

This format is similar to the URL of a web site. scheme can be any type of supported transport, machinename is the server name, port is the port where the service is listening, and path is used essentially to differentiate services running on the same machine. WCF supports several protocols, and each has its own particular addressing format. The default WCF messaging protocol is SOAP, in which endpoints are expressed using WS-Addressing constructs.

Addressing HTTP

Services can be hosted in different ways; you'll learn more about these in Chapter 5. HTTP services can either be self-hosted or hosted on Internet Information Services (IIS). When addressing an HTTP service in a self-hosted scenario, you use the following format:

```
http://localhost:8080/QuickReturns/Exchange
```

When SSL is required, you can replace http with https. In a WCF configuration, you can set the HTTP address as follows:

```
<endpoint
    address="http://localhost:8080/QuickReturns/Exchange"
    bindingsSectionName="BasicHttpBinding"
    contract="IExchange" />
```

We'll cover the bindingsSectionName and contract attributes of the endpoint node in the following sections.

Addressing TCP

The TCP transport uses the `net.tcp:` scheme, but otherwise follows the same rules as described for HTTP addresses. Here is an example:

```
net.tcp://localhost:8080/QuickReturns/Exchange
```

In a WCF configuration, you can set the `net.tcp` address as follows:

```
<endpoint
    address="net.tcp://localhost:8080/QuickReturns/Exchange"
    bindingsSectionName="NetTcpBinding"
    contract="IExchange" />
```

Addressing MSMQ

You can use the Microsoft Message Queuing (MSMQ) transport in an asynchronous one-way (fire-and-forget) or duplex type of messaging pattern, and use the MSMQ features of Windows. MSMQ has public and private queues. Public queues are usually available through Active Directory and can be accessed remotely, whereas private queues are local queues that are available only on the local machine. MSMQ addresses use the `net.msmq` scheme and specify a machine name, queue type, and queue name. Port numbers don't have any meaning in the MSMQ address. A sample MSMQ address is as follows:

```
net.msmq://localhost/private$/QuickReturnSettleTrade
```

In a WCF configuration, you can set the `net.msmq` address as follows:

```
<endpoint
    address=" net.msmq://localhost/private$/QuickReturnsSettleTrade"
    bindingsSectionName="NetMsmqBinding"
    contract="IExchange" />
```

Addressing Named Pipes

Named pipes provide a means to implement inter- or in-process communication. The Named Pipes transport in WCF supports only local communication and uses the `net.pipes` scheme. Port numbers don't have any meaning with the Named Pipes transport. This results in the following address format:

```
net.pipe://localhost/QuickReturns/Exchange
```

In a WCF configuration, you can set the `net.pipe` address as follows:

```
<endpoint
    address="net.pipe://localhost/QuickReturns/Exchange"
    bindingsSectionName="NetNamedPipeBinding"
    contract="IExchange" />
```

Base Addresses

When multiple endpoints are associated with a WCF service, you assign a primary address to the service and a relative addresses to all the endpoints. The primary address is called the *base address*, which shortcuts the duplication of the scheme, host, port, and root path in your configuration. To define two endpoints in a WCF configuration, you would add the following section to express QuickReturns Ltd's base address:

```
<host>
    <baseAddresses>
        <add baseAddress="http://localhost:8080/QuickReturns"/>
        <add baseAddress="net.pipe://localhost/QuickReturns"/>
    </baseAddresses>
</host>
```

This allows you to define the following endpoints:

```
<endpoint
    name="BasicHttpBinding"
    address="Exchange"
    bindingsSectionName="BasicHttpBinding"
    contract="IExchange" />

<endpoint
    name="NetNamedPipeBinding"
    address="Exchange"
    bindingsSectionName="NetNamedPipeBinding"
    contract="IExchange" />
```

Bindings

A binding defines how you can communicate with a service, and as such has the biggest impact in the programming model of WCF. It is the primary extension point of the ABCs of WCF. The binding controls the following:

- The transport (HTTP, MSMQ, Named Pipes, TCP)

- The channels (one-way, duplex, request-reply)

- The encoding (XML, binary, Message Transmission Optimization Mechanism [MTOM])

- The supported WS-* protocols (WS-Security, WS-Federation, WS-Reliability, WS-Transactions)

WCF provides a default set of bindings that should cover most of your requirements. If the default bindings don't cover your requirements, you can build your own binding by extending from CustomBinding class.

Table 3–2 shows the features of each default binding that comes with WCF. These features directly relate to the transport protocols, the encoding, and the WS-* protocols. The Configuration and Element columns relate to the configuration element in the application interoperability; the Transactions, Security, and Default Session columns relate to several of the WS-* protocols described in Chapters 1 and 2. The Duplex column specifies whether the binding supports the duplex messaging exchange pattern. As you can see, each transport we covered earlier has at least one associated predefined binding.

Table 3–2. Predefined WCF Bindings

Binding	Configuration	Security	Default Session	Transactions	Duplex
basicHttpBinding	Basic Profile 1.1	None	No		
wsHttpBinding	WS	Message	Optional	Yes	
wsDualHttpBinding	WS	Message	Yes	Yes	Yes
wsFederationHttpBinding	WS-Federation	Message	Yes	Yes	No
netTcpBinding	.NET	Transport	Optional	Yes	Yes
netNamedPipeBinding	.NET	Transport	Yes	Yes	Yes
netMsmqBinding	.NET	Transport	Yes	Yes	No
netPeerTcpBinding	Peer	Transport			Yes
msmqIntegrationBinding	MSMQ	Transport		Yes	
basicHttpContextBinding	basic Profile 1.1	None	No	No	
NetTcpContextBinding	.NET	Transport	Optional	None	Yes
WebHttpBinding	WS	Transport	No		
WSHttpContextBinding	WS	Transport	No	No	
WS2007FederationHttpBinding	WS-Federation	Message	Yes	Yes	No
WS2007httpBinding	WS	Message	Yes	Yes	

Remember that you can have multiple endpoints defined for a service so that your service supports any combination of these bindings. Only the last six bindings in Table 3–2 (displayed in bold) are predefined bindings that ship with the .NET Framework.

Obviously, only HTTP(S) is truly an interoperable transport. When integration is required with different platforms, you can recognize interoperable bindings with the WS prefix. As mentioned, when you choose a binding, you are often choosing a transport as well. Table 3–3 lists the predefined WCF bindings and the transports they support.

Table 3-3. Predefined WCF Bindings Mapped on the Transports

Binding	HTTP	HTTPS	TCP	MSMQ	Named Pipes
BasicHttpBinding	Yes	Yes	No	No	No
WSHttpBinding	Yes	Yes	Yes	No	No
WSDualHttpBinding	Yes	Yes	No	No	No
WSFederationHttpBinding	Yes	Yes	No	No	No
NetTcpBinding	No	No	Yes	No	No
netTcpContextBinding	No	No	Yes	No	No
NetNamedPipeBinding	No	No	No	No	Yes
NetMsmqBinding	No	No	No	Yes	No
NetPeerTcpBinding	No	No	Yes	No	No
MsmqIntegrationBinding	No	No	No	Yes	No
basicHttpContextBinding	Yes	Yes	No	No	No
NetTcpContextBinding	No	No	Yes	No	No
WebHttpBinding	Yes	Yes	No	No	No
WSHttpContextBinding	Yes	Yes	No	No	No
WS2007FederationHttpBinding	Yes	Yes	No	No	No
WS2007httpBinding	Yes	Yes	No	No	No

BasicHttpBinding is also an interoperable binding that maps very well onto pre-WCF service stacks such as ASMX. The bindings prefixed with Net are Windows-centric; for these, interoperability is expected to be a requirement. In this way, you know up front what your requirements are, and as such, what transport fits best into your scenario.

Contracts

One of the core principles of service orientation is explicit boundaries. When crossing process boundaries in typical RPC technology, you will struggle with issues in which the internals and externals are mixed up. The essence of *contracts* in service orientation is that you agree on what you expose to the outside world in order to decide for yourself how you implement (and change) the inside. Service orientation draws a distinct line between the external interface and the internal implementation. Contracts are the way service orientation achieves true interoperability between different platforms; see Chapter 13 for more details about this.

Contracts come in different flavors. A contract can be a declaration of exposed behavior (the service contract), persistent data (the data contract), or message structure (the message contract). In the following sections, you will learn how to define and use each of these in the WCF programming model.

Message Exchange Patterns

WCF service contracts can express three message exchange patterns that can be used in your services. Note that the binding that you choose will limit the message exchange patterns that are available.

Request-Reply

Request-reply is a two-way operation where each request correlates with a response. The client explicitly waits for a reply. Request-reply is the most common pattern in today's (ASMX) web service (and RPC) world. In WCF, request-reply is the default pattern. Figure 3–2 illustrates the request-reply messaging exchange pattern.

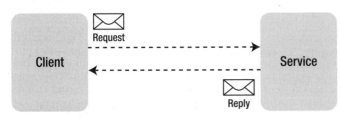

Figure 3–2. Request-reply messaging exchange pattern

One-Way

One-way is a fire-and-forget style of messaging, where the message is transmitted without waiting for a reply from the service. As shown in Figure 3–3, the message is initiated on the client side and passed to the service side, but the client does not expect a reply. This is similar to calling an asynchronous method (a delegate) with a void return type.

Figure 3–3. One-way messaging exchange pattern

Duplex

Duplex messaging is slightly more complex. A duplex channel is really a peer-to-peer connection, with both ends simultaneously acting as both a sender and a receiver (on different channels), as shown in Figure 3–4. A duplex service defines two interfaces—one for each side of the wire. (Refer to Chapter 12 for more information about peer-to-peer and duplex messaging.)

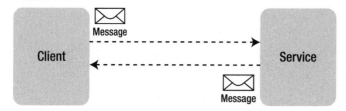

Figure 3–4. *Duplex messaging exchange pattern*

Service Contracts and Operations

The *service contract* expresses the "methods" that are exposed to the outside world. The service contract is also commonly referred to as the *service interface* or the *exposed behavior* of the service. It describes what you can expect from the service, and its policy describes what requirements the service has. Service contracts are implemented as .NET interfaces. The service contracts are implemented as .NET classes implementing the .NET interface. To make the classes WCF service contracts, you must annotate the interface with the [ServiceContract] attribute. The operations need to be annotated with the [OperationContract] attribute. You can find the ServiceContractAttribute and OperationContractAttribute classes in the System.ServiceModel namespace, which you have to include with a using statement. Listing 3–1 shows the service contract defined as a .NET interface for QuickReturns Ltd., including two operation contracts.

Listing 3–1. ServiceContract for the Trade Service

```
using System.ServiceModel;
using QuickReturns.StockTrading.ExchangeService.DataContracts;

namespace QuickReturns.StockTrading.ExchangeService.Contracts
{
    [ServiceContract(Namespace = "http://QuickReturns")]
     interface ITradeService
     {
         [OperationContract()]
         Quote GetQuote(string ticker);

         [OperationContract()]
         void PublishQuote(Quote quote);
     }
}
```

This service is the exchange of the stock-trading application for QuickReturns Ltd. The contract of this service defines the interaction that is going on between the sellers and buyers on a stock market. Sellers offer their stocks by publishing quotes. A quote defines the company the stock is for and what price the seller wants for it. The PublishQuote method is able to publish quotes from sellers on the trade service. The buyers will query the trade service to get a quote on a stock from a specific company. The GetQuote method is able to retrieve published quotes from the service. When the buyer finds an appropriate seller, the actual exchange of stocks can take place by a different service (which will be covered later in this book).

■**Note** When designing a service contract, there are two common approaches: *contract-first* and *code-first*. The contract-first approach ensures interoperability and for most situations is the recommended approach. This ensures that any consumers of the services conform to the published contract. This is especially important if any third parties are involved who need to conform to a predetermined contract. One of the biggest challenges to the contract-first approach is productivity. If in a given situation productivity has a higher precedence than interoperability, then it might make sense to use the code-first approach. (Refer to Chapter 4 for a more detailed discussion of the topic.)

The exchange service is marked with the [ServiceContract] attribute and currently has two operations, GetQuote and PublishQuote. These operations have the [OperationContract] attribute applied. WCF uses these attributes to determine which .NET methods it needs to invoke based on an incoming SOAP message. The attributes also determine the serialization WCF has to do for you—the mapping from SOAP messages to your .NET objects. In Listing 3–1, Quote is a custom .NET type where no mapping is defined yet. For the custom Quote object and any other custom object you want to pass between services and clients, you have to define data contracts. *Data contracts* control the mapping between SOAP messages and .NET objects. We'll cover data contracts in the next section.

To customize the service contract, the ServiceContract attribute has several parameters, as follows:

CallbackContract: Gets or sets the type of callback contract. This is useful when using the duplex messaging exchange pattern.

ConfigurationName: Defines the name as used in the configuration file to store the related configuration settings.

Name: Gets or sets the name for the <portType> element in WSDL. The default value is the name of the .NET interface.

Namespace: Gets or sets the namespace for the <portType> element in WSDL. The default value is the namespace of the .NET interface.

HasProtectionLevel: Defines a (read-only) value that indicates the protection level of the service. At the operation level, it is possible to define that the messages of the operation must be encrypted, signed, or both.

ProtectionLevel: Defines the protection level that the binding must support.

SessionMode: Gets or sets a value that defines whether the contract requires the WCF binding associated with the contract to use channel sessions. SessionMode is an enumeration with possible values of allowed, notallowed, and required. The default value is allowed.

TypeID: Returns a unique identifier when implemented in the derived class.

The same is true for the [OperationContract] attribute. Several parameters are available:

Name: Specifies the name of the operation. The default is the name of the operation.

Action: Defines the (WS-Addressing) action of the request message.

AsyncPattern: Indicates that the operation is implemented asynchronously via a Begin/End method pair.

IsInitiating: Defines a value that indicates whether the method implements an operation that can initiate a session on the server.

IsOneWay: Defines a value that indicates whether an operation returns a reply message.

IsTerminating: Defines a value that indicates whether the operation causes the server to close the session after the reply message is sent.

HasProtectionLevel: Specifies whether a specific protection level is required by the message of this operation.

ProtectionLevel: Defines a value that indicates the protection level of the operation. You can specify that the messages of the operation be encrypted, signed, or both.

ReplyAction: Defines the value of the SOAP action for the reply message of the operation.

If you need full access to the message body and don't want to bother with serialization, another approach is to use the Message object, as shown in Listing 3–2.

Listing 3–2. ITradeServiceMessage Interface Using the Message Object

```
using System.ServiceModel;
using System.ServiceModel.Channels;

namespace QuickReturns.StockTrading.ExchangeService.Contracts
{
    [ServiceContract(Namespace = "http://QuickReturns")]
    interface ITradeServiceMessage
    {
        [OperationContract()]
        Message GetQuote(string ticker);

        [OperationContract()]
        void PublishQuote(Message quote);
    }
}
```

This way, you get access to the SOAP message directly, and WCF doesn't do any type-based serialization. As you can see, the code in Listing 3–2 differs from Listing 3–1. The Quote return type of the GetQuote method and the Quote parameter in the PublishQuote method are now replaced by the generic Message type. So instead of being able to access the properties of the type in an object-oriented way, you can now access the individual elements and attributes directly in the XML message. This can be useful in scenarios where the overhead that comes with serialization is too high.

Data Contracts

As discussed earlier, we are using a custom type called Quote for which you can define a data contract. WCF needs to know how to serialize your custom .NET types. You have two ways of letting WCF know how to do this: via implicit and explicit data contracts. *Implicit* data contracts are mappings of simple types in .NET. WCF has predefined mappings from all .NET simple types to their SOAP counterparts, so you don't have to explicitly define data contracts for the .NET simple types you know in the System namespace (including enums, delegates, and arrays or generics of the simple types in .NET).

Custom types are based on the simple types in .NET, or on types that are themselves built based on the simple types. You can annotate your custom types with the Serializable attribute. This tells WCF to use implicit data contracts. If you use this type of serialization, you don't have to define a data contract. To customize the way you want the serialization to happen, you have to define an explicit data contract for your type. You can do this by defining a simple class with all the properties your type needs, and annotating the class with the DataContract attribute. The DataContract attribute uses an opt-in model, where the .NET method of serializing in combination with formatters determines what gets serialized (public properties, private properties, etc.); as such, you have to specifically annotate each property with the DataMember attribute. In Listing 3–3, we have defined a data contract for the Quote custom type in the stock-trading example.

Listing 3–3. Data Contract for the Custom Quote Type

```
using System;
using System.Runtime.Serialization;

namespace QuickReturns.StockTrading.ExchangeService.DataContracts
{
    [DataContract(Namespace=" http://QuickReturns")]
    public class Quote
    {
        [DataMember(Name="Ticker")]
        public string Ticker;

        [DataMember(Name="Bid")]
        public decimal Bid;

        [DataMember(Name="Ask")]
        public decimal Ask;

        [DataMember(Name="Publisher")]
        public string Publisher;

        [DataMember(Name="UpdateDateTime")]
        private DateTime UpdateDateTime;
    }
}
```

■**Note** The `UpdateDateTime` field is private and attributed, so it will be serialized as part of the SOAP messages that WCF generates. `DataContract` serializes all the properties and variables that are associated with the `DataMember` attribute, and does not take the access specifier into account.

The `DataContract` attribute has several parameters:

`Name:` Defines the name for the data contract, which will also be the name in the XML schema (XSD, WSDL). The default value is the name you defined in .NET.

`Namespace:` Defines the namespace for the data contract. Use this property to specify a particular namespace if your type must return data that complies with a specific data contract or XML schema.

To make versioning possible, you need to be aware of several parameters for the `DataMember` attribute:

`Name:` Defines the name for the data contract, which will also be the name in an XML schema (XSD, WSDL). The default value is the name you defined in .NET.

`IsRequired:` Gets or sets a value that instructs the serialization engine that the member must be present.

`Order:` Gets or sets the order of serialization and deserialization of a member. This can be important if clients rely on the order of the fields.

`EmitDefaultValue:` Gets or sets a value that specifies whether to generate a default value of `null` or `0` for a field or property being serialized.

.NET 4.0 also ships with a `DataContractResolver` class, which provides an option to customize CLR-type mapping for `DataContractSerializer`. With this class you can alter things like names and namespaces on the wire. We will be discussing it in the next chapters.

Message Contracts

Sometimes you require more control over the SOAP envelope than WCF generates. For example, you may want to be able to map fields in your message to the SOAP headers instead of the SOAP body. This is when message contracts come into play. The `MessageContract` attribute allows you to map fields into either the SOAP body or the SOAP headers by means of the `MessageBody` and `MessageHeader` attributes, as shown in Listing 3–4.

Listing 3–4. Quote As a MessageContract

```
using System;
using System.ServiceModel;

namespace QuickReturns.StockTrading.ExchangeService.MessageContracts
{
    [MessageContract]
    public class QuoteMessage
    {
        [MessageBody]
        public string Ticker;
```

```
        [MessageBody]
        public decimal Bid;

        [MessageBody]
        public decimal Ask;

        [MessageHeader]
        public string Publisher;

        [MessageBody]
        private DateTime UpdateDateTime;
    }
}
```

Unlike Listing 3–3, in this example the publisher has now moved from the SOAP body to the SOAP headers. Now you can use this message contract in an operation contract, just like you did with the data contract. So when you need direct control over the SOAP envelope, you can use message contracts to control how properties of your types map to the SOAP headers and SOAP body.

Looking Inside the WCF Layers

WCF is a layered framework similar to the Open Systems Interactive (OSI) model. You will primarily program against the service model layer, and that layer affects the layer underneath it, which is called the *messaging layer*. The messaging layer is the layer where the message transport across the channels on the network becomes reality. The separation between the service model and messaging layers helps you to use programming model without worrying about the actual messaging model.

Figure 3–5 shows how the layering is organized. The messaging layer is the lower-level layer, which contains transports, channels, protocols, and encoding. The service model layer controls behavior, contracts, and policy. Behavior is the most important aspect of the service model layer, whereas in the messaging layer channels are central.

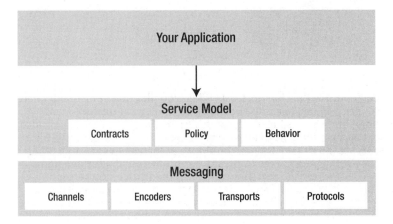

Figure 3–5. WCF layers

The Messaging Layer

The messaging layer is where the actual communication on the wire is happening. This is the layer where transports such as HTTP, MSMQ, TCP, and Named Pipes come into play, as well as the encoding and format of the messages. The transport protocols used inside the messages are implemented as channels; a *channel* allows you to clearly separate the transport from the messaging exchange pattern.

Channels

The address and binding together manifest themselves in the messaging layer of WCF. The address expresses where the message should go, and the binding is the model you use to manipulate the message. Figure 3–6 shows a layered description of the WCF messaging stack.

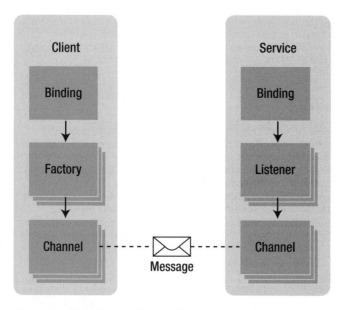

Figure 3–6. *WCF messaging stack*

The binding is the mechanism that controls the channel stack. When you pick one of the predefined bindings mentioned earlier, you are picking, in essence, specific channels. Looking at the bottom of Figure 3–6, you can see that the channels are responsible for transferring a message from the client side to the service side, and vice versa, depending on the messaging exchange pattern used. Obviously, for this to work, the client and service sides should be consistent to be able to exchange messages. In other words, they have to understand the messaging pattern, the transport, the protocols, and the encoding. On the client side, channels are created by factories so that they can talk to the service side across a specific channel or set of channels. On the service side, listeners accept messages from channels.

Channels have input and output handlers that are responsible for consuming messages. *Consuming messages* can mean forwarding the messages across a certain transport, or receiving messages across a certain transport through a specific messaging exchange pattern. The channel also applies security and performs validations. In the default WCF set of bindings, this results in support for the WS-* specifications. Channels can be connected to each other in a pipeline. Therefore, you don't have to rebuild security, reliability, or session state capabilities inside your channels for every transport.

Bindings make it much easier for the client and service sides to work together. The information about the binding is described by the policy in the metadata of the service, and you can rely on this information to align the information by means of imperative code or the more usual configuration. The metadata that is exposed based on the binding allows you to generate proxy code for use on the client side.

Channel Shapes

Channels come in three shapes, which correspond to the messaging exchange patterns described earlier. Given a transport, WCF implements only the messaging exchange patterns that are natural for the transport. This is so that, when using the WCF programming model, you don't need to bother about the transports directly; rather, you can think about the messaging exchange pattern or channel shape. With the interfaces in Listing 3–5, WCF enables the three messaging exchange patterns in code.

Listing 3–5. Channel Interfaces to Support the Different Channel Shapes

```
public interface IOutputChannel : IChannel {
    void Send(Message message);
}

public interface IInputChannel : IChannel {
    Message Receive();
}

public interface IDuplexChannel : IInputChannel, IOutputChannel { }

public interface IRequestChannel : IChannel {
    Message Request(Message message);
}

public interface IReplyChannel : IChannel {
    IRequestContext ReceiveRequest();
}

public interface IRequestContext : IDisposable {
    Message RequestMessage { get; }
    void Reply(Message message);
}
```

The IOutputChannel interface supports sending messages, and the IInputChannel interface supports receiving messages. Together these support the one-way messaging exchange pattern. IInputChannel and IOutputChannel are combined to create the IDuplexChannel interface, which supports the duplex messaging exchange pattern. The IRequestChannel interface supports sending requests, and the IReplyChannel interface supports receiving requests. Together they support the request-reply messaging exchange pattern. Finally, the IRequestContext interface allows you to receive multiple messages over the same channel. This improves concurrency and doesn't limit you from blocking the channel until the reply to a specific request is ready to be transmitted.

Channel Flavors

Channels come in three flavors:

- *Transports*: Transports provide a way to talk to some source on the service side. As you know, WCF supports several transports and allows you to write your own to support other transports, such as SMTP and FTP.

- *Encoders*: WCF supports several typical encoders that are either standards-based (such as MTOM), optimized for reading (binary), or readable (text). You can think of encoders as something that reduces the size of messages and minimizes data (and thus the bandwidth used).

- *Protocols*: WCF supports several protocols, including HTTP, TCP, MSMQ, and Named Pipes. Some of these supported protocols in WCF comply with WS-* standards. In this book, we'll cover several of them, specifically in Chapters 6 through 9.

THE SERVICE MODEL LAYER

Whereas the messaging layer provides total control over the messages flowing around in your application, the service model layer is a higher-level abstraction layer that allows you to customize the messaging through object-oriented programming principles. This is really where the WCF team was able to reach its design goals. The service model layer offers an easy-to-use API with classes, methods, attributes, and configuration to build connected applications. Behaviors are the most important concept in this regard. You can apply multiple behaviors on the client and service sides. Behaviors don't affect the contract in any way; in other words, consumers of services don't know the details about the behavior of the service. Behaviors affect the conversion from messages to .NET types, instancing, throttling, concurrency, and error handling. Up until now in this book, we have covered the generic concepts of the entire API; the rest of this chapter is focused on the service model layer. This is the layer you will use the most.

Using ServiceHost and ChannelFactory

The ServiceHost class gives you access to the WCF hosting infrastructure on the server side, whereas the ChannelFactory class gives you access to the WCF hosting infrastructure on the client side. The following sections cover the basics of ServiceHost and ChannelFactory from a programming model perspective.

In Chapter 4, you will learn about hosting web services in IIS. Chapter 5 covers the complete WCF hosting infrastructure and shows you the different options WCF offers in terms of hosting services in different types of applications and using services in different types of clients. In this chapter, we cover only self-hosting and console applications.

ServiceHost

ServiceHost is instantiated based on a particular service type that you implement, and as such "hosts" your service. When a ServiceHost instance is available, you can do anything you like programmatically in regard to the address, binding, and contracts (ABCs) and behavior (which we will cover later).

Listings 3–6 and 3–7 define and instantiate your first service in a specific service host that is initialized imperatively with an address, a binding, and a contract. We are using the basic examples given earlier, so we use a simple HTTP address and the BasicHttpBinding and ITradeService contracts from earlier.

Listing 3–6. *ServiceHost Instantiation Based on Imperative Calls*

```
using System;
using System.ServiceModel;
using QuickReturns.StockTrading.ExchangeService;
using QuickReturns.StockTrading.ExchangeService.Contracts;

namespace QuickReturns.StockTrading.ExchangeService.Hosts
{
    class Program
    {
        static void Main(string[] args)
        {
        Uri address = new Uri
        ("http://localhost:8080/QuickReturns/Exchange");
        ServiceHost host = new ServiceHost(typeof(TradeService);
        host.Open();
         Console.WriteLine("Service started: Press Return to exit");
         Console.ReadLine();
                }
    }
}
```

Listing 3–7. *TradeService*

```
using System;
using System.Collections;
using System.ServiceModel;
using QuickReturns.StockTrading.ExchangeService.Contracts;
using QuickReturns.StockTrading.ExchangeService.DataContracts;

namespace QuickReturns.StockTrading.ExchangeService
{
    [ServiceBehavior(InstanceContextMode=InstanceContextMode.Single,
                     ReturnUnknownExceptionsAsFaults=true)]
    public class TradeService : ITradeService
    {
        private Hashtable tickers = new Hashtable();
        public Quote GetQuote(string ticker)
        {
            lock (tickers)
            {

                Quote quote = tickers[ticker] as Quote;
                if (quote == null)
                {
                    // Quote doesn't exist
                    throw new Exception(
                        string.Format("No quotes found for ticker '{0}'",
                            ticker));
```

```
            }
            return quote;
        }
    }

    public void PublishQuote(Quote quote)
    {
        lock (tickers)
        {
            Quote storedQuote = tickers[quote.Ticker] as Quote;
            if (storedQuote == null)
            {
                tickers.Add(quote.Ticker, quote);
            }
            else
            {
                tickers[quote.Ticker] = quote;
            }
        }
    }
}
}
```

As you can see, the implementation of the service is simple. It has one member variable (of type Hashtable) that is responsible for keeping the internal state of the service with the provided quotes in memory. In a more realistic scenario, this would of course be kept in some permanent state system (a back end based on a database). To be able to call into the service multiple times, you have to make sure the behavior of the service is a singleton. Therefore, the ServiceBehavior attribute is applied with the InstanceContextMode property set to InstanceContextMode.Single. You will learn more about behaviors in the "Applying Behaviors" section later in the chapter. The ReturnUnknownExceptionsAsFaults property is able to track back an exception that can occur when a quote is requested for an unknown ticker to propagate to the client. For obvious reasons, by default WCF doesn't map .NET exceptions across the wire in SOAP faults. Also, as shown in Listing 3–6, there are no explicit endpoints created in the code. The code automatically takes default endpoints based on the URI exposed. This is done with the new enhancement in .NET 4.0, as we have discussed in Chapter 2's "Default Endpoints" section.

In the "Introducing the Programming Approach" section earlier in this chapter, you learned the approaches you can take in programming WCF; you also learned that as soon as ServiceHost is there, any attributes or configuration will have already been applied. Listing 3–8 shows this in terms of an actual result, but one in which the configuration is much more maintainable.

Listing 3–8. ServiceHost Instantiation Based on Configuration

```
using System;
using System.ServiceModel;
using QuickReturns.StockTrading.ExchangeService;
using QuickReturns.StockTrading.ExchangeService.Contracts;

namespace QuickReturns.StockTrading.ExchangeService.Hosts
{
    class Program
    {
        static void Main(string[] args)
        {
            Type serviceType = typeof(TradeService);
```

```
        ServiceHost host = new ServiceHost(serviceType);
        host.Open();

        Console.WriteLine("Service started: Press Return to exit");
        Console.ReadLine();
    }
  }
}
```

Listing 3–9 provides the App.config file of the service. You can find the TradeService defined with its endpoints. Please note the mexEndpoint mentioned in the App.config file. In .NET 3.x, you could create an IMetadataExchange endpoint in order to allow consumers to retrieve the metadata (WSDL) of the service. The .NET Framework 4.0 ships with a standard endpoint called mexEndpoint to address this need. You just need to specify mexEndpoint in the kind attribute. As discussed in Chapter 2, there are other standard endpoints that ship with .NET 4.0. If you want to use either SvcUtil.exe or the Add Service Reference option in Visual Studio, you need to enable the retrieval of metadata. Also note that serviceBehavior does not have any name attribute attached to it. Since these settings need to be applied to all the services, the name attribute is omitted. In .NET 3.x, even if all the services required the same behavior, we needed to specify servicebehavior with the Name attribute and then apply it to the service. Since this was error-prone, the .NET Framework 4.0 provides the concept of default behavior. The service-wide settings are as follows:

serviceMetadata: This allows you to set whether metadata may be retrieved for the service. You can set some additional attributes as well, including ExternalMetadataLocation, HttpEnabled, HttpsEnabled, HttpGetUrl, HttpsGetUrl, and MetaDataExporter. These are self-explanatory; please refer to the MSDN help for more information.

serviceDebug: These settings allow you to express whether you want to leak specific service exception information and helpful HTML information pages for your services across the service boundary. This should be disabled in production scenarios, but can be helpful during development. You can set some additional attributes such as HttpHelpPageEnabled, HttpHelpPageUrl, HttpsHelpPageEnabled, HttpsHelpPageUrl, and IncludeExceptionDetailInFaults. These are self-explanatory; please refer to the MSDN help for more information.

There are many other service behaviors that can be applied as well depending on the requirement. These include Routing, etwTracking, serviceTimeout, and ServiceThrottling, to name a few. We will be covering all of these in the coming chapters. Here, we have set httpGetEnabled for the metadata and includeExceptionDetailInFaults to true because we need these in the remaining parts of this section and the following section.

Listing 3–9. App.config

```
<?xml version="1.0" encoding="utf-8" ?>
<configuration>
<system.serviceModel>
   <services>
      <service name="QuickReturns.StockTrading.ExchangeService.TradeService"  >
         <host>
             <baseAddresses>
                 <add baseAddress="http://localhost:8080/QuickReturns"/>
             </baseAddresses>
         </host>
         <endpoint address="http://localhost:8080/QuickReturns/Exchange"
             binding="basicHttpBinding"
             contract="QuickReturns.StockTrading.ExchangeService.TradeService">
```

```
            </endpoint>
            <endpoint kind="mexEndpoint" />
        </service>
    </services>
    <serviceBehaviors>
        <behavior  name="">
            <serviceMetadata httpGetEnabled="true"/>
            <serviceDebug includeExceptionDetailInFaults="true"/>
        </behavior>
    </serviceBehaviors>
</system.serviceModel>
</configuration>
```

When you take a closer look at ServiceHost at runtime, you can see that it has two pieces: the ServiceDescription, which is all about the endpoints and behaviors, and the runtime, where you can find listeners, sites, and extensions. The ServiceDescription is built based on the configuration and can be changed with the imperative code you add. Figure 3–7 shows this graphically.

■**Note** It is highly recommended that you download and open the solution for this chapter to get a better understanding of the ServiceDescription. Look at it with the Visual Studio .NET debugger by using the Watches or QuickWatch window.

We'll now explain what the ServiceDescription and runtime can do for you. ServiceHost is always in a certain state (reflected by the State property of type CommunicationState). The possible states are Created, Opening, Opened, Closing, Closed, UnknownMessageReceived, and Faulted. When you start ServiceHost, it activates the runtime and starts creating listeners and extensions. In the debugger, the ServiceDescription looks like Figure 3–8. As you can see, it shows you the same information as Figure 3–7.

In a realistic scenario, you would subclass (extend) ServiceHost by hooking into the API and overriding OnInitialize (and any other methods that are applicable in your scenario) to be able to abstract the logic to build up the description from external configuration or create a more suitable base class for your base library, project, department, or company to use. The OnInitialize method of ServiceHost is a method suitable for doing this type of customization. Listing 3–10 shows you the same example as before, except now ServiceHost is subclassed.

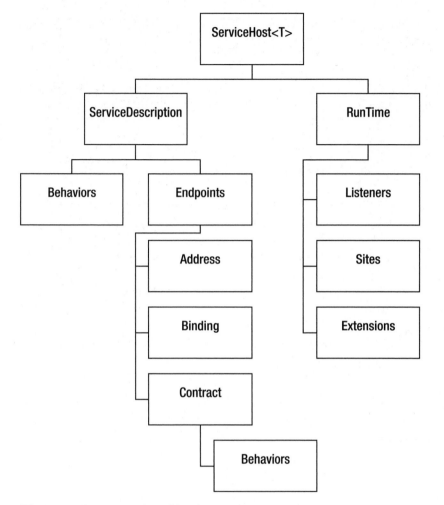

Figure 3–7. Representation of ServiceHost in memory

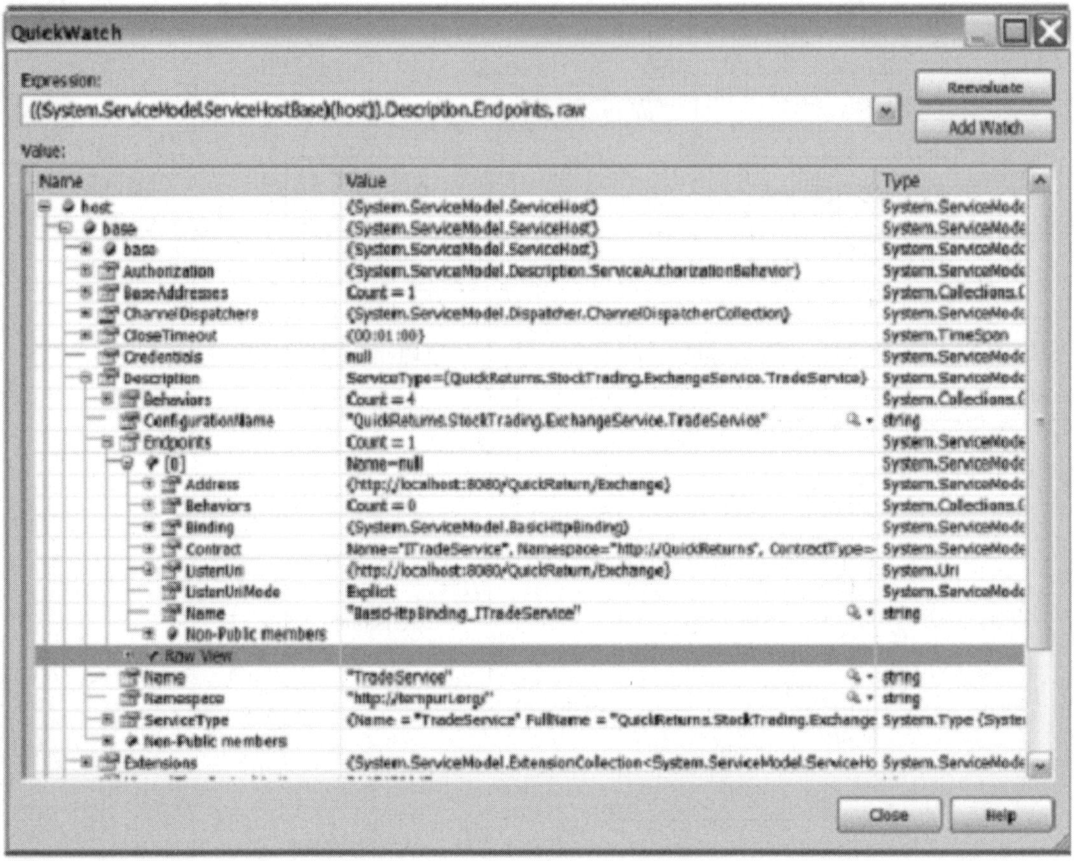

Figure 3–8. QuickWatch window of the ServiceDescription in ServiceHost

Listing 3–10. Subclassed ServiceHost Instantiation Based on Imperative Calls

```
using System;
using System.ServiceModel;
using QuickReturns.StockTrading.ExchangeService;
using QuickReturns.StockTrading.ExchangeService.Contracts;

namespace QuickReturns.StockTrading.ExchangeService.Hosts
{
    public class ExchangeServiceHost
    {
        static void Main(string[] args)
        {
            Uri baseAddress =
                new Uri("http://localhost:8080/QuickReturns");
            CustomServiceHost host =
```

```
            new CustomServiceHost(typeof(TradeService), baseAddress);
        host.Open();
        Console.WriteLine("Service started: Press Return to exit");
        Console.ReadLine();

    }
}

public class CustomServiceHost : ServiceHost
{
    public CustomServiceHost(Type serviceType, params Uri[] baseAddresses)
        : base(serviceType, baseAddresses)
    {
    }

    protected override void OnInitialize()
    {
        BasicHttpBinding binding = new BasicHttpBinding();
        AddServiceEndpoint(typeof(ITradeService), binding, "Exchange");
    }
}
}
```

Although this scenario is not really something you would see in a real application (because you are hard-coding the configuration again), you can imagine its benefits. An example is setting up the description of your service based on a configuration stored in a database.

ChannelFactory

Just like ServiceHost, you instantiate ChannelFactory based on a specific service. There's a difference, though. The client knows only about the exposed contract of the service; it knows nothing about its implementation. Therefore, in this case, the generic that is passed to ChannelFactory is the interface of the contract. In Listing 3–11, we have written a client that instantiates a ChannelFactory to open a channel to the service defined in the previous section about ServiceHost. Listing 3–12 shows the associated configuration files for use on the client side. To handle the third tenet of SOA (sharing the schema, not the class), it is best if you define the contract of the service separately and not create a separate assembly that you use on both the client side and the service side. This way, the service side can evolve without impacting the client side. Of course, the code uses configuration instead of imperative code.

Listing 3–11. The Client Code Using ChannelFactory

```
using System;
using System.ServiceModel;
using System.ServiceModel.Channels;
using System.Runtime.Serialization;


namespace QuickReturns.StockTrading.ExchangeService.Clients
{
    [ServiceContract(Namespace = "http://QuickReturns")]
    interface ITradeService
    {
```

```
        [OperationContract()]
        Quote GetQuote(string ticker);

        [OperationContract()]
        void PublishQuote(Quote quote);
    }

    [DataContract(Namespace = "http://QuickReturns", Name = "Quote")]
    public class Quote
    {
        [DataMember(Name = "Ticker")]
        public string Ticker;

        [DataMember(Name = "Bid")]
        public decimal Bid;

        [DataMember(Name = "Ask")]
        public decimal Ask;

        [DataMember(Name = "Publisher")]
        public string Publisher;

        [DataMember(Name = "UpdateDateTime")]
        private DateTime UpdateDateTime;
    }

    class ExchangeServiceSimpleClient
    {
        static void Main(string[] args)
        {
            EndpointAddress address =
                new EndpointAddress
                    ("http://localhost:8080/QuickReturns/Exchange");
            BasicHttpBinding binding = new BasicHttpBinding();
            IChannelFactory<ITradeService> channelFactory =
    new ChannelFactory<ITradeService>(binding);
            ITradeService proxy = channelFactory.CreateChannel(address);


            Quote msftQuote = new Quote();
            msftQuote.Ticker = "MSFT";
            msftQuote.Bid = 30.25M;
            msftQuote.Ask = 32.00M;
            msftQuote.Publisher = "PracticalWCF";

            Quote ibmQuote = new Quote();
            ibmQuote.Ticker = "IBM";
            ibmQuote.Bid = 80.50M;
            ibmQuote.Ask = 81.00M;
            ibmQuote.Publisher = "PracticalWCF";

            proxy.PublishQuote(msftQuote);
            proxy.PublishQuote(ibmQuote);
```

```
        Quote result = null;
        result = proxy.GetQuote("MSFT");
        Console.WriteLine("Ticker: {0} Ask: {1} Bid: {2}",
            result.Ticker, result.Ask, result.Bid);

        result = proxy.GetQuote("IBM");
        Console.WriteLine("Ticker: {0} Ask: {1} Bid: {2}",
            result.Ticker, result.Ask, result.Bid);

        try
        {
            result = proxy.GetQuote("ATT");
        }
        catch (Exception ex)
        {
            Console.WriteLine(ex.Message);
        }

        if (result == null)
        {
            Console.WriteLine("Ticker ATT not found!");
        }

        Console.WriteLine("Done! Press return to exit");
        Console.ReadLine();

    }
  }
}
```

Listing 3–12. The App.config file for the Client Code

```xml
<?xml version="1.0" encoding="utf-8" ?>
<configuration>
    <system.serviceModel>
        <client>
            <endpoint address="http://localhost:8080/QuickReturns/Exchange"
                binding="basicHttpBinding"
              contract="QuickReturns.StockTrading.ExchangeServiceClient. ITradeService">
            </endpoint>
        </client>
    </system.serviceModel>
</configuration>
```

There is an easier way to consume services without using the ChannelFactory. You can generate the proxies using the SvcUtil.exe utility. The SvcUtil.exe utility retrieves the metadata (WSDL) of the service, and based on that generates the proxy classes that can be used to call the service. In addition, it makes sure the contracts are generated as interfaces as well. Therefore, you can leave out the service contract and data contract you saw in Listing 3–11. The following call to SvcUtil.exe generates a proxy class for use in your client (make sure your service is running before making this call):

```
svcutil.exe http://localhost:8080/QuickReturns
```

The utility will generate a proxy class based on the metadata of the service, which can be retrieved with the following URL:

```
http://localhost:8080/QuickReturns?WSDL
```

The utility will generate a proxy class for you (the file will be named TradeService.cs, and the configuration file will be called Output.config). You can then simplify the client, as shown in Listing 3–13. You can optionally generate the proxy class using the Add Service Reference option, which also internally calls SvcUtil.exe. We will be discussing this in Chapter 4.

Listing 3–13. Simplified Client Code Using the Proxy Generated by SvcUtil.exe

```
using System;
using quickReturns;

namespace QuickReturns.StockTrading.ExchangeService.Clients
{
    class ExchangeServiceClientProxy
    {
        static void Main(string[] args)
        {
            TradeServiceProxy proxy = new TradeServiceProxy();

            Quote msftQuote = new Quote();
            msftQuote.Ticker = "MSFT";
            msftQuote.Bid = 30.25M;
            msftQuote.Ask = 32.00M;
            msftQuote.Publisher = "PracticalWCF";

            Quote ibmQuote = new Quote();
            ibmQuote.Ticker = "IBM";
            ibmQuote.Bid = 80.50M;
            ibmQuote.Ask = 81.00M;
            ibmQuote.Publisher = "PracticalWCF";

            proxy.PublishQuote(msftQuote);
            proxy.PublishQuote(ibmQuote);

            Quote result = null;
            result = proxy.GetQuote("MSFT");
            Console.WriteLine("Ticker: {0} Ask: {1} Bid: {2}",
                result.Ticker, result.Ask, result.Bid);

            result = proxy.GetQuote("IBM");
            Console.WriteLine("Ticker: {0} Ask: {1} Bid: {2}",
                result.Ticker, result.Ask, result.Bid);

            try
            {
                result = proxy.GetQuote("ATT");
            }
            catch (Exception ex)
            {
                Console.WriteLine(ex.Message);
```

```
        }

        if (result == null)
        {
            Console.WriteLine("Ticker ATT not found!");
        }

        Console.WriteLine("Done! Press return to exit");
        Console.ReadLine();
    }
  }
}
```

Listing 3–14 shows the generated Output.config configuration file.

Listing 3–14. *Output.config File Generated by SvcUtil.exe*

```xml
<?xml version="1.0" encoding="utf-8"?>
<configuration>
    <system.serviceModel>
        <bindings>
            <basicHttpBinding>
                <binding name="basicHttpBinding"
                        closeTimeout="00:01:00"
                        openTimeout="00:01:00"
                        receiveTimeout="00:10:00"
                        sendTimeout="00:01:00"
                        allowCookies="false"
                        bypassProxyOnLocal="false"
                        hostNameComparisonMode="StrongWildcard"
                        maxBufferSize="65536"
                        maxBufferPoolSize="524288"
                        maxReceivedMessageSize="65536"
                        messageEncoding="Text"
                        textEncoding="utf-8"
                        transferMode="Buffered"
                        useDefaultWebProxy="true">
                    <readerQuotas maxDepth="32"
                            maxStringContentLength="8192"
                            maxArrayLength="16384"
                            maxBytesPerRead="4096"
                            maxNameTableCharCount="16384" />
                    <security mode="None">
                        <transport clientCredentialType="None"
                                proxyCredentialType="None"
                            realm="" />
                        <message clientCredentialType="UserName"
                                algorithmSuite="Default" />
                    </security>
                </binding>
            </basicHttpBinding>
        </bindings>
        <client>
            <endpoint address="http://localhost:8080/QuickReturns/Exchange"
```

```
                    binding="basicHttpBinding"
                    bindingConfiguration="basicHttpBinding"
              contract="ITradeService" name="basicHttpBinding" />
        </client>
     </system.serviceModel>
</configuration>
```

■**Note** With the code in the `ServiceHost` and `ChannelFactory` discussions, we have finalized the first bit of WCF code that actually compiles and runs. In the code that comes with this book, you can find the `ExchangeService` sample in the `ExchangeService` folder for Chapter 3 (`C:\PracticalWCF\Chapter03\ExchangeService`), complete with two flavors of clients that make some calls to publish and get quotes. The difference between the two clients (`SimpleClient` and `SimpleClientWithProxy`) is that the first uses `ChannelFactory` and the other uses a proxy generated with `SvcUtil.exe`. It is highly recommended that you walk through this code with Visual Studio .NET in debug mode.

Service Description

The *service description* is an important concept when trying to understand WCF. The ABCs of WCF result in a service description, as shown previously in Figure 3–7. In essence, the `ServiceDescription` is an in-memory representation of the environment where your service lives. It is either based on initialization code or a configuration file. Before starting your runtime, you have several options for modifying the service description through the WCF API. Please refer to the earlier `ServiceHost` discussion for details.

Service Runtime

The *service runtime* is an abstraction layer on top of the messaging layer. This layer is the bridge between your application code and the channels in the messaging layer. The messaging layer deals with transport, protocols, and so on, whereas the service runtime or the service model in general deals with the messages flowing through the messaging layer and conforming to certain contracts. The process of passing the message from one end of the wire to other is abstracted from the developer.

The service runtime has typed proxies on the client side and dispatchers on the service side.

- Typed proxies and dispatchers are responsible for handing over messages from the service runtime to the messaging layer, and the other way around. Typed proxies offer methods that are useful to your applications, and it transforms the method calls into WCF messages and hands them over to the messaging layer to transmit them to the service.

- The dispatcher is used on the service side to handle the messages coming in on the channels and is responsible for sending them over to your application code. Figure 3–9 shows this graphically.

As you can see in Figure 3–9, you have proxy operations and a proxy behavior on the client side that are responsible for influencing the channel layer. For every method in your service contract, you have one proxy operation. The operations share one proxy behavior. The proxy behavior deals with all the messages flowing between the channel layer and your application. On the proxy behavior level, you can make interceptions to deal with parameters, serialization, formatting, mapping to real methods, and so on. On the operation behavior level, you can perform such tasks as selecting channels, selecting operations (mapping methods), and inspecting messages.

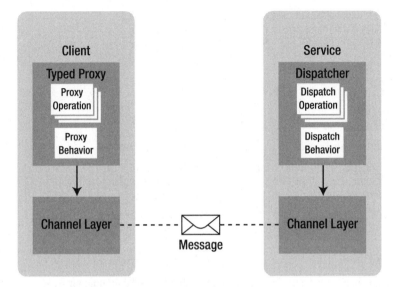

Figure 3–9. *The service model runtime*

On the service side, you'll see a similar concept. At the service level you can perform more powerful tasks because the service side is richer in functionality. The dispatch behavior level allows you to perform tasks such as initializing channels, inspecting messages, handling exceptions, selecting operations, and handling concurrency. The dispatch operation level can handle tasks such as inspecting parameters, serializing, handling transactions, and invoking calls.

Applying Behaviors

Influencing the internals of a service, behaviors are applied at the service, operation, contract, and endpoint levels. WCF comes with several behaviors out of the box, which we'll cover in this section.

With behaviors, it is possible to modify the runtime and eventually affect the internals of each type of concept where it applies (e.g., endpoint, operation, contract, and service). From a programming model perspective, you can apply behaviors through configuration or by using the attributes available to you. Behaviors are something consumers of services have no direct notion of, and they are not expressed in the contract. So, they are all about concepts such as instancing lifetime, concurrency, and transactions.

The behavior interface is defined in such a way that it allows you to affect different aspects of your service. Some of the aspects are validation, bindings, and two methods that do the actual work either on the client side or the server side. Each behavior has the interface shown in Listing 3–15, with one exception. The ServiceBehavior doesn't have the ApplyClientBehavior method because you can only apply the ServiceBehavior at the service level.

Listing 3–15. Generic I...Behavior Interface

```
public interface I...Behavior
{
    void AddBindingParameters(ServiceEndpoint serviceEndpoint,
        BindingParameterCollection bindingParameters);
    void ApplyClientBehavior(ServiceEndpoint serviceEndpoint,
        ClientRuntime behavior);
    void ApplyDispatchBehavior(ServiceEndpoint serviceEndpoint,
        EndpointDispatcher endpointDispatcher, ...);
    void Validate(ServiceEndpoint serviceEndpoint);
}
```

The order in which the methods of the interface are called is as follows:

Validate: This is called when all the information is gathered to build the runtime.

AddBindingParameters: This method is called in the first step of building the runtime and before the underlying channel listener is constructed. This allows you to add the custom parameters expected by the underlying channel implementation.

ApplyClientBehavior/ApplyDispatchBehavior: The actual work takes place in these methods, which are either applied on the client side or the service side (depending on where you are).

■**Note** Although the behavior interfaces look similar, there's no base interface that each of them implements. They were made to look similar so that they could be as intuitive as possible, but they have some minor differences. For example, the IServiceBehavior interface doesn't have the ApplyClientBehavior. In addition, the ApplyDispatchBehavior has some different parameters in certain interfaces. This is why we replaced the specific names of the behaviors with ellipses (...). Please refer to the MSDN help to get more insight into all the behavior interfaces.

Service Behavior

You can define the ServiceBehavior attribute at the service implementation (class) level to specify service-wide execution behavior. You cannot apply this attribute at the interface (contract) level. This distinction is important. The behaviors in WCF have to do with the internals of the implementation, not with the service contract. Listing 3–16 shows the interface of the IServiceBehavior interface that the ServiceBehavior attribute implements.

Listing 3–16. IServiceBehavior Interface

```
public interface IServiceBehavior
{
    // Methods
    void AddBindingParameters(ServiceDescription description,
        ServiceHostBase serviceHostBase,
        Collection<ServiceEndpoint> endpoints,
        BindingParameterCollection parameters);
```

```
    void ApplyDispatchBehavior(ServiceDescription description,
        ServiceHostBase serviceHostBase);
    void Validate(ServiceDescription description,
        ServiceHostBase serviceHostBase);
}
```

As you can gather, the most important method in the `IServiceBehavior` interface is `ApplyDispatchBehavior`, which comes with two parameters. The `ServiceDescription` is mainly provided to inspect the entire service description. However, in practice you could also modify the service and its description, although you wouldn't typically do that at this level. `Validate` is called in order for you to be able to validate the endpoint. WCF will automatically call it for you. `ServiceHostBase` provides the `ChannelDispatchers` collection to inject code into the dispatcher pipeline and affect the dispatching behaviors. This is basically where the translation is made between the .NET objects and the actual sockets underneath the transport. Through the `AddBindingParameters` method and the provided `BindingParameterCollection`, you can pass information about the contract to the channel stack to implement concepts such as security and transactions. This is an important interception and extensibility point if you want to hook into the WCF programming model. This enables you to create even more powerful solutions than you get out of the box.

The default `ServiceBehavior` attribute already provides you with a lot of functionality that can be set through its properties, which are described here (with the exception of `Name`, `Namespace`, and `ConfigurationName`, because they are common across WCF):

`AddressFilterMode` (`AddressFilterMode`): By default, WCF will match messages to their destination endpoints, matching them with the WS-Addressing To header in the SOAP message. For example, setting `AddressFilterMode` to `AddressFilterMode.Prefix` will instruct WCF to match the endpoints on the start of the endpoint URI.

`AutomaticSessionShutdown` (boolean): This specifies whether to automatically close a session when a client closes an output session.

`ConcurrencyMode` (`ConcurrencyMode`): This specifies whether a service supports one thread, multiple threads, or reentrant calls. Valid values are `Reentrant`, `Single`, and `Multiple`. `Single` and `Multiple` correspond to single and multithreaded types of services, and the `Reentrant` service accepts calls that have the same thread context. It is particularly useful when a service calls another service, which subsequently calls back to the first service. In this case, if the first service is not reentrant, the sequence of calls results in a deadlock. The default is `PerCall`, which is typically the best choice because it is best to keep your services stateless to provide scalability.

`IgnoreExtensionDataObject` (boolean): This specifies whether to send unknown serialization data onto the wire.

`IncludeExceptionDetailInFaults` (boolean): This specifies whether you want to leak specific service exception information across the service boundary. This is useful during debugging.

`InstanceContextMode` (`InstanceContextMode`): This gets or sets the value that indicates when new service objects are created. The default is `PerCall`; the other available values are `PerSession`, `Shareable`, and `Single`.

`MaxItemsInObjectGraph` (int): This specifies the maximum amount of items that are to be serialized as part of an object.

`ReleaseServiceInstanceOnTransactionComplete` (boolean): This gets or sets a value that specifies whether the service object is recycled when the current transaction completes.

`ReturnUnknownExceptionsAsFaults` (boolean): By default, WCF doesn't provide the stack trace of issues occurring inside the service, because of the security risks involved. You should set this value only during development to troubleshoot a service; it specifies that unhandled exceptions are to be converted into a SOAP Fault<string> and sent as a fault message. In other words, this translates the world of .NET exceptions to SOAP faults. So, on the wire the details of exceptions can be read, which could potentially expose too many details of the internals of the service.

TransactionAutoCompleteOnSessionClose (boolean): This gets or sets a value that specifies whether pending transactions are completed when the current session closes.

TransactionIsolationLevel (IsolationLevel): This specifies the transaction isolation level. WCF relies on the .NET System.Transactions namespace to enable transactions.

TransactionTimeout (Timespan/string): This gets or sets the period within which a transaction must be completed before it times out (and rolls back).

UseSynchronizationContext (boolean): This gets or sets a value that specifies whether to use the current synchronization context to choose the thread of execution.

ValidateMustUnderstand (boolean): This gets or sets a value that specifies whether the system or the application enforces SOAP MustUnderstand header processing.

Contract Behavior

You can use the IContractBehavior interface to modify the dispatch behavior at the client or service level. IContractBehavior is an extension point you usually need only when you want to customize the dispatch behavior of WCF (see Listing 3–17).

Listing 3–17. IContractBehavior Interface

```
public interface IContractBehavior
{
        void AddBindingParameters(ContractDescription description,
            ServiceEndpoint endpoint,
            BindingParameterCollection parameters);
        void ApplyClientBehavior(ContractDescription description,
            ServiceEndpoint endpoint,
            ClientRuntime proxy);
        void ApplyDispatchBehavior(ContractDescription description,
            IEnumerable<ServiceEndpoint> endpoints,
            DispatchRuntime dispatch);
        void Validate(ContractDescription description,
            ServiceEndpoint endpoint);
}
```

When you implement the IContractBehavior interface in your client-side proxy or service, the ApplyClientBehavior and ApplyDispatchBehavior methods will be called when WCF binds the proxies or dispatchers. You can then customize the passed-in parameters. This is an extension point of the service runtime.

■**Tip** If you want to get a better understanding of what this interface can do for you, just implement it in your service and set a breakpoint in the body of your method. Then you can inspect the passed parameters and get a better understanding of what you can modify.

Channel Behavior

You can use the IEndpointBehavior interface to modify the channel behavior on the client or service side. IEndpointBehavior is an extension point that you usually need only when you want to customize the channel behavior of WCF (see Listing 3–18).

Listing 3–18. IEndpointBehavior Interface

```
public interface IEndpointBehavior
{
        void AddBindingParameters(ServiceEndpoint serviceEndpoint,
            BindingParameterCollection bindingParameters);
        void ApplyClientBehavior(ServiceEndpoint serviceEndpoint,
            ClientRuntime behavior);
        void ApplyDispatchBehavior(ServiceEndpoint serviceEndpoint,
            EndpointDispatcher endpointDispatcher);
        void Validate(ServiceEndpoint serviceEndpoint);
}
```

When you implement the IEndpointBehavior interface in your client-side proxy or service, the ApplyClientBehavior method will be called when WCF applies behaviors at the channel level on the client side; the ApplyDispatchBehavior class does the same on the service side. Obviously, you can then change the passed-in parameters. This is an extension point of the messaging layer.

Operation Behavior

You can apply the OperationBehavior attribute at the operation (method) level; it allows you to specify the specific operation behavior the method has during the execution of an operation. As with all behaviors, the OperationBehavior is internal to the service and has no direct effect on the contract.

Just like the ServiceBehavior attribute, the OperationBehavior attribute supports a few default properties:

TransactionAutoComplete (boolean): Gets or sets a value that specifies whether the transaction in which the method executes is automatically committed if no unhandled exceptions occur.

TransactionScopeRequired (boolean): Gets or sets a value that specifies whether a transaction scope in which the method executes is required. The transaction in which the method executes is automatically committed if no unhandled exceptions occur. The method will enlist the transaction.

Impersonation (boolean): Gets or sets a value that specifies whether the operation can impersonate the caller's identity.

ReleaseInstanceMode (boolean): Gets or sets a value that specifies whether the service objects are recycled during the operation invocation process.

AutoDisposeParameters (boolean): Determines whether the service runtime should dispose all input/output parameters once the operation is invoked.

Service Metadata Behavior

The ServiceMetadataBehavior is a specialized behavior that implements the IServiceBehavior interface. It intercepts requests for the metadata of your service and makes it possible to enable or disable the publication of service metadata using an HTTP GET request (via the HTML page shown in Figure 3–10).

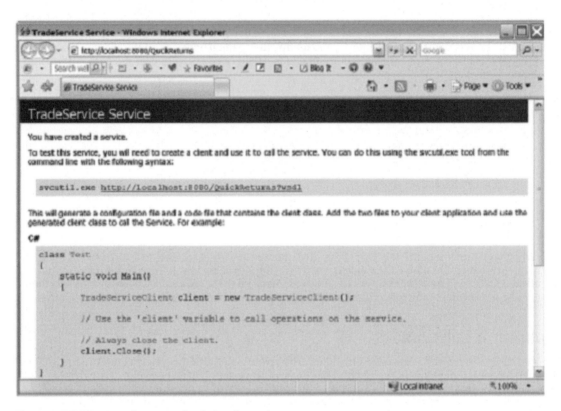

Figure 3–10. *The metadata page for the trade service*

In addition, it is possible to enable or disable the publication of this metadata through a WS-MetadataExchange (WS-MEX) request. If you know the consumers of your service, it makes sense to hand them the metadata rather than making the endpoint address public for others to retrieve. By default, when adding a baseAddress to your service, just like we did in several of our samples, the ServiceMetadataBehavior is added automatically to the Behaviors collection. As expected, you can change this behavior either through configuration or by using imperative code. This way you can appropriately set the properties (httpGetEnabled and httpHelpPageEnabled) of the class. Of course, the best way to do this is by using a configuration file, as in the sample configuration file shown in Listing 3–19. You can retrieve the metadata (WSDL) by retrieving the base address appended with ?wsdl. For example:

http://localhost:8080/QuickReturn?wsdl

Retrieving the base address in a browser results in the page shown in Figure 3–10.

Listing 3–19. Service Metadata in Configuration

```xml
<?xml version="1.0" encoding="utf-8" ?>
<configuration>
<system.serviceModel>
    <services>
        <service name="QuickReturns.StockTrading.ExchangeService.TradeService" >
            <host>
                <baseAddresses>
                    <add baseAddress="http://localhost:8080/QuickReturns"/>
                </baseAddresses>
            </host>
            <endpoint address="http://localhost:8080/QuickReturns/Exchange"
                    binding="basicHttpBinding"
                    contract="QuickReturns.StockTrading.ExchangeService.TradeService">
            </endpoint>
            <endpoint contract="IMetadataExchange"
                        binding="mexHttpBinding"
                        address="mex" />
        </service>
    </services>

    <serviceBehaviors>
        <behavior>
            <serviceMetadata httpGetEnabled="true"/>
            <serviceDebug    includeExceptionDetailInFaults="true"/>
        </behavior>
    </serviceBehaviors>

</system.serviceModel>
</configuration>
```

Using the Configuration Tool

The .NET Framework 3.0 SDK comes with several utilities. One of the most useful utilities is the Microsoft Service Configuration Editor (SvcConfigEditor.exe), shown in Figure 3–11. This utility enables you to open existing and create new WCF configuration files without editing XML files directly. With the tool, you can manage settings for both the client and the service. Additionally, it is possible to configure bindings, behaviors, extensions, host environments, and diagnostics.

■**Tip** By default, the configuration tool is installed in the Microsoft Windows SDK Bin folder (`C:\Program Files\Microsoft SDKs\Windows\v6.0`). It also comes with a help file in that same folder. When you use the configuration editor, we suggest you keep an eye on what it is actually adding to your configuration file. It tends to add more information than you specify, and it is important you know what the configuration settings mean. So, always inspect the results in a text editor after you make changes with the configuration editor and try to understand what it did.

Figure 3–11. Microsoft Service Configuration Editor

Configuring Diagnostics

When you work with WCF, you'll likely run into issues you don't understand completely. To investigate these issues, you will need to know what messages flow through your application, and you'll need to trace them. Luckily, WCF provides integrated support for logging messages and tracing. You can configure diagnostics by using the Microsoft Service Configuration Editor or by manipulating the application configuration manually. Tracing works with listeners, similar to the Microsoft .NET Framework. WCF 4.0 provides trace events that are based on Event Tracing for Windows (ETW), which significantly enhances tracing and diagnostics performance. Each source defined in the <source> section of the config file can have multiple trace listeners associated with it that determine where and how the data is traced. Listing 3–20 gives an example. The code shown in bold is the code for enabling ETW tracing and `ETWTraceListener`. In order to use `ETWTraceListener`, you need to start the ETW trace session, which you can do with a variety of tools. Two of the most popular tools for starting ETW trace sessions are `LogMan.exe` and `Tracelog.exe`, both of which ship with Windows.

Listing 3–20. Application Configuration with Tracing Enabled

```xml
<?xml version="1.0" encoding="utf-8" ?>
<configuration>
<system.diagnostics>
    <sources>

        <source name="System.ServiceModel.MessageLogging"
                switchValue="Warning, ActivityTracing">
            <listeners>
                <add type="System.Diagnostics.DefaultTraceListener"
                     name="Default">
                    <filter type="" />
                </add>
                <add name="ServiceModelMessageLoggingListener">
                    <filter type="" />
                </add>
            </listeners>
        </source>

        <source name="System.ServiceModel"
                switchValue="Warning, ActivityTracing"
                propagateActivity="true">
            <listeners>
                <add type="System.Diagnostics.DefaultTraceListener"
                     name="Default">
                    <filter type="" />
                </add>
                <add name="ETW">
                    <filter type="" />
                </add>
                <add name="ServiceModelTraceListener">
                    <filter type="" />
                </add>
            </listeners>
        </source>
    </sources>
    <sharedListeners>
        <add initializeData="C:\Temp\App_messages.svclog"
            type="System.Diagnostics.XmlWriterTraceListener, System,
            Version=4.0.0.0, Culture=neutral, PublicKeyToken=b77a5c561934e089"
            name="ServiceModelMessageLoggingListener"
            traceOutputOptions="Timestamp">
            <filter type="" />
        </add>
        <add initializeData="C:\App_tracelog.svclog"
            type="System.Diagnostics.XmlWriterTraceListener, System, ➥
            Version=4.0.0.0, Culture=neutral, PublicKeyToken=b77a5c561934e089"
            name="ServiceModelTraceListener"
            traceOutputOptions="Timestamp">
            <filter type="" />
```

```xml
            </add>
              <add type=
                "Microsoft.ServiceModel.Samples.EtwTraceListener, ETWTraceListener"
                name="ETW" traceOutputOptions="Timestamp">
                <filter type="" />
              </add>
          </sharedListeners>

      </system.diagnostics>
      <system.serviceModel>

      <diagnostics>
          <messageLogging logEntireMessage="true"
                          logMalformedMessages="true"
                          logMessagesAtServiceLevel="true"
                          logMessagesAtTransportLevel="true" />
       </diagnostics>

      <services>
        <service    name="QuickReturns.StockTrading.ExchangeService.TradeService">
          <endpoint address="Exchange"
                    binding="basicHttpBinding"
                    bindingConfiguration=""
                    name="basicHttpBinding"
                    contract="QuickReturns.StockTrading.ExchangeService. ➡
                              Contracts.ITradeService" />
          <endpoint address="mex"
                    binding="mexHttpBinding"
                    name="mexHttpBinding"
                    contract="IMetadataExchange" />
          <host>
            <baseAddresses>
              <add baseAddress="http://localhost:8080/QuickReturns" />
            </baseAddresses>
          </host>
        </service>
      </services>
        <behaviors>
          <serviceBehaviors>
            <behavior >
              <serviceMetadata httpGetEnabled="true"/>
              <serviceDebug  includeExceptionDetailInFaults="true"/>
            </behavior>
          </serviceBehaviors>
        </behaviors>
      </system.serviceModel>
      </configuration>
```

You can also edit the configuration file with the configuration tool's Diagnostics window, shown in Figure 3–12.

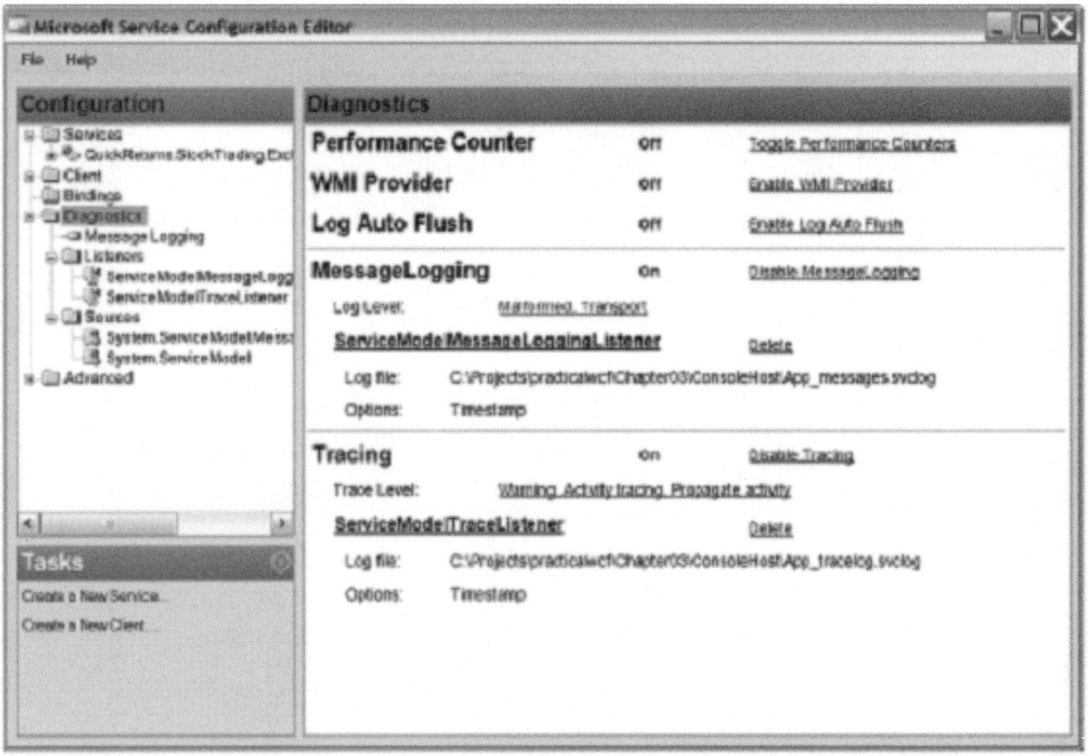

Figure 3–12. Diagnostics window in the configuration tool

In addition, the Windows SDK comes with a small utility that enables you to view the messages flowing through your application. The utility is called the Microsoft Service Trace Viewer (SvcTraceViewer.exe) and is in the same location as the configuration tool, as shown in Figure 3–13.

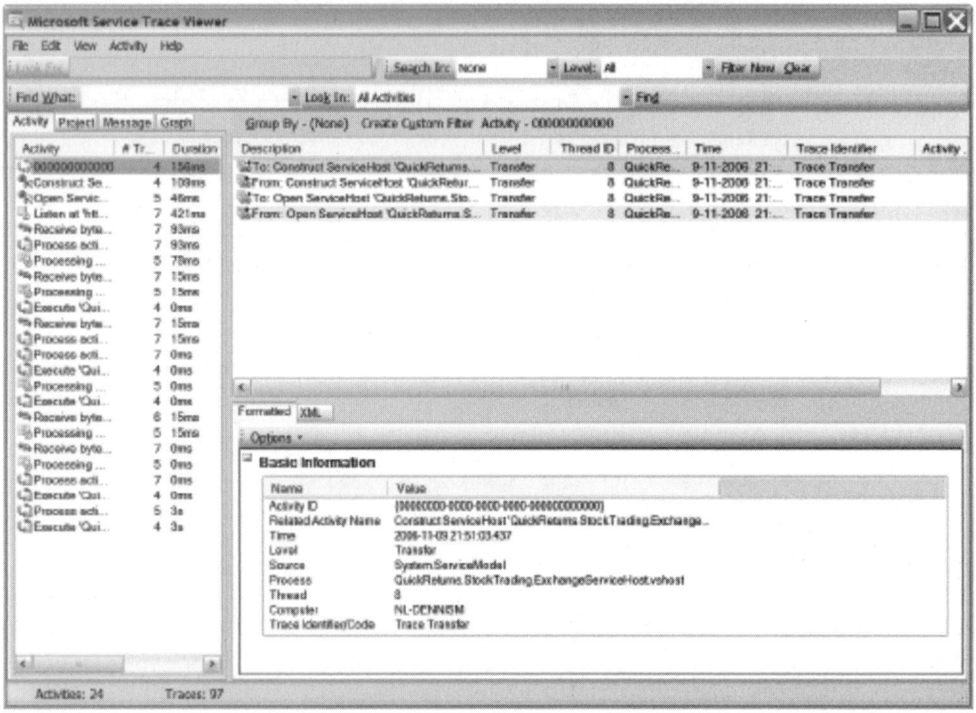

Figure 3–13. Microsoft Service Trace Viewer

The logging capabilities of WCF are extensive; it is possible to log full messages, just headers, malformed messages, messages at the service level or transport level, and so on, as shown in the second bold section of Listing 3–20. You can then use the Service Trace Viewer to view the log files.

■**Tip** By default, the Service Trace Viewer tool is installed in the Microsoft Windows SDK Bin folder (C:\Program Files (x86)\Microsoft SDKs\Windows\v7.0A). It also comes with a compiled help (CHM) file in that same folder. We strongly suggest you run the sample application in this chapter and enable all or at least most of the tracing and diagnostics functionality in the configuration on both the client and service sides, and then inspect the log files you are getting. This will help you understand not only the built-in capabilities regarding diagnostics, but also what is going on under the hood of the WCF programming model.

Configuring Instrumentation

Instrumentation allows activities in an application to give rise to event log and performance counter updates. Just like logging and tracing, you can enable performance counters and WMI (Windows

Management Instrumentation) from within the application configuration or the configuration tool for both the client side and the service side. You can also set the performanceCountersEnabled property to ServiceOnly. Listing 3–21 shows how you do this in an application configuration file.

Listing 3–21. Application Configuration with Instrumentation Enabled

```xml
<?xml version="1.0" encoding="utf-8"?>
<configuration>
   <system.serviceModel>
      <diagnostics wmiProviderEnabled="true" performanceCounters="All" />
      <client>
         <endpoint address="http://localhost:8080/QuickReturns/Exchange"
            binding="basicHttpBinding" bindingConfiguration=""
            contract="ITradeService" name="basicHttpBinding" />
      </client>
   </system.serviceModel>
</configuration>
```

Figure 3–14 shows the Diagnostics window in the Microsoft Service Configuration Editor, which you can use to enable performance counters and WMI events. This results in the changes to the configuration in Listing 3–21 (shown in bold).

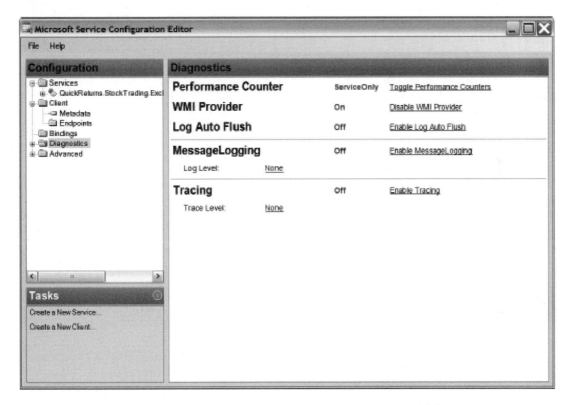

Figure 3–14. Microsoft Service Configuration Editor with instrumentation enabled

Summary

Now that you know how the unified programming model of WCF works and what its architecture is, you should be able to create your first WCF-enabled application. You should also be able to describe where the extension points are, and be able to decide where you should extend in a particular scenario.

In the next part of this book, we'll build on the foundations set in this chapter and cover some more advanced topics in the programming model, including creating, consuming, and hosting services. However, before moving on, make sure you have at least played around with the base services and client that come in the code accompanying this book.

PART II

■ ■ ■

Programming with WCF

Part 1 of this book investigated the basics of SOA and the building blocks of service-oriented computing. It also discussed the evolution of the Microsoft offerings for providing a practical SOA platform to build services on. It focused on the new features of WCF that shipped with the .NET Framework 4.0, and it covered the unified programming model and how WCF provides the best tools to create secure, interoperable web services.

In this part, we'll discuss the technical features of WCF in detail. We'll concentrate on the programming aspects of WCF, again using the fictitious QuickReturns Ltd. stock market application as a learning tool. We'll initially go through installing the WCF components, and then we'll walk through creating services and hosting them with WCF. We will discuss all the hosting options available in WCF in detail. Finally, we'll cover the management options available to manage WCF services to obtain the best return on investment for your application.

CHAPTER 4

■ ■ ■

Installing and Creating WCF Services

This chapter introduces how to implement WCF services. Much can be said about what constitutes a good service and a strong SOA architecture (Chapter 1 addresses those principles). Additionally, many have described web services and SOA as synonyms. I hope I have altered that perspective to clearly indicate that web services are just an implementation model for SOA.

This chapter identifies the installation and configuration requirements of WCF, and then presents a simplified set of examples for creating different types of contracts for services that are part of the QuickReturns Ltd. sample implementation. This chapter focuses primarily on the following:

- The requirements for installing WCF

- Creating WCF services and proxies using Visual Studio 2010 and .NET 4.0 Framework tools

For simplicity, this chapter doesn't discuss the various ways you can host the service. We'll explain that in more detail in later chapters.

WCF allows the abstraction and decoupling of a service's functionality from the actual transport protocols and physical characteristics of the communication interfaces. Prior chapters covered the ABCs of WCF, but here we'll focus on creating services. We will delve more deeply into the technical aspects of the WCF programming model from this chapter onward.

Understanding the Requirements

We'll briefly cover the hardware and software requirements for developing and running .NET 4.0 applications. It's important to note that Microsoft may change or update these requirements over time, so it's best to check Microsoft's web site for the most up-to-date versions.

Hardware Requirements

Generally, the hardware requirements for running WCF as part of .NET 4.0 are different for 32-bit and 64–bit operating systems.

■**Note** The .NET runtime and the .NET SDK have different base requirements. Running the SDK, tools, utilities, and compilers requires additional resources. Given that most developers are using Visual Studio .NET 2010 as their primary development environment, they should have as much memory, CPU, and disk space as they can afford.

Table 4–1 presents the minimum hardware requirements for the processor and RAM (at the time of writing), and Table 4–2 describes the minimum hardware requirements for hard disk space.

Table 4–1. Hardware Requirements: Processor and RAM

Scenario	Minimum Processor	Minimum RAM
.NET Framework 4.0 redistributable	1 GHz Pentium	512 MB
.NET Framework 4.0 SDK	1 GHz Pentium	512 MB

Table 4–2. Hardware Requirements: Hard Disk Space

Scenario	Minimum
32-bit	850 MB
64–bit	2 GB

■**Note** Microsoft publishes its requirements at `www.microsoft.com/downloads/details.aspx?FamilyID=9cfb2d51-5ff4-4491-b0e5-b386f32c0992&displaylang=en` and in the README file installed with the .NET SDK. You can find this in the `Program Files (x86)\Microsoft Visual Studio 9.0\SDK\v3.5` directory if it is installed as part of Visual Studio .NET, or online at `http://download.microsoft.com/download/B/5/7/B57D25A2-B3FD-4668-91B9-DB43B6BD910D/NETFx4RTM.htm`.

Software Requirements

We'll now cover the software platform requirements for both developing and running .NET 4.0 applications. At the time of this writing, the installation order is quite stringent. During research for this book, I installed uninstalled, reinstalled, and even wiped machines numerous times to get the beta and Community Technology Preview (CTP) components operating correctly. It's clear that machine virtualization is a blessing for this type of leading-edge work. Having discussed the "cleanliness" of the

SDK installation process with the Microsoft program managers, they also empathize with the development community and are looking to make the process as tight as possible.

The following are the component requirements to run and develop .NET 4.0 and WCF-based applications:

- Windows Server 2008 R2 or later, Windows 7, Windows 2003 SP2, Windows XP SP3, or Windows Vista SP1

- The .NET Framework 4.0 web installer package

The development environment requires a few extra tools and, as a general recommendation, should be equipped with a few more resources for the hardware:

- Windows Server 2008 R2(not supported on Server Core Role), Windows 7, Windows 2003 SP2, Windows XP SP3, or Windows Vista SP1

- The .NET Framework 4.0 SDK (x86/x64/I64)

- The Microsoft Windows SDK (formerly known as Platform SDK)

- The.NET Framework 4.0 runtime components

- IIS installation (recommended)

- Microsoft Visual Studio 2010 Express Edition (or a more complete version—Pro, Suite, etc.) (recommended)

■**Note** Developing WCF and .NET 4.0 Framework solutions requires only the .NET 4.0 Framework SDK. However, it is expected that most developers will use Visual Studio 2010. All versions of Visual Studio 2010 support the development of WCF (.NET 4.0) applications. You can find the .NET 4.0 runtime and SDK at http://msdn.microsoft.com/netframework/downloads/updates.

Installing the .NET 4.0 Development Components

This section lists the general steps for installing the .NET 4.0 (WCF) development components. This is the required installation order:

1. Install the .NET Framework 4.0.

2. Install Visual Studio 2010.

3. Install the Windows SDK for .NET 4.0.

WCF services can be hosted in any application process that loads the .NET 3.x (or above) runtime, loads the appropriate .NET Framework runtime components, and ultimately instantiates a System.ServiceModel.ServiceHost instance that listens on an endpoint for requests.

> ■**Note** Chapter 5 provides greater detail about hosting, the various options available, the overall mechanics, and the nuances associated with the various hosting options.

This chapter focuses on getting up and running with WCF services and using the simplest of hosts—the ASP.NET development server and IIS. You can use IIS for both developing and deploying WCF services. Most of the mechanics of hosting WCF services inside ASP.NET are handled by an implementation of an `HttpHandler`. This handler is `System.ServiceModel.Activation.HttpHandler`, and is mapped on a per-machine basis in the machine's `web.config` file, which is located in the directory `%windir%\Microsoft.NET\Framework64\v4.0.30319\CONFIG`.

IIS, WCF, AND THE HTTP API

The Windows operating system (from Windows 2003 to Windows Server 2008) provides the HTTP API to allow applications that create HTTP listeners to gain a series of advantages over the traditional Winsock mechanism that was available in prior releases of Windows. WCF is positioned to take full advantage of this capability, which for the most part has been dormant on the client platform.

> ■**Note** All ASP.NET "resources" are mapped to types that implement the `IHttpHandler` interface, as required by the ASP.NET hosting engine.

Within the `httpHandler` section of the machine's `Web.config` file, the mapping appears as shown in Listing 4–1.

Listing 4–1. *.svc Mapping for WCF Handler

```
<add
path="*.svc"
verb="*"
type="System.ServiceModel.Activation.HttpHandler, System.ServiceModel.Activation,
Version=4.0.0.0, Culture=neutral, PublicKeyToken=31bf3856ad364e35"
validate="False"/>
```

The `System.ServiceModel.Activation.HttpHandler` class is responsible for providing the `ServiceHost` environment inside the ASP.NET worker process for applications that are hosted on IIS. This handler, just like handlers that provide for other extensions (*.aspx, *.asmx), is responsible for providing any runtime compilation of source code embedded inside the *.svc files, in addition to providing update detection of the same source code, as is done for the other handler types.

Understanding Service Contracts

Service contracts, one of the Cs in the ABCs of WCF, are what are advertised to the consumers of your services. This advertisement generally takes place through a schema and a contract definition that supports a standardized method for publishing the service contract (along with data contracts). Today, that schema is either a Web Services Description Language (WSDL) contract or a WS-MetadataExchange (MEX) contract. These formats are industry-supported, open specifications. These specifications can be found at the following locations:

- *WSDL*: www.w3.org/TR/wsdl

- *MEX*: http://schemas.xmlsoap.org/ws/2004/09/mex

WSDL AND WS-METADATAEXCHANGE

WSDL is an XML Schema–based description of supported operations and messages for an endpoint. MEX represents a message exchange protocol that allows the discovery of WSDL, WS-Policy, or XML Schema associated with a target namespace. More information is available at http://specs.xmlsoap.org/ws/2004/09/mex/WS-MetadataExchange.pdf

■**Note** For COM interop, a third type of contract exists—a *typed contract*. See Chapter 10 for more details.

Platform and framework vendors have implemented tools and libraries that can leverage these standardized contracts to provide a more seamless integration experience between service providers and the consumers (sometimes referred to as *receivers* and *senders*). WCF provides in its metadata model the ability to define and publish, as well as consume, these standardized schema definitions. It is possible in WCF to leveraging contracts both programmatically at runtime and declaratively at design and configuration time.

WCF provides the standards and tools support primarily through SvcUtil.exe. This utility is the primary code and metadata interpretation tool. That, in combination with the WCF framework's ability to leverage reflection to interrogate types adorned with the appropriate attributes, makes generating and using the WCF framework less complicated than before. Figure 4–1 illustrates how service metadata is consumed by SvcUtil.exe for proxy generation; additionally, the same metadata is leveraged by the WCF framework for runtime interaction.

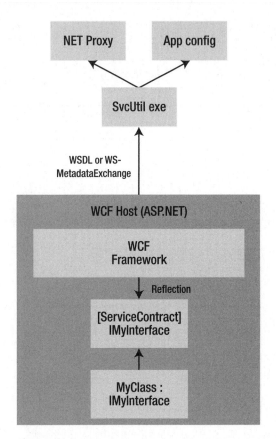

Figure 4-1. Metadata publishing and client code generation

Contract First or Code First?

There have been lots of discussions in SOA communities regarding code-first vs. contract-first service development. I won't say one is better than the other; however, in a true contract-first paradigm, you'll spend all the up-front time generating the schema (WSDL) in XML that supports your service contract implementation. Frankly, I'd rather listen to someone scratch their nails on a blackboard than start with a whole bunch of XML. Although WCF can support a contract- and schema-driven starting point, for the most part you'll spend time adorning your types with attributes in a declarative model and allowing the WCF framework to generate the necessary schema and contract metadata.

The WCF programming model of "code first and then apply attributes to the interface" allows the WCF framework to do all the work of providing a standardized schema to publish to consumers of the service. This model works best in industries or organizations where you're the only provider of the service, or where you're just working on internal solutions that require cross-application integration, and you have full control over the interfaces.

.NET ATTRIBUTES BACKGROUND

.NET uses attributes throughout the framework. Attributes permeate many aspects of how your types are hosted by the .NET CLR. Things such as Code Access Security (CAS) and general assembly metadata all depend upon attributes that are part of the generated Microsoft Intermediate Language (MSIL). This is one of the declarative aspects of .NET.

The ASP.NET 2.0 web service model also relies on class- and method-level attributes that control how the .NET Framework manages the runtime support of web services through the request-reply cycle. For the most part, the declarative model remains the same when moving to WCF.

According to the WCF product team, this was somewhat intentional in order to help the migration and transition of both existing ASP.NET 2.0 web services and developers to the WCF model. That initial transition started with the introduction of Web Services Enhancements (WSE). The transition from out-of-the-box ASP.NET 2.0 web services to WSE web services required no change from a coding perspective. All WSE required was the modification of the application (`web.config`) file that the site was hosted on, in addition to a recompilation to bind to the updated assemblies that were part of the WSE distributions.

WCF supports schema- and contract-first development as well. This might sound like a new model in the .NET world, but it was possible under ASP.NET 1.1 web services as well; it just required some discipline to follow and implement. The paradigm also existed in the COM world; but again, discipline was required and tool support was limited.

The primary tool you'll use in WCF is `SvcUtil.exe`. This chapter introduces how to use `SvcUtil.exe`, and Chapter 5 covers it in more detail.

Service Design

WCF provides the complete design-time decoupling of the service from the service implementation. It does this to allow greater flexibility in choosing the implementation model (which consists of both the service and the ABCs) and greater extensibility for supporting various transports. In other words, you can write and maintain a single instance of your service code without regard for the physical deployment model.

Now, in the real world, you still need to consider what the service provides and what the overall performance is as it relates to marshaling objects across service boundaries and ultimately coupling physical nodes separated by a LAN, a WAN, or the Internet. As a good solution architect, you should consider "Eight Fallacies of Distributed Computing," a set of assumptions written by Peter Deutsch (see http://en.wikipedia.org/wiki/Fallacies_of_Distributed_Computing for more information).

In an ideal implementation, the service providers and service consumers will spend a significant amount of time collaborating from a business perspective. During that collaboration process, a service model will evolve to properly address many aspects of what the service contract will look like, including elements such as the following:

- Granularity

- Coupling

- Cohesion

- Security

- Performance

- Reliability

To be clear, WCF doesn't address these aspects directly; that's up to the solution architect. WCF provides the base framework for implementing service contracts, in conjunction with the rest of the ABCs, for a solid SOA implementation foundation.

Programming Model

Table 4–3 compares WCF's programming model to ASP.NET 2.0 web services.

Table 4–3. Attribute Programming Model Comparison

ASP.NET 2.0 Attribute	WCF Attribute	Description
[WebServiceAttribute]	[ServiceContractAttribute]	Interface, class-level attribute
[WebMethodAttribute]	[OperationContractAttribute]	Method-level attribute
	[DataContractAttribute]	Class-level attribute
	[DataMemberAttribute]	Field, property, event-level attribute

Notice that the attribute-naming conventions have changed from being web oriented to being more SOA oriented (e.g., using terms like *service*, *operation*, and *data*). This was done intentionally to shift the architectural thinking from a web-only mentality to an "any transport" paradigm.

WSE 3.0 provides the ability for different transports to support more complex message exchange patterns, such as duplex channels (through the ISoapDuplexChannel interface). Also, Visual Studio 2008 and later do not provide direct support for WSE 3, and instead rely on WCF for the same functionality. WCF now provides a much more simplistic model for implementation, in addition to a fully extensible framework, as well as support for WS-* specifications, such as WS-Transactions, WS-Reliability, and others.

Hello World

Now we'll demonstrate a simple Hello World example (see Chapter04/Example01 in the downloadable code) in both ASP.NET 2.0 and WCF. This first sample demonstrates a simple service implementation. It uses a "code first with attributes" model, which is *not* a best practice—it's purely an example to show the similarities between ASP.NET 2.0 web services and WCF. The best practice is a contract-first model, in which you define the schema prior to coding the implementation. This removes the designer's bias toward any implementation details or restrictions.

■**Note** With some of the IIS-hosted samples, a set of scripts provides the IIS virtual directory creation and ASP.NET mapping, along with a script to remove the IIS virtual directory when done. The creation/removal scripts are in each example's directory, and are named CreateVirtualDirs.bat and DeleteVirtualDirs.bat, respectively. You must be an administrator on the system to execute these files. Additionally, if you're on Vista or Windows Server 2008, you must run from an elevated command prompt from the directory where these files exist.

To ensure you focus on how the services are created, we will use only IIS as the hosting environment. (Chapter 5 discusses other WCF hosting options.)

ASP.NET 2.0 Web Service: Hello World

Listing 4–2 shows MyService.asmx, which creates a service that return a string with the value "Hello World," along with your name.

Listing 4–2. MyService.asmx

```
<%@ WebService Language="C#" Class="MyService" %>
using System.Web.Services;
[WebService]
public class MyService  : System.Web.Services.WebService
{
    [WebMethod]
    public string HelloWorld ( string yourName )
    {
        return "Hello, World to " + yourName;
    }
}
```

WCF Service: Hello World

Listing 4–3 shows MyService.svc, and Listing 4–4 shows a web.config file containing a WCF service that returns a string with the value "Hello World," along with your name.

Listing 4–3. MyService.svc

```
<%@ ServiceHost Language="C#" Service="MyService" %>
using System.ServiceModel;
[ServiceContract]
public class MyService
{
    [OperationContract]
    public string HelloWorld ( string yourName )
    {
        return "Hello, World to " + yourName;
    }
}
```

Listing 4–4. web.config

```
<?xml version="1.0"?>
<configuration>
  <system.serviceModel>
    <services>
      <service  name="MyService">
        <endpoint   contract="MyService"
      binding="wsHttpBinding"/>
      </service>
```

```
        </services>
        <behaviors>
        <serviceBehaviors>
         <behavior  name="">
            <serviceMetadata httpGetEnabled="true"/>
            <serviceDebug  includeExceptionDetailInFaults="true"/>
         </behavior>
        </serviceBehaviors>
        </behaviors>
      </system.serviceModel>
</configuration>
```

■**Tip** A best practice in WCF is to implement the service contract using an interface; then you implement the interface in a class and update the configuration file to point to the correct type.

From a coding and implementation perspective, the ASP.NET 2.0 web service and the WCF service aren't that different. The method bodies are identical. Deployment under ASP.NET is also nearly identical. When running from Visual Studio 2010, both can leverage the ASP.NET development server. Additionally, if running from IIS and the application mappings are correct, the deployment is identical between the ASP.NET 2.0 web services and WCF services.

The first obvious difference between ASP.NET 2.0 and WCF that you find in the preceding examples is that the WCF implementation requires a configuration (`web.config`) file. The configuration file you see is one of the strengths of building services with WCF—you get almost complete control of the runtime characteristics of a service without forcing a change in the code. In fact, with .NET 4.0, you can create configurationless WCF services. You can make this `web.config` file optional by tweaking `machine.config`, unless you require some specific settings for your WCF services, as discussed in Chapter 2. In later chapters, we'll cover self-hosting and how to manage the WCF runtime characteristics through code as well.

Hello World with Interfaces

A best practice in WCF is to define a contract up front, as an interface, and then provide the implementation of that interface in a concrete class. This provides a clear abstraction of the contract from the implementation. It also provides a clear distinction between that service boundary (remember the "boundaries are explicit" SOA tenet) and the implementation. Although the service interface definition is in code, not in metadata, it's a clear distinction hat permits some flexibility for exposing only what's necessary

The next example (`Example02` in the downloadable code) follows the best practice of implementing the contract in a defined interface, with the implementation provided for separately. The mapping, as you'll soon see, is managed through the framework either programmatically or through configuration options. Listing 4–5 shows `MyService.svc`.

Listing 4–5. MyService.svc

```
<%@ ServiceHost Language="C#" Service="MyService" %>
using System.ServiceModel;

[ServiceContract]
public interface IMyInterface
{
        [OperationContract]
        string HelloWorld ( string yourName );
}

public class MyService : IMyInterface
{
    public string HelloWorld( string yourName )
    {
        return "Hello, World to " + yourName;
    } }
```

■**Note** For Windows Vista and 2008 users, if you run `CreateVirtualDirs.bat` (from an elevated prompt, as required) and attempt to open the Visual Studio 2010 solution file with Visual Studio 2010, you will be presented with a message box indicating that the site is configured with the wrong version of .NET. You can answer either Yes or No to this prompt. To validate the correct version mapped for the virtual site, you must use IIS Manager and ensure that the site is mapped to an application pool configuration with ASP.NET 4.0. The `CreateVirtualDirs.bat` script handles this automatically.

The implementation now provides a clear contract definition, without implementation details, that is required to provide the automatic generation of the metadata (either WSDL or MEX). How the contract is implemented, and ultimately bound, is managed through a configuration file or programmatically. For this example, and probably what is destined to be the norm, we do it via configuration.

In the `web.config` file for the WCF service, shown in Listing 4–6, the mapping between the type and the contract takes place through the `<services>` element inside the `<system.serviceModel>` section. Note the clear contract mapping to the implementation type, which is the interface definition.

Listing 4–6. web.config

```
<?xml version="1.0"?>
<configuration>
  <system.serviceModel>
    <services>
      <service   name="MyService"  >
        <endpoint         contract="IMyInterface"
      binding="wsHttpBinding"/>
      </service>
    </services>
```

```
    <behaviors>
    <serviceBehaviors>
      <behavior  name="">
        <serviceMetadata httpGetEnabled="true"/>
        <serviceDebug   includeExceptionDetailInFaults="true"/>
      </behavior>
    </serviceBehaviors>
    </behaviors>
  </system.serviceModel>
</configuration>
```

If you launch this service in the ASP.NET development server, you'll see something different from Figure 4–2, because the URL will differ by the IP port for the project. The ASP.NET development server dynamically chooses the IP port, unless you override this behavior. If you're using IIS, then the default port (80) is left off, and the URL appears as in Figure 4–2.

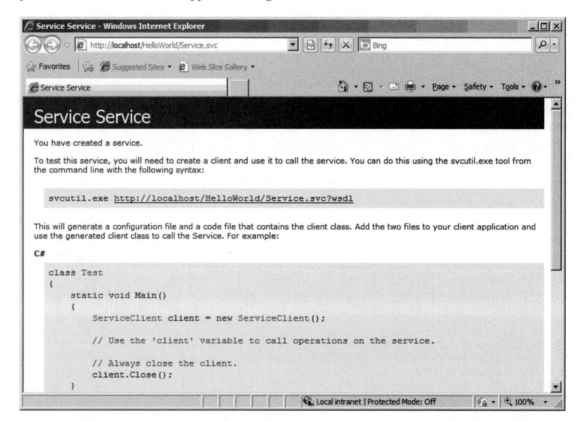

Figure 4–2. Viewing the WCF Hello World service

The initial difference when consuming ASP.NET web services vs. WCF services is the use of different client proxy generation tools. You'll see that step in the following sections using two different methods: Visual Studio 2010 integration and the SvcUtil.exe utility.

Service Client Proxy

Now that you have a service, it's time to define a client for that service. So, add a C# console application, and place the implementation code in a separate file as part of the ASP.NET application. The following is part of the Example03 sample code.

Proxy Generation Using the Visual Studio 2010 Add-In

Similar to ASP.NET proxy creation, if you right-click the project in the IDE, you'll see options for adding references. Select Add Service Reference, as shown in Figure 4–3.

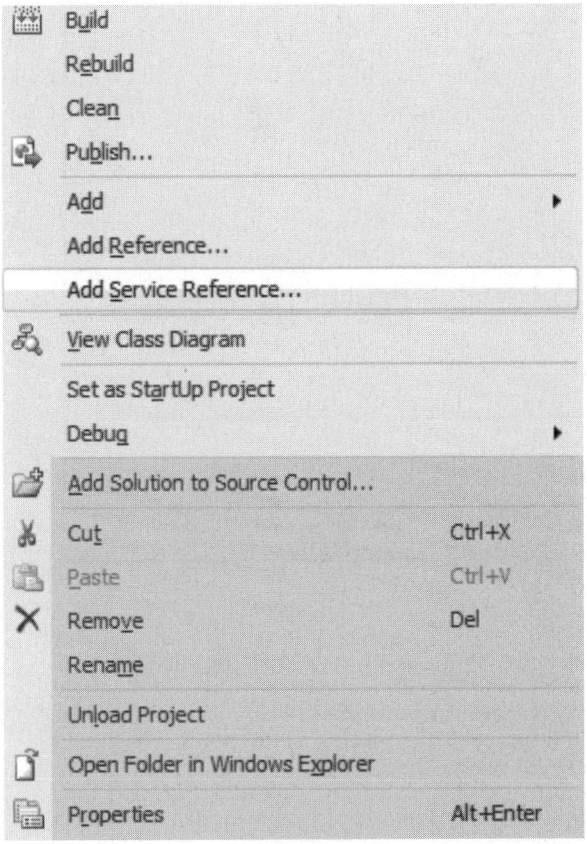

Build	
Rebuild	
Clean	
Publish...	
Add	▶
Add Reference...	
Add Service Reference...	
View Class Diagram	
Set as StartUp Project	
Debug	▶
Add Solution to Source Control...	
Cut	Ctrl+X
Paste	Ctrl+V
Remove	Del
Rename	
Unload Project	
Open Folder in Windows Explorer	
Properties	Alt+Enter

Figure 4–3. Adding a reference to a WCF service

This menu option is a wrapper around the SvcUtil.exe utility, and actually spawns a process with the necessary parameters. Once you've selected the Add Service Reference option, you'll see the Add Service Reference dialog box, as shown in Figure 4–4.

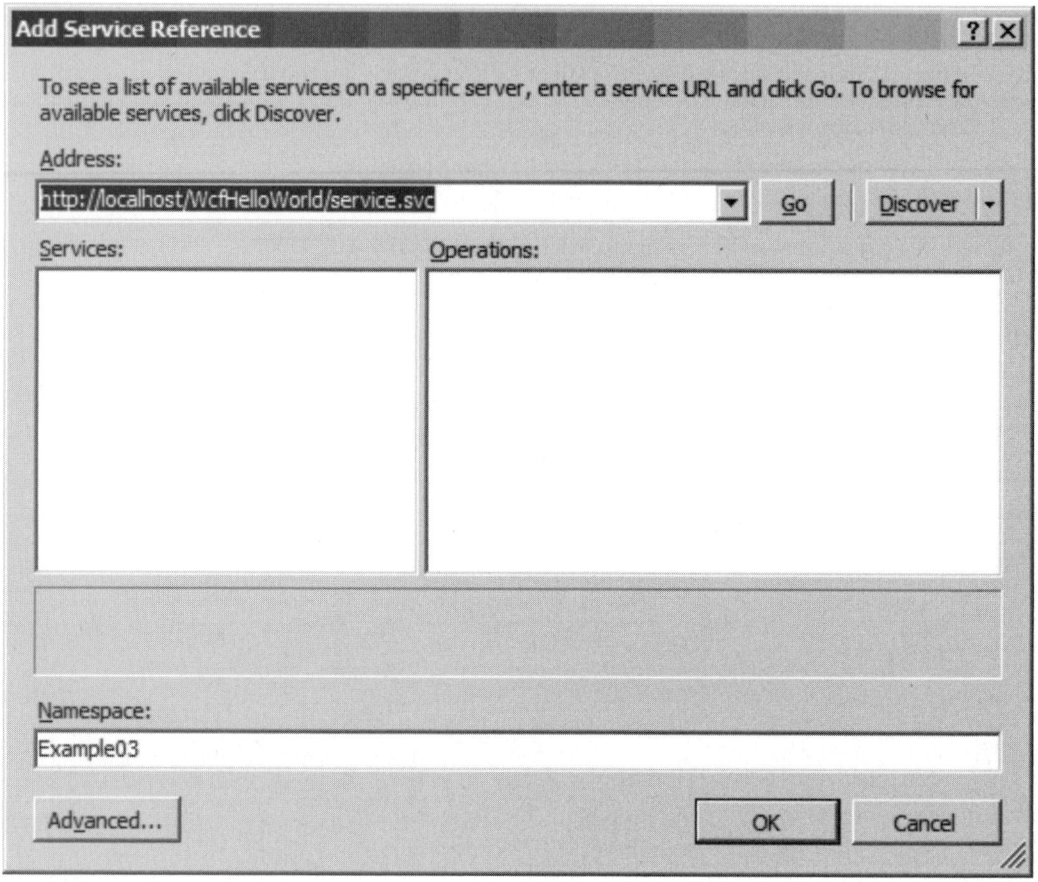

Figure 4–4. Add Service Reference dialog box

Click Go to get a list of services and their associated operations. Click OK, and the add-in will spawn SvcUtil.exe, which will generate (or modify) the necessary proxy class and the required configuration file, and add the necessary references to the project. The project's references will now list the required WCF assemblies: System.Runtime.Serialization and System.ServiceModel. At this point, you should now be ready to program your first service call into your service tier.

A brief explanation of the objects added to the project is necessary. During the SvcUtil.exe (Add Service Reference) call, the utility added the following items and references to the project automatically. Some are only to aid the Visual Studio integration; others are required for using the service directly through the proxy.

Service references: Within this folder, two items were added. The first, a map file, provides support for the generation and regeneration of the proxy through the Visual Studio add-in. The second item—Example03.cs—represents the concrete proxy class implementation that leverages the namespace System.ServiceModel to provide a simple integration class.

Configuration: The second item is the App.config file. An App.config file (automatically renamed during the Visual Studio build process to <assembly name>.config) provides the runtime WCF configuration parameters. If you peer inside this file, you'll notice a tremendous number of settings, many of which are either defaulted or redundant to the default settings. A general approach is to generate the file and then manage it using the WCF SvcConfigEditor.exe editor utility. This utility is located in the Windows SDK Bin directory. Figure 4–5 shows the user interface of the tool as well.

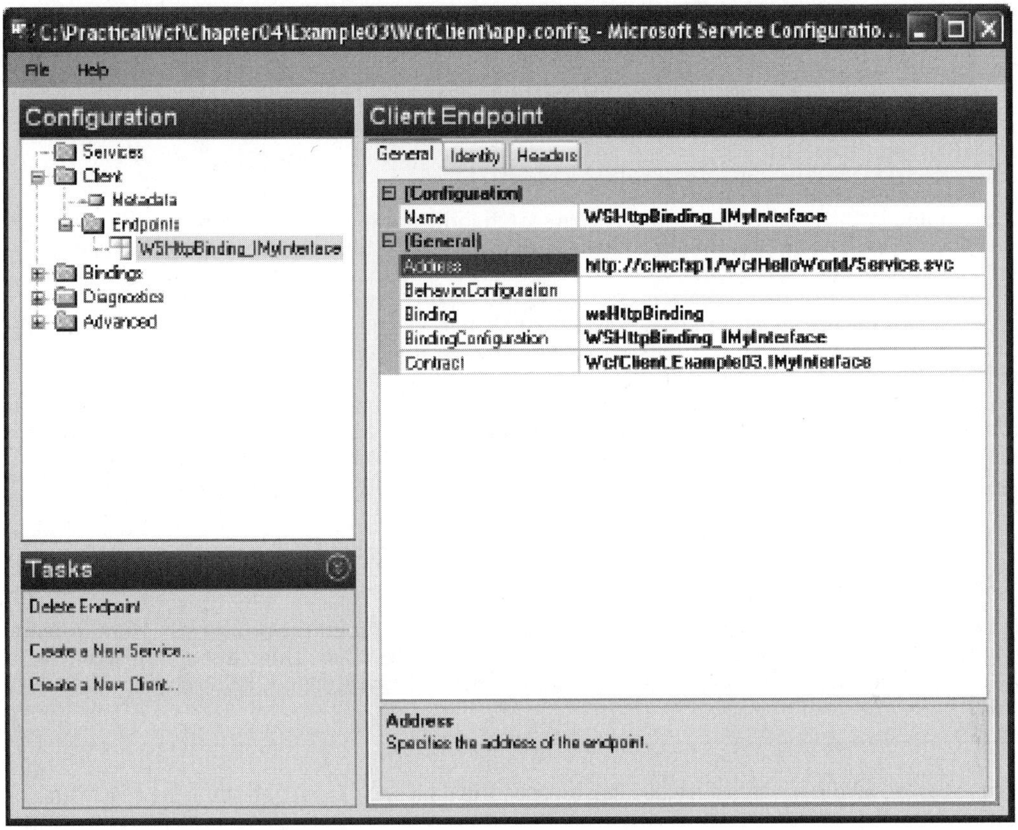

Figure 4–5. *Microsoft Service Configuration Editor, SvcConfigEditor.exe*

As you can see from the figure, you can manage a tremendous number of detailed properties through the Microsoft Service Configuration Editor. This is one of the greatest strengths of WCF—the ability to control many aspects of an implementation without impacting the core service implementation. That a service implementation doesn't need to change in order to migrate from an HTTP-based protocol to another message-oriented one is a core strength of WCF's metadata approach.

You'll see many parts are controllable through the runtime configuration; however, you need to define many aspects of a service implementation at the service contract level.

Proxy Generation Using SvcUtil.exe

An alternative method is to leverage the SvcUtil.exe utility directly, instead of using the Visual Studio add-in. Again, the Visual Studio add-in calls SvcUtil.exe, with parameters, to generate the proxy when executed directly from within Visual Studio. You can see the command line and results of that command by viewing the Output window and setting the Show Output From drop-down list to Service Reference.

To generate the proxy manually, choose Start ➤ All Programs ➤ Visual Studio Command Prompt (2010). This command prompt is useful because its path is set to the binary directory where the SDK tools and utilities are located.

Let's explore how to use the SvcUtil.exe command-line tool to generate two outputs necessary for the example project: the client proxy source code file and the application configuration file. These files are then merged into the client project. SvcUtil.exe can generate both. For this example, the following command (which should appear on a single line) produces both a proxy class and a configuration file:

```
svcutil /config:newConfig.config /out:"Example03.cs"
    /n:*,WcfClient.Example03
    "http://localhost/WcfHelloWorld/Service.svc?wsdl"
```

The command is fairly self-explanatory. The /n switch indicates in which namespace the generated proxy class should fall. The last parameter is the URL of the service endpoint where you can find schema information. Note that you can replace ?wsdl with ?mex because SvcUtil.exe supports both methods of discovery. You can access further help by executing svcutil.exe /? from the command prompt.

The next step is to take the output files Example03.cs and newConfig.config and merge them into the project. You can add the first file, Example03.cs, directly to the project by choosing Add Existing Item from the Project menu in Visual Studio 2010.

You need to add the second file as an application configuration (App.config) file in the project. If the project does not already have an App.config file, you can add one by again choosing Add Existing Item from the Project menu. If there is already an existing App.config file, you need to merge the system.serviceModel section into the existing App.config file, ensuring you take all the appropriate child elements.

Client Code

The client code in Example03, shown in Listing 4–7, is a simple call through the proxy class. Here, you are leveraging the using statement to ensure that the Dispose method is called. The other option is to wrap it in a try...finally block, with a call to the object's Dispose method inside the finally clause.

■**Note** The using keyword is a shortcut method that expands into the try...finally block in the generated MSIL

Listing 4–7. WcfClient program.cs

```
using System;
namespace WcfClient
{
    class Program
    {
        static void Main( )
        {
            // using "block" as a shortcut for a try...finally block
            // with a call to the object Dispose() method in the finally block
            using( Example03.MyInterfaceClient proxy =
```

```
      new Example03.MyInterfaceClient() )
    {
      string result = proxy.HelloWorld( "Nishith Pathak" );
      Console.WriteLine( result );
      Console.WriteLine( "Press <enter> to exit..." );
      Console.ReadLine();
    }
  }
 }
}
```

Hosting on IIS

The previous examples are all included in the downloadable source code with an automated script for creating the virtual directory on IIS. This section shows you how to create a .NET 4.0 WCF service and host it in IIS.

The first step to take is to create an empty solution file. This provides total control over the location of the file. If you bypass this step, Visual Studio 2010 creates the project where you want it to, but the solution file is put in your default location for your Visual Studio projects.

To generate an empty solution file that you'll add your projects to, from within Visual Studio select File ➤ New Project ➤ Other Project Types ➤ Visual Studio Solutions ➤ Blank Solution. Be sure to specify both the name and the location for the blank solution.

After creating the empty solution file, the next step is to add a .NET 4.0 (WCF) service web project. If you immediately add the project to the solution, the project files are created in the default C:\inetpub\wwwroot subdirectory. To gain a little more control, you can create the IIS virtual site before adding the project location to the solution file. The next step is to just create a subdirectory where the solution file is located, as shown in Figure 4–6.

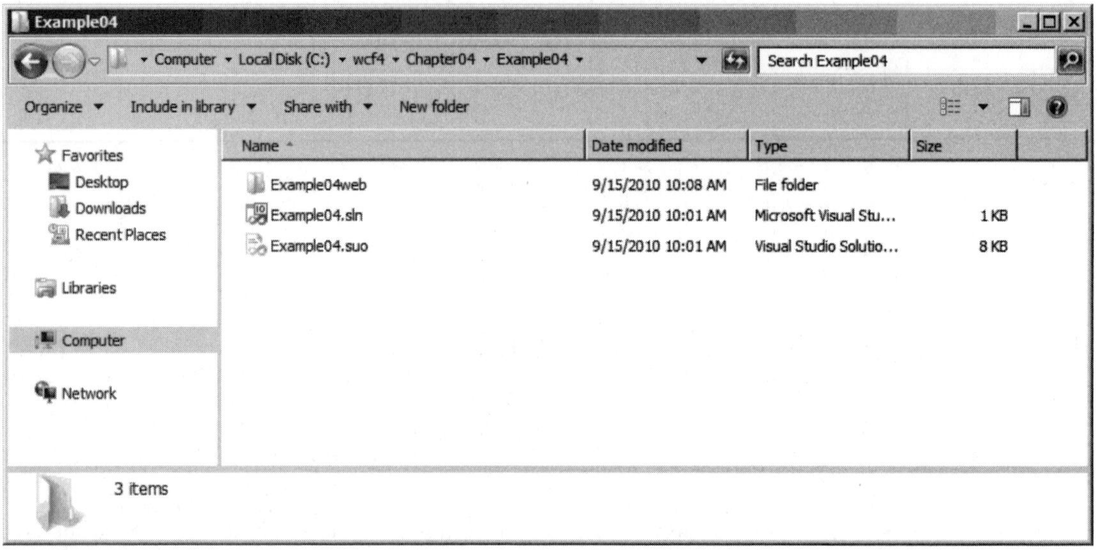

Figure 4–6. Creating a subdirectory in the solution folder

Then you need to create a virtual directory in IIS that points to the directory that you just created. So, launch IIS Manager (Start ➤ Control Panel ➤ Administrative Tools ➤ Internet Information Services). Right-click in IIS and choose the option Add Virtual Directory. Set the alias to Example04web, and point the physical path to the recently created directory. Click OK. Dismiss all open dialog boxes by clicking the OK buttons. At this point, you should have a solution directory with a child project that has, or will have, all its resources (source code files and content) located in a directory of your choosing (that is, not in the default C:\inetpub\wwwroot directory).

Now you're ready to add the project to the solution you created earlier. In Visual Studio, select the solution in Solution Explorer, right-click, and then select Add ➤ New Web Site.

At this point, ensure that you select the .NET 4.0/WCF service template, set HTTP as the location, use the URL that was set on the folder alias using web sharing in Windows Explorer, and set the language of your choice, as shown in Figure 4–7.

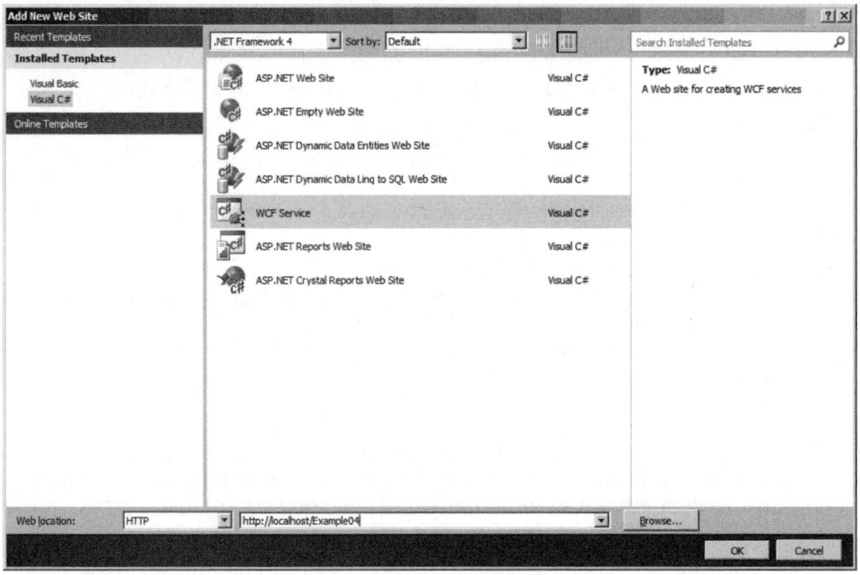

Figure 4–7. Adding a WCF service project to a solution

Click OK. You will get a warning, as shown in Figure 4–8.

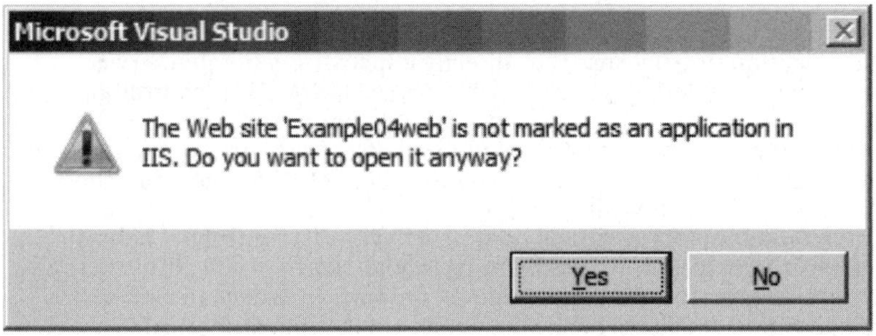

Figure 4–8. Creating an application in IIS through Visual Studio 2010

This warning is evoked because this directory has been a virtual directory until now, and has not been marked as an application. By clicking Yes, you are making this directory an application and also setting its application pool to ASP.NET 4.0 Integrated. Visual Studio 2010 will only open those web site projects that have an application pool set to ASP.NET 4.0. Click Yes, and the Visual Studio .NET 4.0 template system will create a project starting point for your service, giving you a complete project. Notice that the project template leverages the special folder names for the application code and application data. In the previous example, the source code was hosted directly in the *.svc file. The project shown here, which is generated from the .NET 4.0 template, has a distinct source directory, along with a *.cs file that contains the interface and class implementation.

■**Tip** In the real world, it's best to separate the service interface (contract) and implementation types into their own assemblies (DLLs), which translate to projects in Visual Studio. Having the structure as shown previously is a nice feature for ease of use, but from a physical separation perspective, it's better to provide distinct assemblies for the tiers.

If you look at the file system using Windows Explorer or using a command prompt and view the directory you started in, you'll see the same set of files listed under the project in Visual Studio Solution Explorer. At this point, if you browse to the location http://localhost/example04Web/ using Internet Explorer, you'll see a directory listing (as long as the settings are like those in Figure 4–7). If you click service.svc, you will be brought to the default help screen generated by System.ServiceModel.Activiation.HttpHandler for the *.svc extensions, as shown in Figure 4–2. At this point, you follow the same steps as in a client application, either generating a proxy class directly through the use of the SvcUtil.exe utility or by right-clicking the project, or generating the proxy through the Add Service Reference add-in feature, as shown previously. The accompanying solution for this example has a complete console client that makes a call into the WCF service you just created.

ServiceContract Attribute

One of the valuable capabilities of WCF is getting control over how the WCF framework generates the metadata for the service contract. The examples presented so far have been the simplest forms, relying on the default settings and values that are generated by SvcUtil.exe (for the client) or at runtime by the framework.

When designing services, it's important to understand what is generated as metadata. You need an awareness of what the naming conventions are because they directly impact the generated service description metadata. This section helps you identify what capabilities exist in WCF for controlling how this metadata is created.

The ServiceContract attribute is the entry point into the definition of a service. In conjunction with binding and endpoint information (generally through configuration), it is this information that clients (service consumers) apply in order to use your service.

The ServiceContract attribute represents the contract, not the behavior. To control the behavior, you need to leverage the behavior aspect of the WCF programming model. More specifically, you apply the class-level attribute ServiceBehaviorAttribute and the required properties associated with your implementation. Chapter 3 provides more details on behaviors. Table 4–4 lists the properties that are part of the ServiceContract attribute to control metadata generation and runtime capabilities support by WCF.

Table 4–4. ServiceContract Attribute Properties

Class Property	Description
CallBackContract	Designates the contract in duplex message exchange (two-way) pattern implementations.
Name	Controls the naming of the interface in the WSDL or metadata; allows overriding using the interface or class name in the generated metadata.
Namespace	Controls the namespace that is used in the WSDL or metadata from the default of tempuri.org.
SessionMode	Indicates whether this service requires bindings that can support sessions among more complex message exchange patterns. It's used in conjunction with ServiceBehaviorAttribute, which is applied on a class.
ConfigurationName	Controls the name that is used to locate the service in the application configuration file.

At the service contract level, you have a few options that give you a foundation to work upon for managing the emitted metadata. Since types are ultimately turned into XML to support the loosely coupled world of WCF services, you have two choices for serialization, as described in Table 4–5.

Table 4–5. Serialization Options

Attribute Type	Description
DataContractSerializer	Default serialization class that handles serializable types in addition to contract types (data or message). This supports two modes: shared type and shared contract. The first is when both types exist on both sides of the channel—such as with .NET Remoting. The second type is a loosely coupled mode, where the only requirement is that types exist on both sides of the channel that can serialize/deserialize from the XML.
XmlSerializer	Serialization class that handles only serializable types. Use this class when you need greater control over the XML that is emitted from the WCF serialization process.

Let's take a look at a different example, one that's from the QuickReturns Ltd. company (Example05)—specifically the section showing how to implement the exchange's service for TradeSecurity. (Please refer to Chapter 3 for background information on QuickReturns Ltd.)

The core requirement for TradeSecurity is a request-reply message exchange pattern. This pattern is a fairly simple but common interaction between service endpoints. From a high-level view, this method requires a Trade schema, and on return it provides an Execution schema. The examples here just return a decimal for simplicity.

You'll start by implementing the service contract using all the defaults. First, create an empty Visual Studio solution. The Blank Solution template appears under Other Project Types ➤ Visual Studio Solutions after you choose File ➤ New Project.

Second, add a class library—or what's called a .NET 4.0/WCF service library—to the project. To do this, select the solution in Solution Explorer, and right-click. Then choose Add ➤ New Project.

Once the Add New Project dialog box appears, ensure you select the .NET 4.0 grouping along with the .NET 4.0/WCF service library template. Also ensure that you name your project ExchangeService, along with validating the location of where the files are created.

■**Tip** It's a best practice to separate your service library into a discrete compilation unit—a .NET assembly. This allows for greater specialization of the project team because you extend and integrate various parts of the system. Also, it allows for more loosely coupled versioning of system components. Obviously, if the system is simple, it's probably not necessary to take these control steps; however, it generally doesn't hurt to start out this way, because when your system grows beyond the simple stage, you'll be better prepared.

At this point, Visual Studio 2010 adds the project, creating a source file that has a simple WCF implementation with the "get data" method implementation. If you are using a previous version of Visual Studio, you will get the customary Hello World method implementation. The template has embedded comments that provide some basic pointers on how to proceed with your implementation. Additionally, a commented code section provides the necessary steps on hosting the WCF service from your newly created WCF library in another project. The code provided in that commented section is for hosting outside ASP.NET. (Chapter 5 covers hosting options in depth.)

In addition to a sample implementation, the project references have been updated to make it easier to work with WCF applications.

Now, in Solution Explorer, delete the generated Service1.cs and IService1.cs files. Then right-click the project and add a new item. Locate the .NET 4.0/WCF service item. Enter **TradeService** in the Name field, and click Add. In the generated TradeService.cs file, replace the contents with Listing 4–8.

Listing 4–8. TradeService.cs Implementation

```
using System;
using System.ServiceModel;
namespace ExchangeService
{
    [ServiceContract(
        Namespace="http://PracticalWcf/Exchange/TradeService",
        Name="TradeService")
    ]
    public interface ITradeService
    {
        [OperationContract]
        decimal TradeSecurity( string ticker, int quantity );
    }
    public class TradeService : ITradeService
    {
        const decimal IBM_Price = 80.50m;
        const decimal MSFT_Price = 30.25m;
        public decimal TradeSecurity( string ticker, int quantity )
        {
            if( quantity < 1 )
```

```
            throw new ArgumentException(
                "Invalid quantity", "quantity" );
        switch( ticker.ToLower() )
        {
            case "ibm":
                return quantity * IBM_Price;
            case "msft":
                return quantity * MSFT_Price;
            default:
                throw new ArgumentException(
                    "SK security - only MSFT & IBM", "ticker" );
        }
    }
  }
}
```

Remove the `ITradeService.cs` class for this example. Notice that the top of the file contains a reference to the `System.ServiceModel` namespace. This namespace contains the necessary types that provide attribute support for the contract declaration.

This implementation follows the best practice of separating the contract definition from the implementation. In the example, the `ServiceContract` attribute is applied to the `ITradeService` interface. Additionally, the single method signature within `ITradeService` has the `OperationContract` attribute. These attributes signal to the WCF runtime how to generate the metadata and WSDL necessary for discovering supported operations, in addition to managing the actual runtime calls from clients.

The `TradeService` class simply implements `ITradeService`. How does the WCF runtime know what type to load in response to client requests? You'll see in a little bit how this takes place through configuration; specifically how the ABCs are tied together.

Make sure the code compiles before proceeding. If there are no errors, create a simple ASP.NET hosting project for this newly created .NET 4.0/WCF service library.

In Solution Explorer, add a new empty web site—which is just a standard ASP.NET web site—to your solution. Do this either by right-clicking the solution and choosing Add New Web Site or by choosing File ➤ Add ➤ New Web Site from the Visual Studio menu.

Now select the web project you just created in Solution Explorer, right-click, and choose to add a reference. Once the Add Reference dialog box opens, select the Projects tab, and choose the Exchange Service project from the list.

Now right-click the project again and add a `Web.config` file to the project if one does not already exist. Modify the contents of the `web.config` file, ensuring the `<system.serviceModel>` section appears as a child of the `<configuration>` element, as shown in Listing 4–9.

Listing 4–9. Web Site web.config File (Partial)

```xml
<?xml version="1.0"?>
<configuration>
  <system.serviceModel>
    <services>
      <service name="ExchangeService.TradeService">
        <endpoint contract="ExchangeService.ITradeService"
                  binding="wsHttpBinding"/>
      </service>
    </services>
    <behaviors>
      <serviceBehaviors>
        <behavior name="">
```

```
            <serviceMetadata httpGetEnabled="true"/>
            <serviceDebug httpHelpPageEnabled="true"
                          includeExceptionDetailInFaults="true"/>
        </behavior>
      </serviceBehaviors>
    </behaviors>
  </system.serviceModel>
  <appSettings/>
  <connectionStrings/>
<system.web>
...
```

This configuration file contains a system.serviceModel section (shown in bold) that provides the necessary binding and contract information for the sample. The service element identifies the specific .NET type that is exposed through this service endpoint. The endpoint element identifies the specific contract that is bound to the service type listed. Since the example is using IIS activation, the wsHttpBinding is the binding used, which supports request-reply in addition to reliable, secure, and transactional message exchange.

Next, right-click the web project again and add a .NET 4.0/WCF service. Modify the dialog box entries by specifying TradeService.svc as the name of the file and setting C# as the language.

Open the newly created TradeService.svc file and replace the contents with this single line:

```
<%@ ServiceHost Language="C#" Service="ExchangeService.TradeService" %>
```

Note that the Service parameter is now set to a type that resides in the assembly generated from the exchange service project.

First, do a solution build (Build ➤ Build Solution). Then right-click the web project and choose View in Browser (you must have directory browsing enabled, as in Figure 4–6, previously). Once Internet Explorer opens and you see the directory listing, click the TradeService.svc file. At this point, the ASP.NET runtime will begin the compilation process, generating the required assemblies to service your request. After a few seconds (depending upon your machine configuration), you should see the standard help screen shown in Figure 4–9.

Congratulations! You've now created a simple TradeService service using the best practice of separating the service implementation into its own assembly and referencing it from a web project. If you look at the accompanying solution, a simple client console project calls the service for a few securities.

If you enter the following into a browser (ensuring that the ASP.NET development server is running and the port for your site matches), you'll see the differences in the generated metadata for the namespace and name of the service:

```
http://localhost/Exchangeweb/TradeService.svc?wsdl
```

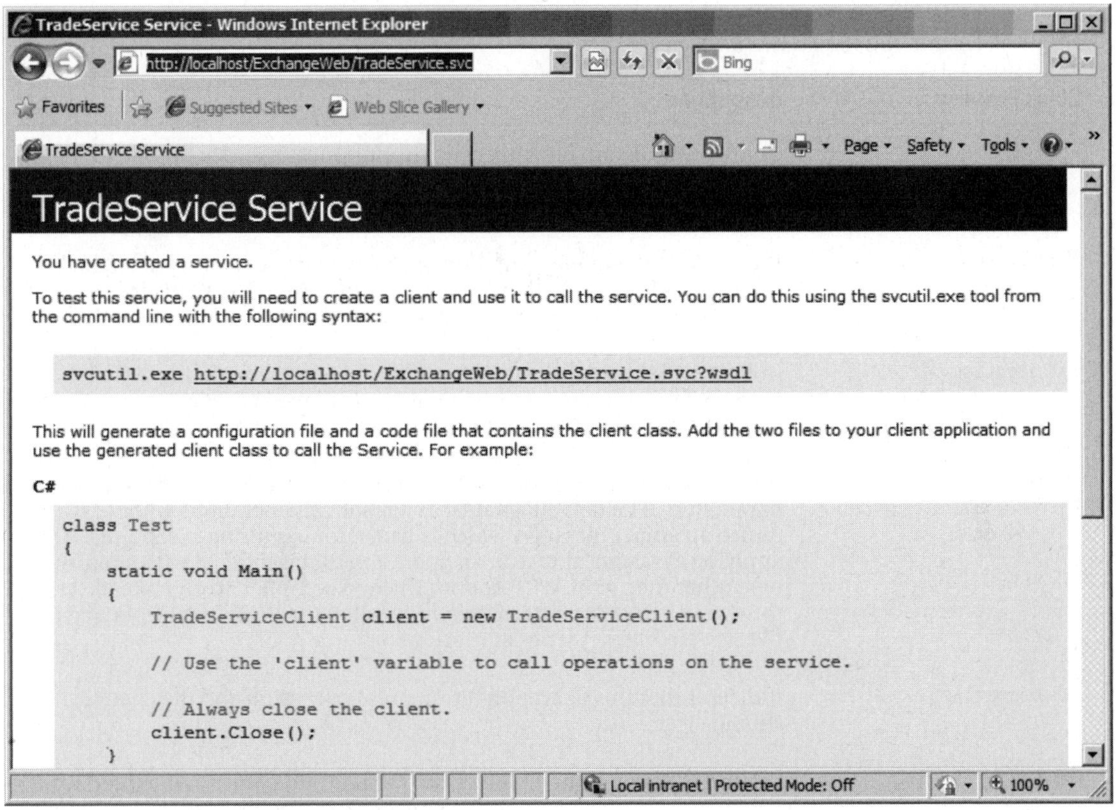

Figure 4–9. Viewing the WCF TradeService service

OperationContract Attribute

The OperationContract attribute, as with the ServiceContract attribute, provides for even greater control over the WSDL generation. Generally, you'll accept most of the defaults, but for certain features, such as duplex messaging, you'll need to use options indicating that the operation is one-way. Additionally, for session management, you'll be leveraging some of the options for overall service session management.

Table 4–6 describes the properties in the OperationContract attribute type.

Table 4–6. OperationContract Attribute Properties

Class Property	Description
Action	Controls the action on the request (input) message. Use this in conjunction with * to indicate that the operation can handle all unmatched operation requests.
AsyncPattern	Provides for the implementation of an asynchronous process on the server, the client, or both tiers. This feature aids .NET clients in supporting operations with the efficiency of using a single client thread.
IsInitiating	Indicates that this operation is an initiation of a session; the default is true, so if you require session initiation, you need to set all operations to false except the initiation operation.
IsOneWay	Indicates that the operation returns nothing (void) or can't accept out parameters. The default is false; as a result, all operations without it return an empty message, which is useful for capturing exceptions. If applying the value of true to an operation that is marked with a return type other than void, WCF doesn't throw a compiler error. Instead, it throws an InvalidOperation exception when the WCF framework inspects the ServiceContract types at runtime.
IsTerminating	Indicates that this operation terminates the session and the channel should close.
Name	Overrides the operation name from the method name on the interface.
ReplyAction	Controls the action on the reply (output) message. Used in conjunction with the Action property.

The solution Example06 has an updated version of the ITradeService service contract. In this version, the OperationContract properties have been explicitly set. Also notice that the ServiceContract attribute now has a new property indicating that it supports sessions. Without the ServiceContract.SessionMode property being set to SessionMode.Required, the OperationContract properties of IsInitiating and IsTerminating would be illogical. This condition is not caught at compile time, only at reflection time.

Listing 4–10 is a snippet from Example06. Notice that some added properties have been set in both the ServiceContract and OperationContract attribute initializations.

Listing 4–10. TradeService.cs with OperationContract Properties

```
[ServiceContract(
    Namespace = "http://PracticalWcf",
    Name = "TradeService",
    SessionMode = SessionMode.Required)
]
public interface ITradeService
{
```

```
[OperationContract(
  Action="http://PracticalWcf/TradeSecurityNow",
  IsOneWay = false,

  IsTerminating = false,
  Name = "TradeSecurityNow"
  )]
decimal TradeSecurity( string ticker, int quantity );
}
```

These changes provide control over the WSDL generated from the metadata on your service contract. If you take a brief before-and-after look, you'll see some of the changes.

If you open the URL that points to the WSDL for the definitions, you'll see the changes and added control. The URL to open is as follows (ensure your ASP.NET development server is running!):

```
http://localhost:/Example04web/TradeService.svc?wsdl=wsdl0
```

■**Note** The generated URL by the .NET Framework may differ from the one shown here. To find the correct URL, look for the `<wsdl:import...>` element in the base URL.

Listing 4–11 is the generated WSDL before the `OperationContract` properties are applied.

Listing 4–11. TradeService.cs WSDL Before Property Changes

```
<wsdl:input wsaw:Action="http://PracticalWcf/TradeService/TradeSecurity"
  message="tns:TradeService_TradeSecurityNow_InputMessage" />
```

Listing 4–12 shows the WSDL definition for a newly modified service contract.

Listing 4–12. TradeService.cs WSDL After Property Changes

```
<wsdl:input
    wsaw:Action="http://PracticalWcf/TradeSecurityNow"
    message="tns:TradeService_TradeSecurityNow_InputMessage"/>
```

Note the updated `Action` names for both the input and output messages. If you look inside the client proxy code generated as part of the project, you'll see the updated matching names for the new contract.

■**Caution** Whenever an update to metadata occurs, ensure you regenerate the proxy. You can do this by selecting the map file in Solution Explorer for the service reference, right-clicking, and choosing Update Service Reference. This resubmits the call through `SvcUtil.exe` for the regeneration of the proxy type in your client project. This assumes you're working with Visual Studio integration.

Inside the client program, the only change required, other than updating the service reference through SvcUtil.exe, is to modify the method name of the proxy class from the following:

```
result = proxy.TradeSecurity( "MSFT", 2000 );
```

to the following:

```
result = proxy.TradeSecurityNow( "MSFT", 2000 );
```

The reason for this change is that the OperationContract.Name property is now set to TradeSecurityNow. As a result, when the call to SvcUtil.exe is made to regenerate the proxy, the new operation name instead of the old is used, which causes a break in the compilation.

ServiceBehavior Attribute

So far, we've focused specifically on the contract definition. We've intentionally avoided any discussion of how a service behaves. Generally, service behavior is an implementation-dependent aspect of a solution. In addition to using ServiceBehavior, you also have the ability to apply behavior at the operation level with the OperationBehavior attribute (covered in the next section).

The ServiceBehavior attribute is applicable only at the class (implementation) level, while the ServiceContract attribute was applicable at both the interface (contract) and class levels. This distinction is important. Behaviors in WCF are not part of the contract; they are implementation-specific.

The capability exists to control service-wide behavior elements such as the following:

- *Concurrency*: Controls threading behavior for an object and whether it supports reentrant calls. It's valid only if the Instancing property is not PerCall.

- *Instancing*: Controls new object creation and manages object lifetime. The default is PerCall, which creates a new object on each method call. Generally, in session-oriented services, providing either PerSession or Shareable may provide better performance, albeit at the cost of concurrency management.

- *Throttling*: Managed through configuration, when concurrency allows for multiple calls, to limit the number of concurrent calls, connections, total instances, and pending operations.

- *Transaction*: Controls transaction aspects such as autocompletion, isolation level, and object recycling.

- *Session management*: Provides automatic session shutdown or overrides default behavior.

- *Thread behavior*: Forces the service thread to have affinity to the UI thread; this is helpful if the underlying service host is a WinForms application and updates to controls on that form may happen in the service implementation.

OperationBehavior Attribute

The other important behavior attribute is the OperationBehavior attribute. Although you have control over the service-wide behaviors using the ServiceBehavior attribute, you have more granular control at the operation level.

Again, these are implementation details applied at the class method level instead of the service interface. Operation aspects controllable through this attribute are as follows:

- *Transactional*: Provides for autocompletion along with transaction flow and the required and supported options

- *Caller identity*: When binding supports, provides the ability to execute under the caller's identity

- *Object recycling*: Provides for overriding the InstanceMode mode of the ServiceContractBehavior

Understanding Data Contracts

Data contracts, in WCF, are the preferred method of abstracting your .NET types from the schema and XML serialized types. With WCF, you have choices for creating the metadata that is used to publish your service and how that impacts the runtime serialization of your .NET types into platform-agnostic schema types that are represented in XML.

The process can be hidden, if you choose, from the developer. Primitive types are easily mapped to leverage the default DataContractSerializer. Other types are controllable through the DataContract attribute capabilities. However, if you still want control, you can always use XmlSerializer to manage the serialization of your types into XML. So, in the following sections, we'll first walk through some of the ways you can work with XmlSerializer before moving on to data contracts.

All the examples so far have used the default DataContractSerializer type for XML serialization/deserialization. We'll take a brief look at using XmlSerializer for managing the XML serialization process.

XML Serialization

WCF supports two primary means of XML serialization. For a majority of scenarios, the DataContract attribute and its corresponding DataContractSerializer type are the preferred means of providing this requirement. However, the secondary method, the XmlSerializerFormat attribute, provides finer control over the XML serialization process. Additionally, by providing your own implementation of IXmlSerializable, effectively overriding .NET default serialization, you can control serialization entirely.

I will stress that you can use the data contract capabilities most of the time when developing enterprise applications. This is especially true when you control—or at least affect—both sides of the wire. Even if you don't have control on both sides of the wire, you can probably gain enough control to emit the XML as required by using data contracts.

In Listing 4–13, the solution (Example07) has been expanded to include a concrete Trade class. This class represents the object (or message) that is presented to the exchange for requesting execution on a market order.

Listing 4–13. TradeService Interface with a Trade Parameter

```
[ServiceContract(
    Namespace = "http://PracticalWcf/Exchange/TradeService",
    Name = "TradeService",
    SessionMode = SessionMode.Required)
]
public interface ITradeService
{
    [OperationContract(
      IsOneWay = false,
      Name = "TradeSecurityAtMarket"
```

```
    )]
  decimal TradeSecurity( Trade trade );
}
```

The TradeSecurity interface is updated to take a Trade object and return a decimal result. Also notice that the Name parameter on the operation is TradeSecurityAtMarket. I chose this name to override the default of TradeSecurity and provide a distinction between market orders and limit orders on the metadata.

The Trade class looks like Listing 4–14 (notice the absence of either a Serializable attribute or a DataContract attribute at the top of the class).

Listing 4–14. The First Few Lines of the Trade Class

```
namespace ExchangeService
{
    public class Trade
    {
        string _ticker;
        char _type;
        string _publisher;
        string _participant;
        decimal _quotedPrice;
        int _quantity;
        DateTime _tradeTime;
        decimal _executionAmount;


        /// <summary>
        /// Primary exchange security identifier
        /// </summary>
        public string Ticker
        {
            get { return _ticker; }
            set { _ticker = value; }
        }
```

If you launch the ASP.NET development server and view TradeService.svc in the browser, you'll see the error shown in Figure 4–10.

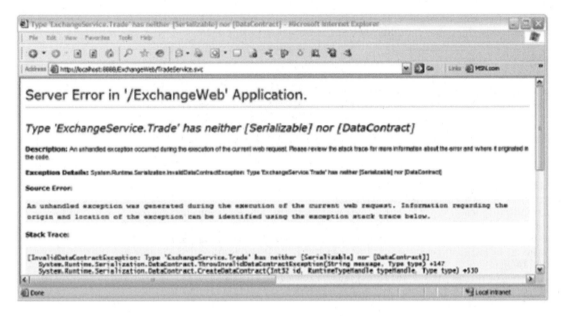

Figure 4–10. Error page for a nonserializable or missing data contract

At this point, WCF doesn't know what to do. Therefore, let's apply the Serializable attribute to the Trade type and take a look at the generated schema, as shown in Listing 4–15.

Listing 4–15. Trade Type with the Serializable Attribute

```
namespace ExchangeService
{
    [Serializable]
    public class Trade
    {
        string _ticker;
        char _type;
        string _publisher;
...
```

To view the generated schema for the modified contract, first navigate to the following page: http://localhost:8888/ExchangeWeb/TradeService.svc?wsdl. Once at that page, if you locate the schema import, using the XPath /wsdl:definitions/wsdl:import, you'll see another reference to a schema. You need to load that schema as well. That location should be, depending upon your host and IP port, as follows: http://localhost:8888/ExchangeWeb/TradeService.svc?wsdl=wsdl0.

■**Note** Again, you need to first open the base WSDL and search for the <wsdl:import> element, which will provide the correct location for the imported WSDL.

Notice the addition of the wsdl0 parameter to the original WSDL request. Viewing that page, you should see something that contains XML and is similar to Listing 4–16.

Listing 4–16. *TradeService WSDL Definition*

```
<xsd:import
  schemaLocation="http://localhost:8888/ExchangeWeb/TradeService.svc?xsd=xsd2"
  namespace="http://schemas.datacontract.org/2004/07/ExchangeService" />
```

You need to go a little deeper, opening the schemaLocation URL from Listing 4–16 to get to the type's schema. If you browse to the schemaLocation from Listing 4–16, the code in Listing 4–17 appears.

Listing 4–17. *Trade Schema Serializable (Trade.cs)*

```
<?xml version="1.0" encoding="utf-8"?>
<xs:schema elementFormDefault="qualified"
  targetNamespace="http://schemas.datacontract.org/2004/07/ExchangeService"
  xmlns:xs="http://www.w3.org/2001/XMLSchema"
  xmlns:tns="http://schemas.datacontract.org/2004/07/ExchangeService"
  xmlns:ser="http://schemas.microsoft.com/2003/10/Serialization/">
  <xs:import
    schemaLocation="http://localhost:8888/ExchangeWeb/TradeService.svc?xsd=xsd1"
    namespace="http://schemas.microsoft.com/2003/10/Serialization/"/>
  <xs:complexType name="Trade">
    <xs:sequence>
      <xs:element name="_executionAmount" type="xs:decimal"/>
      <xs:element name="_participant" nillable="true" type="xs:string"/>
      <xs:element name="_publisher" nillable="true" type="xs:string"/>
      <xs:element name="_quantity" type="xs:int"/>
      <xs:element name="_quotedPrice" type="xs:decimal"/>
      <xs:element name="_ticker" nillable="true" type="xs:string"/>
      <xs:element name="_tradeTime" type="xs:dateTime"/>
      <xs:element name="_type" type="ser:char"/>
    </xs:sequence>
  </xs:complexType>
  <xs:element name="Trade" nillable="true" type="tns:Trade"/>
</xs:schema>
```

First, note the targetNamespace that was used. Since we didn't override the namespace using .NET XML serialization support, we get what DataContractSerializer defaults to: http://schemas.data.coontract.org/2004/07/<serviceName>. This is probably not desired, but we'll get to this issue in a moment.

Second, the elements chosen by DataContractSerializer aren't the public properties, but the fields (private or public), along with the underscore as part of the name; this is also an undesirable result. This is the default behavior, and fortunately you can control this by utilizing the XML serialization support that's part of the .NET Framework.

Finally, note the order of the elements—they're in alphabetical order, which is the default processing rule for DataContractSerializer.

■Note This code is provided in the Begin folder as part of Example07 on the Apress web site (www.apress.com).

To control the WSDL generation, you need to switch from using DataContractSerializer to leveraging XmlSerializer; you can do this by decorating the service contract at the interface level with the XmlSerializerFormat attribute, as shown in Listing 4–18.

Listing 4–18. TradeService with XmlSerializer Support (TradeService.cs)

```
namespace ExchangeService
{
    [ServiceContract(
        Namespace = "http://PracticalWcf/Exchange/TradeService",
        Name = "TradeService",
        SessionMode = SessionMode.Required)
    ]
    [XmlSerializerFormat(
        Style = OperationFormatStyle.Document,
        Use = OperationFormatUse.Literal)]
    public interface ITradeService
    {
        [OperationContract(
          IsOneWay = false,
          Name = "TradeSecurityAtMarket"
          )]
        decimal TradeSecurity( Trade trade );
    }
```

Now, if you rerequest the imported namespace using the following URL, you'll see the schema updated with your targetNamespace attribute (check the schema import in the generated WSDL for the correct location):

```
http://localhost:8888/ExchangeWeb/TradeService.svc?xsd=xsd0
```

■**Note** Again, I need to emphasize that to find the nested WSDL, you must search the base WSDL for the <wsdl:import> element, and then the nested import of type schema shown in Listing 4–19.

Listing 4–19 shows the new schema.

Listing 4–19. New Schema with XmlSerializer Support

```
<?xml version="1.0" encoding="utf-8"?>
<xs:schema
    elementFormDefault="qualified"
    targetNamespace="http://PracticalWcf/Exchange/TradeService"
    xmlns:xs="http://www.w3.org/2001/XMLSchema"
    xmlns:tns="http://PracticalWcf/Exchange/TradeService">
  <xs:import
    schemaLocation="http://localhost:8888/ExchangeWeb/TradeService.svc?xsd=xsd1"
    namespace="http://microsoft.com/wsdl/types/"/>
  <xs:element name="TradeSecurityAtMarket">
    <xs:complexType>
      <xs:sequence>
```

```
        <xs:element minOccurs="0" maxOccurs="1" name="trade" type="tns:Trade"/>
      </xs:sequence>
    </xs:complexType>
  </xs:element>
  <xs:complexType name="Trade">
    <xs:sequence>
      <xs:element minOccurs="0" maxOccurs="1"
        name="Ticker" type="xs:string"/>
      <xs:element
        minOccurs="1" maxOccurs="1"
        name="Type" type="q1:char"
        xmlns:q1="http://microsoft.com/wsdl/types/"/>
      <xs:element
        minOccurs="0" maxOccurs="1"
        name="Publisher" type="xs:string"/>
      <xs:element
        minOccurs="0" maxOccurs="1"
        name="Participant" type="xs:string"/>
      <xs:element
        minOccurs="1" maxOccurs="1"
        name="QuotedPrice" type="xs:decimal"/>
      <xs:element
        minOccurs="1" maxOccurs="1"
        name="Quantity" type="xs:int"/>
      <xs:element
        minOccurs="1" maxOccurs="1"
        name="TradeTime" type="xs:dateTime"/>
      <xs:element
        minOccurs="1" maxOccurs="1"
        name="ExecutionAmount" type="xs:decimal"/>
    </xs:sequence>
  </xs:complexType>
  <xs:element name="TradeSecurityAtMarketResponse">
    <xs:complexType>
      <xs:sequence>
        <xs:element
          minOccurs="1" maxOccurs="1"
          name="TradeSecurityAtMarketResult" type="xs:decimal"/>
      </xs:sequence>
    </xs:complexType>
  </xs:element>
</xs:schema>
```

You now have a targetNamespace that reflects the namespace requirement; additionally, the elements within the Trade complexType are all the public property names and types. The XmlSerializer includes only the public properties or fields; additionally, they are serialized in the order presented in the class, as requested through reflection.

■**Note** This code is provided in the accompanying code as Step1 in Example07.

It's possible to gain further control over the generated schema by continuing to leverage the capabilities of .NET XML serialization. If you want to modify or exclude public properties or fields and control the order and nullability, you can use the various attributes, as described in the MSDN documentation under the topic "Attributes That Control XML Serialization." As a quick example just for fun, let's exclude the participant, modify the element name for TradeTime, and cause Ticker to be an attribute instead of an XML element. The example code now generates a schema, as shown in Listing 4–20.

■**Tip** To get a full understanding of the capabilities of XML serialization in .NET, please refer to MSDN and search for "attributes that control XML serialization."

Listing 4–20. Trade Schema Using XML Serialization Control Attributes

```
<xs:complexType name="Trade">
  <xs:sequence>
    <xs:element minOccurs="1" maxOccurs="1"
      name="Type" type="q1:char"
      xmlns:q1="http://microsoft.com/wsdl/types/"/>
    <xs:element minOccurs="0" maxOccurs="1"
      name="Publisher" type="xs:string"/>
    <xs:element minOccurs="1" maxOccurs="1"
      name="QuotedPrice" type="xs:decimal"/>
    <xs:element minOccurs="1" maxOccurs="1"
      name="Quantity" type="xs:int"/>
    <xs:element minOccurs="1" maxOccurs="1"
      name="ExecutionTime" type="xs:dateTime"/>
    <xs:element minOccurs="1" maxOccurs="1"
      name="ExecutionAmount" type="xs:decimal"/>
  </xs:sequence>
  <xs:attribute name="Ticker" type="xs:string"/>
</xs:complexType>
```

You'll notice now that the Ticker property appears as an XML Schema attribute instead of an element, the property TradeTime is now ExecutionTime, and the element Participant no longer appears in the schema.

■**Note** The complete solution is provided in the accompanying code in the folder End as part of Example07.

So, with XmlSerialization support through the use of the XmlSerializer attribute on the service contract, it is possible to gain control over the XML Schema generation. In addition to the extensibility provided by the implementation of the .NET interface IXmlSerializable on your .NET class, the capabilities to support just about any format required are also available.

Data Contracts

Data contracts are the preferred means (because of their simplicity) for controlling what and how .NET type members are serialized to and from XML. Again, it's important to emphasize that one size does not fit all. Sometimes data contracts can't support the required schema generation. This is most likely to happen when you have no control over the schema and you must provide messages that match a published schema.

The first step in leveraging data contract capabilities in the WCF framework is to modify the `Trade` class by decorating it with the `DataContract` attribute, as shown in Listing 4–21.

Listing 4–21. Trade Class with the DataContract Attribute

```
using System;
using System.Runtime.Serialization;
namespace ExchangeService
{
    [DataContract(
        Namespace = "http://PracticalWcf/Exchange/Trade" )]
    public class Trade
```

If you rerequest the schema for the `TradeService` contract, you now have a `Trade` type that leverages `DataContractFormatter` support (`DataContractFormatter` is the default formatter type on the service contract if no `Formatter` attribute is present). The issue now is that you have no members of the trade that appear in the schema, as shown in Listing 4–22.

Listing 4–22. Trade Class Schema with No Members

```
<xs:complexType name="Trade">
  <xs:sequence/>
</xs:complexType>
<xs:element name="Trade" nillable="true" type="tns:Trade"/>
```

`DataContractSerializer` by default serializes only member fields or properties, either public or private, that are decorated with the `DataMember` attribute. This is in further support of the "boundaries are explicit" base tenet of SOA that the WCF team followed.

■**Note** This example is part of the accompanying code in the folder `Example08`.

So, once you have determined which `DataContract` members should be present on the service contract interface, you must adorn those members with the `DataMember` attribute, as shown in Listing 4–23.

Listing 4–23. Trade with DataMember Attributes on Fields and Properties

```
namespace ExchangeService
{
    [DataContract(
        Namespace = "http://PracticalWcf/Exchange/Trade" )]
    public class Trade
    {
        string _ticker;
```

```csharp
char _type;
string _publisher;
string _participant;

[DataMember( Name = "QuotedPrice", IsRequired = false, Order = 1 )]
internal double _quotedPrice;

[DataMember( Name = "Quantity", IsRequired = true, Order = 0 )]
private int _quantity;

[DataMember( Name = "TradeTime", IsRequired = false, Order = 9 )]
Nullable<DateTime> _tradeTime;

double _executionAmount;


[DataMember(IsRequired = true, Order = 3)]
public string Ticker
{
    get { return _ticker; }
    set { _ticker = value; }
}

[DataMember(IsRequired = true, Order = 4)]
public char Type
{
    get { return _type; }
    set { _type = value; }
}

[DataMember(IsRequired = true, Order = 10)]
public string Publisher
{
    get { return _publisher; }
    set { _publisher = value; }
}

public string Participant
{
    get { return _participant; }
    set { _participant = value; }
}
```

Pay special attention to the mix of fields and properties that have the DataMember attribute. As stated, you can apply the DataMember attribute to either fields or properties. Additionally, the accessibility level of these fields or properties can be either public or private. So, regardless of the accessibility level (public, private, internal), DataContractSerializer serializes those member fields or properties. We've also applied additional properties to several of the DataMember attributes (there are only three properties—a case for simplicity). These properties control the following:

- XML Schema optional support: IsRequired

- Physical order in the schema: Order

- *Name of element*: Name

Now, if you rerequest the schema for the DataContract type, you see the code in Listing 4–24.

Listing 4–24. Trade Data Contract with DataMember Properties

```
<xs:complexType name="Trade">
  <xs:sequence>
    <xs:element
        name="Quantity" type="xs:int"/>
    <xs:element
        minOccurs="0" name="QuotedPrice" type="xs:double"/>
    <xs:element
        name="Ticker" nillable="true" type="xs:string"/>
    <xs:element
        name="Type" type="ser:char"/>
    <xs:element
        minOccurs="0"
        name="TradeTime" nillable="true" type="xs:dateTime"/>
    <xs:element
        name="Publisher" nillable="true" type="xs:string"/>
  </xs:sequence>
</xs:complexType>
<xs:element name="Trade" nillable="true" type="tns:Trade"/>
```

You can see the generated schema that is produced, which includes members marked with the DataMember attribute, regardless of the accessibility level or whether the members are fields or properties. The primary reason for this method of processing data contracts is that the WCF team understands that many systems are developed by looking at predefined business classes—a code-first model. This gives designers and developers the flexibility for defining what should be included via a declarative model, without forcing them down a significant refactoring path or back to design.

Another interesting aspect of DataMember is the Order property. The WCF framework (DataContractSerializer specifically) isn't as rigid as the XmlSeriaization framework in regard to specifying the order the elements appear in. In fact, you can skip around (as shown in the example) and even duplicate Order values.

Message Contracts

Message contracts in WCF give you control over the SOAP message structure—both header and body content. You leverage the MessageContract attribute along with the MessageHeader, MessageBody, and Array variants of both (MessageHeaderArray and MessageBodyArray) to provide structure along with additional control over the content. With message contracts you can designate optional SOAP headers. With message body elements you can designate ProtectionLevel settings that provide WCF-enforced policies of signing and encrypting on those elements decorated with the ProtectionLevel property.

Message contracts work with either DataContractSerializer or XmlSerializer, and provide you with additional control over the WSDL generation, specifically SOAP headers and body content. Additionally, message contracts provide support for SOAP header requirements designating specific endpoints for processing the message via the MessageHeader.Actor property. Additionally, the MessageHeader.Relay property indicates that the actor should continue to pass messages to the next endpoint after processing the request.

In this section, we'll present a quick example of message contracts related to QuickReturns Ltd. Remember, three fields are required to be set to predefined values in the SOAP header. Why would you mandate headers in the SOAP request? One common scenario is to apply policies and rules based upon the content of the SOAP request. If you can promote or present some attribute of the request to the

SOAP header, it can be easily validated before any downstream code processes the request in your service implementation.

If you take a look at the Trade class in Listing 4–25 (part of the accompanying code in Example09), you can see that it has been updated with a specific namespace, in addition to being decorated with the DataMember attribute with a mix of fields and properties. Additionally, the Execution class, shown in Listing 4–26, has been similarly decorated.

Listing 4–25. *Trade Data Contract (Partial)*

```
namespace ExchangeService
{
    [DataContract(
        Namespace = "http://PracticalWcf/Exchange/Trade" )]
    public class Trade
    {
        string _ticker;
        char _type;
        string _publisher;

        [DataMember(
            Name = "Participant", IsRequired = true, Order = 0 )]
        string _participant;

        [DataMember(
            Name = "QuotedPrice", IsRequired = false, Order = 1 )]
        internal double _quotedPrice;

        [DataMember(
            Name = "Quantity", IsRequired = true, Order = 1 )]
        private int _quantity;

        [DataMember(
            Name = "TradeTime", IsRequired = false, Order = 9 )]
        Nullable<DateTime> _tradeTime;

        double _executionAmount;

        /// <summary>
        /// Primary exchange security identifier
        /// </summary>
        [DataMember( IsRequired = true, Order = 3 )]
        public string Ticker
        {
            get { return _ticker; }
            set { _ticker = value; }
        }
```

Listing 4–26. *Execution Data Contract (Partial)*

```
namespace ExchangeService
{
    [DataContract(
        Namespace = "http://PracticalWcf/Exchange/Execution" )]
    public class Execution
```

```
{
    [DataMember(Name= "SettleDate")]
    DateTime _settlementDate;

    [DataMember( Name = "Participant" )]
    string _participant;

    [DataMember( Name = "ExecutionAmount" )]
    double _executionAmount;

    [DataMember( Name = "TradeSubmitted" )]
    Trade _trade;
```

Message contracts allow the encapsulation of data contracts in addition to specifying what part of the message is in the message header and message body. So, for this example, I've added a single source code file that contains the definition of two additional classes: TradeSecurityRequest and TradeSecurityResponse. These classes are then decorated as required with the MessageContract attribute. Additionally, the members are then decorated with either the MessageHeader attribute or the MessageBody attribute, as shown in Listing 4–27.

Listing 4–27. MessageHeader and MessageBody Attributes in TradeSecurityRequest (Partial)

```
[MessageContract]
public class TradeSecurityRequest
{
    Trade _trade;
    string _particpant;
    string _publisher;
    string _ticker;

    [MessageHeader(MustUnderstand=true)]
    public string Participant
    {
        get
        {
            return _particpant;
        }
        set
        {
            _particpant = value;
        }
    }

    [MessageBody]
    public Trade TradeItem
    {
        get
        {
            return _trade;
        }
        set
        {
            _trade = value;
        }
    }
```

Look at the `MessageHeader` attribute on `Participant`; the `MustUnderstand` property transfers the responsibility of enforcing this header on the SOAP request to the WCF framework. So, with a simple attribute and property value, we've now provided a simple validation. Listing 4–28 illustrates how to use the `MessageContract` and `MessageBody` attributes as applied to the `TradeSecurityResponse` message in this example.

Listing 4–28. TradeSecurityResponse Message

```
[MessageContract]
public class TradeSecurityResponse
{
    [MessageBody]
    public Execution ExecutionReport;
}
```

The response message is simply an encapsulation of the execution data contract. We've simply encapsulated the data contracts and promoted certain fields or properties as header values.

If you take a look at the updated `TradeService` implementation shown in Listing 4–29, you'll see several changes.

Listing 4–29. Updated TradeService (Partial)

```
[ServiceContract(
    Namespace = "http://PracticalWcf/Exchange",
    Name = "TradeService"
    )
]
public interface ITradeService
{
    [OperationContract(
    Action = "http://PracticalWcf/Exchange/TradeService/TradeSecurityAtMarket"
    )]
    [FaultContract( typeof( ArgumentException ) )]
    TradeSecurityResponse TradeSecurity( TradeSecurityRequest tradeRequest );
}
```

The first change is the explicit specification of the `Action` property of `OperationContract`. The second is the addition of the `FaultContract` attribute to the `TradeSecurity` method. And finally, the `TradeSecurity` interface itself, as defined in `ITradeService`, has been updated to take the respective message contracts from the classes defined in `Messages.cs`.

Specifically, the first change, the addition of `Action`, is for illustrative purposes only, to show how you can control these values. The WCF framework would provide default WS-Addressing and SOAP headers as required based upon the `ServiceContract` namespace, name, and operation name.

The second change is the `FaultContract` attribute. So far, all the examples have had limited exception processing. However, it's important to note that .NET exceptions and SOAP exceptions are different. Therefore, the `FaultContract` capability of WCF provides a way to map, encapsulate, and override how faults are handled and reported. This is important because given the cross-platform capability of WCF, it would not be feasible to enforce knowledge of .NET types. Therefore, in this example, we've wrapped the `TradeService` implementation in a `try...catch` block and provided a throw of `FaultException` in the catch block as follows:

```
throw new FaultException<ArgumentException>( ex );
```

The final change is the modification to the `TradeSecurity` operation. The signature has been updated to receive and respond to the corresponding `TradeSecurityRequest` and `TradeSecurityResponse` messages, respectively.

With the service contract change, the `TradeSecurity` implementation changes to match the interface signature. You now have direct and simple property-level access to the SOAP headers that the client of the service contract must present. Although we are using in our examples WCF-generated proxies and .NET clients, this requirement is a SOAP standard, and regardless of the implementation technology (Java, C++, or some other SOAP framework), as long as they implement the specifications, you have enforcement of your `MustUnderstand` rule.

Listing 4–30 provides the simple value validation of the three headers presented using .NET properties from the message contract.

Listing 4–30. TradeService Header Check Implementation (Partial)

```
public class TradeService : ITradeService
{
    const double IBM_Price = 80.50D;
    const double MSFT_Price = 30.25D;
    public TradeSecurityResponse TradeSecurity( TradeSecurityRequest trade )
    {
        try
        {
            //Embedded rules
            if( trade.Participant != "ABC" )
                throw new ArgumentException( "Particpant must be \"ABC\"" );

            if( trade.Publisher != "XYZ" )
                throw new ArgumentException( "Publisher must be \"XYZ\"" );

            if( trade.Ticker != "MSFT" )
                throw new ArgumentException( "Ticker must be \"MSFT\"" );
```

The completed solution provides for client-side trapping of the fault exceptions leveraging the WCF capabilities. On the client side, using WCF, we apply the `FaultException` generic with the `ArgumentException` type to trap and process exceptions as required by the fault condition, as shown in Listing 4–31.

Listing 4–31. Client program.cs Catch Block on Fault Exception (Partial)

```
catch( FaultException<ArgumentException> ex )
{
    Console.WriteLine( "ArgumentException Occurred" );
    Console.WriteLine( "\tAction:\t" + ex.Action );
    Console.WriteLine( "\tName:\t" + ex.Code.Name );
    Console.WriteLine( "\tMessage:\t" + ex.Detail.Message );
}
```

The `FaultException` type provides access to the SOAP fault headers through simple properties, allowing exception handling or reporting as needed.

You can extend the service contract side of the channel by providing your own implementation of the `IErrorHandler` interface. This interface, when extended, is added to your own service contract implementations. Alternatively, you can add it to the `DispatchBehavior.ErrorHandlers` collection, which can override how messages are transformed into objects and dispatched to methods.

Summary of Service Contracts

We'll now summarize some characteristics of the service contract capabilities and the types that are available for managing the generation of the schema and the serialization process.

- DataContractSerializer

  - Default serialization manager in WCF

  - Works with the DataContract, MessageContract, Serializable, and IXmlSerializable types

  - Default namespace is http://schemas.data.coontract.org/2004/07/<serviceName>

  - Defaults to fields (public or private)

  - Defaults to alpha sort

  - XmlSerialization (XmlSerializerFormat)

  - Works with the Serializable and IXmlSerializable types

  - Is controlled through .NET XML serialization rules—a host of XML attributes that provides an explicit override of default behavior

  - Can control attributes and elements through the simple use of XML serialization attributes

  - Can control order (but the Order property is rigid in .NET XML serialization)—again, through XML serialization attributes

- DataContract

  - Works with DataContractSerializer

  - Includes only DataMember in serialization

  - Can override the Name or Namespace properties

  - Default order is reflection-based

- DataMember

  - Works with DataContractSerializer and DataContract

  - Can only override Name, IsRequired, and Order

  - Order property is not rigid

- MessageContract

  - Works with the DataContractSerializer and XmlSerializerFormat attributes

  - Provides control over SOAP message structure—header or body content

  - Leverages the MessageHeader, MessageBody, MessageHeaderArray, and MessageBodyArray attributes for customization

Summary

In this chapter, we stepped through the initial installation and configuration of your first WCF services. We then provided background on service contracts, data contracts, different aspects of how WCF deals with serialization, and important aspects of distributed computing.

We focused purely on the implementation details, not the actual hosting. The samples for this chapter all run either within IIS hosting or directly under the ASP.NET development server that comes with Visual Studio 2010.

The next chapter will cover the hosting options and the details associated with some of those options. What's important to take away from this chapter is the separation between and decoupling of those that implement the service logic and those responsible for deployment and hosting. This provides solution designers with a framework that reduces bias based upon platform or implementation restrictions.

CHAPTER 5

■■■

Hosting and Consuming WCF Services

When your business relies on SOA, you need to make sure your services are robust. The most important driver behind the robustness of your application is where/how you host your service. You need to ask yourself several questions when thinking about hosting services:

- What are the availability requirements of my services?

- How am I going to manage and deploy my services?

- Do I need to support older versions of my services?

- How am I going to scale up my services?

Learning how to cover these business requirements is essential to developing successful services. As you learned in Chapter 3, you have to host services on your own host. WCF doesn't come with its own host, but instead comes with a class called `ServiceHost` that allows you to host WCF services in your own application easily. You don't have to think about any of the network transport specifics to ensure that your services are reachable. It's a matter of configuring your services' endpoints either programmatically or declaratively and calling the `Open` method of `ServiceHost`. All the generic functionality regarding bindings, channels, dispatchers, and listeners that you learned about in Chapter 3 is baked into `ServiceHostBase` and `ServiceHost`. This means that the responsibility of the application you use to host your service (the application where `ServiceHost` is running) is significantly less than you would expect up front.

This chapter describes the types of applications you can use to host `ServiceHost`. In addition, you will learn about the differences that exist when you want to consume these services when they're hosted in different applications. In this chapter, you will learn about the following:

- The different hosting options available to you

- The advantages and disadvantages of each hosting option

- When to choose which hosting option

- How Microsoft has implemented the different hosting options, and the extensibility points each option has

On the Microsoft .NET platform, there are several types of managed Windows applications that you can create with Visual Studio .NET:

- WinForms applications

- Console applications

- Windows services

- Web applications (ASP.NET) hosted on Internet Information Services (IIS)

- WCF services inside IIS 7.0

- Windows Activation Services (WAS)

- Windows Azure platform

If you look through the project templates that come with Visual Studio 2010, you will find other options at your disposal. For obvious reasons, we don't consider any of the other templates to be viable options to use in the services world. It is worth noting, however, that WCF doesn't block you from running your service in any other type of application as long as it provides you with a .NET application domain. If you don't know the concepts behind a .NET application domain, please refer to the "Understanding .NET Application Domains" sidebar. Depending on the requirements you have for your host, there are four general categories for hosting your WCF services, as follows:

- Self-hosting in a managed .NET application

- Hosting in a Windows service

- Hosting in different versions of IIS

- Hosting on the Windows Azure platform

As you can imagine, all these have associated project templates in Visual Studio, as mentioned earlier in this section, and all of them have their own characteristics. To get a better understanding of which host is the best in each situation, you need to understand the requirements and the features hosts typically have. This chapter will walk you through each hosting option individually.

UNDERSTANDING .NET APPLICATION DOMAINS

Assuming you understand the role of Windows processes and how to interact with them from managed code, you need to investigate the concept of a .NET application domain. To run your managed .NET code in a process, you create assemblies. These assemblies are not hosted directly within a Windows process. Instead, the Common Language Runtime (CLR) isolates this managed code by creating separate logical partitions within a process called an *application domain*. A single process may contain multiple application domains, each of which hosts distinct pieces of code encapsulated in assemblies. This subdivision of a traditional Windows process offers several benefits provided by the .NET Framework. The main benefits are as follows:

domains provide the operating system–neutral nature of the .NET Application platform by abstracting the concept of an executable or library.

Application domains can be controlled and (un)loaded as you want.

Application domains provide isolation for an application or within a process where multiple application domains live. Application domains within a process are independent of each other, and as such one can remain functional when another fails.

Hosting Environment Features

A .NET application requires a hosting Windows process. Inside that Windows process you can host multiple .NET application domains. An application domain is the means for the .NET CLR to isolate the managed code from Windows. The CLR automatically creates one default application domain in each worker process. The default application domain is not unloaded until the process in which it runs shuts down. The CLR controls the shutdown of the default application domain. In most hosts, no code runs inside the default application domain. Instead, hosts (or *processes*) create a new application domain so the application domain can be closed independently of the process. In a lot of applications, it is desirable that the client-side and server-side code execute in different application domains. Often these desires stem from reasons such as security and isolation.

The relationship between processes and application domains is similar to the relationship between applications and application domains and the WCF ServiceHost. As Figure 5–1 illustrates, every process has at least one application domain, and each application domain can host zero or more WCF ServiceHost instances. WCF requires at least an application domain hosted inside a Windows process.

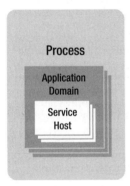

Figure 5–1. The relationship between processes, application domains, and the WCF ServiceHost

■**Note** Although you can instantiate multiple instances of ServiceHost, it is easier to maintain one instance of ServiceHost per application domain. You can use multiple endpoints to expose multiple service interfaces in one host. More advanced hosts such as IIS and WAS do instantiate multiple instances of ServiceHost to provide isolation and different security contexts.

The main responsibility of the host is to provide a Windows worker process and an application domain to the WCF ServiceHost. In addition, WCF relies on the security and configuration features provided by an application domain. A Windows process always runs under a default identity that WCF uses out of the box. However, WCF comes with features to impersonate users on several levels (which is covered in Chapter 7). If you don't use these features, then the Windows process that your service runs under provides the security context. As you know from previous chapters, by default WCF relies on the configuration features in the .NET Framework that are accessible through the application domain.

Some hosts come with additional features for managing applications running under them. Most notably, IIS comes with automatic process recycling, resource throttling, logging, health indicators, and other features.[1] You will learn more about these topics throughout the chapter.

Hosting Environment Requirements

Microsoft did a good job ensuring that you as a service developer don't have to care much about the hosting environment. ServiceHost abstracts all the technological difficulties so you can focus on your service logic instead of the plumbing involved in hosting services. Based on your requirements, you have to choose a host.

WCF is written primarily as a programming model, and it's host-agnostic. ServiceHost doesn't care where it is instantiated as long as it is running when you want your services to be reachable. It requires a process that runs a .NET application domain.

You need to consider certain requirements when choosing a hosting environment (such as whether it's a console application, a WinForms application, etc.). Each hosting environment has certain merits and drawbacks, and we'll cover these in the next few sections. Depending on your hosting environment, you may need to instantiate ServiceHost where your services live. Typical .NET applications, such as console and WinForms applications, run on user desktop machines—environments that don't run all the time. While these types of environments allow hosting of services, they're not typical enterprise-ready hosts. Enterprise-ready hosts are able to support a larger-scale service-oriented architecture, where services expose key business functionality on which multiple systems rely. These enterprise-ready hosts typically fulfill requirements such as high availability. As such, console or WinForms applications shouldn't be considered enterprise-ready hosts.

Services usually run on servers and are managed and operated by operators. Usually the operators that manage servers don't like starting console applications or WinForms applications by hand when servers are rebooted. For your service applications to be ready to run in a data center, the only viable options for enterprise service-oriented scenarios are hosting your services on IIS, a Windows service, or the Windows Azure platform.

Sometimes you'll require interprocess communication on a user's desktop machine. In this scenario, the service is active only when the user is using the application. Typical applications where you see interprocess communication requirements are console applications and WinForms applications. These applications are suitable for hosting these types of services.

To determine which host is the most applicable for your scenario, you should refer to your nonfunctional requirements. Typically, *nonfunctional requirements* are technical requirements that your application must meet to ensure a certain level of quality and maintainability. For WCF applications, nonfunctional requirements concern the following topics:

Availability: When do you want to be able to reach your service?

Reliability: What happens when your service somehow breaks? How does this affect other consumers?

Manageability: Do you need easy access to information about what is happening on the host where the WCF services live?

---

[1] Different IIS versions have different manageability features that are supported by WCF. Most notably, IIS 5.1 on Windows XP comes with several limitations in the management user interface.

Versioning: Do you need to support older versions of the service? Do you know who is consuming your services?

Deployment: What is your deployment model? Are you installing through the Microsoft Installer process and Visual Studio deployment packages, or is Xcopy sufficient?

State: Are your services stateless? Do you need sessions?

Agility: How can your service respond faster to growing customer needs? Do you know how to expand your service to reach new markets and have your services achieve a richer online presence?

Efficiency: How can you reduce the total cost of operation of some workloads of a service? Do you know the ways to ensure that your service is more productive and can increase operational efficiency over a period of time?

Based on these nonfunctional requirements, you can decide which host meets your needs. To help you with this choice, for the remainder of the chapter we'll discuss the different hosting environments and their advantages and disadvantages.

■**Note** The WCF programming model is host-agnostic, so you can always switch to a different host later without having to change your service implementation. Typically, you'll start with a self-hosted scenario in a console application to test-drive and prototype your services.

Self-Hosting Your Service

The most flexible and easiest way to host WCF services is by self-hosting. To be able to self-host your services, you have to meet two requirements:

- You need the WCF runtime.

- You need a managed .NET application in which you can host ServiceHost.

It is your own responsibility to write the code that starts and stops the host. The following are the advantages of self-hosting:

It is easy to use: With only a few lines of code, you can have your service running.

It is flexible: You can easily control the lifetime of your services through the Open and Close methods of ServiceHost<T>.

It is easy to debug: Debugging WCF services that are hosted in a self-hosted environment provides a familiar way of debugging, without having to attach to separate applications that activate your service.

It is easy to deploy: In general, deploying services hosted in a self-hosted environment is as easy as using Xcopy. You don't need any complex deployment scenarios on server farms and the like to deploy a simple Windows application that serves as a WCF ServiceHost.

It supports all bindings and transports: Self-hosting doesn't limit you to out-of-the-box bindings and transports. On Windows XP and Windows Server 2003 and later, IIS limits you to HTTP only.

Self-hosting also has the following disadvantages:

Limited availability: The service is reachable only when the application hosting the service is running. In a practical scenario, these applications might not be running all the time.

Limited features: Self-hosted applications have limited support for high availability, easy manageability, robustness, recoverability, versioning, and deployment scenarios. WCF doesn't provide these out of the box, so in a self-hosted scenario you have to implement these features yourself; IIS, for example, comes with several of these features by default.

In other words, you shouldn't consider self-hosting for enterprise scenarios. Self-hosting is suitable during the development or demonstration phases of your enterprise project. You also might want to self-host your services when you want applications on a user desktop to communicate with each other, or in peer-to-peer scenarios, as described in Chapter 12.

You saw several examples of self-hosting scenarios in Chapter 3. These examples used simple console applications. To better illustrate self-hosting in a real-life scenario, this chapter presents a WinForms application that hosts a service that tracks published quotes for the market makers actors in the QuickReturns Ltd. case study.

For this scenario, you have two distinct WinForms applications. One is the Market Makers Manager application that market makers can use to publish quotes and trade their securities. The other is a separate WinForms application that tracks published quotes. It does this by exposing a service that implements the ITradeTrackingService contract, as described in Listing 5–1. The Market Makers Manager application calls this service when it successfully publishes a quote through the TradeService.

Listing 5–1. Service Contract for the Trade-Tracking Service

```
using System.ServiceModel;
using QuickReturns.StockTrading.ExchangeService.DataContracts;

namespace QuickReturns.StockTrading.TradeTrackingService.Contracts
{
    [ServiceContract()]
    interface ITradeTrackingService
    {
        [OperationContract()]
        void PublishQuote(Quote quote);
    }
}
```

Hosting in Windows Services

Hosting a WCF service in a Windows service is a logical choice. Windows services shouldn't be confused with WCF services. A *Windows service* is a process managed by the operating system. Windows comes with the Service Control Manager, which controls the services installed on the operating system. Windows uses services to support operating system features such as networking, USB, remote access, message queuing, and so on.

Writing a Windows service that hosts your WCF service is pretty easy, and comes with several benefits over the self-hosting scenario discussed earlier in this chapter. The following are the advantages:

- *Automatic starting*: The Windows Service Control Manager allows you to set the startup type to automatic so that as soon as Windows boots, the service will be started, without an interactive login on the machine.

- *Recovery*: The Windows Service Control Manager has built-in support to restart services when failures occur.

- *Security identity*: The Windows Service Control Manager allows you to choose a specific security identity under which you want the service to run, including built-in system or network service accounts.

- *Manageability*: In general, Windows operators know a lot about the Service Control Manager and other management tools that can work with Windows service installation and configuration. This will improve the acceptance of Windows services in production environments; however, to make services maintainable, you would probably have to add some instrumentation and logging features.

- *Support for all bindings and transports*: Self-hosting doesn't limit you to using out-of-the-box bindings and transports. On Windows XP and Windows Server 2003, IIS limits you to HTTP only.

Windows services also have the following disadvantages:

- *Deployment*: Services need to be installed with the .NET Framework Installutil.exe utility or through a custom action in an installer package.

- *Limited features*: Windows services still have a limited set of out-of-the-box features to support high availability, easy manageability, versioning, and deployment scenarios. Essentially, you have to cover these requirements yourself through custom code while, for example, IIS comes with several of these features by default. Windows services do add recoverability and some security features, but you still have to do some work yourself.

- You can use Visual Studio 2010 to create a Windows service using the Windows service project template shown in Figure 5–2.

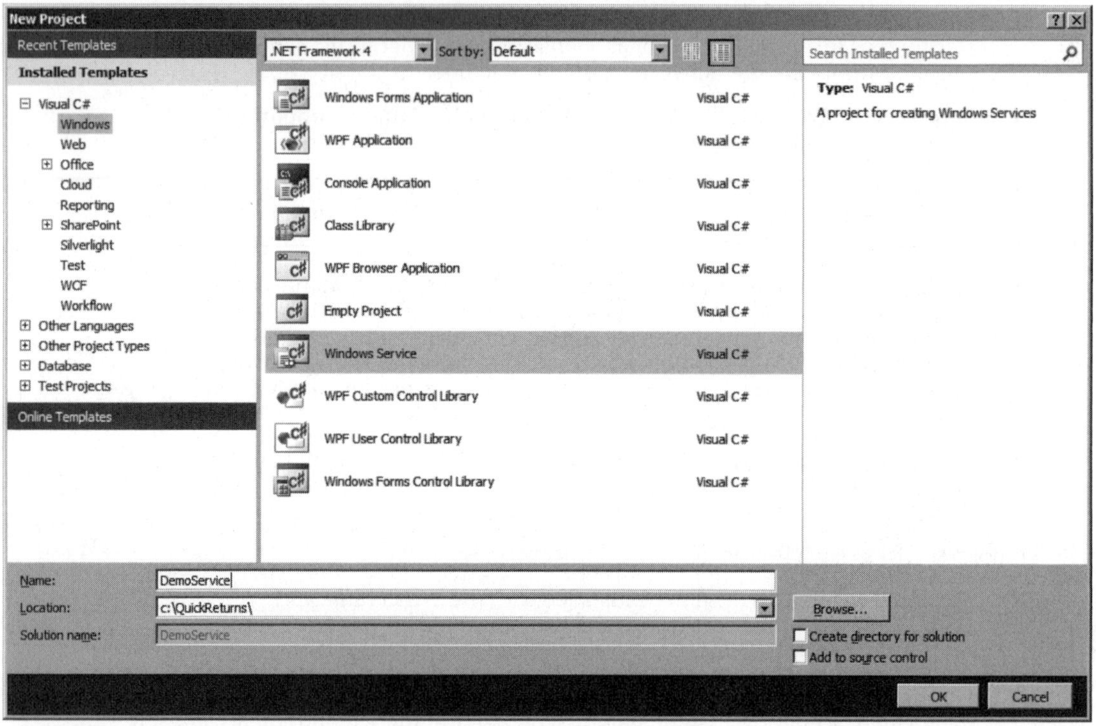

Figure 5–2. *Visual Studio 2010 Windows service project template*

The Windows service project template generates a project that contains two files: the service1.cs file, which that contains the service implementation, and the program.cs file, which instantiates and essentially hosts the Windows service. To host your WCF service inside a Windows service, you merely need to implement the Start and Stop methods of the Windows service, as shown in Listing 5–2. Since starting Windows services is similar to starting your services inside a WCF ServiceHost, you end up tying the lifetime of your WCF service to the lifetime of your Windows service.

Listing 5–2. *Windows Service Hosting the WCF ServiceHost*

```csharp
using System;
using System.ServiceModel;
using System.ServiceProcess;
using QuickReturns.StockTrading.ExchangeService;


namespace QuickReturns.StockTrading.ExchangeService.Hosts
{
    public partial class ExchangeWindowsService : ServiceBase
    {
        ServiceHost host;

        public ExchangeWindowsService()
        {
```

```
        InitializeComponent();
    }

    protected override void OnStart(string[] args)
    {
        Type serviceType = typeof(TradeService);
        host = new ServiceHost(serviceType);
        host.Open();
    }

    protected override void OnStop()
    {
        if(host != null)
            host.Close();
    }
}
}
```

___

■**Tip** If you want to debug your startup (or shutdown) code, just insert the following line in your code:
`System.Diagnostics.Debugger.Break();` (potentially surrounded by some logic to do this only in debug builds).

___

To install a service in the Service Control Manager, you have to add an installer to the project. Visual Studio 2010 allows you to do this easily:

1. Open the Designer view of the Service class in your Windows service project.

2. Click the background of the designer to select the service itself, rather than any of its contents.

3. In the Properties window, click the Add Installer link in the gray area beneath the list of properties, as shown in Figure 5–3. By default, this adds a component class containing two installers to your project. The component is named ProjectInstaller, and the installers it contains are the installer for your service and the installer for the associated process of the service.

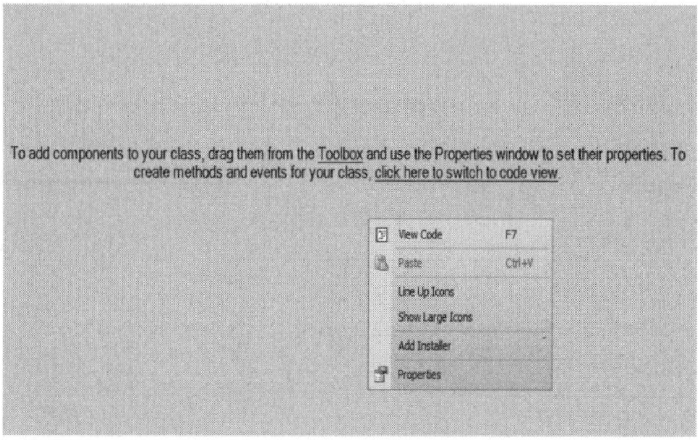

Figure 5–3. The Add Installer function of a Windows service project

4. Access the Designer view for ProjectInstaller, and click ServiceInstaller1.

5. In the Properties window, set the ServiceName property to QuickReturns Exchange Service.

6. Set the StartType property to Automatic, as shown in Figure 5–4.

Figure 5–4. The Properties window of the QuickReturns Exchange Service

7. Access the Designer view for ProjectInstaller, and click serviceProcessInstaller1.

8. In the Properties window, set the Account property to Network Service, as shown in Figure 5–5.

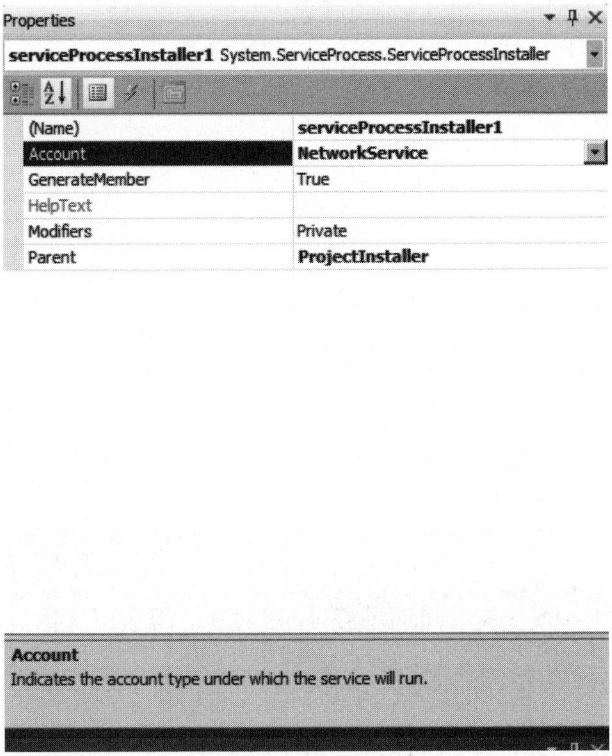

Figure 5–5. *The Properties window of the QuickReturns Service ProcessInstaller*

To create a setup that can be used to install your Windows service, you need to add a Visual Studio setup and deployment project to the solution. The following steps describe how to add a setup and deployment project to your solution.

1. Select File ➤ Add ➤ New Project.

2. In the New Project dialog box, select the Other Project Types category, select Setup and Deployment, select Visual Studio Installer, and then select Setup Project, as shown in Figure 5–6.

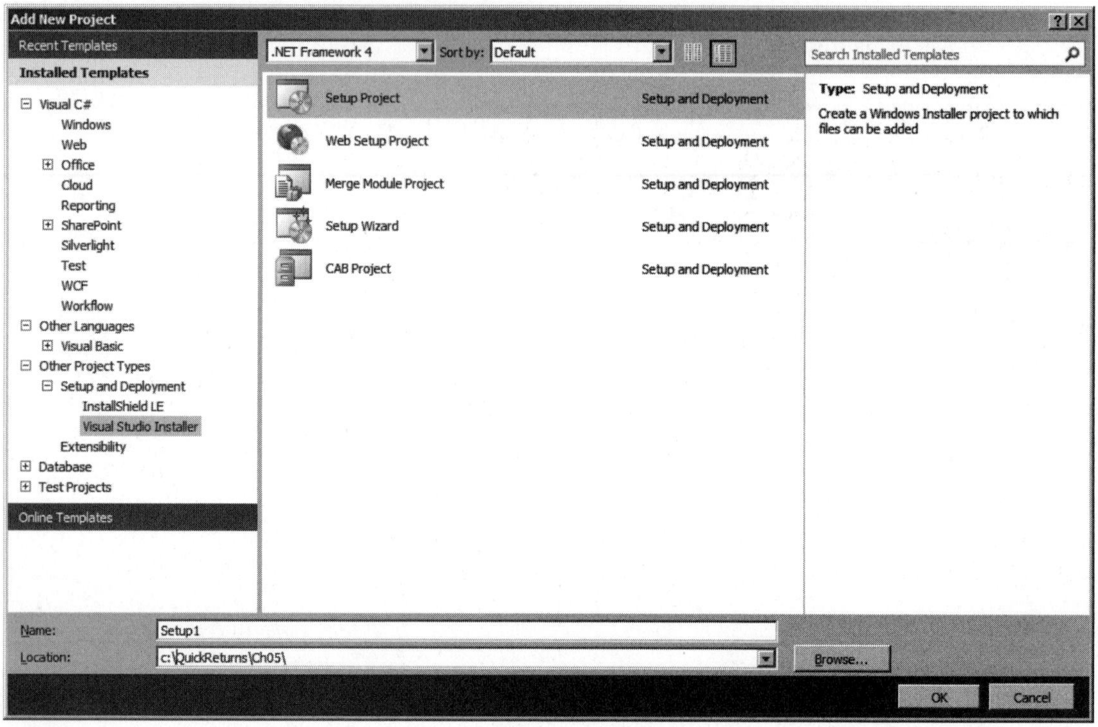

Figure 5–6. Visual Studio 2010 setup project template

3.   In Solution Explorer, right-click the setup project, point to Add, and then
      choose Project Output, as shown in Figure 5–7. The Add Project Output Group
      dialog box will appear.

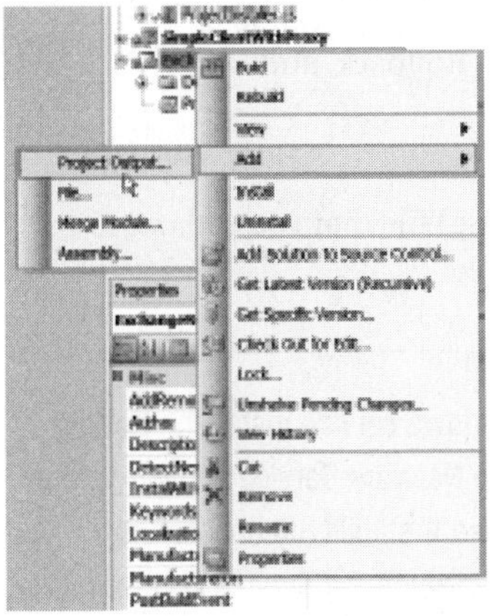

Figure 5–7. Adding the Windows service project output

4. Select the Windows service project.

5. From the list box, select Primary Output, and click OK.

This adds a project item for the primary output of your Windows service to the setup project. Next, you'll add a custom action to install the executable file. To add a custom action to the setup project, follow these steps:

1. In Solution Explorer, right-click the setup project, point to View, and then choose Custom Actions, as shown in Figure 5–8. The Custom Actions view will appear.

Figure 5–8. Opening the Custom Actions view

2. Right-click Custom Actions, and select Add Custom Action.

3. Double-click the application folder in the list box to open it, select Primary Output from the Windows service project, and click OK. The primary output is added to all four nodes of the custom actions: Install, Commit, Rollback, and Uninstall.

4. Build the setup project.

When you compile the project, the output is a Microsoft Installer (.msi) file that you can use to install the service into the Windows Service Control Manager.

■**Note** This chapter describes the basics of building Windows services and Windows service installers. Setting your Windows services to run under the unrestricted Localsystem account or the Network Service account is not always the best choice in terms of security best practices. Usually, operators have the ability to choose the credentials during setup or adjust the security identity settings after installation through the Service Control Manager Management Console snap-in that can be accessed through Windows Computer Management. Refer to Chapter 7 of this book, the MSDN help, or a book dedicated to .NET development for more details and best practices regarding developing Windows services.

Hosting Using IIS

Web service development on IIS has long been the domain of ASP.NET. When ASP.NET 1.0 was released, a web service framework was part of it. Microsoft leveraged the ASP.NET HTTP pipeline to make web services a reality on the Windows platform. Unfortunately, this tight coupling between ASP.NET and web services comes with several limitations in the service orientation world; the dependency on HTTP is the main culprit. Running the ASP.NET HTTP pipeline on a different host is hard, and is therefore an uncommon scenario. Even then, ASP.NET web services (aka ASMX services) stay very web-oriented in terms of deployment scenarios and configuration dependencies. Microsoft initially released several versions of Web Services Enhancements (WSE) to cover some of the limitations of ASP.NET web services, and especially to address the limitations in the implementation of the WS-* protocols. However, WSE was very dependent on the ASP.NET web service implementation.

As discussed in previous chapters, WCF services take a totally different approach to making service orientation a reality. The unified programming model of WCF is based on a strictly layered model to break the web-oriented paradigm and disconnect the service model and channel layer from the supported transports. This model allows WCF to support several different hosts, of which IIS is the most important.

WCF was built to support all operating systems from Windows XP onward. Since IIS 5.1, which was released with Windows XP, a lot has changed. Still, Microsoft has succeeded in supporting WCF on older versions of IIS, due to the features provided by the .NET Framework and the CLR. The following sections will discuss the differences between the process models of different IIS versions, and what these differences mean for your WCF services.

Core IIS Features

To fully describe IIS functionality, we first have to explain the core features of IIS. IIS has long been able to support multiple sites and multiple applications on one machine. To enable this, IIS introduced a common address model that is split into three main areas:

- Sites

- Applications

- Virtual directories

Sites are bound to a particular scheme, network address, and port combination. IIS supports not only HTTP, but also (depending on the version) FTP, NNTP, and SMTP. You can run multiple applications under the same site, and under the same scheme, network, and port combination. A typical URI for an application is `http://localhost/MyApplication`. A virtual directory is simply a folder that is mapped to the network space of the site, which could be somewhere else on the file system. This way, you can keep the actual content or code of an application separate from the other applications that are part of the same site.

In IIS 6.0, Microsoft made some significant changes in the IIS process model. The IIS process model was split into application pools that could be shared among sites and applications, where each application runs in its own application domain. An *application pool* is a separate Windows worker process called `W3wp.exe` and is started only when it needs to start. IIS comes with an application activation model that allows IIS to start up an application pool when it receives a request for a particular application that is bound to that application pool. This enables IIS to host several thousands of applications on one server without keeping several thousand processes running. The activation architecture of IIS is an interesting model in the service world, as you will see in the "WAS" section of this chapter.

Figure 5–9 shows the core IIS 6.0 architecture on the bottom of the HTTP protocol stack, and at least four different processes on top of that:

- `Lsass.exe` (Local Security Authority Subsystem Security) is part of the operating system and is responsible for the security features in IIS.

- `Inetinfo.exe` is the process that hosts the non-HTTP services and the IIS admin service, including the metabase.

- `SvcHost.exe` is the process that can host operating system services; in the case of IIS, it hosts the web (HTTP) service.

- `W3wp.exe` is a worker process. IIS can have multiple `W3wp.exe` processes—one for each application pool. To support web garden scenarios where one application is split into separate processes, you can have multiple instances of the same worker process. This can provide additional scalability and performance benefits.

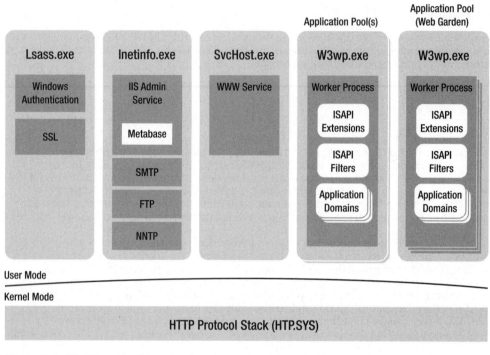

Figure 5–9. IIS 6.0 core architecture

■**Note** IIS 6.0 was the most widely used version of IIS before the release of WCF. In addition, WCF supports IIS 6.0, and the model closely resembles the implementation that was chosen with IIS 7.0 and WAS, as you will learn in the remainder of this chapter. The main difference between IIS 5.1 and IIS 6.0 is the limitation in the amount of sites and application pools. IIS 5.1 supports only one site bound to one application pool.

Hosting WCF Services in IIS

To host a WCF Service in IIS, you need a new physical file with the .svc extension. The file associates a service with its implementation and is the means for IIS to create ServiceHost for you. IIS takes over the interaction between your service and ServiceHost; you no longer have to instantiate and start ServiceHost yourself. The first line of the .svc file contains a directive enclosed in the ASP.NET <% Page %> directive that tells the hosting environment to which service this file points. The service code can then reside inline, as shown in Listing 5–3, in a separate assembly registered in the GAC, in an assembly that resides in the application's Bin folder, or in a C# file that resides under the application's App_Code folder. The most common scenario is to define endpoints in a configuration file. In IIS, you have to define your endpoints in the web.config file, as explained in the next section.

Listing 5–3 shows a sample `.svc` file based on the `TradeService` service shown earlier. It has the service code defined inline. Listing 5–4 shows an example `.svc` file where the code resides in the `App_Code` folder.

Listing 5–3. ExchangeServiceInline.svc File with Inline Code

```
<%@ServiceHost Language="C#"
Service="QuickReturns.StockTrading.ExchangeService.TradeServiceInline" %>

using System;
using System.Collections;
using System.ServiceModel;
using QuickReturns.StockTrading.ExchangeService.Contracts;
using QuickReturns.StockTrading.ExchangeService.DataContracts;

namespace QuickReturns.StockTrading.ExchangeService
{
    [ServiceBehavior(InstanceContextMode=InstanceContextMode.Single,
                     IncludeExceptionDetailInFaults=true)]
    public class TradeServiceInline : ITradeService
    {
        public Quote GetQuote(string ticker)
        {
            ...
        }

        public void PublishQuote(Quote quote)
        {
            ...
        }
    }
}
```

Listing 5–4. ExchangeService.svc File with External Code

```
<% @ServiceHost language="C#"
Service=" QuickReturns.StockTrading.ExchangeService.TradeService"
CodeBehind="~/App_Code/TradeService.cs" %>
```

■**Note** The sample code that comes with this book contains the `TradeService` service hosted inline and comes with an implementation in the `App_Code` folder to illustrate the concepts in this section. You can find it by opening the Chapter 5 solution file.

Configuring WCF Services in IIS

Hosting in IIS means you will have to set up the WCF configuration in the `web.config` file of the application where you want to host your service. The service configuration in the `web.config` file is similar to that of self-hosted services. Listing 5–5 shows an example of a `web.config` file for the `TradeService` service.

Listing 5–5. web.config Used to Configure a Service Hosted in IIS

```xml
<?xml version="1.0"?>
<configuration xmlns="http://schemas.microsoft.com/.NetConfiguration/v2.0">
    <system.serviceModel>
        <services>
            <service name="QuickReturns.StockTrading.ExchangeService.TradeService"
                    behaviorConfiguration="tradeServiceBehavior">
            <endpoint name="basicHttpBinding"
                        address=""
                        binding="basicHttpBinding"
                        contract="QuickReturns.StockTrading.ExchangeService.➥
                                Contracts.ITradeService"/>
            <endpoint name="mexHttpBinding"
                        contract="IMetadataExchange"
                        binding="mexHttpBinding"
                        address="mex" />
            </service>

            <service name="QuickReturns.StockTrading.ExchangeService.TradeServiceInline"
                    behaviorConfiguration="tradeServiceBehavior">
                <endpoint name="basicHttpBinding"
                            address=""
                            binding="basicHttpBinding"
                            contract="QuickReturns.StockTrading.ExchangeService.➥
                                    Contracts.ITradeService"/>
                <endpoint name="mexHttpbinding"
                            contract="IMetadataExchange"
                            binding="mexHttpBinding"
                            address="mex" />
            </service>
        </services>
        <behaviors>
            <serviceBehaviors>
                <behavior name="tradeServiceBehavior" >
                    <serviceMetadata httpGetEnabled="true" />
                </behavior>
                <behavior name="returnFaults"
                            returnUnknownExceptionsAsFaults="true"/>
            </serviceBehaviors>
        </behaviors>
    </system.serviceModel>
</configuration>
```

Please note that the address attribute of the service is empty. The `.svc` file determines the *base* address of the service. You can, however, provide an additional string that would set the endpoint's address relative to the `.svc` file. For example, you can use `http://localhost:8080/QuickReturns/Exchange.svc/ExchangeService`.

The service's name attribute is specified in the config file functions as a lookup key for the corresponding ExchangeService.svc file. It tells the hosting environment to which service this configuration belongs. The other attributes at the endpoint level are the same, as explained previously.

In IIS, web configuration files can be nested in sites, applications, and virtual directories. WCF takes all the configuration files into account and merges services and their endpoints together. This means nested web.config files are added such that the last file read on the bottom of the hierarchy takes precedence over files higher in the hierarchy.

Accessing ServiceHost in IIS

The default behavior of hosting your WCF services in IIS is that IIS controls the instantiation of ServiceHost. This avoids the use of any startup or shutdown code before a message reaches your service. The advantage of this is of course that less code will introduce fewer potential errors. IIS provides you with an easier hosting environment, in terms of lines of code, than a console application. However, sometimes you need a way to circumvent this limitation. To do this and customize IIS in instantiating ServiceHost, you can build a factory that creates your custom host. This way, you can access any of the events or override any of the methods you like.

To support custom ServiceHost activation, you should implement your own Factory, which inherits from the ServiceHostFactory class. That class is provided to allow you to hook up the events for ServiceHost; you can use this class and set the type to the Factory attribute in the .svc file, as shown in Listing 5–6. By overriding the CreateServiceHost method of the ServiceHostFactory class, you can perform tasks similar to those in self-hosting scenarios, as discussed in Chapter 3. This enables you, among other things, to abstract the logic to build up the description from the external configuration or create a more suitable base class for your base library, project, department, or company to use.

Listing 5–7 shows the code of TradeServiceCustomHost and TradeServiceCustomHostFactory, which create the host.

Listing 5–6. *.svc File with a CustomServiceHostFactory*

```
<% @ServiceHost Language="C#" Debug="true"
    Service="QuickReturns.StockTrading.ExchangeService.TradeService"
    Factory="QuickReturns.StockTrading.ExchangeService.
TradeServiceCustomHostFactory" %>
```

Listing 5–7. *TradeServiceCustomHostFactory and TradeServiceCustomHost*

```
using System;
using System.ServiceModel;
using System.ServiceModel.Activation;

namespace QuickReturns.StockTrading.ExchangeService
{
    public class TradeServiceCustomHostFactory : ServiceHostFactory
    {
        protected override ServiceHost CreateServiceHost(
            Type serviceType, Uri[] baseAddresses)
        {
            TradeServiceCustomHost customServiceHost =
                new TradeServiceCustomHost(serviceType, baseAddresses);
            return customServiceHost;
        }
    }

    public class TradeServiceCustomHost : ServiceHost
    {
        public TradeServiceCustomHost(Type serviceType, params Uri[] baseAddresses)
            : base(serviceType, baseAddresses)
        {
```

```
        }

        protected override void ApplyConfiguration()
        {
            base.ApplyConfiguration();
        }
    }
}
```

Recycling

When you host WCF services on IIS, the WCF services enjoy all the features of ASP.NET applications. You have to be aware of these features because they can cause unexpected behavior in the services world. One of the major features is application recycling, which includes application domain recycling and process recycling. Through the IIS Management Console, you can configure different rules when you want the recycling to happen. You can set certain thresholds on memory, time, and the amount of processed requests, as shown in Figure 5–10. When IIS recycles a worker process, all the application domains within the worker process will be recycled as well. Usually, when critical files in an ASP.NET-based web application change, the application domain also recycles. This happens, for example, when changing the web.config file or assemblies in the Bin folder.

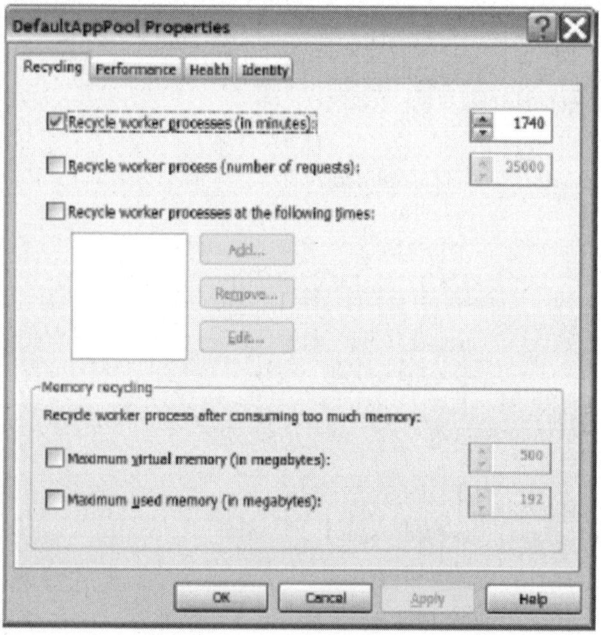

Figure 5–10. Application pool recycling settings

> ■**Note** The process recycling described here covers recycling in Windows Server 2003. To enable process recycling in Windows XP and IIS 5.1, you can download the IIS 5.0 process recycling tool from the Microsoft web site. The process recycle tool runs as a service on a computer running IIS 5.0 or 5.1.

After modifying an `.svc` file, the application domain is also recycled. The hosting environment will try to close all the WCF services' open connections gracefully in a timely manner. When services somehow don't close in time, they will be forced to abort. Through the `HostingEnvironmentSettings` configuration settings, you can modify the behavior of recycling, as shown in Listing 5–8. The `idleTimeout` setting determines the amount of idle time in seconds for an application domain to be recycled. The `shutdowntimeout` setting determines the amount of time in seconds to gracefully shut down an application. After this timeout, the applications are forced to shut down.

Listing 5–8. web.config with hostingEnvironment Section for Recycling Settings

```
<system.web>
    <hostingEnvironment idleTimeout="20"
                        shutdownTimeout="30"/>
</system.web>
```

When you use WCF sessions, these recycling features are critical to understand. This is typically the case in the security and reliable messaging scenarios, as you will read in Chapters 6 and 8. By default, WCF stores session state in memory. This is a different implementation from ASP.NET session state and doesn't come with a configuration to switch over to persistent session state storage. However, in the security and reliable messaging scenarios, you can and should benefit from the ASP.NET implementation. Using the ASP.NET compatibility features of WCF provides you with the SQL Server and state server implementations of ASP.NET session state to support enterprise-ready scenarios. In the next section, you will learn how to benefit from the WCF ASP.NET compatibility mode.

ASP.NET Compatibility Mode

When hosting your WCF services in a load-balanced or web garden environment, where subsequent requests in a session can be processed by different hosts or processes in the environment, you need out-of-process persistent storage for your session state. Out of the box, WCF doesn't support persistent storage for session state. Instead, WCF stores all its session state in memory. When your WCF services are hosted in IIS, you can end up with recycling scenarios, as described in the previous section. Instead of building persistent storage for sessions all over again, WCF relies on the ASP.NET implementation for session state. This approach has one serious limitation: you limit your services to HTTP.

ASP.NET session state is not the only feature that is supported by the ASP.NET compatibility mode. It also supports features such as the `HttpContext`, globalization, and impersonation, just like you are used to with ASP.NET web services (ASMX). Refer to the MSDN help for the ASP.NET-specific features to enable out-of-process session state.

To see the limitation of ASP.NET compatibility mode, you have to explicitly mark your services with the `AspNetCompatibilityRequirements` attribute, as shown in Listing 5–9.

Listing 5–9. The AspNetCompatiblityRequirements Attribute

```
namespace QuickReturns.StockTrading.ExchangeService
{
    [ServiceBehavior(InstanceContextMode=InstanceContextMode.Single,
                     ReturnUnknownExceptionsAsFaults=true)]
    [AspNetCompatibilityRequirements(
     RequirementsMode=AspNetCompatibilityRequirementsMode.Allowed)]
    public class TradeService : ITradeService
    {
    ...
    }
}
```

The AspNetCompatibilityRequirementsMode attribute has the following allowed values:

- NotAllowed: Indicates that your services may *never* be run in ASP.NET compatibility mode. You have to set this in scenarios where your service implementation doesn't work in ASP.NET compatibility mode, such as when your services are not built for HTTP.

- Allowed: Indicates that your services *may* be run in ASP.NET compatibility mode. Choose this value only when you know your service can work in this mode.

- Required: Indicates that your service *must* be run in ASP.NET compatibility mode. Use this value when your service requires persistent session storage.

When you choose the Required option, WCF will verify that all the supported endpoints for the services are HTTP endpoints, and will throw an exception during ServiceHost initialization if they aren't. In addition to the AspNetCompatibilityRequirements attribute, you must set aspNetCompatibilityEnabled, as shown in Listing 5–10.

Listing 5–10. Configuration with aspNetCompatibilityEnabled

```
<?xml version="1.0"?>
<configuration xmlns="http://schemas.microsoft.com/.NetConfiguration/v2.0">
    <system.serviceModel>
        <serviceHostingEnvironment aspNetCompatibilityEnabled="true"/>
        <services>
        ...
        </services>
        <behaviors>
        ...
        </behaviors>
    </system.serviceModel>
</configuration>
```

■**Note** The sample code that comes with this book contains the TradeService service hosted in the ExchangeServiceInline.svc file, which is configured to run in ASP.NET compatibility mode. You can find it by opening the Chapter 5 solution file.

Windows XP and IIS 5.1

IIS 5.0, which came as part of Windows 2000, split the process model of IIS and introduced worker processes. The primary reason for this change was to isolate applications so that IIS could host different applications that were independent of each other. IIS 5.0 was released with Windows 2000, and IIS 5.1 was released with Windows XP. WCF doesn't support hosting services on Windows 2000 with IIS 5.0; because of that, we will take a closer look at IIS 5.1 only. IIS 5.1 is supported, but has the limitation of only one site per process, and each application in IIS runs in a worker process called aspnet_wp.exe. IIS 5.1 is a great version for developing ASP.NET web sites and WCF services; however, it is not suitable for enterprise use because it has connection limits and runs only on a client version of earlier Windows versions or Windows XP.

Figure 5–11 shows the process model of IIS 5.1. The architecture is split into two pieces. W3svc.exe on the left hosts an HTTP listener, launches worker processes, and manages the configuration. The worker processes on the right enable IIS 5.1 to host managed .NET applications, where ASPNET_ISAPI.dll is responsible for creating managed .NET application domains. Note that on Windows XP, the W3svc.exe Windows service is hosted in the SvcHost.exe process, together with the SMTP and FTP services.

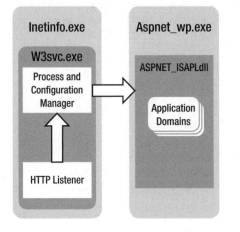

Figure 5–11. IIS 5.1 process model architecture

■**Note** You aren't required to have IIS to run ASP.NET and WCF services. For example, you can use the ASP.NET development web server that is provided with Visual Studio 2005. When Windows XP was released, however, Visual Studio didn't have this feature. You were required to work with IIS 5.1 to be able to develop web applications on Windows XP.

Windows Server 2003 and IIS 6.0

With Windows Server 2003, Microsoft introduced HTTP.SYS, the kernel mode HTTP stack. HTTP.SYS is plugged into the IIS 6.0 architecture through W3svc.exe, which is a user-mode component that bridges the kernel-mode implementation of HTTP.SYS and connects this to the process and configuration management system that was already there in IIS 5.1. And as of IIS 6.0, the concept of application pools became more generalized. While in IIS 5.1, only managed (ASP.NET) applications could be hosted in separate application pools, in IIS 6.0 all types of applications can be hosted in separate application pools. ASPNET_ISAPI.dll is still responsible for starting application domains in the managed ASP.NET world. Figure 5–12 illustrates the process model in IIS 6.0.

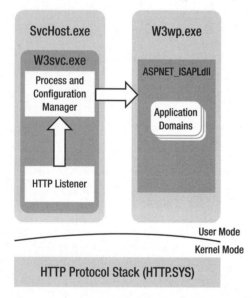

Figure 5–12. IIS 6.0 process model architecture

Refer to Chapter 4 for details about hosting your services in IIS 6.0.

Hosting in IIS 7.0

IIS 7.0 has marked another big evolution in the web server world. As shown in Figure 5–13, two big changes were made. First, protocol-specific listener adapters support all four WCF transports, instead of only HTTP (as in IIS 6.0). In addition, WAS, a new operating system service, was introduced. Both W3svc.exe and WAS run inside an operating system host called SvcHost.exe. To be able to use the power of the IIS 6.0 process model in conjunction with WCF, these changes were necessary. You might be asking that if WCF services also work in IIS 5.1 and IIS 6.0, what benefits do you get by generalizing the process model and activation features in IIS? Simple—by generalizing the activation concept to make it protocol-agnostic instead of bound to HTTP, you expand the activation features of the platform to basically all transports.

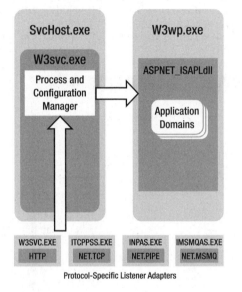

Figure 5–13. IIS 7.0 process model architecture

With the release of Windows Vista and Windows Server 2008, Microsoft moved the process management and configuration features of IIS and made them generally available inside the operating system. This enables any application built on top of that model to use the power of runtime activation and spawning worker processes based on messages coming in.

The protocol-specific listener adapters for HTTP, TCP/IP, Named Pipes, and MSMQ live inside their own process, and bridge the specific transports to WAS. Listener adapters ask WAS to activate worker processes and then hand over the actual communication to the specific protocol handler inside these worker processes. So, WAS now has all the features that used to be part of W3svc.exe. By splitting this responsibility into separate processes, the three other transports also benefit from the process model and activation features that used to be built into IIS 6.0, but only for HTTP. To summarize, with IIS 7.0 you can host any WCF service across any transport that is provided out of the box inside IIS. In the next section, you will learn how WAS activation works and what you need to be aware of when you want to host your WCF services inside IIS 7.0 and WAS on Windows Vista or Windows Server 2008.

To host the TradeService that you have been using throughout this book inside IIS 7.0, all you have to do is configure IIS and place the .svc file created for IIS 6.0 in the site you will create. The following steps will enable you to configure IIS 7.0, WAS, and the .NET Framework 3.x or later on Windows Server 2008 and get your TradeService running inside IIS 7.0:

1. Start the Server Manager (found in Administrative Tools).

2. Add the Web Server (IIS) role to the server.

3. Note that the web server installation automatically adds WAS.

4. On the Detailed Settings screen for IIS, select ASP.NET, and under Security select Basic and Windows Authentication. Keep the rest of this default settings.

This will install IIS and WAS. Now you are all set to run your WCF services on IIS 7.0. The next step is to create an application in IIS in which to run your service. For this you need Internet Information Services (IIS) Manager. You can find the IIS management tool in Administrative Tools on the Start menu. Once you've started Internet Information Services (IIS) Manager, navigate to your server, then to your web sites, and finally to the default web site. Right-click the default web site, and select Add Application, as illustrated in Figure 5–14.

Figure 5–14. Creating a new application in Internet Information Services (IIS) Manager

Now you need a folder on your local machine to host your application's `.svc` files. As illustrated in Figure 5–15, you can give the application a name where the service can be reached (`http://localhost/<chosenname>`) and specify the folder where the files reside, and you can select the application pool.

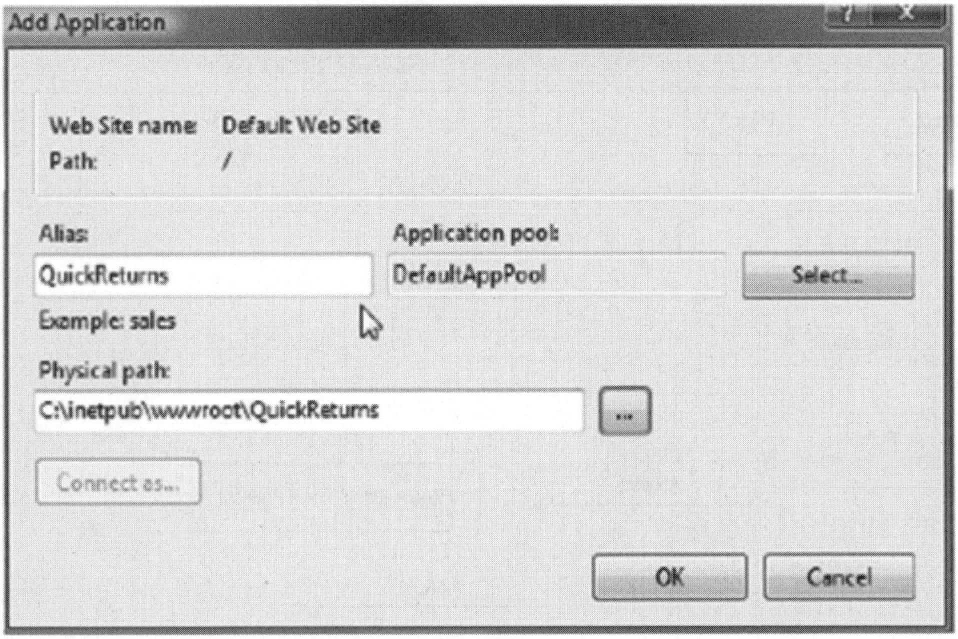

Figure 5–15. Setting the properties for a new application in Internet Information Services (IIS) Manager

If you did everything correctly, your service should be reachable through IIS 7.0. You can test this by navigating to your newly created application—for example, `http://localhost:8080/QuickReturns/Exchange.svc/ExchangeService`.

WAS

WAS enables you to host any WCF service and support any transport inside the IIS model. WAS takes over creating worker processes and providing the configuration from the original `W3svc.exe` Windows service that you know from IIS 6.0 (and runs inside the `Inetinfo.exe` process). WAS and IIS now share the configuration store that defines sites, applications, application pools, and virtual directories. In this section, we'll walk you through the process of activation with WAS, as shown in Figure 5–16.

By default, when no requests are being made to a newly booted server, Windows runs five services (if all the protocols are enabled). These Windows services are

- WAS

- World Wide Web Publishing Service (hosting the listener adapter)

- NET.TCP listener adapter

- NET.PIPE listener adapter

- NET.MSMQ listener adapter

When the listener adapters start, they register themselves with WAS and receive the WAS/IIS configuration for their specific protocols. In this way, the listener adapters are aware of the sites and applications they should support. Each listener adapter then starts listening on the appropriate ports provided with the configuration so it can dispatch the requests coming in to the appropriate application.

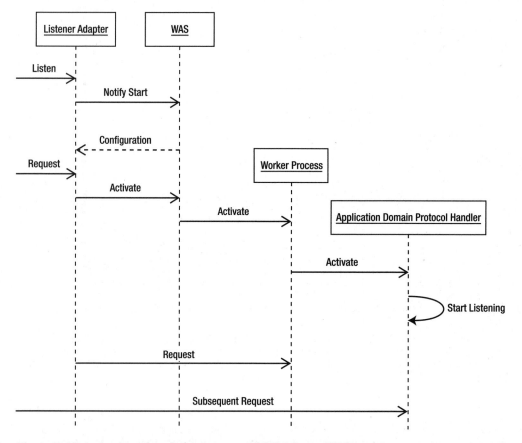

Figure 5–16. *Activation of worker processes with WAS for an HTTP request*

As soon as the first request comes in, the listener adapter will call WAS to activate the worker process, including a managed .NET application domain for the specific application for which the request is destined.

The request is then handed over to the so-called application domain protocol handler inside the worker process to handle the request and return the response to the client. It doesn't matter whether the request is a WCF service request, an ASP.NET request, or any other request for IIS 7.0. The activation process is created to enable worker processes to start when requests come in.

To start the WCF ServiceHost inside the application domain, the application domain protocol handler must call the EnsureServiceAvailable static method. This method is protocol-agnostic and activates the entire service, including all endpoints and transports (not only the transport for the protocol handler that calls the method).

■**Note** Inside the listener adapters and protocol handlers, some true magic happens for HTTP and TCP in particular. Sockets are opened inside the listener adapters hosted in a separate process. Then, when the first request comes in, the socket is actually handed over from the listener adapter to the application domain protocol handler to be able to handle the first and any subsequent requests!

Hosting WCF Services in Windows Azure

Microsoft Windows Azure platform is a cloud computing platform that allows applications to be hosted and run at Microsoft data centers. It became commercially available on February 1, 2010.

UNDERSTANDING CLOUD COMPUTING

Cloud computing is a real buzzword these days, and has lot of promise for becoming the next-generation delivery model for IT services. In raw terms, cloud computing is an Internet-based computing model through which you can avail yourself of on-demand resources, software, and information. These resources and software can be accessed via a web service, a web browser, or any application that has Internet availability. I often refer to cloud computing as the next step in extending Software as a Service (SaaS) to Platform as a Service (PaaS). It facilitates deployment of applications without the cost and complexity of buying and managing the underlying hardware and software layers.

Cloud computing provides a sheer level of abstraction to the end user, who does not need to worry about the technology infrastructure supporting the cloud. The end consumer does not need to own the physical infrastructure, but instead rents it from service providers. There are lots of cloud service providers, including Microsoft, Amazon, Salesforce, and Google. The infrastructures they provide include hosting multiple VMs on which your services can run. These providers also provide different renting models—such as a utility- or subscription-based models—to provide their services to end consumers. Over the last few years, all of these service providers have made huge investments in cloud computing. Amazon, for example, did a fabulous job in the field of cloud computing when they released Amazon Web Services (AWS) way back in 2006.

Users can purchase Windows Azure service time from the Azure web site (www.microsoft.com/azure). This platform also provides an operating system called Windows Azure that serves as a runtime for the application and provides a set of services that allows the development, management, and hosting of an application.

You need the Windows Azure SDK to develop an application that will be deployed in Windows Azure. In order to use Visual Studio 2010 to develop, debug, execute, and deploy WCF services in Windows Azure, you also need to download Windows Azure Tools for Microsoft Visual Studio. This not only installs the Windows SDK but also installs an integrated set of tools for developing Windows Azure services in Visual Studio. As of this writing, it can be downloaded from http://msdn.microsoft.com/en-us/windowsazure/cc974146 To get the most up-to-date link, visit http://msdn.microsoft.com/en-us/windowsazure/cc974146.aspx. Click Download, and then install VSCloudService.exe. Click OK and Run. You will see the welcome screen, as shown in Figure 5–17.

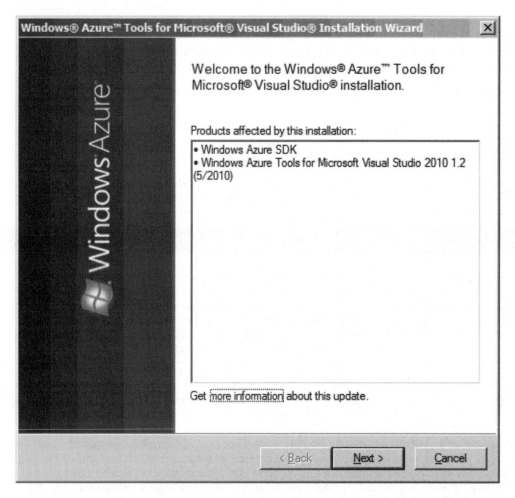

Figure 5–17. Installation wizard for Windows Azure Tools for Microsoft Visual Studio

Click Next, and you will see the licensing terms window, as shown in Figure 5–18.

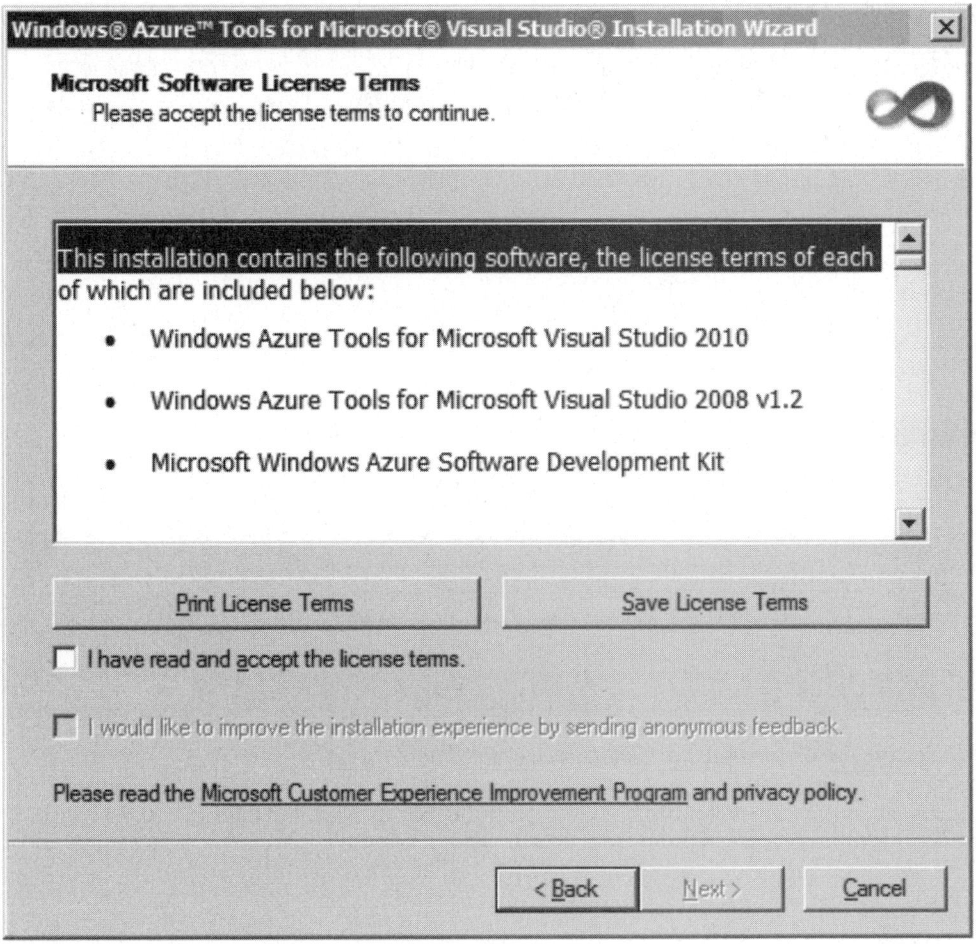

Figure 5–18. The licensing terms screen

Click the first check box, and then click Next. Windows Azure Tools for Microsoft Visual Studio will start installing on your machine. Click OK to complete the installation.

Let's now host our TradeService service in a development fabric, which is a simulation environment of Windows Azure. A *development fabric* allows you to build, test, and debug the service locally before deploying to Windows Azure.

Create a new project by opening Visual Studio 2010, select File, select New Project, and then select the Windows Azure Cloud Service template, as shown in Figure 5–19. Be sure to specify the name and location for your project. For our service, we have used the name CloudQuickReturns, as shown in Figure 5–19.

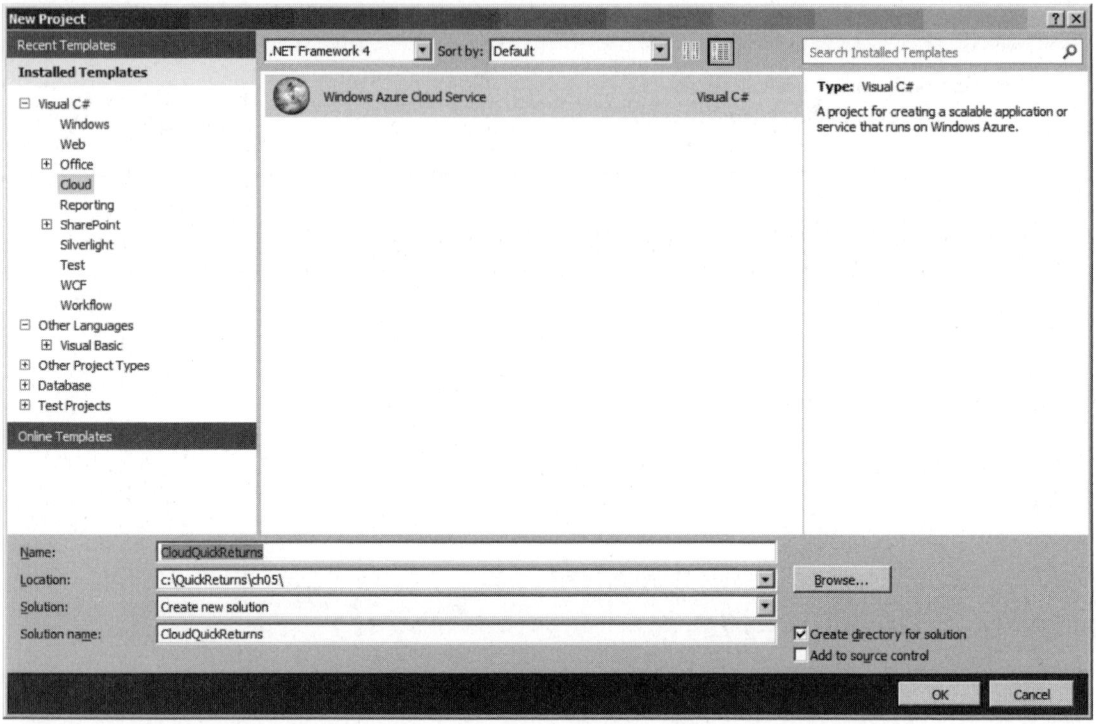

Figure 5–19. Selecting the Windows Azure Cloud Service template

Click OK. Visual Studio 2010 will prompt you to select the role, as shown in Figure 5–20. A service must implement one or more roles in order for it to be hosted in Windows Azure. The roles are mainly of two types:

- Web role

- Worker role

The web role is mainly for web application programming. Most of the time, users prefer this web role. The worker role is mostly used for doing background processing for the web role.

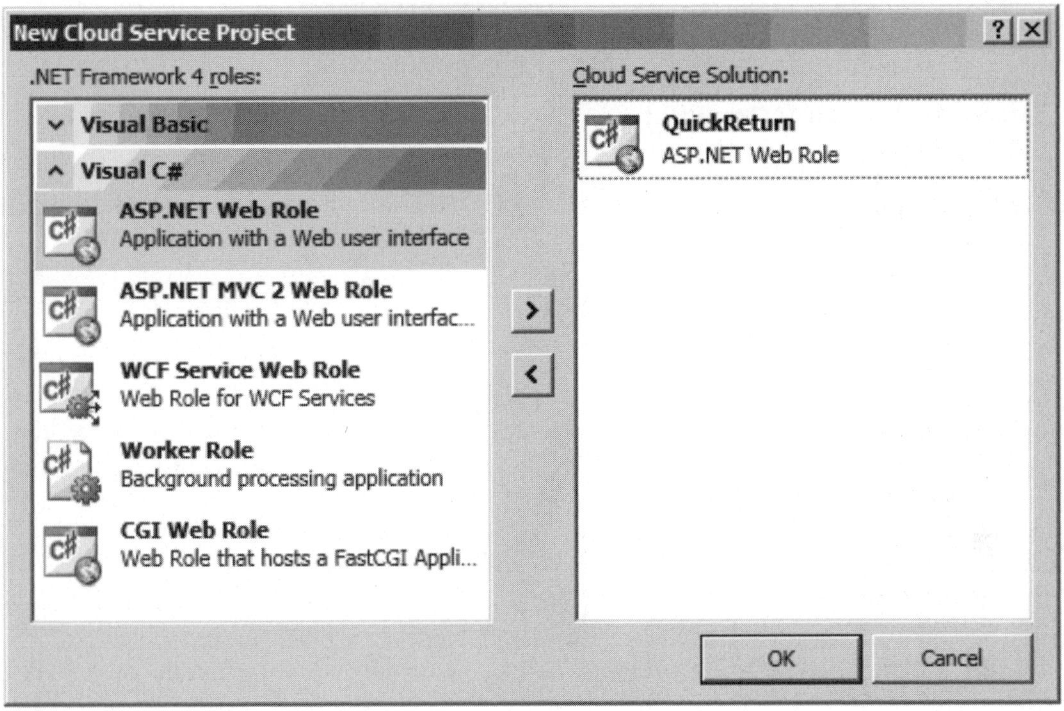

Figure 5–20. Selecting a role for the CloudService project

Select ASP.NET Web Role, and then click the > button. Rename the role QuickReturn, as shown in the preceding figure, and click OK. Visual Studio 2010 will create two projects for you, as shown in Figure 5–21.

Figure 5–21. Solution Explorer for cloud computing

The next step is to add a WCF service to the web project by right-clicking QuickReturn, clicking Add New item, and then selecting WCF Service. Name the service TradeService.svc, as in Chapter 3. We will be hosting the very same TradeService service in fabricated cloud. Click OK. This will create two files in your solution: ITradeService.cs and TradeService.svc. Copy the code from Listings 5–11 and 5–12 to each of these files, respectively.

Listing 5–11. Interface Code for ITradeService.cs

```
namespace QuickReturn
{
    [ServiceContract(
        Namespace = "http://PracticalWcf/Exchange/TradeService")
    ]
    public interface ITradeService
    {
        [OperationContract]
        decimal TradeSecurity(string ticker, int quantity);
    }
}
```

Listing 5–12. *TradeService Class TradeService.svc.cs*

```
namespace QuickReturn
{
    public class TradeService : ITradeService
    {
        const decimal IBM_Price = 80.50m;
        const decimal MSFT_Price = 30.25m;
        public decimal TradeSecurity(string ticker, int quantity)
        {
            if (quantity < 1)
                throw new ArgumentException(
                    "Invalid quantity", "quantity");
            switch (ticker.ToLower())
            {
                case "ibm":
                    return quantity * IBM_Price;
                case "msft":
                    return quantity * MSFT_Price;
                default:
                    throw new ArgumentException(
                        "SK security - only MSFT & IBM", "ticker");
            }
        }
    }
}
```

Build the solution. Set CloudQuickReturns as your startup project. Run the application. This will package your service, start the development storage, and then deploy the service to the development fabric.

■**Note** Make sure that you have configured the development storage of the fabricated server. By default, it is SQL Server Express. If you need to install SQL Server Express, or if you need to configure development storage to run with your local instance, configure the fabricated server storage with the DSInit utility, which ships with Windows Azure. The SDK can be accessed through the Windows Azure SDK command prompt. For more information about DSInit, visit http://msdn.microsoft.com/en-us/library/dd179457.aspx.

This will start your fabricated server and will enable you to host your service in your development fabricated server. The service will be shown in a browser, as shown in Figure 5–22.

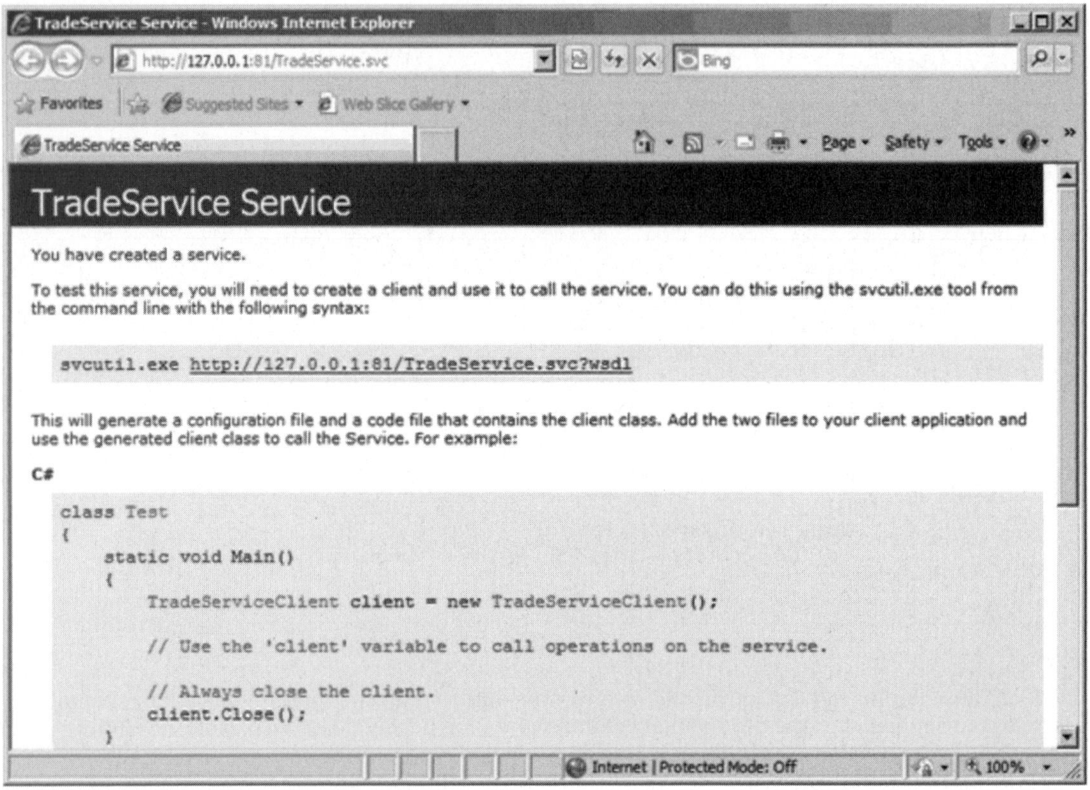

Figure 5–22. TradeService hosted in a fabricated server

Congratulations! You have now hosted your WCF service in a development fabric.

Windows Azure Tools also comes with the Development Fabric UI, as shown in Figure 5–23, which provides an interactive way to view the service deployment. This UI enables you to view logging and diagnostic information, and also allows you to debug your service locally by attaching a debugger through the UI. In order to access the Development Fabric UI, right-click the Windows Azure simulation monitor icon of the fabricated server in the Windows taskbar, and then click Show Development Fabric UI to open the user interface, as shown in Figure 5–23.

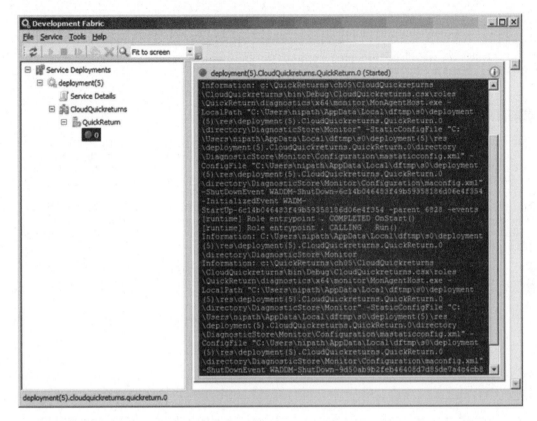

Figure 5–23. Development Fabric UI

In order to deploy your service to Windows Azure, you need to right-click your CloudQuickReturns project and choose Publish. This will create the service package. If you are not using Visual Studio 2010, you can create the service package using the CSPack utility, which ships with the Azure SDK. Once a service package has been created, you can upload it through Visual Studio 2010 or by using the Windows Azure portal. For more details on how to deploy your WCF service to Windows Azure, visit http://msdn.microsoft.com/en-us/windowsazure/ff798117.aspx.

Hosting Options

Earlier in this chapter, you learned about the different options you have to host your services. In addition, you learned which business requirements (or nonfunctional requirements) can be covered by which hosting scenario. In general, you can apply a "Why not IIS?" approach. IIS provides the best match in terms of features, in particular in scenarios where your services expose key business functionality on which multiple systems rely. When you choose IIS and then have to choose between IIS 6.0 and IIS 7.0, you should obviously choose the latter because of the new activation features. In scenarios where you need interprocess communication, both WinForms and console applications are viable options. Windows services and hosting in Windows Azure are essentially the only alternatives to IIS, and will typically be used when you are building a server product or when you need advanced control over the activation and lifetime of your services. Hosting your service in Windows Azure can also require a business decision, but this option is definitely going to be the best way to host your enterprise-ready service.

In the next section, we will go through the options for consuming your services, and what the hosting options means for the consumer side.

Consuming WCF Services

In the previous sections, you learned about the different hosting options you have.. You can consume WCF services in several ways depending on the hosting option. If you are using WCF on the client side, you will be very productive because WCF comes with tools that can generate proxy classes to call WCF services. WCF provides standards and tools support primarily through `SvcUtil.exe`. You'll use this as the primary metadata interpretation tool. That, in combination with the WCF framework's ability to leverage reflection to interrogate types adorned with the appropriate attributes, makes the generation and use of the WCF framework less complicated than with existing frameworks. In addition, Visual Studio 2010 comes with easy-to-use features to add service references to your projects and seamlessly generate proxy classes. Essentially, you have the following options:

- Retrieving the WSDL from the service, and handcrafting a proxy to call the service. This is a typical scenario when you don't have WCF on the client side. For this scenario, please refer to Chapter 13.

- Using the Add Service Reference features of Visual Studio 2010, and letting them generate a proxy to use in your client.

- Using the `SvcUtil.exe` tool to generate proxy classes.

Service Proxies

A *service proxy* enables you to work with services in an object-oriented way. Proxy classes abstract the communication model used by the service so you as a client developer are not directly aware you are talking to a (remote) service. It is as if you are calling local code. The proxy class implements the service interface of the service and thus enables you to call methods on the service interface as if these were local methods. Proxies are generated for any custom type that is used in the service interface. Listing 5–13 contains pieces of a generated proxy for the TradeService service in the QuickReturns Ltd. sample. It illustrates that on the client side a Quote is available that maps to the Quote object on the server side, although they are distinct classes. The Quote object serializes according to the contract so that, on the service side, it can be serialized into the service-side version of the Quote data contract. In addition, you can see the GetQuote and PlaceQuote methods calling a base class that will eventually make the call across the service boundary via the configured transport.

Listing 5–13. Sample Generated Proxy for the TradeService Service

```
namespace SimpleClientWithProxy.ExchangeService
{
    [DataContract()]
    public partial class Quote : object, IExtensibleDataObject
    {
        // Left out the Quote Datamembers in printed code, see sample code
    }
}
```

```
[GeneratedCode("System.ServiceModel", "4.0.0.0")]
[ServiceContract()]
public interface ITradeService
{
  [
     OperationContract(Action = "http://tempuri.org/ITradeService/GetQuote",
        ReplyAction = "http://tempuri.org/ITradeService/GetQuoteResponse")]
  Quote GetQuote(string ticker);

  [
     OperationContract(Action = "http://tempuri.org/ITradeService/PublishQuote",
        ReplyAction = "http://tempuri.org/ITradeService/PublishQuoteResponse")]
  void PublishQuote(Quote quote);
}


[GeneratedCode("System.ServiceModel", "4.0.0.0")]
public interface ITradeServiceChannel : ITradeService, IClientChannel
{
}

[GeneratedCode("System.ServiceModel", "4.0.0.0")]
public partial class TradeServiceClient : ClientBase<ITradeService>, ITradeService
{
   // Left out some constructors in printed code, see sample code

   public SimpleClientWithProxy.ExchangeService.Quote
      GetQuote(string ticker)
   {
      return base.Channel.GetQuote(ticker);
   }

   public void PublishQuote(
      SimpleClientWithProxy.ExchangeService.Quote quote)
   {
      base.Channel.PublishQuote(quote);
   }
}
```

We have already covered how to add a service reference in Visual Studio 2010 and generate a proxy via a command-line tool in Chapter 4. Please refer to the "Proxy Generation Using the Visual Studio 2010 Add-In" section of Chapter 4 for more details.

Summary

Now that you know all about your alternatives in terms of hosting, you should be able to build WCF applications and host them anywhere you like. In addition, you should understand the benefits of hosting in the most recent environments available: IIS 7.0 on Windows Vista, and Windows Server 2008 in combination with WAS. You also learned some of the benefits of hosting in Windows Azure and how to host your WCF service in a development fabric. In the next chapter, you will learn about managing WCF services.

CHAPTER 6

■ ■ ■

Managing WCF Services

Any new technology goes through numerous phases in its life cycle. The most exciting phase is the envisioning or evangelizing phase, where you are exposed to snazzy marketing material and promises of higher productivity. Then the technology graduates to the phase of gradual implementation by the industry. Many people get caught up in the euphoria of technical features in these two phases. Senior managers (i.e., CIOs and CTOs) of organizations are keen to deliver the "latest and greatest" technology to their shareholders. However, developers tend to focus their attention on implementing the technology. The development cycle for most of these new applications is much shorter than the expected life span of the systems. All these systems need to be maintained efficiently to justify the return on investment (ROI) over a long period of time. Unfortunately, in most cases people tend to overlook the management and operation of new technology. Specifically, how do you continue to support the new system? What are the operational processes that can assist in managing each component? Often, these questions are not appropriately answered when trying to promote new technology.

In fact, organizations often spend millions of dollars building the most state-of-the-art technical solutions but are reluctant to consider a substantial budget for operating and managing the new technology. This dilemma was once described eloquently by a Microsoft speaker—he compared operating and managing a new technology to raising a baby. The most exciting part for the parents is conceiving and giving birth to the baby. However, the difficult part of parenting starts after the baby is born. This is similar to the technology life cycle. A lot of emphasis is put on the conception and first implementation of a new technology. However, you achieve most of the effort and the value-added activity (the return to the business stakeholders) by carefully managing and monitoring the system. With the latest trend of outsourcing operational activities to overseas developer centers, the issue of managing the day-to-day operations of any technology is gaining more attention every day. Microsoft has recognized this industry trend and invested in WCF service management to address this issue.

You investigated the WCF architecture and learned how to create and host WCF services in the previous chapters. In this chapter, you will learn how to manage and monitor a WCF service. This chapter will do the following:

- It will illustrate the WCF management tools available to developers so they can be more productive. It will also cover new features available in .NET 4.0, including ETW tracing and new performance counters.

- It will discuss the value of building custom code, implementing logging and tracing, using performance counters, and using WMI (Windows Management Instrumentation) objects.

- It will illustrate the value of message logging, tracing, WMI, and performance monitors for system administrators in monitoring their IT systems and maintaining them efficiently.

- It will explain the custom performance monitors that business users can work with to cater to different business activities.

- It will explain the custom performance counters and WMI tools available to senior management for monitoring their ROI.

We'll first cover the business drivers for managing and monitoring WCF services.

Exploring the Business Drivers

You need to justify the business value of any IT investment before stakeholders approve the costs to implement it. Stakeholders expect several important features from any new IT investment. The typical questions they will ask are as follows:

- How do I track the new technology's performance? The business may need to produce statistics for ROI figures or be aware of saleability issues. It may need to know whether the new solution will process 100,000 requests a day. Can you track and log these 100,000 requests and data-mine to derive valuable business information?

- Can the system administrators monitor the activity? Most important, does the system have the capability of letting the system administrators know when the system fails? Is it an expensive exercise to manage these activities? How much extra effort is involved in building a separate IT system to monitor the new application?

- How extensible is the technology? Do you need a complete code rewrite to modify simple business logic? Or is it a simple task through a configuration setting? What happens when the upgrades become available? Will the new technology be backward compatible?

The WCF service management tools address all these business drivers. WCF provides the user interface to the back-office system when it comes to the traceability of business activities. This can take place in many ways. You can utilize configuration files to create the plumbing for services and clients. WCF also makes deploying the services and clients easy. When the application is operational, you can use runtime tools to monitor its activity. You can use specific WCF performance counters (and custom-built ones) to track server activities. You can also use WMI to monitor the applications.

What happens if your service fails? Is there a way to trace the origin of the failure? You can utilize message logging and tracing to evaluate how each message is processed using WCF tools. These tools are also helpful when the system administrator tries to pinpoint a failure of the system. WCF also utilizes the event log to record errors and warnings for easier diagnosis of issues by a system administrator. The same tools can also assist developers in validating and debugging their code. The WCF tools provide a complete record of the service's activities(including those occurring on UI screens and back-office systems). These tools and defined processes will assist an organization's senior management in addressing the proper governance and accountability for IT systems in their organizations.

You will learn how to utilize these tools throughout this chapter. Specifically, you will begin your journey by implementing a custom monitoring system built using an "interfaces" approach. You will learn how to manage WCF services by writing custom code similar to any other .NET application. You will look at the current code required to manage an application in this manner, and contrast this with how the WCF tools can reduce overhead. You will appreciate the flexibility and power of the tools, which can produce extensive tracing information quickly and easily. In addition, you will investigate configuration files, tracing and message-logging activities, performance counters, and WMI objects in this chapter. However, this chapter does not cover the Windows event log implementations.

Building Custom Code to Monitor Activity

The most common implementation option among developers is to develop their own custom code for monitoring. Developers can utilize interfaces in C# or Visual Basic .NET to build monitoring classes to audit, trace, and manage their services. This was common with ASMX and other previous technologies because of the lack of tools available out of the box from the Windows platform. This method also delivers the flexibility to concentrate on the features the developer prefers to monitor. In this section, you'll investigate how you can utilize custom code building to implement some monitoring functionality in the QuickReturns Ltd. example. Specifically, you will create an ITradeMonitor interface that will act as a framework monitor to the ExchangeService service requests.

■ **Note** We are using Chapter 4's Example04 to build these monitoring examples, and we are self-hosting the service. This is different from Chapter 4's implementation of the service being hosted as an IIS service. The design change is simply to facilitate the ease of creating sample code. The self-host concepts will facilitate IIS hosting without any major modifications (i.e., you need to make some trivial changes, such as creating a web.config file as opposed to an App.config file). We are using Visual Studio 2010 as the IDE for these examples.

Here are the steps for implementing the code:

1. Open the Visual Studio 2010 IDE (Start ➤ Programs ➤ Microsoft Visual Studio 2010 ➤ Microsoft Visual Studio 2010).

2. Create a blank solution in Visual Studio 2010 (File ➤ New ➤ Project).

3. You will see the New Project dialog box. Select Other Project Types, then select Visual Studio Solutions, and finally choose Blank Solution. Name this solution WCFManagement, and point to your preferred directory (in this case we have chosen C:\PracticalWCF\chapter06), as shown in Figure 6–1.

Figure 6–1. *Creating a blank solution file*

4. Add the ExchangeService project from Chapter 4's Example04 folder. Now you need to make some changes to the code. Specifically, add a new C# file to the project by right-clicking ExchangeService and selecting Add ➤ New Item. When the Add New Item dialog box appears, name it ITradeMonitor.cs, as shown in Figure 6–2.

Figure 6–2. Adding the ITradeMonitor class to ExchangeService

Listing 6–1 illustrates the code in this class.

Listing 6–1. ITradeService.cs

```
Using System;
using System.Collections.Generic;
using System.ServiceModel;
using System.Text;

namespace ExchangeService
{
    [ServiceContract]
    public interface ITradeMonitor
    {
        [OperationContract]
        string StartMonitoring(string ticker);
        [OperationContract]
        string StopMonitoring(string ticker);
    }
}
```

The ITradeMonitor interface is simple. You are implementing two methods: StartMonitoring and StopMonitoring. What is the objective of this interface? You are forcing the classes that implement this interface to address monitoring activities that occur before and after implementing the business logic. Therefore, alter TradeService.cs to implement this interface, as shown in Listing 6–2.

■ **Note** We are showing how to use custom-built interfaces as monitoring utilities in order to illustrate WCF managing and monitoring concepts. We aren't implementing best practices or optimizations for running in a production environment. Instead, this exercise is intended to illustrate the pain developers will encounter when implementing management logic. Then we will walk through the WCF tools available that can deliver more efficient and productive outcomes with a simple configuration file switch.

Listing 6–2. Altering the TradeService.cs Code

```
using System;
using System.ServiceModel;

namespace ExchangeService
{
    [ServiceContract(
        Namespace = "http://PracticalWcf/Exchange/TradeService",
        Name = "TradeService")
    ]
    public interface ITradeService
    {
        [OperationContract]
        double TradeSecurity(string ticker, int quantity);
    }
    public class TradeService : ITradeService, ITradeMonitor
    {
        // Same code as Example 4, Chapter 4

        public string StartMonitoring(string ticker)
        {
            lock (this)
            {
                // Start the monitoring process here. In other words, you can
                // configure this function to start a manual log file
                // or send information to the event log. For this example, we are
                // returning a string to indicate the monitoring has commenced.
                return "Monitoring has started for " + ticker;
            }
        }
        public string StopMonitoring(string ticker)
        {
            lock (this)
            {
                // End the monitoring process here
```

```
            return "Monitoring has finished for " +ticker;
        }
    }
}// End of TradeService class
}// End of Namespace
```

This code implements the ITradeMonitor interface in TradeService.cs and will display a message and the ticker name as the functionality of these methods. Traditionally, developers utilized this mechanism to create log files, implement auditing, and enable trace information. The WCF service is operational now, so let's try to host it (refer to Chapter 5 for detailed descriptions of various hosting options in WCF).

As mentioned, we will show how to utilize the self-hosting option for this example. First, create a new console project (select File ➤ Add ➤ New Project ➤ Console Application) called TradeServiceHost, and add it to the WCFManagement solution. Rename the program.cs file host.cs. You will need to add a reference to the ExchangeService project and a reference to the System.ServiceModel namespace. Listing 6–3 illustrates the code for host.cs.

Listing 6–3. Self-Hosting Code

```
using System;
using System.Collections.Generic;
using System.ServiceModel;
using System.Text;

namespace ExchangeService
{
    public class Program
    {
        public static void Main(string[] args)
        {
            using (ServiceHost host = new ServiceHost(typeof(
                TradeService),
                new Uri[] { new Uri("http://localhost:8000/") }))
            {
                host.Open();
                Console.WriteLine("The WCF Management trading
                    service is available.");
                Console.ReadKey();
            }
        }
    }
}
```

This code creates a WCF self-hosted service on port 8000 on the localhost machine. It displays a message indicating that the service is functioning after you start the host with the host.Open method. You also need to add the endpoints for ITradeService and ITradeMonitor. Both these endpoints will use wsHttpBinding as the preferred binding mechanism.

Next, you need to detail this information in the App.config file. You can add App.config by right-clicking the solution and choosing Add New Item. Listing 6–4 shows the code for App.config.

Listing 6–4. Configuration File for host.cs

```
<?xml version="1.0" encoding="utf-8" ?>
<configuration>
  <system.serviceModel>
```

```
      <services>
       <service name="ExchangeService.TradeService"
              >
         <endpoint address="http://localhost:8000/TradeService"
              binding="basicHttpBinding"
           contract="ExchangeService.ITradeService" />
         <endpoint address=http://localhost:8000/TradeMonitor
            binding="wsHttpBinding"
            contract="ExchangeService.ITradeMonitor" />
       </service>
      </services>
      <behaviors>
       <serviceBehaviors>
        <behavior name="">
          <serviceMetadata httpGetEnabled="true"/>
          <serviceDebug httpHelpPageEnabled="true"
             includeExceptionDetailInFaults="true"/>
        </behavior>
       </serviceBehaviors>
      </behaviors>
     </system.serviceModel>
</configuration>
```

Now you'll concentrate on the client that consumes these services. You will reuse the WCFSimpleClient project from Example04 from Chapter 4. You will alter the code to implement the ITradeMonitor interface and utilize the StartMonitoring and EndMonitoring code. You need to right-click the solution file and select the Add Project option to achieve this. You also need to add references to System.SystemModel and System.Runtime.Serialization. Listing 6–5 shows the client code.

Listing 6–5. Client Code for the Trade Service

```
ITradeService proxy = new System.ServiceModel.ChannelFactory
    <ITradeService>("TradeServiceConfiguration").CreateChannel();
ITradeMonitor monitor = new System.ServiceModel.ChannelFactory
    <ITradeMonitor>("TradeMonitorConfiguration").CreateChannel();
Console.WriteLine( "\nTrade IBM" );
    Console.WriteLine(monitor.StartMonitoring("IBM"));
double result = proxy.TradeSecurity( "IBM", 1000 );
Console.WriteLine( "Cost was " + result );
    Console.WriteLine(monitor.StopMonitoring("IBM"));
```

Finally, you need to add the configuration code for the client, as shown in Listing 6–6.

Listing 6–6. Client Configuration Settings for the Trade Service

```
<?xml version="1.0" encoding="utf-8"?>
<configuration>
  <system.serviceModel>
    <client>
      <endpoint name="TradeServiceConfiguration"
            address="http://localhost:8000/TradeService"
           binding="wsHttpBinding"
          contract="ExchangeService.ITradeService"/>
      <endpoint name="TradeMonitorConfiguration"
            address="http://localhost:8000/TradeMonitor"
```

```
        binding="wsHttpBinding"
          contract="ExchangeService.ITradeMonitor"/>
    </client>
  </system.serviceModel>
</configuration>
```

Now you are ready to test your new monitoring code, so right-click the solution file and select Build All. Start the service, browse to the Bin\debug directory of the TradeServiceHost project, and double-click TradeServiceHost.exe. You should see the screen shown in Figure 6–3.

Figure 6–3. TradeServiceHost running

Let's execute the client now. Browse to the Bin\debug directory of the WCFSimpleClient project, and execute WCFSimpleClient.exe. You should see the screen shown in Figure 6–4.

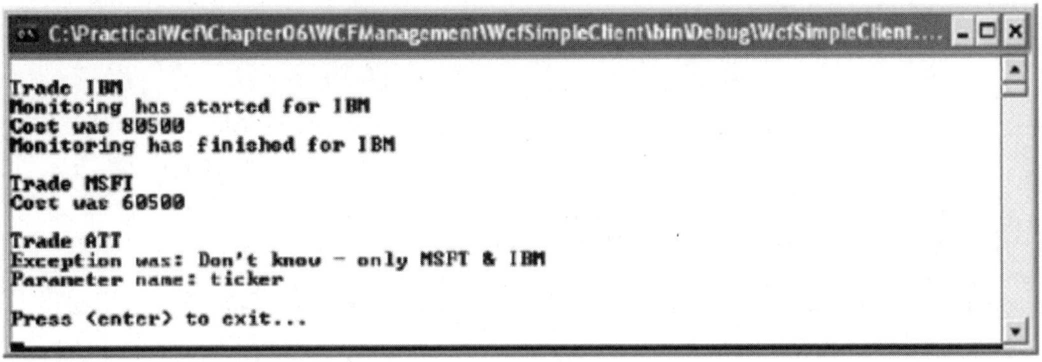

Figure 6–4. TradeServiceClient running

As you can probably gather, creating custom code to manage a web service is a tedious task, and you must consider the developer effort that goes into creating these modules. You would be better served to use this time and effort to solve more business problems (as opposed to building a custom framework that manages services). You probably are saying, "There must be a better way to perform these monitoring activities. What does WCF offer?"

One of the most appealing features about WCF is its management functionality. WCF provides the greatest breadth and depth of all Microsoft's service offerings when it comes to service management. In this regard, WCF can assist you with the following:

- Using configuration files
- Using tracing functionality
- Using message logging

- Using performance monitors (both built-in WCF counters and custom-made counters)

- Implementing WMI

Using Configuration Files

You have already been exposed to the concept of using a configuration file in an application. Configuration files usually take the form of `App.config` or `web.config` files for WCF services. These are great tools for altering the behavior of programs without changing code. These runtime tools are extensively used in WCF. You can manage settings for WCF bindings, behaviors, services, and diagnostics without manually modifying the configuration files in a text editor. As discussed in Chapter 4 as well, the executable used for altering the behavior of the program without changing code is `SvcConfigEditor.exe`. You can find it in the `<Drive Name>:\Program Files\Microsoft SDKs\Windows\v7.0A\Bin` directory. The main features of this tool are as follows:

- You can create new configuration files for services and clients using a wizard approach. This process will guide you to choose binding, behavior, contract, and diagnostic settings.

- You can validate an existing configuration file against the standard `System.Configuration` schema.

- You can modify and manage configuration settings for services, executables, COM+ services, and web-hosted services.

You'll now investigate how you can use `SvcConfigEditor.exe` to improve the QuickReturns Ltd. example.

Configuration Editor: SvcConfigEditor.exe

Open the `App.config` file of the `WCFSimpleClient` project (refer to Listing 6–6). You will use `SvcConfigEditor.exe` to modify the content and add a new binding to the client. Here are the steps:

1. Navigate to `<Drive Name>:\Program Files\Microsoft SDKs\Windows\v7.0A\Bin`, and open `SvcConfigEditor.exe`. You can also refer to the help file in the same directory.

2. Select File ➤ Open ➤ Config File, navigate to the directory of the `App.config` file for the `WCFSimpleClient` application, and open the file.

You can view and modify every element of the configuration file using this graphical user interface. You can simply select the element you want to modify and type in the new value. For this example, let's change the `wsHttpBinding` setting of the client to `basicHttpBinding`. To do this, select the `Binding` element and change the value to `basicHttpBinding` for the `TradeService` endpoint. Save the settings using File ➤ Save. You also need to change the binding settings for the `TradeServiceHost` `App.config` file for the same endpoint information, and change `wsHttpBinding` to `basicHttpBinding`. Otherwise, an error will occur because of a binding mismatch. Now open the new configuration file, and view the changes in Visual Studio 2010. You can see the changes in Listing 6–7 performed by `SvcConfigEditor.exe` and compare them to Listing 6–6.

Listing 6–7. WCTSimpleClient App.config File After the Service Configuration Editor Change

```
<?xml version="1.0" encoding="utf-8"?>
<configuration>
  <system.serviceModel>
    <client>
      <endpoint address=http://localhost:8000/TradeService
            binding="wsHttpBinding"
            bindingConfiguration=""
            contract="ExchangeService.ITradeService"
            name="TradeServiceConfiguration" />
      <endpoint address=http://localhost:8000/TradeMonitor
            binding="wsHttpBinding"
            contract="ExchangeService.ITradeMonitor"
            name="TradeMonitorConfiguration" />
    </client>
  </system.serviceModel>
</configuration>
```

The configuration file changes are quite trivial with WCF services (refer to Chapter 3 for more details). You will also utilize SvcConfigEditor.exe in the rest of the chapter to apply numerous configuration file changes to implement message logging, tracing, performance counters, and WMI providers. Now you'll concentrate on adding tracing and message-logging capabilities to a WCF service.

Using Tracing and Message-Logging Capabilities

Implementing tracing and implementing message-logging capabilities are similar tasks in WCF. Therefore, we will cover them together. We'll first clarify what circumstances dictate message logging and then cover where you use tracing.

Message Logging

You can use message logging to monitor the activity of incoming and outgoing messages from a service. This will enable you to view and evaluate the message content that is received by the services. This is valuable in tracking malformed messages for system administrators and developers. The business users will also be interested in the content that describes the user's input requests that are derived through the message log. Several options are available for message logging in WCF.

Message logging occurs at two levels: the service level and the transport level. At the service level, messages get logged as soon as they enter or leave the application's code. At the transport level, messages are logged when the WCF runtime calls the transport mechanism to transfer the messages. WCF provides the option to log malformed messages as well. Malformed messages are those messages that are rejected by the WCF runtime during processing. WCF messaging offers three switches to manage these activities. They are logMessagesAtServiceLevel, logMalformedMessages, and logMessagesAtTransportLevel, and they are set in the messageLogging element. These three categories are independent of each other. You can activate each of them in configuration files independent of each other; you can also utilize *filters* to set the boundaries for capturing messages.

At the service level, all messages are logged even if filters are defined. If they are defined, only the messages that agree with the filters are logged. This happens before the WCF runtime is called. The transport layer messages are ready to be encoded after reaching the WCF runtime. If the filters are defined, the WCF runtime will log only those messages that correspond to the filter. Otherwise, it will record all messages. You'll now learn how to activate message logging and define filters.

■ **Caution** You need to be careful with assigning read access to message logging and tracing. Typically, only system administrators should have the privileges to activate or deactivate these processes. Giving others these privileges could cause a security breach in your solution architecture.

Enabling Message Logging

WCF does not log messages by default. To activate message logging, you need to perform two steps. First, you must add a listener to the System.ServiceModel.MessageLogging source. It is important to define the listener. If no listener is defined, no logging output is generated. Then you must set attributes for the messagelogging element in the configuration file.

The following are the steps for using SvcConfigEditor.exe to enable message logging.

■ **Note** We are using the TradeServiceHost project's App.config file to demonstrate message logging and tracing. It is important to note that production services should not be targeted to rigorous tracing and message logging. This will affect the productivity of the service, which primarily should facilitate the business processes, not tracing and message logging.

1. Open SvcConfigEditor.exe.

2. Open the TradeServiceHost project's App.config file (File ➤ Open).

3. Navigate to the Diagnostics window, and click the Enable Message Logging link. This action will add a ServiceModelMessageLoggingListener class to the project to enable message logging. You can also configure the extent of the logging (where the log is stored on disk). Your screen should look like Figure 6–5.

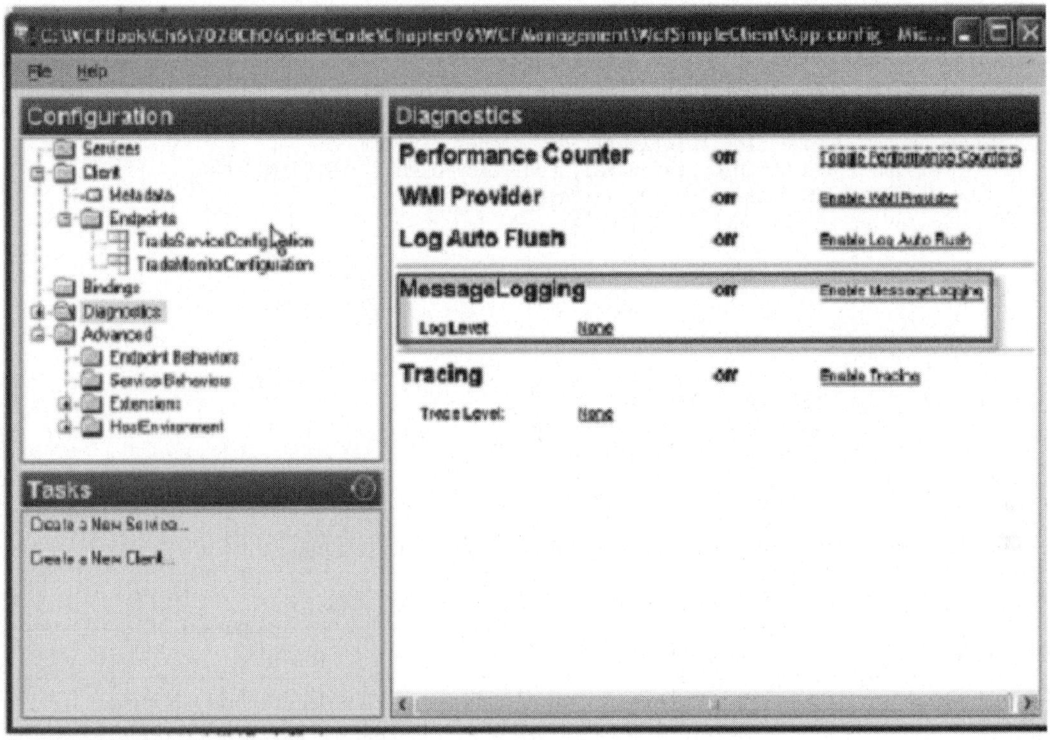

Figure 6–5. Enabling message logging

4. Save the file in the Service Configuration Editor. Build the solution, and run the server and the client. You should view the message log file in the specified location. You can revisit the App.config file to view the changes made by enabling message logging, as shown in Listing 6–8.

Listing 6–8. Additional Code in the TradeServiceHost App.config File

```
...
  <system.diagnostics>
    <sources>
      <source name="System.ServiceModel.MessageLogging"
            switchValue="Warning, ActivityTracing">
        <listeners>
          <add type="System.Diagnostics.DefaultTraceListener"
                      name="Default">
            <filter type="" />
          </add>
          <add name="ServiceModelMessageLoggingListener">
            <filter type="" />
          </add>
        </listeners>
      </source>
```

```
    </sources>
    <sharedListeners>
      <add initializeData="
          C:\PracticalWcf\Chapter06\WCFManagement\\WcfSimpleClient\
          App_messages.svclog"
        type="System.Diagnostics.XmlWriterTraceListener, System,
          Version=4.0.0.0, Culture=neutral, PublicKeyToken=b77a5c561934e089"
        name="ServiceModelMessageLoggingListener"
          traceOutputOptions="Timestamp">
        <filter type="" />
      </add>
    </sharedListeners>
  </system.diagnostics>
  <system.serviceModel>
    <diagnostics>
      <messageLogging logMalformedMessages="true"
              logMessagesAtServiceLevel="false"
        logMessagesAtTransportLevel="true" />
    </diagnostics>
...
```

Table 6–1 shows the list of options available during the message logging.

Table 6–1. Logging Options for Message Logging

Logging Option	Description
LogEntireMessage	If set to true, the entire message (the header and body) is logged. If set to false, only the message header is logged. By default, this option is set to false. This setting affects all message-logging levels: service, transport, and malformed messages.
LogMalformedMessages	This specifies whether malformed messages are logged or not. By default, malformed messages are logged.
LogMessagesAtServiceLevel	This specifies whether messages are logged at the service level or not. By default, messages are *not* logged at the service level. If this option is set to true, all the infrastructure messages are logged (except reliable messaging).
LogMessagesAtTransportLevel	This specifies whether messages are logged at the transport level or not. By default, messages are logged at transport level. If this option is set to true, all the infrastructure messages are logged.
maxMessagesToLog	This specifies the maximum number of message to log. All types of messages are counted. By default, this value is 10,000. Once the limit specified is reached, tracing is used to inform the user, and no additional messages are logged.
maxSizeOfMessageToLog	This specifies the maximum size of messages to log in bytes. By default, the value for the service and transport level is 262144 bytes (256 KB), and the value for malformed messages is 4 KB. Messages exceeding the limit are not logged.

You can further customize message logging by adding filters. If no filters are defined, all messages are logged. If any filters are defined, only messages that match at least one of the filters are logged. In order to add filters, you need to add the `filters` section to the `messageLogging` section of the `App.config` file. Filters support the XPath syntax and are applied in the order they appear in the configuration file. You can just include XML tags that direct the WCF runtime to log the images that correspond to this namespace, and ignore the others. Listing 6–9 details the modification to the `App.config` file.

Listing 6–9. *Adding a Filter to the Message Log*

```
<messageLogging logEntireMessage="true"
     logMalformedMessages="true" logMessagesAtServiceLevel="true"
     logMessagesAtTransportLevel="true" maxMessagesToLog="420">
     <filters>
        <add xmlns:soap="http://www.w3.org/2003/05/soap-envelope">
                        /soap:Envelope/soap:Headers
        </add>
     </filters>
</messageLogging>
```

You can also specify the node quota while defining filters, which indicates the maximum number of nodes that can be examined to match the filter. To view these message log files, you can use the `SvcTraceViewer.exe` utility (this topic is discussed later in this chapter). We'll now cover how to enable tracing.

Enabling Tracing

How does tracing differ from message logging? Tracing mechanisms act as the instrumentation for service messages and fault monitoring. Tracing is similar to the Visual Studio debugger, which helps you step through and into code. Therefore, tracing is a great tool to track the message flow of the application.

WCF tracing is based on Event Tracing for Windows (ETW) and is built on top of the `System.Diagnostics` namespace. As with messaging, trace data is emitted by the trace source identified by the name. To emit the trace data from any of these sources, you need to add *trace listeners* to the source. Trace listeners define the format in which trace data is logged. If no listeners are defined, no message will be traced.

WCF does not trace messages by default. To enable tracing in WCF, follow steps 1 through 4 in the previous section. You need to click the Enable Tracing hyperlink to enable tracing, as in Figure 6–6. This will add a `ServiceModelTraceListener` instance to the runtime. You must configure the name and location for your trace file if you have specific requirements. WCF defines the trace source for each of the assemblies. Also, the trace level for each of the listeners must have a value other than `off`. By default, the trace level is `off` and no trace is emitted. One more thing to keep in mind is that you need to start the ETW trace session before using any ETW trace listener. You can use a tool like `logman.exe` or `Tracelog.exe` to start the ETW session.

Next, build the solution, and run the server and client. The communication for initializing the host, the communication between the host and the client, and the destruction of the host instance will be recorded in this trace file. You can use `SvcTraceViewer.exe` to view the trace file content.

Using SvcTraceViewer.exe

The `SvcTraceViewer.exe` utility will enable you to view both message log files and trace files. You can find it at `<Drive Name>:\Program Files\Microsoft SDKs\Windows\v7.0A\Bin`. Open the trace file from the `TradeServiceHost` with the `WCFSimpleClient` console application. (Navigate to the correct directory, and select File ➤ Open to open the file.) You should see a screen similar to Figure 6–6.

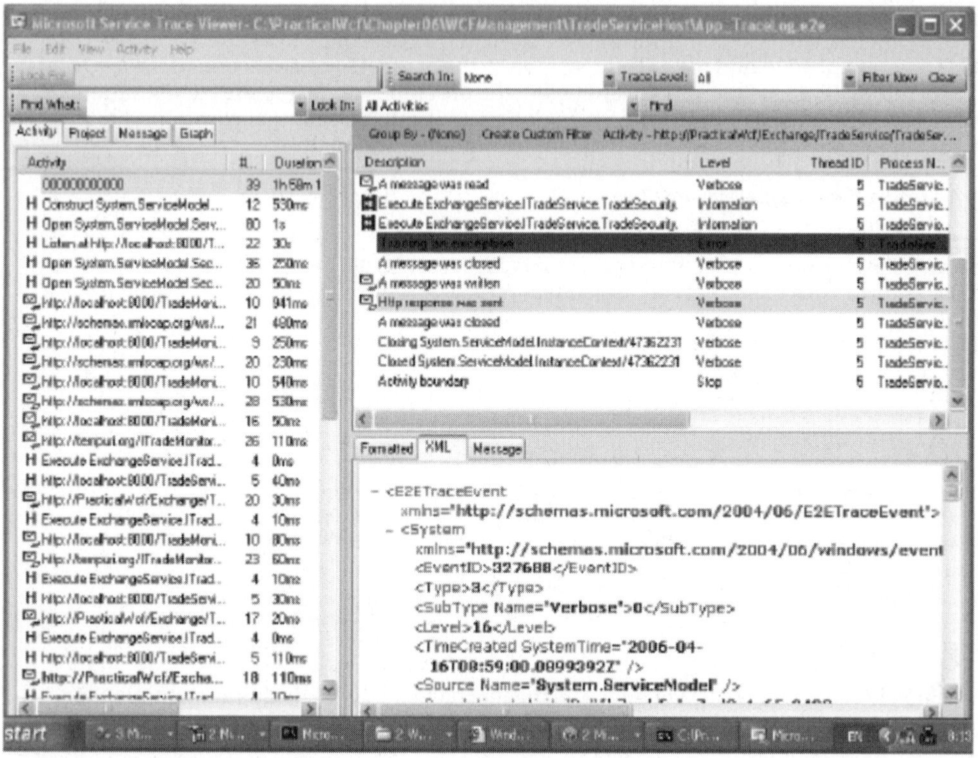

Figure 6–6. *SvcTraceViewer.exe reading the trace file*

This is a comprehensive implementation of the step-by-step process of the WCF service. It starts with the object creation at the top and records each interaction with the WCF runtime and the clients. It clearly details object activities, message sends, and all errors in the host's life cycle. You can view each of the XML messages in the bottom pane. It also records the duration of each activity. You can also get a graphical timeline representation by clicking the Graph tab. This is a comprehensive tool that adds a lot of value for developers and system administrators who are investigating tracing and message log files. Please refer to the SvcTraceViewer help file (in the same directory) for further information.

Using WCF Performance Counters

WCF implements out-of-the-box performance counters to assist developers and system administrators in monitoring WCF services. You can use these performance counters for business uses to justify the costs, risks, and ROI of software systems. WCF performance counters address four major areas: AppDomain, ServiceHost, Endpoint, and Operation. All operation counters monitor activities on "calls per second" and "call duration" items. The following are some other important WCF counters; most of them are self-explanatory:

- Calls: Total Number of Calls
- CallsOutstanding

- CallsSucceeded

- CallsErrored

- CallsDuration

These are some security-related counters:

- SecurityCallsNotAuthenticated

- SecurityCallsNotAuthorized

- SecurityCallsTampered

- SecurityImpersonationsFailed

These are some important transaction and messaging performance counters:

- TxCommitted

- TxAborted

- TxInDoubt

- RMSessionsStarted

- RMSessionsCompleted

- RMSessionsFaulted

- RMMessagesDiscarded

- RMQPoisonedMessages

- RMBufferSize

A few new performance counters have been added in .NET 4.0 as well:

- PercentOfMaxCalls

- PercentOfMaxSessions

- PercentOfMaxInstances

■ **Note** Performance counters consume a lot of memory. Therefore, make sure you allocate substantial memory when you run performance counters. It is good practice to add the `<performanceCounters fileMappingSize="1000000" />` line to the `App.config` file to increase the memory size. This will replace the default size of 524288 bytes.

Enabling Built-In WCF Performance Counters

Enabling WCF performance counters is a pretty straightforward process. The easiest way is to open the configuration file in `SvcConfigEditor.exe`. In the Diagnostics window in the Service Configuration

Editor, you just need to click the Toggle Performance Counters link and save the file to enable built-in WCF counters in your code. This will enter the following line in the App.config file:

```
<diagnostics performanceCounters="All">
```

You'll now see some performance counters in action. Specifically, you will monitor the TradeServiceHost service activity using these counters. Here are the steps:

1. Open the App.config file of TradeServiceHost using the Service Configuration Editor, and change the diagnostic element to include performance counters. You can do this by checking the Enable Performance Counter box.

2. Build the WCFManagement solution. Run TradeServiceHost and the WCFSimpleClient module as the client. This will create the instances for the performance counters to track against.

3. Open Performance Monitor by selecting Start ➤ Control Panel ➤ Administrative Tools ➤ Performance, or by entering **perfmon.exe** at the Start ➤ Run command. You should see something similar to Figure 6–7.

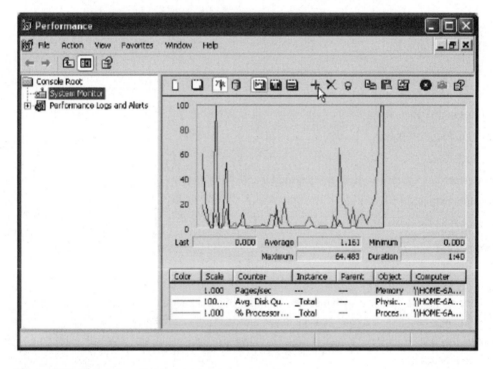

Figure 6–7. Adding a performance counter

4. Click the + button to add a performance counter.

You will see the screen shown in Figure 6–8. You can see the WCF-related counters under the Processor section (they're the ones prefixed with *ServiceModel*).

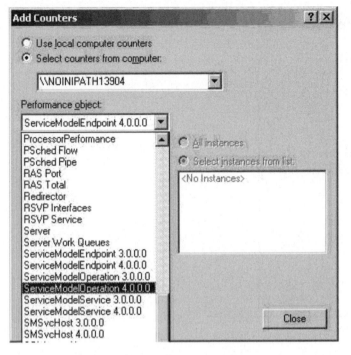

Figure 6–8. Selecting WCF performance counters

Select the ServiceModelService 4.0.0.0 family of counters. This will select all the counters that are built into the WCF ServiceModel namespace. You will see the screen shown in Figure 6–9 when you try to add one of these counters. You can pick any counter (e.g., Calls Total, Calls Faulted, etc.) from the list. This will instruct you to choose the WCF instances on the right side of the Add Counters dialog box. Since you are currently monitoring the TradeServiceHost service, you can pick the TradeService HTTP instance (since you are using the HTTP binding variation) to monitor, and click Add to include it in the graph.

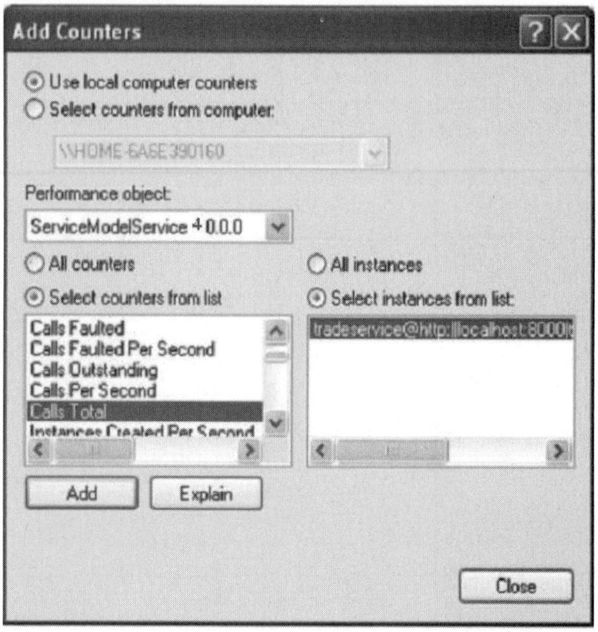

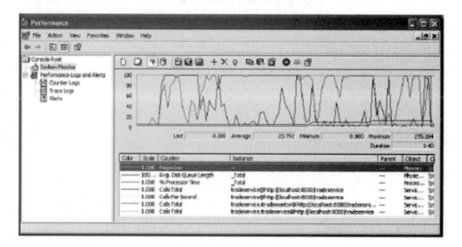

Figure 6–9. Picking performance counters for the TradeServiceHost instance

Figure 6–10 shows the Calls Total counters for both the `TradeService` and `TradeMonitor` services in the `WCFManagement` solution. These are built-in performance counters provided by Microsoft. However, you can build custom counters to address specific business needs.

Figure 6–10. Performance counters for TradeService and TradeMonitor

Creating Custom Performance Counters

You can also create custom counters for WCF. This also assists business users in monitoring business information by leveraging the Performance Monitor utility. This utility is appealing to the senior management of an organization because it gives them a set of tools to measure the success or failure of their IT systems.

QuickReturns Ltd. is a stock-brokering house that will have many stockbrokers dealing in multiple securities. How will management track the total value of the stockbrokers' daily trades? Let's say this firm has a particular interest in Microsoft stock. It thinks that Microsoft stock is a good buy and wants to keep an eye on the fluctuation of the price. How do you accommodate this scenario? Will you be able to utilize performance counters to address these business needs?

You will be addressing these business needs by implementing performance counters in WCF, which isn't too tedious a task. You will create a new console application called TradingServicePerfMonHost and use this project to create the performance counters. However, you will not create any new clients for this service. You will utilize the self-hosting method and invoke the service calls from the main function. This is the same as having multiple clients trying to send requests to the host. The following are the steps:

1. First, add a class to the ExchangeService project. You could have modified the TradeService.cs class, but it is cleaner to add a new class and implement the code (and we want to leave TradeService.cs for you to experiment with—feel free to modify the code available on the Apress web site [www.apress.com]).

2. Right-click the ExchangeService project, and select Add ➤ New Item. Call this class TradePerfMon.cs. You need to add references to System.ServiceModel, System.Diagnostics, and System.Runtime.InteropServices. Listing 6–10 shows the code for the new class.

Listing 6–10. TradePerfMon.cs

```
using System;
using System.Collections.Generic;
using System.Diagnostics;
using System.Management;
using System.Management.Instrumentation;
using System.Runtime.InteropServices;
using System.ServiceModel;
using System.ServiceModel.Description;
using System.Text;
using System.Threading;

namespace ExchangeService
{
    [ServiceContract(
        Namespace = "http://PracticalWcf/Exchange/TradeService",
        Name = "TradeService")
    ]

    public interface ITradePerfMonService
    {
        [OperationContract]
        double TradeSecurity(string ticker, int quantity);
    }
    [ServiceBehavior(InstanceContextMode = InstanceContextMode.Single)]
    public class TradePerfMon : ITradePerfMonService
```

```
    {
        private double totalValue = 0;
        private double microsoftVolume = 0;
        private const string CounterCategoryName =
            "Trade Service PerfMon";
        private const string TotalCounterName = "Trade Total Value";
        private const string MicrosoftCounterName =
            "Microsoft Trade Volume";

        private PerformanceCounterCategory counterCategory = null;
        private PerformanceCounter totalCounter = null;
        private PerformanceCounter microsoftCounter = null;
        const double IBM_Price = 80.50D;
        const double MSFT_Price = 30.25D;

        public TradePerfMon()
        {
            if (PerformanceCounterCategory.Exists(CounterCategoryName))
            {
            PerformanceCounterCategory.Delete(CounterCategoryName);
            }

CounterCreationData totalCounter = new CounterCreationData
    (TotalCounterName, "Total Dollar value of Trade Service
    transactions.",PerformanceCounterType.NumberOfItemsHEX32);
 CounterCreationData microsoftCounter = new
    CounterCreationData(MicrosoftCounterName, "Total Microsoft
    securities being traded", PerformanceCounterType.NumberOfItemsHEX32);
CounterCreationDataCollection counterCollection = new
    CounterCreationDataCollection(new CounterCreationData[]
    { totalCounter, microsoftCounter });
 this.counterCategory = PerformanceCounterCategory.Create(
    CounterCategoryName,"Trade Service PerfMon Counters",
    PerformanceCounterCategoryType.MultiInstance,counterCollection);
 totalValue = 0;
 microsoftVolume = 0;
        }
    }
}
```

In this code, you first initialize the variables to implement the Total Value counter and the Microsoft Volume counter. Then you create the foundations for the performance counters in the TradePerfMon constructor. You will first check whether the performance counter category (that is, Trade Service PerfMon) is available. If so, delete it because you will create it again. Then you create the Total Value counter and the Microsoft Volume counter and add them to the performance counter collection.

The next step is to initialize the counters. The following code illustrates this concept:

```
public void InitializeCounters(
    System.ServiceModel.Description.ServiceEndpointCollection endpoints)
{
    List<string> names = new List<string>();
    foreach (ServiceEndpoint endpoint in endpoints)
    {
        names.Add(string.Format("{0}@{1}",
```

```
                this.GetType().Name, endpoint.Address.ToString()));
    }

    while (true)
    {
        try
        {
            foreach (string name in names)
            {
                string condition = string.Format("SELECT * FROM
                    Service WHERE Name=\"{0}\"", name);
                SelectQuery query = new SelectQuery(condition);
                ManagementScope managementScope = new
                    ManagementScope(@"\\.\root\ServiceModel",
                    new ConnectionOptions());
                ManagementObjectSearcher searcher = new
                    ManagementObjectSearcher(managementScope, query);
                ManagementObjectCollection instances = searcher.Get();
                foreach (ManagementBaseObject instance in instances)
                {
                    PropertyData data = instance.Properties["
                        CounterInstanceName"];

                    this.totalCounter = new PerformanceCounter(
                        CounterCategoryName, TotalCounterName,
                        data.Value.ToString());
                    this.totalCounter.ReadOnly = false;
                    this.totalCounter.RawValue = 0;
                    this.microsoftCounter = new PerformanceCounter(
                        CounterCategoryName, MicrosoftCounterName,
                        data.Value.ToString());
                    this.microsoftCounter.ReadOnly = false;
                    this.microsoftCounter.RawValue = 0;

                    break;
                }
            }
            break;
        }
        catch(COMException)
        {

        }

    }
    Console.WriteLine("Counters initialized.");
}
```

In this code, you use a WMI Query Language (WQL) query to select the counters that are available to the runtime. Therefore, the query at runtime for totalCounters will be SELECT * FROM Service WHERE Name= "tradeperfmon@http://localhost:8000/tradeperfmonservice. This query is executed in the scope of the root\ServiceModel namespace to retrieve data about the TradePerMon service from WMI. From the data that is retrieved, the code extracts the value of the CounterInstanceName property. That property value provides the name by which the current instance of the service is identified within the Windows performance counter infrastructure. Then you initialize the totalValue and microsoftCounter counters.

The next step is to code the TradeSecurity function:

```
public double TradeSecurity(string ticker, int quantity)
{
    double result = 0;
    if (quantity < 1)
        throw new ArgumentException(
            "Invalid quantity", "quantity");
    switch (ticker.ToLower())
    {
        case "ibm":
                result = quantity * IBM_Price;
                totalValue = +result;
                if (this.totalCounter != null)
                    this.totalCounter.RawValue = (int)totalValue;
                return result;
          case "msft":
                result = quantity * IBM_Price;
                totalValue = +result;
                microsoftVolume = +quantity;
                if (this.totalCounter != null)
                    this.totalCounter.RawValue = (int)totalValue;
                if (this.microsoftCounter !=null)
                    this.microsoftCounter.RawValue = (int)microsoftVolume;
                return result;
        default:
            throw new ArgumentException(
                "Don't know - only MSFT & IBM", "ticker");

    }
    }

  }
}
```

This is similar to the previous TradeSecurity function. The only difference is that you add the logic to increment the totalValue and microsoftVolume fields. Then the function is used as the source for the counters.

The next step is to create a self-hosting application to invoke the TradeSecurity function so you can record values against the custom counters.

Create a new console project called TradingServicePerfMonHost (right-click the WCFManagement solution and select Add ➤ New Project). You also need to add a reference to the System.ServiceModel namespace. Put the code in Listing 6–11 in the Program.cs file.

Listing 6–11. Code for Program.cs File in TradingServicePerfMonHost

```
using System;
using System.Collections.Generic;
using System.Messaging;
using System.ServiceModel;
using System.Text;

namespace ExchangeService
```

```
{
    public class Program
    {
        public static void Main(string[] args)
        {
            TradePerfMon trade = new TradePerfMon();
            using (ServiceHost host = new ServiceHost(typeof(
                TradePerfMon), new Uri[] { new Uri("
                    http://localhost:8000/TradePerfMonService") }))
            {
                host.Open();
                trade.InitializeCounters(host.Description.Endpoints);
                Console.WriteLine("The WCF Management trading
                    service is available.");
                for (int index = 1; index < 225; index++)
                {
                    Console.WriteLine("IBM - traded " + (index+100) +
                        " shares  for " + trade.TradeSecurity("IBM",
                        (index+100)) + " dollars" );
                    // you are deliberately increasing the total volume
                    of trades to view the difference in the
                    Perfomance Monitor)
                    Console.WriteLine("MSFT - tradedtrade " + index +
                        " shares for " + trade.TradeSecurity("MSFT",
                        index) + " dollars");
                    System.Threading.Thread.Sleep(1000);
                }

                Console.ReadKey();
            }
        }
    }
}
```

In this code, you first instantiate an object type of TradePerfMon. Then you create a host type of TradePerfMon and open the host. The configuration settings are read from the App.config file. Then you invoke the IntializeCounters function to initialize the counters. Then you use a loop to create a series of trades. This is done so that you can view the custom performance counters in action. Note that we have tweaked the index variable in Listing 6–11 to differentiate the counters when they become available (for cosmetic changes, to view them as separate entities from each other).

The next step is to create the App.config file for the host application, as shown in Listing 6–12. (Please ignore the wmiProviderEnabled="true" flag, which will be discussed in the next section.) This is similar to the previous host application.

Listing 6–12. App.config File for the Host Application

```
<?xml version="1.0" encoding="utf-8" ?>
<configuration>
  <system.serviceModel>
    <diagnostics wmiProviderEnabled="true"
        performanceCounters="All">
      <messageLogging logEntireMessage="true"
          logMalformedMessages="true"
        logMessagesAtServiceLevel="true"
```

```
        logMessagesAtTransportLevel="true" />
    </diagnostics>
    <services>
      <service name="ExchangeService.TradePerfMon">
        <endpoint address=http://localhost:8000/TradePerfMonService
                binding="basicHttpBinding"
          contract="ExchangeService.ITradePerfMonService" />
      </service>
    </services>
  </system.serviceModel>
</configuration>
```

Now you'll build the WCFManagement solution and make the TradeServicePerfMonHost the startup application:

1. Right-click the WCFManagement solution and select Set As Startup Project. Compile the solution and run the code. You should see a screen similar to Figure 6–11, indicating that trading takes place in a loop structure.

2. Now you are ready to capture these custom counters in Performance Monitor. Open Performance Monitor (select Start ➤ Run and enter **perfmon.exe**), and click the Add button.

Figure 6–11. TradeServicePerfMonHost application running

3. In the Add Counters dialog, choose Trade Service PerfMon from the Performance Object drop-down in order to view the collection, and also view the two counters, Trade Total Value and Microsoft Trade Volume, under the collection. You should also see the existing instances of the host application. Your screen should be similar to Figure 6–12.

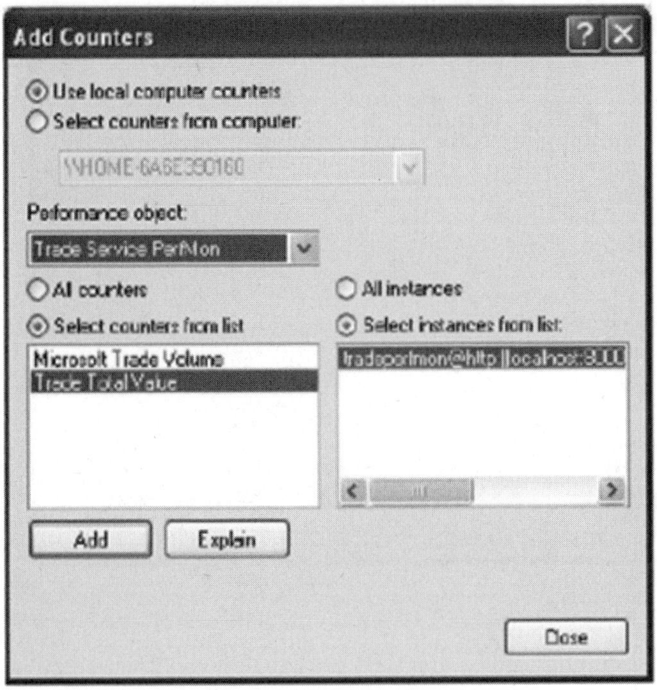

Figure 6–12. Custom TradeService counters

4. Select both of these counters, and look at how the total trade value and
    Microsoft volume are doing. This information will be valuable for business
    users to make decisions about Microsoft stock and the state of the business.
    Since you are using a loop to trade stocks, both the total value and the
    Microsoft volume are increasing steadily. Note that we are using different
    scales for the total value and the Microsoft volume, since the total value will be
    far greater than the Microsoft volume, as shown in Figure 6–13.

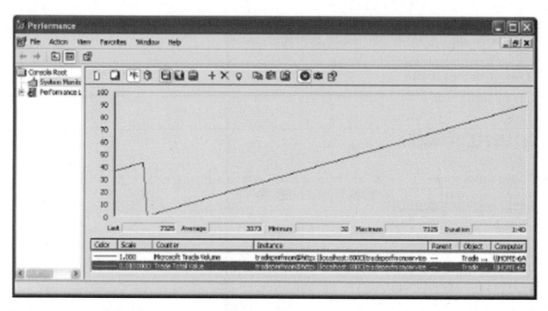

Figure 6–13. Custom performance counters in action

This is how you utilize Performance Monitor to manage your WCF service. Now you'll learn how you can use WMI to facilitate WCF management.

Using WMI

WMI is an add-in component to the Windows operating system that enables monitoring on a variety of object models. WMI was created as a web-based enterprise management (WBEM) tool that you can use to monitor and maintain complex enterprise applications over web browsers. You can invoke WMI from many technologies, such as C++, Visual Basic, C# (and any managed code implementation, such as J# or Visual Basic .NET), ODBC, and so on. It integrates seamlessly with the WCF programming model for monitoring and managing WCF services also.

You can enable WMI with the flip of a switch in WCF. WCF services provide information to WMI at runtime. Therefore, you can use existing WMI tools to monitor and manipulate these services. You can use the WMI programming interfaces to construct custom network and business operation consoles for your WCF applications. It is easy to enable WMI monitoring in WCF services. All you have to do is include the following line in the configuration file:

```
<diagnostics wmiProviderEnabled="true">
```

This enables all the WMI objects for WCF. To view this information, you need to install WMI CIM Studio. This is a free download available from Microsoft (http://www.microsoft.com/downloads/en/details.aspx?FamilyID=6430f853-1120-48db-8cc5-f2abdc3ed314&displaylang=en). It is an ActiveX component that plugs into Internet Explorer. Here are the steps to utilize WMI for WCF services:

1. Run TradeServicePerfMonHost.exe (since you need a live instance to monitor).

2. Open WMI CIM Studio (Start ➤ Programs ➤ WMI Tools ➤ WMI CIM Studio).

3. You will be asked to enter the starting point for the namespace in which you are interested. Enter **root\ServiceModel**. Your screen should be similar to Figure 6–14.

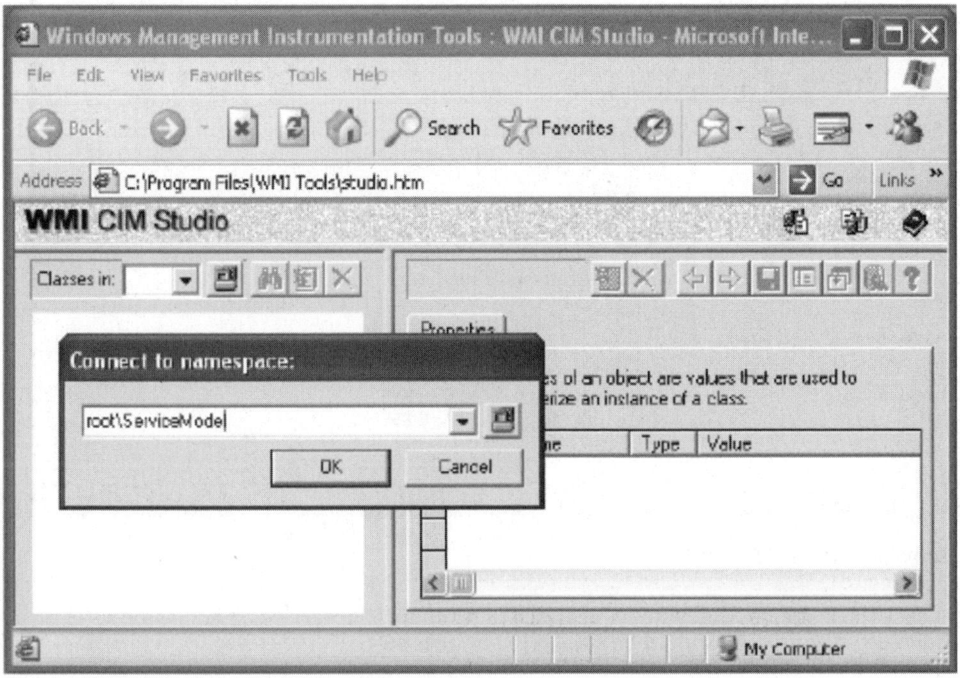

Figure 6–14. *Opening WMI CIM Studio with the correct namespace*

You will be asked to select your user details, and you will then be presented with a comprehensive view of every WMI interface that deals with WCF. You can monitor bindings, services, behaviors, contracts, and so on from this interface. As such, you can monitor the TradeService instance with this interface as well. You can get a list of all running services by clicking the instance icon, as shown in Figure 6–15.

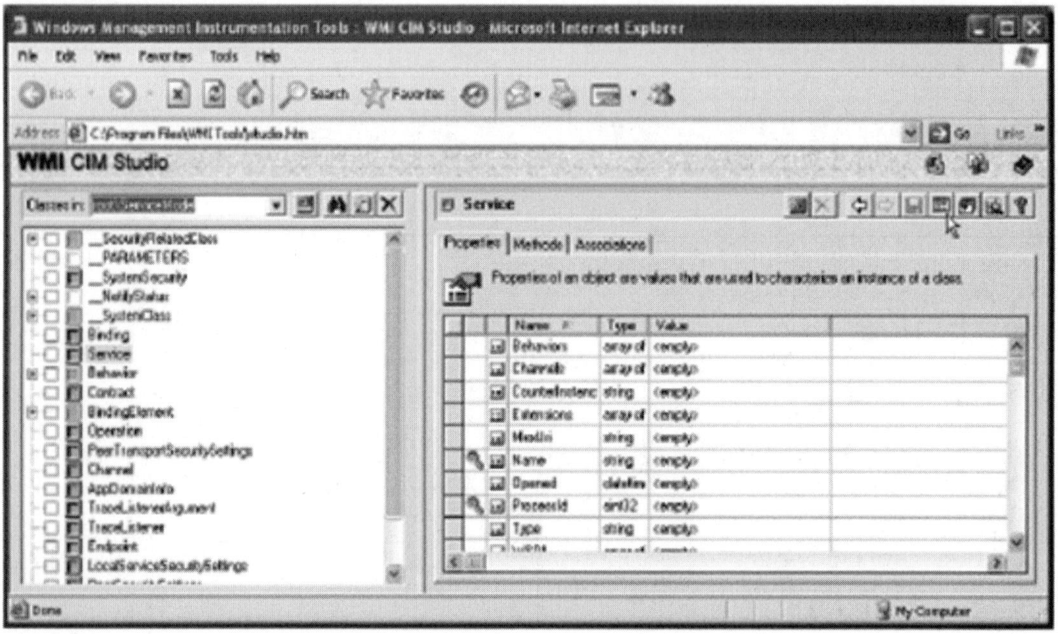

Figure 6–15. Services in WMI CIM Studio

When you click the instance icon, you will see a list of running WCF services. Choose the TradeService instance. Your screen should be similar to Figure 6–16.

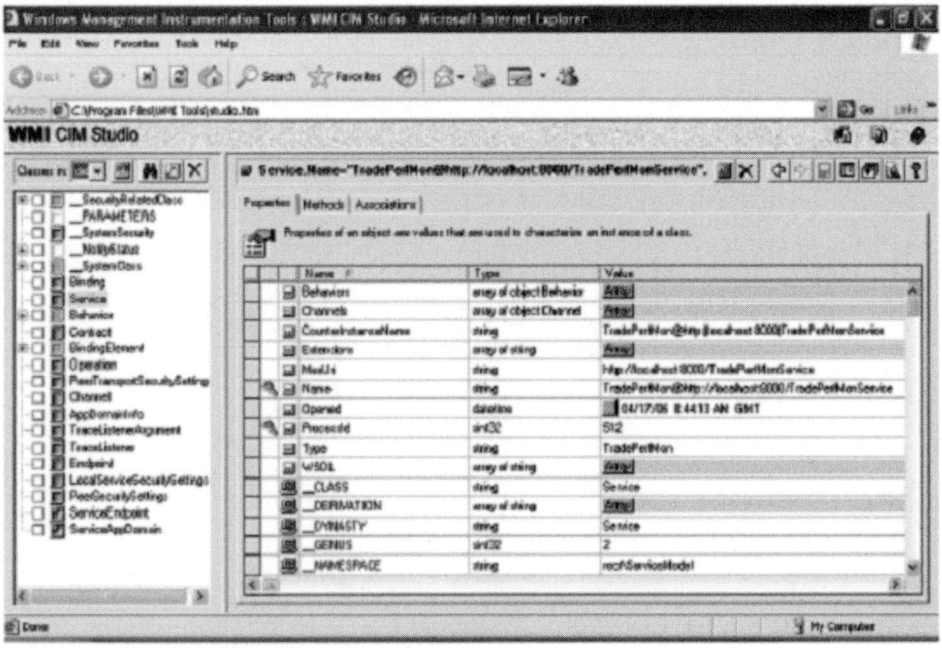

Figure 6–16. *Currently running TradeService instances*

You can navigate to each WMI element and query the WCF service in great detail. This is a great monitoring tool for system administrators and developers.

Summary

You have learned a lot about WCF management and monitoring in this chapter, including the following:

- Developers can use custom-built interfaces to monitor the service activity.

- Developers and system administrators can utilize message logging and tracing in WCF to track and debug WCF services. They can use SvcTraceViewer.exe to view message logs and trace data.

- Developers and system administrators can use the SvcConfigEditor.exe tool to modify configuration files.

- Business users, system administrators, and developers can use out-of-the-box performance counters to monitor service activity, and they can also build custom performance counters to facilitate business needs.

- Developers and system administrators can use WMI CIM Studio to monitor WMI activity on WCF services.

Now that you are familiar with how to manage and monitor web services, the next chapter will shed some light on WCF security, one of the most intriguing and important topics in WCF.

■ ■ ■

Advanced Topics in WCF

You have investigated the basics of creating services, evaluated the out-of-the-box hosting options, and learned how to consume the services using clients. You have also learned about the management tools available in WCF to efficiently manage these WCF services. These features will assist you in creating simple WCF applications. However, real-world SOA applications will have many other demanding features to implement.

These complex real-world web service implementations will address security issues (both client and service), reliable messaging, transactions, COM+ integration, data integration issues, and peer-to-peer communications. An enterprise can achieve its value propositions by utilizing these advanced features of WCF. In this part of the book, you will concentrate on these topics. In addition, in Chapter 13 you'll investigate the WCF interoperability options available for seamlessly communicating with non-Microsoft platforms.

CHAPTER 7

■ ■ ■

Implementing WCF Security

Security is one of the fundamental features of any software platform. In fact, security requirements have grown exponentially in the past decade because of the increasing popularity of public networks. Securing a distributed enterprise (one that is physically scattered around the world) using a public network such as the Internet is a challenging task. Malicious hackers, identity fraudsters, and disgruntled employees cost organizations millions of dollars every year. What does WCF offer in the security space to combat these issues?

You can secure your enterprise in many ways. Initially, you need to secure an organization at the physical level. You need to ensure your server farms are behind locked doors and are carefully monitored for access. You should restrict access to resources as much as possible. One emerging option is to outsource server farms to reputable third parties, which set up stringent measures to limit physical access to the farms. These outsourced hardware facilities have strict access controls to prevent any unauthorized access to the servers. They are in most cases built underground and without any windows or external access points. When you are comfortable with the level of security of your hardware devices, you can turn your attention to software practices.

You can address security requirements for applications in many aspects of software development. Some of these aspects are the platform, the data, the hosts, and the communications between clients and services. In this chapter, we will discuss only platform-level security. Our main focus will be to show the mechanisms available to protect your messages between services and clients.

WCF is a distributed application platform based on SOAP. Basically, WCF addresses the communication between multiple nodes and multiple applications, and you utilize SOAP to achieve the communication in WCF. Bindings in WCF (e.g., HTTP, TCP, MSMQ, etc.) provide you with different options to optimize SOAP messages depending on your business requirements. In this chapter, we will address messages traveling from one node to another through intermediaries (with firewalls) and messages traveling on public networks (the Internet). These scenarios introduce many security threats. We will discuss these threats in the next section. In a nutshell, this chapter discusses the following items to illustrate the WCF security concepts:

- Why you need to be concerned about security in SOAP messages

- The WCF security features that address the following issues:

    - Credentials and claims

    - Transport-level security

    - Message-level security

    - Mixed-mode (transport-level and message-level) security

    - The federated security model in WCF

- Authorization

- Auditing
- Windows CardSpace (formerly known as InfoCard)

You'll start your journey by learning why you need to address WCF security, and about the business drivers behind addressing security on the latest Microsoft platform offerings. The next section will also discuss the value that WCF adds to solve the security concerns of CTOs and CIOs.

Business Drivers

WCF is based on the communication mechanism between clients and services using messages. These messages are vulnerable on numerous fronts. An authorized party must create the client message to conform to a standard that the service can comprehend. In most cases, the messages need to be encrypted and signed to verify the authenticity of the sending party. The communication line between the client and the service needs to be secure. The receiver should also be able to decrypt the messages and verify the integrity of the sender. Therefore, security plays a major part in any enterprise architecture solution.

Here are some other examples of business drivers:

- You need to audit and track the communication between clients and services to prevent malicious acts. In the QuickReturns Ltd. example, an intruder can intercept the messages between the clients and the service. If the intruder can use the valid client details to initiate trades on the market and withdraw funds from the client's account, this can have disastrous implications for QuickReturns Ltd. How do you stop these malicious attacks, and what is available in WCF to prevent them?

- How can you guarantee that the messages arrived from the client (i.e., how do you implement nonrepudiation)? How do you know whether messages were intended for the correct service? Can the client sign the messages with the private key, and can the service verify the authenticity by utilizing a public key?

- Do you know whether a purchase order was submitted only once? What happens if a rogue intruder replays the same order to generate bogus orders for the service? What measures are in place to stop these attacks? If these attacks continue, how do you eradicate the threat before it escalates to a denial of service attack?

We'll take a closer look at what WCF has to offer to address these concerns and counter these issues in the next section.

Introducing the WCF Security Features

Microsoft has invested a lot of effort in guaranteeing security on Vista and other later operating system such as Windows Server 2008. Microsoft counterparts viewed its security as a weakness in the early 1990s. Since then, Microsoft has done a commendable job combating that stigma. You may remember the initiative to ensure "secure code," and the "trusted access security" campaigns that Microsoft implemented to address this issue. Microsoft's objective was to educate developers so they could address security needs in the fundamental design.

In Windows 2003 Server, Microsoft set security to the highest level by default. You had to downgrade the security privileges to obtain access to resources. WCF is also based on the "guilty until proven innocent" and "all user input is evil" concepts.

Any distributed application is prone to many forms of malicious attacks by intruders. Modern distributed software architectures use public networks such as the Internet to send business-sensitive information. This information can be compromised in various ways (such as by packet sniffing on the wire, malicious systems administrators at routing destinations, etc.). The security model for WCF needs to be comprehensive to handle all these threats. The core of WCF security is to address four important features:

Confidentiality: Is the information confidential between the sender and the receiver? This feature will ensure that unauthorized parties do not get the opportunity to view the message. You can usually achieve this by using encryption algorithms.

Integrity: This feature ensures that the receiver of the message gets the same information that the sender sends without any data tampering. You usually sign messages using digital signatures to achieve integrity.

Authentication: This is to verify who the sender and receiver are, and whether they're known to the system or application.

Authorization: At the authorization stage, you know who the sender or receiver is. But you also need to know whether they are authorized to perform the action they are requesting from the application.

These are the key features the WCF security model attempts to address. You achieve the physical implementation of addressing these issues by configuring bindings and behaviors in WCF. WCF offers a rich set of bindings to address these security issues. It also gives you the flexibility to extend or create custom bindings to address specific security needs if necessary. In the next section, you'll investigate how to use bindings in WCF to implement security.

Security Features of Bindings

Bindings define one or more WS-* protocols that WCF supports. Every binding addresses two important aspects of messaging. These aspects are the encoding and transport of the message. *Encoding* defines the way messages are serialized. *Transport* defines the mechanisms that get the messages from the sender to the receiver. Let's look at the BasicHttpBinding binding as an example. It uses the WS-I Basic Profile XML encoding and HTTP for transport. This binding is designed to support interoperable scenarios with other platforms. Therefore, it does not implement any means of security by default. (However, you can extend this binding to implement security by utilizing custom code.) You can also use WsHttpBinding or WsDualHttpBinding to implement security.

■ **Note** Please consult Chapter 3 for an extensive discussion of bindings. This chapter focuses on the security implications and extensions of bindings. However, it is important to note that the binary-encoded bindings (i.e., Net*Binding) require WCF on both the sender and the receiver ends because of optimization and performance reasons. NetMsmqBinding is used for asynchronous scenarios. NetTcpBinding and NetNamedPipeBinding support reliable sessions and transactions.

You can also build custom bindings using the `System.ServiceModel.Channels` namespace. You can define security features, encoding, and serialization options that are suitable to your requirements using the classes available in this namespace. Similarly, you can also use the `ProtectionLevel` binding property to enforce integrity and confidentiality. The options available for the `ProtectionLevel` property are as follows:

> `None`: The binding is authenticated only. This option disables message-based protection.
>
> `Sign`: This ensures integrity in the transmitted data. It signs but does not encrypt the message.
>
> `EncryptAndSign`: This ensures both confidentially and integrity.

Protection Levels

WCF security encrypts and signs messages by default. This can be overkill in some instances, such as during debugging. To avoid this, you can just implement integrity when confidentiality is not a requirement. In such cases, WCF provides the facility to set the protection level on the message. Also note that protection levels can only be set for messages. WCF does not allow the disabling of protection levels for transport security. The following application file snippet illustrates how to achieve this using configuration files; the messages are required to be signed only before they are sent:

```
<bindings>
  <wsHttpBinding>
    <binding name="test">
      <security mode="Message">
        <message defaultProtectionLevel="Sign"/>
      </security>
    </binding>
  </wsHttpBinding>
</bindings>
```

You can also specify the `protectionLevel` property through code at `ServiceContract` and `OperationContract` as well.

Message exchange patterns (MEPs) determine how the messages are sent from the sender to the receiver. WCF does implement security support for both one-way and request-reply MEPs. However, duplex MEPs are available only in `WsDuaHttpBinding`, `NetTcpBinding`, and `NetNamedPipeBinding`.

How do you present your rights to the WCF runtime via bindings? What are the mechanisms available in WCF to pass on your requests to access resources? These questions are answered by the implementation of credentials and claims in WCF, which will be discussed in the following section.

Credentials and Claims

WCF security is based on credentials. A *credential* is an XML compatible entity that assists the Windows runtime in identifying a user. Credentials consist of one or more claims. A *claim* can be a username, a digital certificate, or a custom token that specifies the holder's right to access the application. This information will assist the Windows runtime in granting or denying access to the WCF application. The Windows runtime will verify the claims by the user. Therefore, if the user is using a certificate, the runtime will inspect the certificate information and verify whether the user is who they say they are. This relates to the authentication concept discussed earlier. Once the user is authenticated, the certificate key can be used to decrypt the data. This will fulfill the integrity feature discussed earlier. This can be followed by an authorization check that will verify whether the user has access to the data and functions of the application.

There are several *claim sets* set up in WCF (certificates, usernames, Kerberos tickets, and custom tokens). They are mapped to a standard internal claim set in the WCF runtime. The user can alternate between one claim and another (i.e., between the username and the custom token pair) without any issues with the Windows runtime. After the first communication with the server, the user session will commonly use a *token* to present the claim set information without checking for authentication, authorization, and integrity on subsequent requests. This is designed to improve response times.

■ **Note** In WCF, the highest security level is activated by default. Therefore, the user needs to decrease the security level if they want to accommodate certain security requirements. Also, the security model facilitates configuration-level changes without requiring any code or runtime modifications (which is the same as reliable messaging, transaction support in WCF, and so on). Therefore, if you alter your MSMQ binding to replace the WsHttpBinding binding, the application will seamlessly integrate with the same security context.

Next, we'll examine how you can extract claim information in WCF and investigate it using code, with the assistance of the QuickReturns Ltd. sample application.

■ **Note** You will reuse the Chapter 6 code in this example. The service and client functionality will be the same. Specifically, the server will expose a security trading service, and the client will make requests to trade securities. Please consult the code that accompanies this chapter to guide you along.

The most significant code changes will be in the ExchangeService class. You will modify the code to reflect the claims that the client will make to gain access to the service. Here are the steps:

1. Open Visual Studio 2010 (select Start ➤ Programs ➤ MS Visual Studio 2010 ➤ Microsoft Visual Studio 2010).

2. Create a blank solution in Visual Studio 2010 (select File ➤ New ➤ Project).

3. Select Visual Studio Solutions ➤ Other Project Types, and then select Other Visual Studio solutions and choose Blank Solution. Name this solution WCFSecurity, and point to your preferred directory (C:\PracticalWcf\Chapter07 in this example).

4. Add the ExchangeService project from Chapter 6 (right-click the WCFSecurity solution, and select Add ➤ Existing Project). The next step is to make some changes to the TradeSecurity code. As shown in Listing 7–1, modify the code to gain access to claim information. The rest of the class is identical to the Chapter 6 code.

Listing 7–1. Adding Claim Access Code to the ExchangeService Class

```
public double TradeSecurity(string ticker, int quantity)
        {
            Console.WriteLine("Claim made at " + System.DateTime.Now.TimeOfDay);
            System.ServiceModel.OperationContext opx;
            opx = OperationContext.Current;
            if (opx != null)
            {
                System.IdentityModel.Policy.AuthorizationContext ctx =
                    opx.ServiceSecurityContext.AuthorizationContext;
                foreach (System.IdentityModel.Claims.ClaimSet cs in ctx.ClaimSets)
                {
                    Console.WriteLine("Claim Issued by : " + cs.Issuer);
                    foreach (System.IdentityModel.Claims.Claim claim in cs)
                    {
                        Console.WriteLine("Claim Type - " + claim.ClaimType);
                        Console.WriteLine("Claim Resource name - " +
claim.Resource);
                        Console.WriteLine("Claim Right - " + claim.Right);
                    }
                }
            }
            if (quantity < 1)
                throw new ArgumentException(
                    "Invalid quantity", "quantity");
            switch (ticker.ToLower())
            {
                case "ibm":
                    return quantity * IBM_Price;

                case "msft":
                    return quantity * MSFT_Price;
                default:
                    throw new ArgumentException(
                        "Don't know - only MSFT & IBM", "ticker");
            }
        }
```

Initially you need to gain access to the authorization context, which you can
get from the current operation context by using the
ServiceSecurityContext.AuthorizationContext property. Then you go
through all the ClaimSets the user is presenting to the service. These ClaimSets
are comprised of individual claims. These are the claims that the client needs
to present to the service to gain access to the QuickReturns Ltd. application.
This claim information is printed on the console for you to read. You are
printing only the ClaimType, Resource (that the claim is for), and Right
information for the purpose of this example. The next step is to create the host
console application to host this newly modified ExchangeService class.

5. This example uses the self-hosting option. Create a new console project by right-clicking and selecting Solution ➤ Add ➤ New Project ➤ Console Application. Name it ClaimHost, and add it to the WCFSecurity solution. Rename the program.cs file host.cs. You are creating a WCF self-hosted service on port 8000 on the localhost machine. You display a message to inform the user that the service is functioning after you start the host with the host.Open method. The code and the config file are identical to those for the Chapter 6 TradeServiceHost project. You will utilize the WsHttpBinding to communicate with the service endpoints (Refer to Listings 6-2 and 6-4 in Chapter 6 for the host.cs code and App.config file, respectively.)

6. Let's concentrate on the client that consumes this service now. Create a new console project called ClaimClient, and add it to the WCFSecurity solution. The code for the client is identical to Listing 6-5 in Chapter 6. You will also use WsHttpBinding to bind with the service endpoint. The App.config file is also identical to Listing 6-5.

7. Build the solution to create executables for ClaimHost and ClaimClient. Let's run the service first. Your screen should be similar to Figure 7–1.

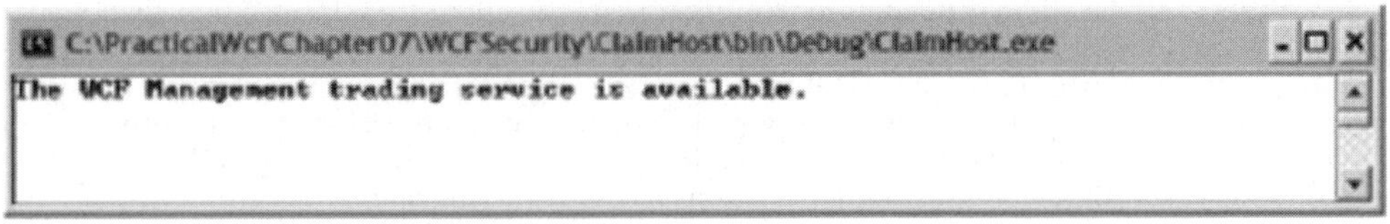

Figure 7–1. ClaimHost application running

The next step is to run the client. Let's navigate to the client's directory and execute the client. Your screen should look like Figure 7–2.

Figure 7–2. ClaimClient application running

Notice that while the client was running, the ClaimHost window recorded all the claims the client was presenting over the WsHttpBinding. The screen will display the Issuer for the ClaimSet and the ClaimType, Resource, and Right information for each claim. Your screen should look like Figure 7–3.

Figure 7–3. Displaying claim information at the service host console

This screen displays all the claim information to authenticate the client (the ClaimClient instance) to the service (ClaimHost). The issuer of the ClaimSet is Self in this scenario (i.e., the services and the client are running on the same machine). Then all the claims are looped through one by one. ClaimType is displayed first, followed by the Resource that the claim is for, followed by the Right for the resource.

Now that you're familiar with the mechanisms the client utilizes to submit claims to WCF services, we'll look into the options available to present these claims to the WCF runtime.

Presenting Credentials and Claims to WCF

The user's credentials can be presented to the Windows runtime in one of two ways: by utilizing the transport level or by utilizing the message level. The *transport level* will provide the credentials as part of the message transport. This is similar to Secure Sockets Layer (SSL) communication. The transport-level protocols will verify the credentials with the Windows runtime and establish a secure session between the client and the service. However, there is no explicit security for the messages that travel using the protected transport layer. Unfortunately, the transport security also terminates at the destination SSL gateway. The messages will be exposed to malicious intruders as soon as they exit the destination's SSL gateway. This may not be the actual hosting web server. Many companies implement SSL accelerators on proxy servers in their DMZ. This leaves the message's subject open to possible hijacking in the network between their accelerators and their servers. However, this is a common and proven security feature that the industry has utilized successfully (provided the destination organization takes steps to secure the messages as soon as they enter their organization).

The second option is to implement credentials at the *message level*, where the credentials are embedded in the message. No credentials are transported at the transport layer. The message will not be exposed to malicious hackers until the receiver can decrypt the message using a special key known to the receiver. However, this method is slower than the transport-level method because of the extra encryption involved. The messages will also be larger than the transport-level messages. The first message between the sender and receiver initiates the authentication and authorization between the two entities. The subsequent messages will have an optimized token to replace the complete credentials, in order to counter the slow response times. This mechanism will attempt to reduce the size limitation and increase the speed of the communication. The credentials of the service and client are specified in the binding information. You can have the following as credential type options in WCF:

None: No security is provided via the transport level or messaging level. BasicHttpBinding uses this mode by default, but the other bindings do not use it. (In other words, their security mode needs to be specified explicitly.)

Transport: This uses transport-level security (i.e., SSL) and provides mutual authentication and message protection at the transport level.

Message: This uses SOAP messages to provide authentication, authorization, integrity, and confidentiality. These SOAP messages are WS-Security compliant.

Mixed mode: This uses both transport-level and message-level security. Confidentiality and integrity are delivered by the transport layer. Authentication and authorization are provided at the message level.

Both: This is available only in the NetMsmqBinding binding. It provides authentication at both the message level and the transport level.

TransportWithMessageCredential: This provides client authentication at the message level and service authentication at the transport level.

TransportCredentialOnly: This does not provide any message protection, only transport-level security. This option is available with basicHttpBinding only.

Binding Support for Credentials

Table 7–1 lists the most common bindings and whether they support transport, message, or mixed mode.

Table 7–1. Binding Support for Credential Types

Binding	Transport Mode?	Message Mode?	Mixed Mode?
BasicHttpBinding	Yes	Yes	Yes
wsHttpBinding	Yes	Yes	Yes
wsDualHttpBinding	No	Yes	No
netTcpBinding	Yes	Yes	Yes
netNamedPipeBinding	Yes	No	No
netMsmqBinding	Yes	Yes	No
MsmqIntegrationBinding	Yes	No	No
netPeerTCPBinding	Yes	Yes	Yes
WS2007HttpBinding	Yes	Yes	Yes
wSFederationHttpBinding	No	Yes	No
WS2007FederationHttpBinding	No	Yes	No

In addition to the bindings shown in the table, The .NET Framework 3.5 and later provide a set of bindings commonly known as *relay bindings*, specifically for cloud computing. Each of these relay bindings resides under the Microsoft.ServiceBus client framework, and each has a one-to-one mapping with its standard WCF binding equivalent. For example, basicHttpBinding has basicHttpRelayBinding as its equivalent. The key distinction between the standard WCF bindings and their relay equivalents is that the relay equivalents listen on the cloud-based service bus while the standard bindings listen to the local Windows computer. Also, all the relay bindings reside in the Microsoft.ServiceBus namespace. Now that you're familiar with bindings and the modes they support, how do you set the modes in code? You can do this by setting the binding credentials in the binding's Mode property, which you can find in the Security property of the binding. You can also set the credentials using the bindingCredentials property of the Binding object. Figure 7–4 illustrates the security mode being set using a WsHttpBinding at the message level.

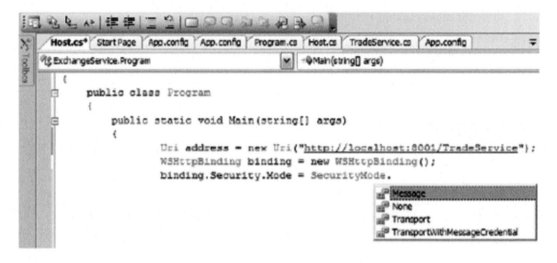

Figure 7–4. Adding the security mode

Note that this TradeService instance is scheduled to run on port 8001. However, all the examples in this chapter utilize port 8000 as the endpoint. In the next section, you'll look at these credential security levels in more detail with some sample code.

Transport-Level Security

Under the transport-level model, the credentials are applied at the transport level. Therefore, the messages between the sender and the receiver are not visible to intruders. This works effectively in point-to-point scenarios. It is difficult to implement transport-level security when there are multiple routing mechanisms to multiple recipients. Multiple gateways will expose the messages to intruders when the messages are transferred from one SSL provider to another. This feature makes transport-level security unrealistic for non-point-to-point scenarios. However, you can use hardware accelerators to achieve quick response times under this model. This feature also allows transport-level security to have high throughput and fast response times. Since every transport protocol has its own mechanism for passing credentials, this allows for fewer authentication options as compared to message security.

Transport-level security provides mechanisms to authenticate both the service and the client so they adhere to confidentiality, integrity, and authorization.

CODE VS. CONFIGURATION FILES REGARDING SECURITY

One of the most flexible features in WCF is the ability to implement the same task by either coding explicitly or using configuration files. It is helpful to use configuration files in WCF security. Configuration files give you the flexibility to alter the security features without recompiling the code. This is common when the security standards get superseded by the latest security offerings. However, for the purposes of the next example, you will use explicit code on the service side. The client is configured using application configuration files. This was intentionally done to illustrate the flexibility of the WCF security model.

Transport-level security (specifically SSL) is a proven concept and has wide acceptance in the technical community. Also, SSL hardware accelerators allow for fast message transmission. However, SSL supports only a subset of claim types. These are Windows authentication, digest authentication, and certificates. SSL does not support the rich WS-Security or Security Access Markup Language (SAML) token claim types in WCF. SAML tokens are key elements for achieving distributed computing security on multiple platforms. WCF offers several transport credential types:

None: This is for anonymous clients. This setting specifies that the service does not need to authenticate the client, and the client does not need to present any credentials to the service. This is not a recommended settings, and should be avoided wherever possible.

Basic: This specifies Windows Basic authentication. This is implemented according to RFC 2617 (which is available at www.rfc-editor.org). This type is only available with the HTTP protocol, and the client is authenticated against the Microsoft Active Directory service.

Digest: This specifies digest authentication between the service and the client.

Ntlm: This specifies NTLM authentication. NTLM is well suited for workgroup environments, and the service is authenticated using an SSL certificate. This authentication is more secure than Basic authentication.

Windows: This setting uses Windows Kerberos authentication in a domain environment and NTLM in a workgroup environment.

Certificate: This performs client authentication using an X.509 certificate. This option is mainly preferred in business-to-business (B2B) scenarios where Windows authentication is not possible.

How do you implement transport-level security in WCF? In the following exercise, you will reuse the TradeServiceHost and WcfSimpleClient projects from Chapter 6. Specifically, you will add these two projects to the WCFSecurity solution. Here are the steps:

1. Add the TradeServiceHost project and the WcfSimpleClient project to the WCFSecurity solution (right-click the WCFSecurity solution and select Add ➤ Existing Project).

2. Modify the code for the host.cs file in the TradeServiceHost project. Listing 7–2 shows the code.

Listing 7–2. Code for the host.cs File in the TradeServiceHost Project

```
using System;
using System.Collections.Generic;
using System.ServiceModel;
using System.Text;


namespace ExchangeService
{
    public class Program
    {
        public static void Main(string[] args)
        {
                Uri address = new Uri("https://localhost:8000/TradeService");
                WSHttpBinding binding = new WSHttpBinding();
                binding.Security.Mode = SecurityMode.Transport;
                // The clients of the service do not need to be
                // authenticated - since we are running over SSL
                binding.Security.Transport.ClientCredentialType =
            HttpClientCredentialType.None;
                Type contract = typeof(ExchangeService.ITradeService);
                ServiceHost host = new ServiceHost(typeof(TradeService));
                host.Open();
                Console.WriteLine("The WCF Management trading
              service is available.");
                Console.ReadKey();
        }
    }
}
```

Initially you will create a new URI and WsHttpBinding for your endpoint. It is important to know that the URI is an HTTPS endpoint—not an HTTP endpoint. This is to utilize SSL as a transport credential provider. Then you set the binding security credential to Transport. You are not requesting the client to authenticate over SSL, so you use HttpClientCredentialType.None. Finally, you specify the contract and then activate the service. Now you'll work on the client code.

3.   You don't need to alter any code in the WcfSimpleClient project's program.cs file. Instead, you use the App.config file of the project to enhance the security. The App.config file of the WcfSimpleClient project should be similar to Listing 7–3. (Please note that you are altering code only for the TradeService functions. The TradeServiceMonitoring functions are not altered as a result of this exercise. The code is similar, so we won't reiterate the same concepts. (As such, we've deleted the monitoring code from the sample code for this chapter.)

Listing 7–3. App.config File for the WcfSimpleClient Project

```xml
<?xml version="1.0" encoding="utf-8"?>
<configuration>
  <system.serviceModel>
    <client>
      <endpoint
        address="https://localhost:8000/TradeService"
        binding="wsHttpBinding"
        bindingConfiguration="TradeWsHttpBinding"
        contract="ExchangeService.ITradeService"
        name="TradeServiceConfiguration" />

    </client>

    <bindings>
      <wsHttpBinding>
        <binding name="TradeWsHttpBinding">
          <security mode="Transport">
            <transport clientCredentialType="None"/>
          </security>
        </binding>
      </wsHttpBinding>
    </bindings>
  </system.serviceModel>
</configuration>
```

This is similar to the Chapter 6 TradeService configuration file. However, you have altered the binding information to facilitate transport security. You have declared a new TradeWsHttpBinding section to detail the binding information. This section details that you are utilizing Transport as the security mode and you are not requiring the client to authenticate against the service.

4. Compile and build the TradeServiceHost and WcfSimpleClient projects. Navigate to the service, and start the service first. You will see output similar to Figure 7–1 (shown previously). Then start the client, and you will be presented with something like Figure 7–2. You should also see the ClaimSet activity in the service console. (This looks like Figure 7–3. However, the claim data will be different because you are utilizing transport-level security.)

Next, we'll examine what message-level security provides in WCF.

Message-Level Security

Message-level security relies on the message itself to secure the communication. The authentication, authorization, integrity, and confidentiality are met using the message data. It does not rely on the transport mechanism to provide any security for it. The message mode provides an end-to-end security context for the enterprise. This also works well with multiple hops and recipients. Since you are not relying on the transport layer, you can expand the message headers to implement multiple security assertions. This is a great tool to build federation services. Persistence of message headers will enable you to utilize integrity and confidentiality checks. You can also have rich claim support in message-level security (via SAML, custom tokens, WS-Trust, etc.). You can utilize multiple authentication mechanisms at different gateways. However, the downside is that messages can get considerably larger because of the additional header information. Therefore, the throughput will be slower than with transport-level security. Message-level security also provides mechanisms to authenticate and authorize both services and clients. You can also implement message-level security as utilizing binding by explicit coding or configuration files. The message credential types available in WCF are as follows:

None: This provides no message-level security with the client and the service. Therefore, the user is anonymous.

Windows: The client uses Windows credentials in SOAP messages to authenticate with the service. Depending on whether you use a domain or workgroup environment, this credential gets authenticated using either Kerberos authentication or NTML authentication, respectively.

Username: The client needs to be authenticated using the username credentials. However, WCF does not provide any encryption to protect the username credentials. The service can use Windows Credentials, SQL Server Membership Provider, or a custom validator to get authenticated.

Certificate: The client needs to be authenticated using an X.509 certificate.

Issue Token: The client and service depend on a security token service (STS) to issue a token that the client and server can trust. One example of an STS is Windows CardSpace. (This is discussed later in the "Windows CardSpace" section.)

You'll now learn how to implement message-level security in WCF. You will modify the `TradeServiceHost` service to utilize a certificate to authenticate the service to the Windows runtime. You will call this certificate `localhost`. You will also use another certificate called `WCFUser` to authenticate the client to the service. Therefore, when the message leaves the client, it will be protected until it gets to the service machine's Windows runtime. You will use explicit code (as opposed to configuration files) in both the client and service for this exercise.

The first step is to create two certificates for `localhost` and `WCFUser`. Let's use `makecert.exe` to create these certificates:

```
makecert.exe -sr CurrentUser -ss My -a sha1 -n CN=localhost -sky
exchange  -pe
certmgr.exe -add -r CurrentUser -s My -c -n localhost -r CurrentUser -s
TrustedPeople
```

This command will make a certificate called `localhost` in the store location `CurrentUser` and use the store name `My`. Then the following command adds the newly created certificate to the `TrustedPeople` container. These steps will ensure that you have a valid service certificate. The client will also be based on the local machine for the purposes of this example. The following command will create the `WCFUser` certificate for the client to authenticate against the server:

```
makecert.exe -sr CurrentUser -ss My-a sha1 -n CN=WCFUser -sky
exchange  -pe
certmgr.exe -add -r CurrentUser -s My -c -n WCFUser -r CurrentUser -s
TrustedPeople
```

You can verify that the certificate is created without any errors by invoking the MMC console for certificates by selecting Start ➤ Run, typing **certmgr.msc**, and pressing Enter. (Or you can select Start ➤ Run, type **mmc**, press Enter, and select "Add Certificates" snap in if the view is not available.) Your screen should look like Figure 7–5.

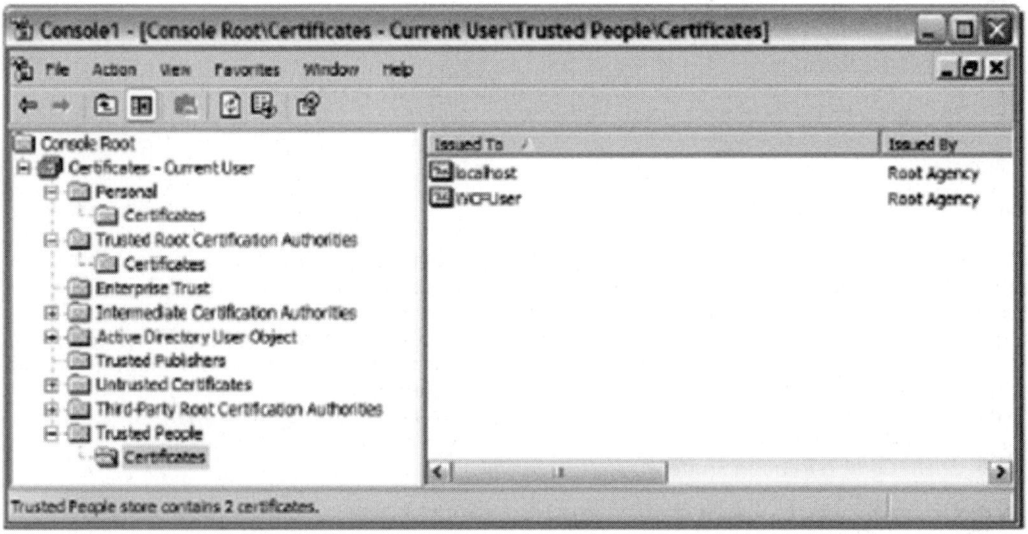

Figure 7–5. *Verifying certificates for the service and client authentication*

Listing 7–4 shows the code for the host.cs file on TradeServiceHost.

Listing 7–4. *host.cs File of the TradeServiceHost Project*

```
using System;
using System.Collections.Generic;
using System.ServiceModel;
using System.Text;
using System.Security.Cryptography.X509Certificates;

namespace ExchangeService
{
    public class Program
    {
        public static void Main(string[] args)
        {
                Uri address = new Uri("http://localhost:8001/TradeService");
                WSHttpBinding binding = new WSHttpBinding();
                // Set the security mode
                binding.Security.Mode = SecurityMode.Message;
                binding.Security.Message.ClientCredentialType =
                    MessageCredentialType.Certificate;

                Type contract = typeof(ExchangeService.ITradeService);
                ServiceHost host = new ServiceHost(typeof(TradeService));
                host.AddServiceEndpoint(contract, binding, address);
                // Set the service certificate
                host.Credentials.ServiceCertificate.SetCertificate(
                    StoreLocation.CurrentUser,
                    StoreName.My,
```

```
                    X509FindType.FindBySubjectName,
                    "localhost");
                host.Open();
                Console.WriteLine("The WCF Management trading service
                is available.");
                Console.ReadKey();
            }
        }
}
```

You need to import System.Security.Cryptography.X509Certificates into the code first. This is mandatory for utilizing certificate-related functions. Then you specify the client credential type as Certificate. Then you set the certificate for the service. You can use this certificate to authenticate against the Windows runtime to validate that the service has access to the business data. Therefore, even if an intruder hacks into the service, the intruder will not be able to access business information without the certificate information. You'll now see how the client is implemented.

Next, modify the program.cs file in the WcfSimpleClient project according to Listing 7–5.

Listing 7–5. Client Code to Run the TradeServiceHost Service

```
using System;
using System.ServiceModel.Channels;
using System.ServiceModel;
using System.Security.Cryptography.X509Certificates;

namespace ExchangeService
{
    class Program
    {
        static void Main( string[] args )
        {
            EndpointAddress address =
                new EndpointAddress("http://localhost:8001/TradeService");
            WSHttpBinding binding = new WSHttpBinding();
            binding.Security.Mode = SecurityMode.Message;
            binding.Security.Message.ClientCredentialType =
                MessageCredentialType.Certificate;


            System.ServiceModel.ChannelFactory<ITradeService> cf =
                new ChannelFactory<ITradeService>(binding,address);
            cf.Credentials.ClientCertificate.SetCertificate(
                StoreLocation.CurrentUser,
                StoreName.My,
                X509FindType.FindBySubjectName,
                "WCFUser");
            cf.Credentials.ServiceCertificate.SetDefaultCertificate(
                StoreLocation.CurrentUser,
                StoreName.My,
                X509FindType.FindBySubjectName,
                "localhost");
            ITradeService proxy = cf.CreateChannel();

    //.... The rest of the code is unchanged.
```

```
        }
    }
}
```

This code is similar to the service code. You initially set the security mode to Message. Then you inform the runtime that the clients will be using certificates to authenticate themselves. Then you set the WCFUser certificate credentials. You use the SetCertificate method that specifies the StoreLocation and StoreName and ask the certificate to be found using the subject name. This certificate will give all the information a client will need to present to the server to authenticate.

Then you set the server's certificate. Remember that the service needs to authenticate itself to the Windows runtime. This certificate information will only be available to a valid client. This way, you minimize the risk of an intruder getting access to the service by presenting a single compromised client certificate (i.e., the client needs to know both the client and server certificate information to gain access to the service).

The App.config files for the service and client are simple. They just have to define the endpoint of the TradeService, since you have already implemented the security settings in the code.

Compile and build the service and the client. First run the service, and then the client. You should see content similar to that in Figures 7–1 through 7–3 earlier in the chapter.

It is also beneficial to analyze the messages that travel between the service and the client. You will be able to view the encrypted message data using SvcTraceView.exe. (Consult Chapter 6 for a refresher on SvcTraceViewer.exe, how to implement it, and its location.) This view will enable you to analyze every message transferred between the client and the service. This will enhance your knowledge of the under-the-hood WCF implementation to facilitate message-level security.

Figure 7–6 illustrates how the certificate claim set in the message header is understood by the server authentication system.

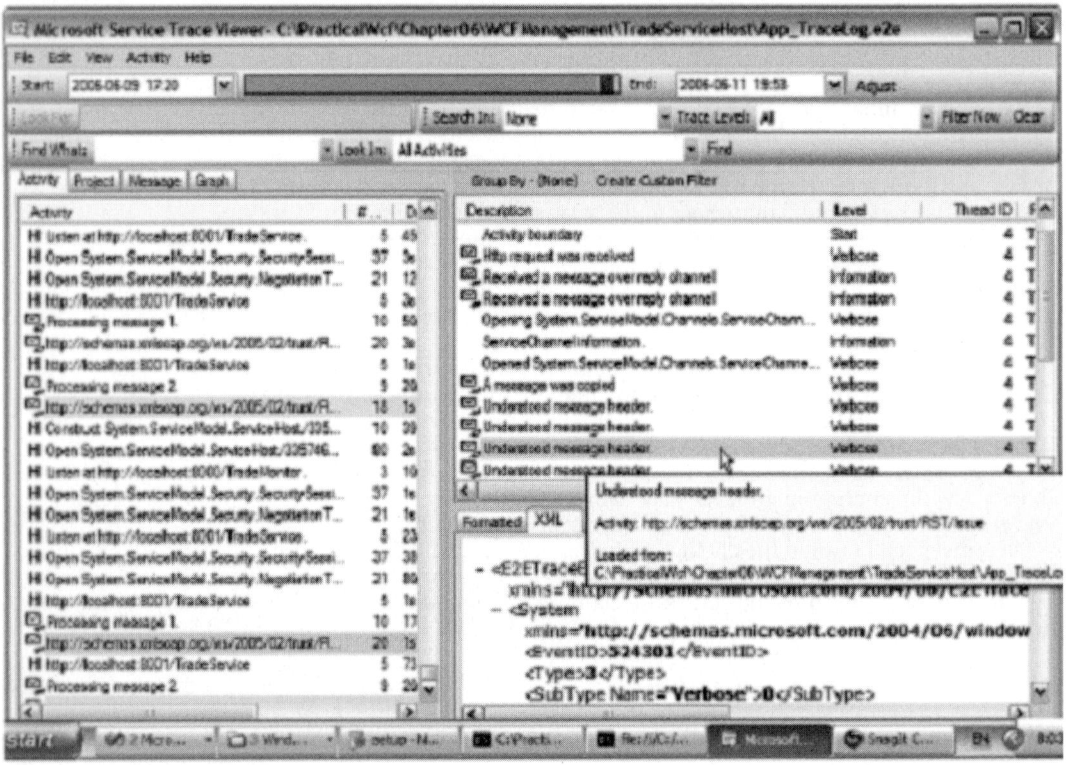

Figure 7–6. Using SvcTraceView.exe to analyze message-level security

In the next section, we'll look at mixed-mode security.

Mixed-Mode Security

Transport mode security is faster than message-level security. However, it has limited credential types (e.g., it has no SAML tokens). Message-level security has a richer set of credentials, but because of XML serialization and deserialization, it is slower than transport mode. With mixed-mode security, however, WCF offers the rich claims and federation advantages that message-level security offers, and supports multifactor authentication using rich credentials as well. You can also use custom tokens in mixed mode. In general, mixed mode offers a secure and fast way of transmitting data between services and clients.

Mixed mode performs integrity and confidentiality at the transport level, and authentication and authorization at the message level. You can use the TransportWithMessageCredential property (refer to Figure 7–4) to specify mixed mode with the binding.Security.Mode setting. It is simple to implement mixed code; the service code is similar to Listing 7–6.

Listing 7–6. *Implementing Mixed Mode in the Service*

```
using System;
using System.Collections.Generic;
using System.ServiceModel;
using System.Text;
using System.Security.Cryptography.X509Certificates;

namespace ExchangeService
{
    public class Program
    {
        public static void Main(string[] args)
        {
                Uri address = new Uri("https://localhost:8001/TradeService");
                WSHttpBinding binding = new WSHttpBinding();
                // Set the security mode
                binding.Security.Mode = SecurityMode.TransportWithMessageCredential;
                binding.Security.Message.ClientCredentialType =
                    MessageCredentialType.Certificate;

                Type contract = typeof(ExchangeService.ITradeService);
                ServiceHost host = new ServiceHost(typeof(TradeService));
                host.AddServiceEndpoint(contract, binding, address);
                // The rest of the code is the same
```

It is important to note that the URL is HTTPS. You are relying on SSL for integrity and confidentiality. Then you set the security mode to TransportWithMessageCredential and dictate that the client must authenticate using a certificate to gain access to the service. The program.cs file of the WcfSimpleClient looks like Listing 7–7.

Listing 7–7. *Client Code for Mixed-Mode Security*

```
using System.Net
namespace ExchangeService
{
    class Program
    {
        static void Main( string[] args )
        {
            ServicePointManager.ServerCertificateValidationCallback =
                delegate(Object obj, X509Certificate certificate,
                X509Chain chain, SslPolicyErrors errors)
                { return true;
                    // Need to implement company-specific validations
                };

            EndpointAddress address =
                new EndpointAddress("https://localhost:8001/TradeService");
            WSHttpBinding binding = new WSHttpBinding();
            binding.Security.Mode =
                SecurityMode.TransportWithMessageCredential;
            binding.Security.Message.ClientCredentialType =
                MessageCredentialType.Certificate;
```

```
System.ServiceModel.ChannelFactory<ITradeService> cf =
    new ChannelFactory<ITradeService>(binding,address);
cf.Credentials.ClientCertificate.SetCertificate(
    StoreLocation.CurrentUser,
    StoreName.My,
    X509FindType.FindByThumbprint,
    "43 5d 98 05 7b a1 73 87 66 ca 89 a1 ae 0e 3c 76 2c 12 2b 95");
```

You need to inform the client to initiate the SSL session with the service first. You do this by utilizing the ServicePointManager.ServerCertificateValidationCallback delegate. This delegate will initialize the SSL connection. The implementation of this delegate can be different from company to company (i.e., every organization will have a different matrix to validate its digital claims. Usually, the code will check for a CN=CompanyName entry). Therefore, true is returned for the purposes of this example. Next, you set the security mode and the client certificate. This time you are using the FindByThumbprint function (as opposed to FindByName). You can derive the thumbprints by accessing the properties of the certificate. Build the server and client, and your output should be similar to Figures 7–1 through 7–3.

Most often, you need to authenticate and authorize every time you send a SOAP message to the server. You may need to verify the identity of the sender when the sender has already established its identity using claims. You can handle this scenario in WCF by using *secure sessions*.

A secure session is established when the first call is made from the client to the server. The client will initially present the credentials to the service to authenticate. The service will create a special token that will be inserted into the SOAP header to keep track of the client's credentials. The subsequent requests from the client will present this special token to the service to gain access to the service. If you take a look at Listing 7–7 (shown previously) and navigate through the messages between the client and the server, you will find this token information in the header of the SOAP message.

We have discussed security mainly in point-to-point client and service scenarios. However, large enterprises employ thousands of employees. Certificates are commonly used to authenticate these employees. This mean employees needs to know other employees' certificate information to send a message to one of them. What happens when one enterprise merges with another enterprise? Does an employee from enterprise A need to know all the enterprise B certificate details? You can use federated credentials to address these issues in WCF.

Federated Security Model in WCF

The concept of federated credentials is important in the modern age of distributed computing. It means you can delegate the "verification" of a claim to a third party. The third party will in return give you a key that you can use to communicate with a service. The third party (commonly referred to as the *broker* or *security token service*) has a trust relationship with the service. Therefore, whenever a client comes with a certified credential from the broker, the service will trust the client's credentials. Figure 7–7 explains this scenario further.

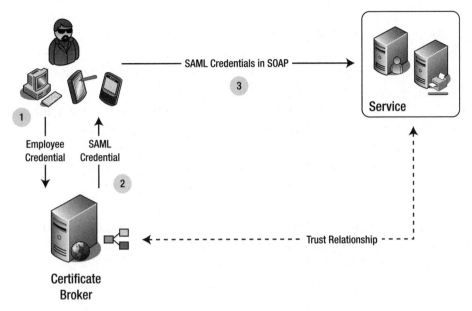

Figure 7–7. Federated credentials in action

You are assuming the client employee is using a certificate in this scenario. The employee may use multiple devices (a computer, a PDA device, etc.) to make a request of a service that is part of an external enterprise. The employee will first liaise with the certificate broker by providing the employee certificate stating his intentions of consuming the service. The broker will analyze the certificate and confirm its authenticity. Then the broker will issue an SAML-based credential set to the user to communicate with the service. This SAML token is signed with the special key from the broker to validate the token. This key is known only to the service that the employee is attempting to consume.

The client uses the SAML token in the SOAP request message header to send a request to the service. The service will analyze the SAML token and verify it is from a known certificate broker to the service (e.g., using the special key from the broker). The service will check the trust relationship between the service and the certificate broker and proceed with the client request.

Federated credentials play a key role in future security implementations. You can use the flexibility of proving one set of credentials (a certificate from the client) to a user and converting it to another set of credentials (an SAML token) in many scenarios to add value for customers. You also have the flexibility of altering your internal security mechanisms (i.e., the client can provide a username password pair to replace the certificate). However, your external implementation of the claims will not be changed. The broker will still create the same SAML token with the username/password pair. You do this by utilizing WSFederationHttpBinding in WCF. The next section will investigate authorization.

Authorization in WCF

This section will describe how to authorize users in WCF and discuss the differences between authentication and authorization. This section will first investigate the fundamentals of the .NET application security model and later cover some of the .NET offerings to handle authentication and authorization.

■ **Note** The .NET Framework offers a rich set of APIs (based on the IPrincipal interface) to manage authentication and authorization. They allow you to create a specialized, static (once-only) Principal object after the Active Directory authentication is approved. This Principal object will live securely on the client's desktop and attend to authorization requests during the life span of the user session. The authorization and authentication are provided by different providers. The provider information is usually based in configuration files. The objective of keeping separate providers for authorization and authentication is to seamlessly transfer the user context from one authorization or authentication provider without any code changes. It is important to note that WCF does not explicitly address authentication and authorization. What WCF does is evaluate claims, and authenticate and authorize claim sets utilizing the .NET Framework to satisfy the security requirements.

The cornerstones of the .NET security models are the IPrincipal interfaces. Developers can build objects that extend IPrincipal (usually called Principal) to incorporate the authentication and authorization information regarding a specific user.

Before we go any further, it's important to understand the differences between authentication and authorization:

- Authentication is the process of identifying users. This is commonly performed by requesting a username/password pair or a certificate to verify the authenticity of the user.

- Authorization happens after authentication. Authorization addresses the question of what the user will have access to after the authentication. If a user is known to the Windows runtime, authorization determines what the user can access in the system (e.g., a user who logs in under the Manager role might be provided delete access for purchase orders).

Authentication is mainly performed by API calls to Active Directory. Active Directory will return with a confirmation of the user's identity or deny their access to the system. The authorization details in most cases have to be explicitly coded. Authorization in .NET is based on roles (e.g., a user in the SeniorManager role might be able to delete purchase orders, while a user in the Manager role cannot). For example, if a tries to delete a purchase order, you need to check whether they have the SeniorManager role attached to their profile. You do this by utilizing the IsInRole function. This code queries whether the currently logged-in user has the SeniorManager role and is able to delete a purchase order:

```
Using System;
Using System.Threading;
if (Thread.CurrentPrincipal.IsInRole("SeniorManager"))
{
    // Code to delete purchase order
}
```

You can also utilize .NET Framework security to force the runtime to authorize entities at the function level. The following code snippet will demand the permissions you need to check before the user can execute the function. This is an alternative to the IsInRole feature of the .NET Framework.

```
using System.Security.Permissions;
...
[PrincipalPermission(SecurityAction.Demand, Role="SeniorManager")]
public bool DeletePurchaseorder()
{
    // Code to delete purchase order
}
```

It is important to understand the basics of authentication and authorization to grasp the security concepts in WCF and the .NET Framework. You'll now learn how to implement authorization in WCF security. Here are the steps:

1. The first step is to add the authorization information to the ExchangeService module. You have not enforced any authorization check to the code until now; you have relied on the Windows authentication models to authenticate the user. As soon as the authentication is valid, the client is able to extract the stock prices from the service. Let's tie authorization to the user's Windows credentials. Let's assume you are going to restrict access to the TradeService function to administrators, such that any user not part of the Administrator group will not be able to access the service. To do this, you'll code the logic into ExchangeService, as illustrated in Listing 7–8. The code explicitly instructs the .NET runtime to check whether the user is in the Administrator role.

Listing 7–8. ExchangeService Code to Include Authorization

```
using System;
using System.ServiceModel;
using System.Security.Permissions;

namespace ExchangeService
{


    // Same code as before

    public class TradeService : ITradeService, ITradeMonitor
    {
        const double IBM_Price = 80.50D;
        const double MSFT_Price = 30.25D;

        // Invokers must belong to the Administrator group
        [PrincipalPermission(SecurityAction.Demand,
        Role = "Administrators")]
        public double TradeSecurity(string ticker, int quantity)
        {
            Console.WriteLine("Claim made at " + System.DateTime.Now.TimeOfDay);
            System.ServiceModel.OperationContext opx;
            opx = OperationContext.Current;
        // Same code as before
```

2. Now you'll create the service. Add a new project to the WCFSecurity solution by right-clicking the WCFSecurity solution and then selecting Add ➤ New Project. Call it AuthAuditHost. (Note that we will use the same project to illustrate auditing in the next section.) The code will be similar to Listing 7–9.

Listing 7–9. Code for the host.cs File of the AuthAuditHost Project

```
using System;
using System.ServiceModel;
using System.ServiceModel.Description;

namespace ExchangeService
{
    public class Program
    {
        public static void Main(string[] args)
        {
            Uri address = new Uri("http://localhost:8001/TradeService");
            WSHttpBinding binding = new WSHttpBinding();
            Type contract = typeof(ExchangeService.ITradeService);
            ServiceHost host = new ServiceHost(typeof(TradeService));
            host.AddServiceEndpoint(contract, binding, address);
            host.Open();
            Console.WriteLine("The WCF Management trading service is available.");
            Console.ReadKey();
        }
    }
}
```

3. Now you'll create the client. Create a new console application called
    AuthAuditClient, and add it to the WCFSecurity solution. (Right-click the
    WCFSecurity solution and select Add ➤ New Project.) Take a look at Listing 7–
    10, in which we'll add some exception management code to address the
    exceptions that arise if the user is not in the Administrator role.

Listing 7–10. Code for the program.cs File of the AuthAuditClient Project

```
using System;
using System.ServiceModel.Channels;
using System.ServiceModel;

namespace ExchangeService
{
    class Program
    {
        static void Main( string[] args )
        {
            EndpointAddress address =
                new EndpointAddress("http://localhost:8001/TradeService");
            WSHttpBinding binding = new WSHttpBinding();
            System.ServiceModel.ChannelFactory<ITradeService> cf =
                new ChannelFactory<ITradeService>(binding, address);
            ITradeService proxy = cf.CreateChannel();

            Console.WriteLine("\nTrade IBM");
            try
            {
                double result = proxy.TradeSecurity("IBM", 1000);
                Console.WriteLine("Cost was " + result);
```

```
                Console.WriteLine("\nTrade MSFT");
                result = proxy.TradeSecurity("MSFT", 2000);
                Console.WriteLine("Cost was " + result);
            }
            catch (Exception ex)
            {
                Console.Write("Can not perform task. Error Message -
                " + ex.Message);
            }
            Console.WriteLine("\n\nPress <enter> to exit...");
            Console.ReadLine();
        }
    }
}
```

4. Now execute the service, and then run the application. Your screen should be similar to Figure 7–1. Since you are currently logged in as an user who is part of the Administrator group, when you execute the client, you should get a screen that looks like Figure 7–8.

Figure 7–8. AuthAuditClient running under an Administrator account

We'll now show how to run this client under a different account without administrator access. We have created a user account called chris without any administrator access. Use the following runas command to run the client:

```
runas /noprofile /user:local\chris AuthAuditClient.exe
```

This command will execute AuthAuditClient.exe as the chris account. You don't need to load the user profile in this case. Therefore, you use the /noprofile flag. You will be asked to enter the password for the chris account. When the password is validated, the client will run under the new account (chris). Your screen should look like Figure 7–9.

Figure 7–9. Using the runas command to execute the client under a different account

Since the chris account is not part of the Administrator group (and does not have a role to reflect this in its Windows profile), you should see the screen shown in Figure 7–10, which denies access to the service.

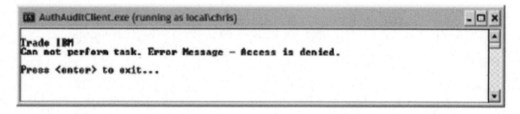

Figure 7–10. Access is denied for users who do not have the correct roles.

Authorization Options for One-Way Communications

What happens when the message is only one-way? Is there a requirement to authorize the sender at the receiver's end? Does WCF support this functionality? WCF implements mechanisms that do not require any negotiation between the client and service. WCF supports a one-shot, or nonnegotiated, security mode for this purpose. To support the one-shot security mode, you will set the flag negotiateServiceCredential="false" at the message level. However, you need to provide valid credentials to authenticate the request. This will ensure that the message is initiated from a trusted source even when the authorization is ignored at the service end. The following configuration snippet illustrates this feature:

```
<bindings>
  <wsHttpBinding>
    <binding name="test">
      <security mode="Message">
        <message negotiateServiceCredential="false"
                 clientCredentialType="Certificate"/>
      </security>
    </binding>
  </wsHttpBinding>
</bindings>
<behaviors>
```

```
  <behavior name="credentialConfig">
    <clientCredentials>
      <!-- Other configuration not shown. -->
      <serviceCertificate storeLocation="CurrentUser" storeName="My"
      x509FindType="FindBySubjectDistinguishedName"
      findValue="localhost"/>
    </clientCredentials>
  </behavior>
</behaviors>
```

WCF also implements multiple membership providers to assist developers in integrating Active Directory, LDAP, and custom directory structures. You can also create your own providers to suit specialized scenarios. WCF also ships with multiple role provider classes that will reduce developer effort.

We have investigated the WCF security model, authentication, and authorization in detail. The next section will discuss how to track these security-related features, and it will also discuss WCF's auditing mechanism for tracing and monitoring security activities.

Auditing for Security Features in WCF

WCF has a rich set of utilities to address security auditing. It uses the Event Viewer extensively to record security-related events. It also provides access to a rich set of APIs that will enable you to directly communicate with the Event Viewer. Let's examine how you can leverage the Event Viewer now. You will enhance AuthAuditHost to record all the security events to the Event Viewer. Listing 7–11 shows the code for the modified host.cs file of AuthAuditHost.

Listing 7–11. Enabling Auditing for the Service

```
using System;
using System.ServiceModel;
using System.ServiceModel.Description;

namespace ExchangeService
{
    public class Program
    {
        public static void Main(string[] args)
        {
            Uri address = new Uri("http://localhost:8001/TradeService");
            WSHttpBinding binding = new WSHttpBinding();
            Type contract = typeof(ExchangeService.ITradeService);
            ServiceHost host = new ServiceHost(typeof(TradeService));
            host.AddServiceEndpoint(contract, binding, address);

            // Add auditing to the service
            ServiceSecurityAuditBehavior auditProvider =
                host.Description.Behaviors.Find<ServiceSecurityAuditBehavior>();
            if (auditProvider == null)
            {
                auditProvider = new ServiceSecurityAuditBehavior();
            }
            auditProvider.AuditLogLocation = AuditLogLocation.Application;
            auditProvider.MessageAuthenticationAuditLevel =
```

```
                AuditLevel.SuccessOrFailure;
            auditProvider.ServiceAuthorizationAuditLevel =
                AuditLevel.SuccessOrFailure;

            host.Description.Behaviors.Add(auditProvider);
            host.Open();
            Console.WriteLine("The WCF Management trading service is available.");
            Console.ReadKey();
        }
    }
}
```

Auditing is available in WCF using ServiceSecurityAuditBehavior from the System.ServiceModel.Description namespace. To enable auditing, you first check whether the audit provider is available in the current context. If it doesn't already exist, then you create an audit provider using the ServiceSecurityAuditBehavior class. Next, you specify the audit location. This can be either the application or the security log. Choose the application log for this example. Then you can specify the audit level. The available levels are success, failure, and success and failure. This example uses the success and failure option. You can set these levels using the MessageAuthenticationAuditLevel and ServiceAuthorizationAuditLevel properties for the message. Once you do this, all the auditing information regarding messages and server authorization will be recorded on the server's application log. Finally, you add the audit provider to the service.

Now run the service and then the client. Let's check whether the information is available in the event log. Choose Start ➤ My Computer ➤ Manage ➤ System Tools ➤ Event Viewer, or choose Start ➤ Run ➤ Eventvwr.exe. Look under the application log under the event log, as shown in Figure 7–11.

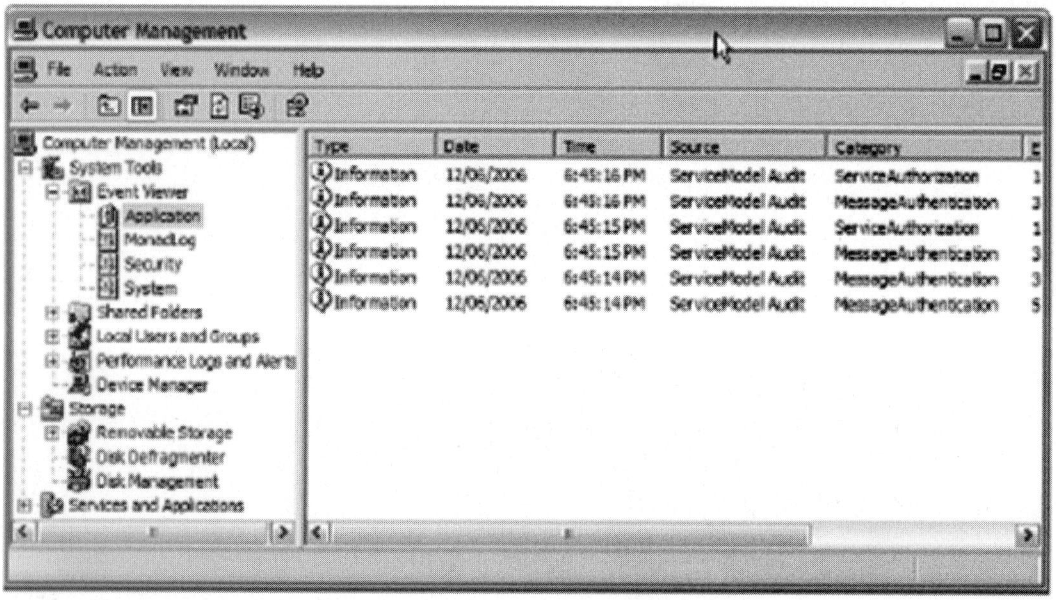

Figure 7–11. Application log entries for the AuthAuditHost service

Let's look at one log entry to verify the details. Your screen should be similar to Figure 7–12. This entry describes a successful authorization call made by the `AuthAuditClient` instance.

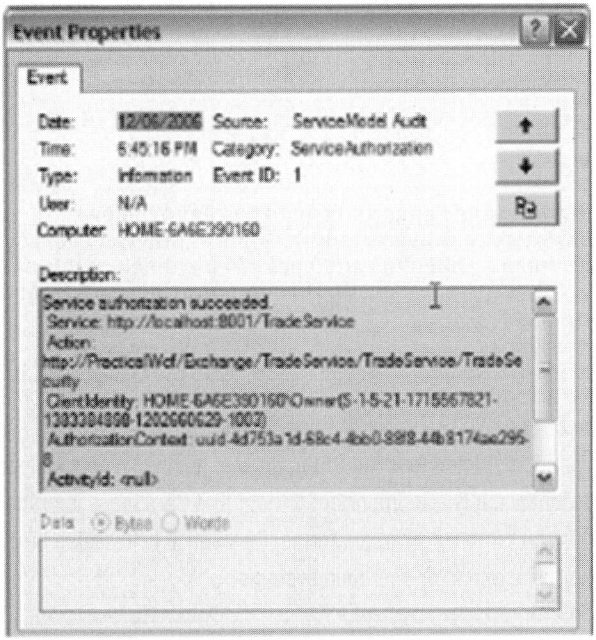

Figure 7–12. Audit log entry that illustrates successful authorization by AuthAuditClient

You should now be familiar with WCF authentication, authorization, and auditing concepts. But how do you manage your identity in a distributed environment? Is it fair to conclude that the identities are all scattered over a public network such as the Internet? For example, some of our information is stored in Amazon accounts. You might also have a .NET Passport identity to sign into your Hotmail account. Are you also an avid buyer and seller on eBay? Is there a way you can leverage all these identities at once? Or can you present your eBay identity to convince Amazon to upgrade your membership? Perhaps you want to manage all these identities centrally. WCF does offer a programming model to make this vision a reality.

Windows CardSpace

Windows CardSpace is a specialized identity metasystem that helps you manage multiple identities. Let's take an everyday example. You use your driver's license to prove you are a valid driver on the road. How do you prove this to a suspecting police officer who inquires about it? You show them a valid driver's license *card*. Likewise, you use a card to prove to an ATM that you have the correct credentials to withdraw money. You use different physical cards to accommodate different situations, and if you have a lot of cards, you need a mechanism to manage them. A common practice is to store all the cards in a wallet. In this way, the wallet becomes your identity metasystem in everyday life.

You can use the same concept in distributed computing. The .NET Passport system provides an e-mail address and password to validate you. This is similar to the bank providing a card to withdraw cash.

Similarly, your employees will give the administration digital signature that proves they are legitimate employees of the company. How do you store all these identities and extract them on demand to facilitate your needs? The answer lies in Windows CardSpace.

A *card* is a digitally signed entity that illustrates a user's claims to a system. In general, two types of cards exist. The first one is a *personal card*, which a user can issue to herself. This is similar to picking an e-mail address and a password for a Passport account. The second type is the *provider card*, which is provided by a trusted third party. This is similar to a bank card that is given to you by the bank.

How Windows CardSpace Works

The magnetic strip on the back of your bank card stores your claims to the bank system. Windows CardSpace works similarly to this magnetic strip. CardSpace converts your personal or provider cards to special tokens and validates their authenticity on demand. Different card types can use different tokens for these validations. Personal cards use SAML 1.1 token types by default. However, provider card tokens are subject to an organization's technology preferences.

■ **Note** It is important to note that CardSpace is based on the WS-Trust specification. Windows CardSpace can use SAML tokens to validate user claims. However, it is not restricted to using SAML tokens. It can use any custom token algorithm as long the server can validate the credentials. It is also important to note that CardSpace isn't the only identity metasystem there is; there are others based on other software platforms. CardSpace is available on Windows XP SP2, Windows Server 2003 SP1, Windows Vista, and later operation systems.

It's important to understand the difference between Passport and CardSpace. Microsoft .NET Passport is an identity system that enables access to multiple Microsoft resources. Passport's single-identity system fits well into the identity metasystem of CardSpace. Microsoft has also indicated that a identity metasystem that supports multiple identities is more scalable than a single-identity system such as Passport. CardSpace is already supported by a Java toolkit from Ping Identity (a major player in the identity space). Therefore, you can utilize multiple identities on heterogeneous platforms to validate identities with CardSpace.

You can verify whether CardSpace is available on your system by navigating to Start ➤ Control Panel. You should have an icon called Digital Identities, as shown in Figure 7–13.

When you double-click the icon, you will see a wizard that will assist you in creating personal cards and exporting provider cards. This interface acts as a container for all your identity needs.

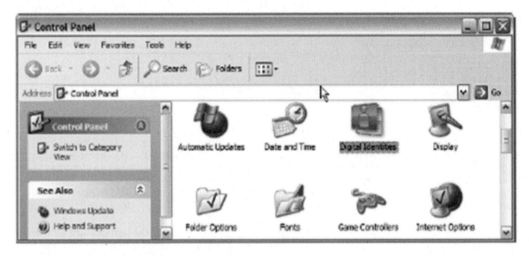

Figure 7–13. Checking whether CardSpace is available on your system

The next section will describe how to use CardSpace in WCF.

Enabling Windows CardSpace in WCF

CardSpace is one of the client credential types in WCF. CardSpace is used as an authentication mechanism on the client side. The server receives a token that summarizes the claims in the personal or provider card. However, the service side must authenticate itself using an X.509 certificate to verify the authenticity. (In other words, since you rely on a foreign token, you need to make sure you have valid credentials on the server side to execute the service.) The configuration file will be similar to Listing 7–12.

Listing 7–12. Service Application Configuration File for CardSpace Support

```
<?xml version="1.0" ?>
<configuration>
    <system.serviceModel>
    <services>
            <service type="ExchangeService.TradeService"
                <endpoint address="http://localhost:8000/TradeMonitor"
                    binding="wsFederationBinding"
                    bindingConfiguration="wsBinding"
                    contract="ExchangeService.ITradeMonitor">
                    <identity>
                        <certificateReference findValue="localhost"
                            storeLocation="LocalMachine"
                            storeName="TrustedPeople"
                            x509FindType="FindBySubjectName" />
                    </identity>
                </endpoint>
            </service>
        </services>
    </system.serviceModel>
```

```
<wsHttpBinding>
    <binding configurationName="wsBinding">
        <security mode="Message">
            <message clientCredentialType="IssuedToken" />
        </security>
    </binding>
</wsHttpBinding>
</configuration>
```

You will use the localhost certificate to authenticate the service to the server runtime. CardSpace also utilizes message-level security. The client credential type you use for CardSpace is called IssuedToken. The client configuration file is similar to the server configuration file. You need to make sure you set the server certificate properly. When the service is built and running, you can execute the client instance. When the client instance runs for the first time, the screen shown in Figure 7–14 will appear. This is a confirmation request by the Windows CardSpace instance to proceed to choose a card to communicate with the service. You can navigate through the wizard and select the appropriate card to use.

Then you can select the CardSpace controller to use to communicate with the service. The Windows runtime will then create a special token that embeds the user's claims and sends it to the service to validate the claims. Figure 7–15 shows the dialog box that requests the user to select one of his cards to submit to the service.

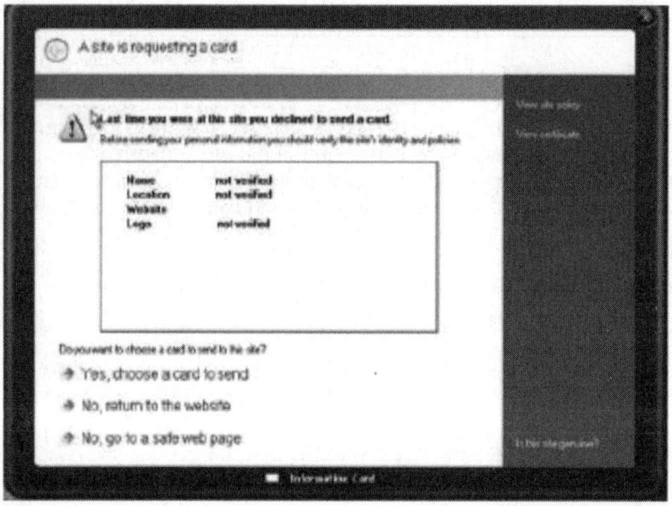

Figure 7–14. Windows CardSpace request dialog box

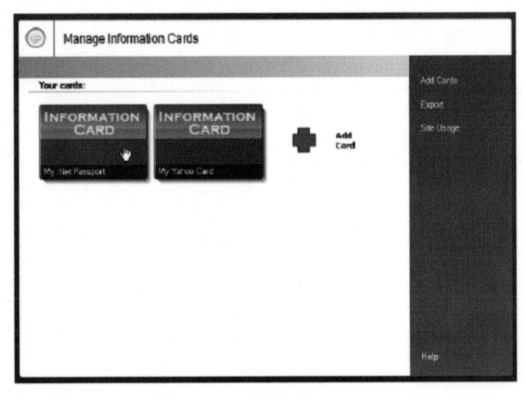

Figure 7–15. Selecting a CardSpace card to authenticate against the service

Summary

This chapter discussed the essentials of WCF security, including the following concepts:

- WCF security is based on four important concepts: authentication, authorization, integrity, and confidentiality.

- You can utilize WCF security at the transport layer, message layer, or both.

- Transport-layer security depends on the transport layer (specifically SSL) to protect the communication between the client and the service. This method is faster than message-based security, but the credential types supported for it in WCF are limited (i.e., it doesn't support rich SAML tokens). Transport-layer messages can also be vulnerable in the recipient's domain after the messages leave the SSL gateway.

- Message-level security is slower than transport-level security. However, it allows developers to use a rich set of credentials. Message mode will guarantee that a message will get to the receiver without being exposed at the transport level.

- Mixed mode supports integrity and confidentiality at the transport layer, and authentication and authorization at the message layer.

- WCF supports federated claims and Windows CardSpace. WCF uses CardSpace as a client credential type. Both personal cards and provider cards are supported.

- WCF enables authorization at the Windows level and will support multiple membership providers as role providers. It also supports a comprehensive auditing and tracing API.

The next chapter discusses reliable messaging and how it is implemented in WCF. Reliable messaging is an important concept in distributed computing; it enables reliable communication channels between multiple enterprises (on heterogeneous platforms) with failover mechanisms.

CHAPTER 8

■ ■ ■

Implementing Reliable Messaging and Queue-Based Communications

WCF helps you implement reliable communications over an infrastructure that might be unreliable. Application infrastructure is prone to failure. Network connectivity often breaks, services might not always be available, and messages get lost. WCF provides you with the functionality to overcome these limitations in the infrastructure.

You will learn in this chapter how to ensure reliable communication in a distributed environment where the application endpoints might be available only intermittently. Reliable messaging in WCF helps developers solve a number of challenges that have plagued them for many years. You will learn about the following in this chapter:

- The need for reliable messaging

- Challenges in implementing reliable messaging

- Reliable sessions

- Queuing support in WCF

- How to integrate with legacy applications using MSMQ

Let's consider our QuickReturns Ltd. scenario. Say you decide to sell a stock that has declared a loss. You put in your order to sell. However, the message never reaches the trading application, and the stock loses more value before you realize what has happened. This could potentially cost you thousands of dollars. Alternatively, say you put in a buy order, which may accidentally be sent multiple times. This can occur for a number of reasons, prime among them being the lack of an acknowledgment from the receiving end. You could end up buying stocks that you didn't really plan to buy. Further, say you want to apply the proceeds of the sale of one stock to buy a second stock. The message to buy goes through, but the sell message fails. This can cause a lot of problems in your portfolio.

You could also experience network-related issues. For example, say the network is clogged by buy/sell orders, and the router is overcome. Or say the wireless connection on your laptop blinks, and your order does not go through. Moreover, since the application is working over the Internet, the congestion is completely out of anyone's control and can result in messages being lost, causing you a real monetary loss. All of these scenarios are real and problematic, and need to be addressed successfully to achieve reliability.

Reliable messaging helps overcome some of these issues since WCF also tracks the liveliness of the available resources. This helps both the reliability and the scalability of your application. An additional piece of functionality that reliability offers is a network adaptive rate of sending messages. In other words, WCF monitors the network congestion and will either speed up or slow down the rate at which messages flow across the network, thus providing a pseudo-load-balancing functionality.

Let's dive into the implementation of reliable messaging in WCF.

The Need for Reliable Messaging

Why should you be excited about reliable messaging? It certainly does not seem at first to be cool, interesting, or even something to get mildly excited about.

Providing reliability to messages has been somewhat of a nightmare in distributed applications, irrespective of the transport. A lot of issues are associated with it. For example, the servers or a network connection might not be available. Even worse, the connection itself might be disrupted for reasons that are not readily predictable. As the developer and architect, you must design around these issues. If you look at the concepts of SOA in general, a key requirement that really should be the fifth tenet of SOA is reliability. (Refer to Chapter 1 for the four tenets of SOA.) It is of little value to have an architecture that does not provide reliability at its core for message communications.

Reliable messaging in the context of SOA guarantees that a message will actually be received at the destination. To do this, you need to ensure that a destination is available. In the SOA world, this option does not exist, since you might not control the destination. In the scenario of reliable messaging, you need to compensate for the fact that messages may not arrive at the destination as intended because of unforeseen and unknown reasons. Hence, you need to hold onto a message until the destination is available and the entire message has in fact passed successfully. Finally, should something go wrong, you need to detect that an error has occurred, recover from it, and then resend the message, which will then be reprocessed. This has been extremely difficult to do in the past, and when a custom implementation has been delivered, it has been prohibitively expensive to implement and maintain.

To remedy these issues, software industry leaders including Microsoft, IBM, BEA, and TIBCO created the WS-ReliableMessaging standard. This addresses the problem of being able to allow messages to be delivered reliably between applications despite failures within software components, networks, or systems. You accomplish this by standardizing on the SOAP and WSDL requirements to identify the application endpoints and bindings.

WCF allows for reliable messaging in a web service environment by ensuring that messages are delivered only once (in other words, without duplicates) and in order. However, since a standard for message queues is not in place across the industry, Microsoft decided to build this capability on top of MSMQ, which provides a buffer mechanism between the client and the service, and in essence decouples them. However, reliable messaging can also be something of a misnomer, since it does not provide for durability, unless you use MSMQ as the container.

For example, if the server application is down for a period of time longer than the timeout defined in the client application, the message will indeed never be delivered. Or, if you persist messages to a durable store—that is, if you write these to the disk on the client side but no such strategy exists on the server side—there really is no reliability. Although the implementation does in fact take into account the requirements for reliability, at least for version 1 of WCF, there is no real support for durability. The WS-ReliableMessaging specification specifies only that the receiving endpoint is required to send an acknowledgment that the message has indeed been received.

Despite these limitations, in a scenario where both ends of the application—that is, the client endpoint and the server endpoint—are indeed up and running, reliable messaging offers you a host of advantages. The failures at the transport level are overcome more often than not without the need to write a single line of additional code.

Challenges of Implementing Reliable Messaging

Implementing reliable messaging has multiple challenges. We'll broadly categorize them into communication issues and processing issues. More often than not, these are interrelated challenges that are nontrivial in nature to solve.

Communication Issues

Communication issues typically revolve around the physical transport. In a service-oriented world, the quality of the communication layer is often not within our control. The main communication issues are the following:

Network issues: The actual physical network is not available. For example, the server may be down or the router may be struggling to cope with high levels of network congestion. In these cases, what happens to your messages, and how do you compensate for this?

Connection drops: You send the message; however, the connection to the destination is lost before the message arrives at the destination. For example, say your machine has its network cable unplugged, or the wireless card on your laptop momentarily blinks. How do you detect the drop, and more importantly, how do you recover from this? Prior to WCF, the messages would be lost, unless of course you had envisioned this and wrote lots of code to overcome the scenario.

Lost messages: This is much like the load of laundry that loses one sock. You don't know what happened to your message. You sent it, the network was available, and your connection was stable, but for some reason the message didn't arrive at the destination. How do you prevent this situation?

Out-of-order messages: You put in a sell order for MSFT stock, the proceeds of which you want applied to the purchase of a really hot energy stock. Naturally, the sell order needs to arrive before the purchase; otherwise, your account will not have adequate funds to buy the energy stock. How do you go about avoiding this scenario?

Processing Issues

Processing issues have to do with the internal applications. When an error occurs, how is it handled internally by the application? Let's look at the main processing challenges:

Messages are lost when an error occurs: Your message was received at the location. However, before it actually entered the system, an error occurred, and the message vanished into the network. How do you prevent this? Take a sell order for MSFT, for example, which is received by the QuickReturns Ltd. application. Before the entire message is actually received, the network drops some packets. Though you have sent the sell order and it has been received at the server, it never enters the sell application.

Interrelated messages are processed individually: You might have a set of messages that need to be processed as one transaction. However, these are treated as individual requests by your system. Once again, the order to sell for MSFT and the order to buy for the energy stock could be processed as a single transaction. Both the messages are related to each other and need to be processed as such.

Failure leads to an inconsistent state: The failure of the delivery of a message in some scenarios leads to an inconsistent state, whereby the client is actually expecting a response. However, since the service might be unavailable, this leads to the client continuing to wait until a timeout occurs.

Messages cannot be retired: Your sale of the marketing stock netted you more money than you expected, which you would like to apply toward the energy stock. So, you resubmit the buy order with a changed quantity. How do you handle this scenario?

The good news is that WCF enables you to overcome these challenges fairly easily with its built-in support for reliable messaging and reliable sessions. Moreover, providing this functionality is fairly straightforward and does not require the services of a highly skilled programmer or reams of code.

WCF makes adding reliability to the distributed application somewhat of a nonevent. This is especially true in an environment where both ends of the application are likely to be available, and WCF provides this functionality at no extra cost or effort. However, WCF version 1 does lack a durable store for messages, although durability can be provided via MSMQ. At the same time, it is important to keep in mind that the reliable messaging feature set in WCF is not a silver bullet, and it wasn't designed to be one. The reliable messaging feature set in the end is about as reliable or unreliable as the network available to it.

Reliable Sessions

WCF reliable messaging provides reliability between two given endpoints regardless of the number of intermediaries between the two. This also includes intermediaries that might use alternatives such as HTTP proxies or SOAP. A great benefit of WCF is that it allows you to switch from one transport mechanism to another using configuration settings. For example, you might start by using TCP with binary encoding and then change to reliable messaging over HTTP by modifying only the configuration files. It really is pretty much as simple as that.

WCF provides reliability and resilience. This means the following:

Guaranteed delivery: Messages are guaranteed to be delivered once and only once. What this means is that your message will get to its destination without any chance of failure, vanishing into the ether, or duplications.

In-order delivery: The messages will be delivered in the same order as they were sent.

Resilience: WCF offers resilience to network outages, delivery destinations being unavailable, SOAP errors, and failures at the intermediaries. Features such as `AcknowledgementInterval`, `FlowControl`, and `InactivityTimeout` help the application be more aware of its environment.

Reliable sessions essentially support interactive communication between endpoints. The reliable session channel runs under a condition of low latency, and the exchange of messages happen at fairly short intervals. Internally, reliable sessions handle the two main issues facing reliable messaging: lost or duplicated messages, and messages arriving in an order different from the one in which they were sent. Reliable sessions provide SOAP messages with functionality that is almost analogous to that provided by TCP in the TCP/IP stack to the IP packets. A TCP socket connection provides the infrastructure for once-only delivery of IP packets between nodes. However, there are significant differences between reliable messaging and the implementation of TCP.

The reliability provided by WCF reliable sessions is at the SOAP message level, rather than the packet level, which is arbitrarily defined. This reliability provided by WCF reliable sessions is the implementation from the WS-ReliableMessaging standard, which is an interoperable industry-standard implementation. The reliability is provided in a transport-neutral manner, and not just for TCP. Additionally, it is not tied to a particular transport session (i.e., TCP session), but is for the lifetime of the session, which may or may not be over a single transport. Reliable sessions provide you with the means to use multiple transport sessions concurrently or sequentially without any fuss. Moreover, the reliability provided is for end-to-end delivery, not just between two nodes of a transport. What this means is that when compared to TCP, which ensures reliability between only two ends of a connection, WCF ensures end-to-end reliability from a sender node to a receiver node, irrespective of the number of intermediaries. Also, reliable sessions can support out-of-order delivery—also knows as *first-in, first-out (FIFO)*, which means that the messages should be processed in the order they arrive, rather than the logical order).

WCF provides a number of settings to implement a fairly sophisticated means of applying network congestion detection, timeout intervals, retry counts, ordering, and so on. These can do a lot more than just the simple retry events you are familiar with, and they can help overcome issues by responding quickly to the loss of a message. (For further details on this, please refer to the WCF SDK documentation.)

Let's now dive into how you actually implement reliable sessions.

■**Note** The code in this chapter is slightly different from the code in Chapter 7. The reasoning behind this is to reinforce the concepts within this chapter. For complete listings of the code, please refer to the solution files.

Enabling WCF Web Services with Reliable Sessions

Assume you have an interface implemented that is called ITradeService, as shown in Listing 8–1.

Listing 8–1. ITradeService

```
using System;
using System.Collections.Generic;
using System.ServiceModel;
using System.Text;

namespace QuickReturns
{
    [ServiceContract]
    public interface ITradeService

    {
        [OperationContract]
        string BeginTrade();
        ...
        void Buy();
        [OperationContract]
        void EndTrade();
    }
}
```

The AddTrade and EndTrade parameters that are provided for the OperationContract attribute ensure that any sequence of invocations to the operation begin with the AddTrade method and complete with the CompleteDeal method. The client application invokes BeginTrade and then invokes AddTrade twice. It has a Buy method followed by an EndTrade method. Let's now assume that one of the AddTrade invocations never reaches the service. In this case, the service would still operate in a valid manner, and the application would not miss AddTrade. Similarly, consider a scenario in which both the invocations arrived at the destination. For whatever reason, one of them was delayed and arrived after CompleteDeal was invoked. The execution sequence would still execute in a valid manner. However, it would not be in the sequence intended by the client. Overcoming these problems is a fairly simple task.

To begin, make the changes shown in Listing 8–2 to ITradeService in order to ensure that you do not have a scenario where messages could potentially be received out of order.

Listing 8–2. ITradeService Changes

```
[ServiceContract(SessionMode=SessionMode.Allowed)]
public interface ITradeService
```

This change will ensure that the messages are delivered in the order you intended. That is practically all you need to do to ensure that you avoid the scenario where messages are received out of order.

You now need to make the same change to the definition of ITradeService in the client, as shown in Listing 8–3.

Listing 8–3. Modifying ITradeService

```xml
<?xml version="1.0" encoding="utf-8" ?>
<configuration>
  <system.serviceModel>

    <client>
      <endpoint
          address="http://localhost/servicemodelsamples/service.svc"
          binding="wsHttpBinding"
          bindingConfiguration="Binding1"
          contract="Microsoft.ServiceModel.Samples.ICalculator" />
    </client>


    <!-- binding configuration - configures WSHttp binding for reliable sessions -->
    <bindings>
      <wsHttpBinding>
        <binding name="Binding1">
          <reliableSession enabled="true" />
        </binding>
      </wsHttpBinding>
    </bindings>


  </system.serviceModel>

</configuration>
```

You will now modify the App.config file of the host project to incorporate the implementation of the WS-ReliableMessaging standard as implemented in the WCF framework. You can do this by double-clicking the App.config file in the IDE or by simply opening it in Windows Notepad. Add the lines shown in Listing 8–4 to the file.

Listing 8–4. Modifying the Service Host App.config File

```xml
<?xml version="1.0" encoding="utf-8" ?>
<configuration>
    <appSettings>
        <!-- use appSetting to configure base address provided by host -->
        <add key="baseAddress" value="http://localhost:8000/TradeService" />
    </appSettings>
    <system.serviceModel>
        <services>
```

```
            <service name="QuickReturns.TradeService">
                <endpoint address="" binding="wsHttpBinding"
                    contract="QuickReturns.ITradeService"/>

                <!-- Must have an HTTP base address for this -->
                <endpoint address="mex"
                    binding="mexHttpBinding"
                    contract="IMetadataExchange" />
            </service>
        </services>

        <!-- binding configuration - configures WSHttp binding
             for reliable sessions -->
        <bindings>
            <wsHttpBinding>
                <binding name="Binding1">
                    <reliableSession enabled="true" />
                </binding>
            </wsHttpBinding>
        </bindings>
    </system.serviceModel>
</configuration>
```

You will make similar changes to your client `App.config` file as well.

Test this application using multiple machines. Put the server application on one machine and the client on the other. Ensure that you can invoke the service; once you have verified this, you can simulate problems. For example, remove the network cable from the server to simulate an intermittent connection, and try calling the service. If the executing thread blocks until the connection becomes available, then as soon as you plug the server back in, you will notice that the call will complete successfully. The magic of reliable sessions is in fact implemented by the `ReliableSessionBindingElement` class, which we will look at more in depth next.

MOVING LARGE VOLUMES OF DATA RELIABLY

Moving large amounts of data between endpoints is somewhat of a sticky situation. Assume that you have a requirement to move files that are 2 GB in size between endpoints in your application. Under most circumstances, streaming offers you an ideal solution.

However, imagine that you are streaming this data across the wire, and because of a network outage you lose the connection. Given that you have implemented reliable messaging in your solution, the message will be recovered. Here you have a small issue. When streaming data, the file is considered to be a single message. Let's assume you transferred 1 GB prior to the outage. In this case, the message will be resent from the beginning when the transmission resumes. You will be starting over, which is annoying, but can be avoided.

The solution is to implement chunking instead of streaming in this scenario. With *chunking*, the sending application will divide the message into smaller files (e.g., 1,000 files of 2 MB each). The downside of this approach is that the throughput is likely to be lower than that of streaming because of the overhead of reliable messaging and the chunking taking place. When you need reliability while moving large files, use chunking. You should be aware that chunking per se is not a feature of WCF, even though it can be implemented fairly easily. In the end, where to set the threshold that will trigger the switch from streaming to chunking is a decision you as an architect will make based upon the operational environment. Refer to `http://msdn.microsoft.com/en-us/library/ms789010.aspx` to learn more about streaming.

The ReliableSessionBindingElement Class

The `ReliableSessionBindingElement` class provides the implementation of the reliable session and ordering mechanisms as defined in the WS-ReliableMessaging specification.

This is provided on all of the standard protocols, such as `netTCPBinding`, `wsHttpBinding`, and `wsDualHttpBinding`. The default values are `false`/`off` for the first two of these.

You can also provide reliable sessions for custom bindings quite easily. You define the reliable session in the same manner as you did for the HTTP protocol in the previous section. Your code will look like Listing 8–5.

Listing 8–5. *Changing the Bindings*

```
<bindings>
    <customBinding>

        <binding configurationName="ReliabilityHTTP">
            <reliableSession/>
            <httpTransport/>
        </binding>

    </customBinding>
</bindings>
```

We discuss the actual implementation of custom bindings in greater detail in Chapter 3.

Some Pointers on Reliable Messaging

When using the functionality of reliable messaging, it is important to follow some basic principles to ensure the scalability of the application.

It is advisable to keep your network in mind, and this includes the transports, firewalls, proxies, and whatever else might be between the client application and the server application.

Internally in WCF, a transfer window is used to hold messages on the client as well as on the server in the event of either not being reachable. This is a volatile cache and is fully configurable. You can find the property in `System.ServiceModel.Channels.ReliableSessionBindingElement.MaxTransferWindow`; the value of this property is the number of messages that can be held within the transfer window. On the client side, this sets the number of messages held awaiting acknowledgments, while on the server it indicates the number of messages that can be buffered for the service in a given transfer window. By default, the value on this is eight messages; however, you can configure this size depending on the utilization, bandwidth, and latency of your network infrastructure.

For example, even if the sender keeps up with the data rate, latency could be high if there are several intermediaries between the sender and the receiver, Thus, the sender will have to wait for acknowledgments for the messages in its transfer window before accepting new messages to send on the wire. The smaller the buffer with high latency, the less effective the utilization of the network is. On the other hand, too high a transfer window size may impact the service because the service may have to catch up to the high rate of sends from the client.

Optimally, your network should have the lowest latency possible, but this is often not the case. The transfer window can actually help out here. Keep in mind that setting the latency value to 1, for example, might actually cause lost messages or dropped messages, thus defeating the entire purpose of reliable messaging. Buffering, when used correctly, will increase the concurrency of your application. If you are in doubt as to what you should set this value at, it is advisable to leave it at its default setting.

■**Note** Before you decide to change any of the default settings, you should test and benchmark the different settings for your environment using various instrumentation, including performance counters and WMI. Some of the important WCF performance counters are Calls: Total Number of Calls, CallsOutstanding, PercentOfMaxInstances, PercentOfMaxCalls, and RMQPoisionedMessages. To learn more about performance counters and WMI, refer to the Chapter 6 section "Using WCF Performance Counters."

Should you decide on a nondefault value, you should configure it on both the client and the server. The correct value will in all likelihood require a measure of trial and error, as well as some degree of understanding of the network.

Another aspect to keep in mind is flow control, which is a mechanism to help the sender and receiver more or less keep pace with each other. Although the TransferWindow property does help in this regard, another tool is available to you: the FlowControlEnabled property. This is a piece of magic pulled off by the WCF team that allows the client and service to either speed up or slow down, depending on how quickly each of them can produce and consume messages. It is recommended that you set this to true.

■**Note** To learn more about FlowControlEnabled, refer to http://msdn.microsoft.com/en-us/library/system.servicemodel.channels.reliablesessionbindingelement.flowcontrolenabled.aspx.

On the next logical level in concurrent applications, the response of the service is governed by the MaxPendingChannels property. This property sets the number of client sessions with which the service can do a handshake. It is possible that a service might not have enough channels available, and in this scenario, when a client attempts to establish a session, it will be refused. That is not something you want. On the other hand, setting this value too high could have adverse effects as well. The default value for the System.ServiceModel.Channels.ReliableSessionBindingElement.MaxPendingChannels property is 4. What you should set it to depends on your infrastructure.

When hosting your application, it is important to take into account a few more points. Reliable sessions are stateful, and the state is maintained in the application domain. This means that all messages that are part of a reliable session must be processed within the same application domain. This is a constraint if you're planning to use a web farm, or in any scenario where the number of servers is more than one. Additionally, when you use dual HTTP channels, each client might require more than two connections (two is the default). Duplex reliable connections in certain cases could require two connections each way. The problem with this is that you could enter a potential deadlock situation by using dual HTTP reliable sessions. This is easily overcome by setting the MaxConnections property to a suitably high number in your configuration files. You do this by simply adding <add name = "*" maxconnection = "nn" /> to the connection management element. Keep in mind that nn is the number of maximum connections you would like to set.

Message queuing is used primarily when you require true asynchronous messaging where the lifetimes of the client and the service might not overlap. Message queuing should also be used when you require reliability. In the real world, applications go down, and services are not always available, especially in scenarios where you face poor network infrastructures. WCF uses the underlying MSMQ technology to provide you with the means of leveraging the available technology to implement reliability, as you will see in the next section.

Reliable messaging, as you have seen, does not provide you with a silver bullet. In particular, the WS-ReliableMessaging standard–compliant implementation does not provide you with any durable storage for your messages. Using MSMQ, which is supported out of the box in WCF, allows you to overcome the infrastructure unreliability to a certain extent. Queuing enables you to effectively decouple the transport for the messages from their actual processing. Moreover, the reliability provided is really only as reliable as the underlying infrastructure in an environment where you do not have control over both endpoints of your application. Figure 8–1 shows conceptually what happens when using persistent stores to utilize the MSMQ communication between a WCF application and an MSMQ legacy application.

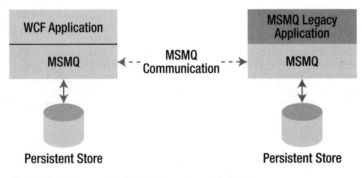

Figure 8–1. Conceptual MSMQ usage with WCF

Queuing in WCF

When designing distributed applications, selecting a transport is fairly important. Factors that you should consider include the requirements of the client and the service, but more importantly whether you need a direct transport or a more isolated one. Instead of using a direct transport (such as HTTP or TCP), where all the communication will fail if the network goes down, you may want more resilience in the transport to overcome this issue. Typically, using a queued transport will achieve this, since queued transports are backed by a store (i.e., a durability container).

Out of the box, WCF provides the ability to use MSMQ, which is the Microsoft implementation of queued transports at the operating system level. Queues store messages from a sending application on behalf of a receiving application and later forward these messages to the receiving application. They ensure the reliable transfer of messages between queues. WCF provides support for queuing by using MSMQ as a transport and enables the following features:

Loosely coupled applications: The sending and receiving applications do not need to know whether each other is available. Moreover, both ends can send and receive messages without being dependent upon how quickly the messages are actually processed. This in effect also makes the overall application achieve higher levels of availability.

Failure isolation: Loose coupling enables messages to be sent to or received from the queue without the endpoints running, which adds a level of failure isolation. For example, imagine a scenario where the server side of the application is unavailable and the client can continue to send messages to the queue. Once the server (receiver) is available, it will pick the messages up and process them.

Load leveling: Multiple instances of the server application are able to read from the same queue and help the application scale out to meet the additional load. Additionally, a high rate or volume of transactions is unlikely to overwhelm the receiver, since the messages will remain in the queue until processed by the receiving application at a rate completely independent of the client application.

Disconnected operations: As discussed, reliability can suffer greatly in environments with unreliable network availability. Queues allow these operations to continue even when the endpoints are disconnected by providing a durable, albeit transient, message store. When the connection to the receiver application is established again, the queue will simply forward the messages to the receiver application for further processing.

It is also important to keep in mind that WCF uses MSMQ not only as the transport channel when communicating with WCF endpoints, but also as a means of integrating with legacy applications. Legacy applications in this context are anything written prior to the release of WCF. These are applications that originally used MSMQ in order to provide a degree of reliability in the world before WCF.

In addition, queuing in WCF is not synonymous with MSMQ. MSMQ is supported out of the box in WCF (but is a feature of the Windows operating system), which makes its usage easy. If you wanted to implement your own version of queues, you could do that using the custom transport properties.

Durable storage, again, is not available out of the box with WCF since the WS-ReliableMessaging standard does not specify any rules about this. Durable storage, however, is possible using persistent queues, which are features of MSMQ, not WCF. This is a somewhat subtle but important distinction. The "reliable" aspect of reliable messaging really depends on how stable your network is. It is more about the actual transport than trying to ensure 100 percent delivery. It simply is not possible to achieve 100 percent delivery without having control over both ends of the application infrastructure (sender and receiver), which in turn opens up an entirely different set of questions quite beyond the scope of this book. NetMsmqBinding offers you a solution, but be aware that it is not WS-ReliableMessaging compliant for the very reasons we have discussed.

Having stated that, you must also weigh the advantages offered by the NetMSMQ binding stack, including durable storage, transactional I/O, and reliable guaranteed delivery of messages. The trade-offs of using the NetMSMQ binding stack are that you lose interoperability as offered by a web service environment, and they in essence operate on a Windows infrastructure only.

The NetMSMQ binding in WCF offers two distinct scenarios. One is where it is used as a transport channel between two WCF application endpoints, and the second is where MSMQ is actually used to integrate with legacy applications that use MSMQ (also known as the *integration channel*). Hence, you could integrate a WCF receiver or client endpoint into your legacy application using MSMQ. This is possible since the queue channel in WCF is actually independent of MSMQ behavior and is in effect only abstracting it.

To get started with MSMQ, you first need to install it on your machine if you have not already done so.

Installing MSMQ

To install MSMQ, choose Add or Remove Programs from the Windows Control Panel to open the dialog box shown in Figure 8–2.

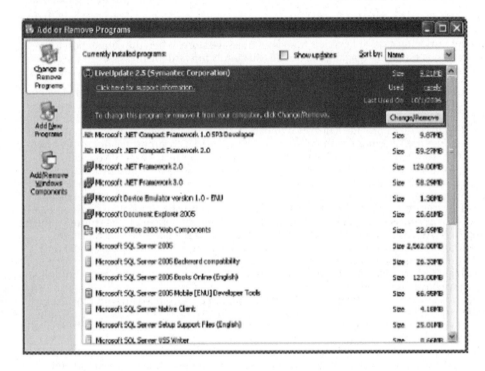

Figure 8–2. *The Add or Remove Programs dialog*

Click Add/Remove Windows Components, and then select Application Server in the Windows Components wizard, as shown Figure 8–3. Then click the Details button.

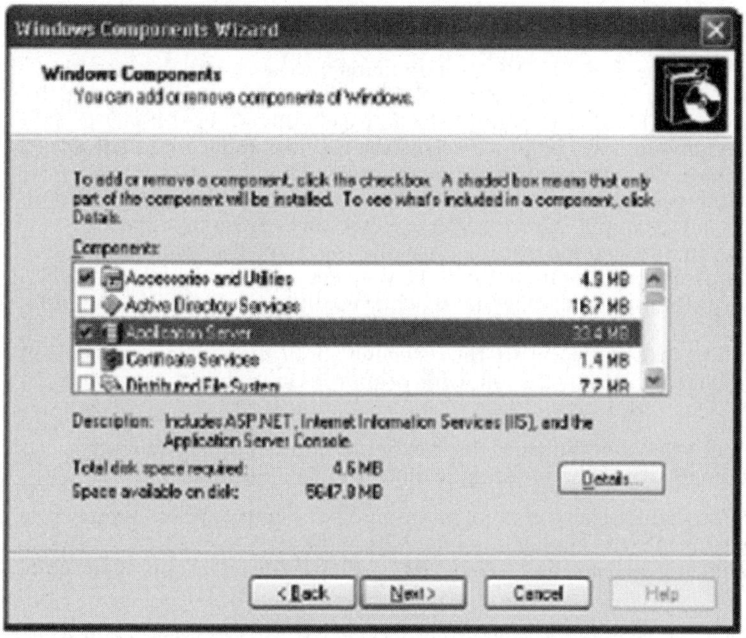

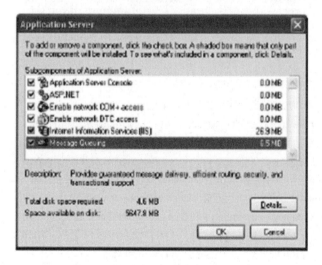

Figure 8–3. *Selecting Application Server*

If Message Queuing is not checked in the Application Server dialog box (as indicated in Figure 8–4), then check it and click OK. Then click the Next button in the Windows Components wizard, and follow the instructions on the subsequent screens to install MSMQ.

Figure 8–4. *Selecting Message Queuing*

Microsoft Message Queues in Windows Server 2008

WCF abstracts out MSMQ, though the behavior of MSMQ itself remains the same, with the exception of MSMQ under Windows Server 2008. If you have worked with MSMQ in the past, you will recognize the familiar queue and the dead letter queue (DLQ). The *queue* is the active channel where MSMQ actually stores the messages that are relevant and that will be processed by the receiver application. The *DLQ* is where the messages end up if they have timed out or have become irrelevant.

Windows Server 2008 also introduces the concept of a *poison queue*. A poison message is one that has exceeded the number of retries. For example, say a receiver application is trying to process a message, but it encounters an error. In this scenario, the message queue will retry delivery until the timeout occurs. At this point, the message will end up in the DLQ. With WCF on Windows Server 2008, a message will continue its set of retry attempts, and once that is achieved, the message will be put onto the poison queue.)

In WCF, poison message handling provides a way for the receiving application to deal with poison messages. Poison message handling is provided by the following properties in each of the available queued bindings:

MaxImmediateRetries: An integer value that indicates the maximum number of times to retry delivery of the message from the main queue to the application. The default value is 5.

MaxRetryCycles: An integer value that indicates the maximum number of retry cycles. A retry cycle consists of putting a message back into the application queue from the retry queue to attempt delivery again. The default value is Max Value or 2,147,483,647, which is the largest possible value for an int32.

RetryCycleDelay: The time delay between retry cycles attempting to deliver a message again. The default value is 10 minutes. The retry cycle and the retry cycle delay together provide a mechanism to address the problem of handling poison messages, which involves a retry after a periodic delay.

RejectAfterLastRetry: A Boolean value that indicates what action to take for a message that has failed delivery after the maximum number of retries has been attempted. If this property is set to true, the message is dropped, and a negative acknowledgment is returned to the sender. If it's set to false, the message is sent to the poison message queue. The default value is false. This property is used when the receiving application cannot process the message after several attempts. If you set the value to false, the message is moved to the poison queue. A queued WCF service can then read the messages out of the poison queue for processing. Negative acknowledgments to the sender are as yet unsupported, so will be ignored under MSMQ 3.0.

■**Note** The poison message feature is supported only on Windows Server 2008 at the time of writing. Another major difference area in Vista and later operating system over previous operating system is in the DLQ. Under the currently supported versions of Windows, there exists a single DLQ on a system-wide basis. However, with Vista you have the option of having DLQs on a per-application basis. Windows Server 2008 also introduces the concepts of the subqueue and transactional remote receives. *Transactional remote receives* allow receiving applications to get messages in a transactional manner. MSMQ did not support this before Windows Server 2008, though you could implement the functionality in a convoluted manner by using the peek method or by writing a custom dispatcher. Refer to `http://msdn.microsoft.com/library/default.asp?url=/library/en-us/wcecomm5/html/wce50lrfmsmqqueuepeek.asp` for further documentation on the *peek* method.

In Figure 8–5, you can see how a message is retried a predefined number of times (in this case three times) and then sent to the poison queue. You can implement your own logic for how you want to handle messages in the poison queue. Please refer to http://msdn.microsoft.com/library/default.asp?url=/library/en-us/msmq/html/42fe2009-310b-42fa-a65e-6d395c15ada5.asp for further details. As an MSMQ veteran, you will also miss the peek method that was available in previous MSMQ implementations. WCF does not support the peek method; however, MSMQ retains the behavior, which has nothing to do with WCF per se.

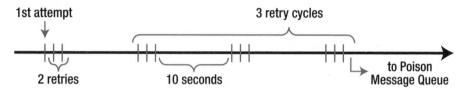

Figure 8–5. *Retries in queues*

The requirement for application-wide queues in the past depended upon the use of public queues. This in turn required Active Directory. Utilizing private queues was not an option, particularly when you needed to cross authentication boundaries. WCF no longer requires public queues, since the behavior of the MSMQ channel is akin to that of the HTTP channel.

The channel stack, as described in earlier chapters, is where WCF actually sends and receives its messages. The transport channels, as you know, are where the messages get exchanged between WCF endpoints, and the MSMQ transport channels, as you will see, are really no different from the HTTP transport channels.

Transport Channels

The MSMQ transport channel is really geared toward allowing two WCF endpoints to communicate with each other using MSMQ. The transport channel supports using SOAP within a message over MSMQ. You will typically use this when your network is inherently unreliable or you want to ensure that your messages are delivered irrespective of infrastructure issues. In other words, you should use it when you are more concerned about transacted I/O and absolute guaranteed delivery than interoperability. You can accomplish this by using NetMsmqBinding, which is predefined in WCF.

Let's look at how you can use queuing in a WCF service as the transport channel. We'll use a self-hosted version of TradeService to illustrate the exchange of messages using the MSMQ transport and its failover.

■**Note** Keep in mind that the code snippets in the following listings are incomplete; you should refer to the code samples for the complete listings. You can find the complete listing under \ProWCF\Chapter8\QueueMessaging.

Begin by modifying TradeService as shown in Listing 8–6 to make it a self-hosted service. Then utilize NetMsmqBinding, and create the queues as required.

Listing 8–6. Modifying TradeService for MSMQ

```
using System;
using System.Configuration;

using System.Messaging;

using System.ServiceModel;

namespace QuickReturns
{
    // Define a service contract
    [ServiceContract]
    public interface ITradeService
    {

        [OperationContract(IsOneWay=true)]

        void DoTrade(string BuyStock, string  SellStock, int Amount);

    }

    // Service class that implements the service contract
    // Added code to write output to the console window
    public class TradeService : ITradeService
    {
        [OperationBehavior(TransactionScopeRequired=true,TransactionAutoComplete=true)]
[ReceiveContextEnabled(ManualControl=true)]
        public void DoTrade(string BuyStock, string SellStock, int Amount)
        {
        ReceiveContext receiveContext;
            if(!ReceiveContext.TryGet(OperationContext.Current.IncomingMessageProperties, out
receiveinContext)
{
Console.WriteLine("Receive context is not available for the message");
return;
}
            Console.WriteLine("Received Request to Sell Stock {0}
                with  the quantity of {1} from And Buy {2}",
                SellStock.ToString() , Amount.ToString(),
                BuyStock.ToString());
        If (Amount >= 50)
{
receiveContext.Complete(TimeSpan.MaxValue)
Console.WriteLine("Amount is more than 50");
}
else
{
receiveContext.Abandon(TimeSpan.MaxValue)
}
Console.WriteLine();

        }
        // Host the service within this EXE console application
```

```
public static void Main()
{
    // Get MSMQ queue name from app settings in configuration
    string queueName = ConfigurationManager.AppSettings["queueName"];
// Create the transacted MSMQ queue if necessary

    if (!MessageQueue.Exists(queueName))
        MessageQueue.Create(queueName, true);

    // Get the base address that is used to listen for
    // WS-MetaDataExchange requests
    // This is useful to generate a proxy for the client
    string baseAddress = ConfigurationManager.AppSettings["baseAddress"];
    // Create a ServiceHost for the TradeService type
    using (ServiceHost serviceHost = new ServiceHost(
            typeof(TradeService), new Uri(baseAddress)))
    {
            serviceHost.Open();
                    Console.WriteLine("The Trade Service is online.");
            Console.WriteLine("Press <ENTER> to terminate service.");
            Console.WriteLine();
            Console.ReadLine();
            // Close the ServiceHost to shut down the service
            serviceHost.Close();
    }
}
}
```

Notice that you add a reference to the System.Messaging namespace, which provides the support for MSMQ. While implementing a service contract, it is important to enable the transaction on each operation. In the preceding example, the DoTrade method has been decorated with the appropriate transaction attributes. This ensures the that transaction gets completed automatically on executing the method, without any errors. This also ensures that the messages are delivered exactly once by using transactional queues. If exceptions are thrown, WCF ensures that the message is not lost by returning it back the queue.

Though this functionality works fine in normal scenarios, it creates a few issues if you are working on load balancing on queues where multiple services or service instances are waiting to process the message from the queue. Consider a scenario where a service returns a message back to the queue for another retry later. The preceding model does not guarantee that the same instance of the service will get the message the next time service requests the message from the queue. This means that other services or service instances would start processing the message without knowing how many times it's already been tried. Also, this means that the message will be pulled from the queue and rewritten again and again for each retry—a costly operation.

To address this issue, WCF 4.0 introduced a new API called ReceivedContext, which prevents a message from being pulled from the queue until the message has been successfully processed by the service. The ReceivedContext class resides in the System.ServiceModel.Channels namespace. This class enables you to look at message content without removing it from the queue(also known as peeking). Peeking does not remove the message from the queue; instead, it makes it invisible so that no other service or service instance sees it as an available message. Peeking also works a way of locking the message to a specific service or service instance. Additionally, peeking prevents the message from having to be repeatedly read from and rewritten to queues over the network.

The first thing you do to utilize ReceiveContext is enable the receiveContext for processing the messages in queues. This is done by decorating the operations with ReceiveContextEnabled, as shown previously in Listing 8–6. Once this is done, you get the receiveContext of the message by calling TryGet method. Once you have the receiveContext, depending on application logic, you can either complete the operation later or abandon it, by calling the complete or abandon method, respectively. Table 8–1 lists some of the important methods in the ReceivedContext class.

Table 8–1. *Important ReceivedContext Methods*

Method Name	Description
Abandon(TimeSpan)	Marks the method as abandoned with the specified timeout value
Abandon(Exception, Timespan)	Marks the method as abandoned with the specified exception and timeout values
Complete(TimeSpan)	Marks the operation as complete with the specified timeout value and removes the message from the underlying queue
EndComplete	Completes an asynchronous complete operation
EndAbandon	Completes an asynchronous abandon transaction
TryGet(MessageProperties, ReceiveContext)	Attempts to get the receive context from the specified message property collection
TryGet(Message, ReceiveContext)	Attempts to get a receive context from the specified message

You also add code to create a message, should one not exist. You create the host service as described in Chapter 4. Define the App.config file that specifies the service address and uses the standard NetMsmqBinding binding for TradeService. The code looks like Listing 8–7.

Listing 8–7. *TradeService NetMsmqBinding*

```xml
<?xml version="1.0" encoding="utf-8" ?>
<configuration xmlns="http://schemas.microsoft.com/.NetConfiguration/v2.0">
        <system.serviceModel>
              <services>
        <service
           behaviorConfiguration="MyServiceTypeBehaviors"
           name="QuickReturns.TradeService">

           <endpoint address="net.msmq://localhost/private/TradeQueue"
                      binding="netMsmqBinding"
                      bindingConfiguration="DomainlessMsmqBinding"
                      contract="QuickReturns.ITradeService"
                      />
           <!-- Add the following endpoint.  -->
           <!-- Note: your service must have an http base
                      address to add this endpoint. -->
```

```
        <endpoint contract="IMetadataExchange" binding=
                    "mexHttpBinding" address="mex" />

    </service>
</services>

<bindings>
    <netMsmqBinding>
        <binding name="DomainlessMsmqBinding" >
        <security>
          <transport
            msmqAuthenticationMode="None"
            msmqProtectionLevel="None"/>
        </security>
        </binding>
    </netMsmqBinding>
</bindings>
...

</configuration>
```

You then modify the client to be able to use the NetMSMQ bindings, as shown in Listing 8–8.

Listing 8–8. Modifying the Client

```
using System;
using System.Data;

using System.Messaging;

using System.Configuration;
using System.Web;
using System.Transactions;
namespace QuickReturns
{
    class Client
    {
        static void Main()
        {
            // Create a proxy for the client
            using (TradeServiceClient proxy = new TradeServiceClient())
            {
                // Create a transaction scope
                using (TransactionScope scope = new TransactionScope
                    (TransactionScopeOption.Required))

                {

                    proxy.DoTrade("MSFT", "IBM", 60);
                    Console.WriteLine("Selling 60 stocks of IBM and Buying MSFT ");

                    proxy.DoTrade("ACN","ABN", 100);
                    Console.WriteLine("Selling 60 stocks of ABN and Buying ACN ");
```

```
                        // Complete the transaction
                        scope.Complete();
...
}
```

As you have seen, you add a transaction scope around the DoTrade method in order to have the service use the NetMSMQ binding correctly. You will learn more about transactions in the next chapter. Next, you modify the App.config file for the client in order to use MSMQ, as per Listing 8–9.

Listing 8–9. Modifying the Client App.config File

```xml
<?xml version="1.0" encoding="utf-8"?>
<configuration>
    <system.serviceModel>
        <bindings>

            <netMsmqBinding>
                <binding name="NetMsmqBinding_ITradeService" closeTimeout="00:01:00"

                    openTimeout="00:01:00" receiveTimeout="00:10:00"
                        sendTimeout="00:01:00"
                    deadLetterQueue="System" durable="true"
                        exactlyOnce="true"
                    maxReceivedMessageSize="65536" maxRetryCycles="2"
                        receiveErrorHandling="Fault"
                    receiveRetryCount="5" retryCycleDelay="00:30:00"
                        timeToLive="1.00:00:00"
                    useSourceJournal="false" useMsmqTracing="false"
                        queueTransferProtocol="Native"
                    maxBufferPoolSize="524288" useActiveDirectory="false">
                    <readerQuotas maxDepth="32" maxStringContentLength=
                        "8192" maxArrayLength="16384"
                        maxBytesPerRead="4096" maxNameTableCharCount=
                            "16384" />
                    <security mode="Transport">
                        <transport msmqAuthenticationMode="None"
                            msmqProtectionLevel="None" />
                        <message clientCredentialType="Windows" />
                    </security>

                </binding>
            </netMsmqBinding>
        </bindings>
        <client>
            <endpoint address="net.msmq://localhost/private/
                    TradeQueue" binding="netMsmqBinding"
                bindingConfiguration="NetMsmqBinding_ITradeService"
                    contract="ITradeService"
                name="NetMsmqBinding_ITradeService" />
        </client>

    </system.serviceModel>
</configuration>
```

In this code, you set timeouts, the DLQ (should the message time out), the number of retries, and several related parameters. You also define that the client should use the NetMsmqBinding elements.

Right-click the solution, and set the client, TradeService, as the startup project. Run the application. Close TradeService, and let the client send messages. You can then browse the MSMQ queues in the Computer Management console and see the messages in the queue, as shown in Figure 8–6.

Start another version of TradeService, and you should be able to see the same messages being processed by the service.

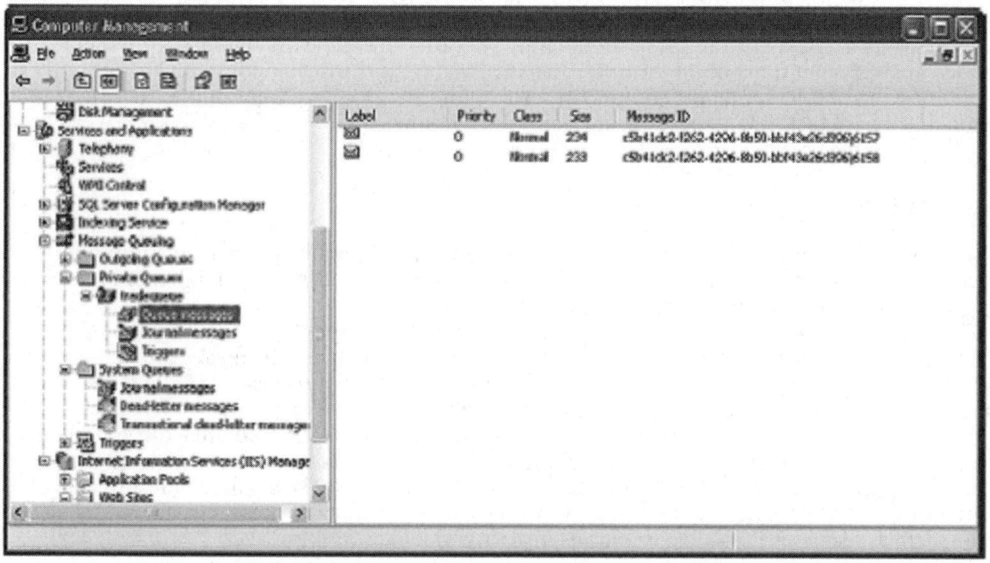

Figure 8–6. *Messages in the trade queue*

The scenario here addresses the use of discrete transactions; however, in some cases you'll need to use batch processing—for example, when dealing with back-end applications such as order-clearing systems. For further details on batch processing with queues, refer to the "Batch Processing with Queues Using Sessions" sidebar.

BATCH PROCESSING WITH QUEUES USING SESSIONS

When messages are processed together or in a specified order, you can use a queue to group them to facilitate batch processing by a single receiving application. Here's an example that may help you understand this better. Say you are selling products online and want to process orders that consist of multiple line items. The client application stores each of these line items as messages in a queue to be processed by a back-end order-processing system implemented as a WCF service. In a farmed back-end order-processing system, if each line item message is processed by a different back-end server, the performance will suffer. In a nonfarmed system with only a single back-end server, the server must process unrelated order line items as they come out of the queue. This complicates the business logic and degrades performance because the server switches between processing different orders.

For performance and correctness, it is best to have a single back-end system to process all line items associated with an order. WCF provides the concept of a session, which allows a server to maintain state for a client over a series of interactions. You can use a session to group all the messages related to an order so that a single receiving application and the same service instance can process all the related messages.

The MSMQ transport channel at the sender places the body of the WCF message within the MSMQ message and sends it via the MSMQ transport. It is the job of the MSMQ transport channel stack at the receiver to unpack the WCF message from the MSMQ message and then dispatch it as an invocation operation on the WCF service. The common theme in WCF is that the real work of messaging is in the channel, which abstracts out most of the complexities involved from the developer to make life simpler.

Implementing the MSMQ transport channel in WCF to integrate two WCF endpoints, as you have seen, is a straightforward task. Let's now look at integration channels.

Integration Channels

Massive amounts of applications have already been deployed, and will not be thrown away simply because of an emerging set of tools has been introduced. We would prefer the world to become WCF compliant overnight, but the chances of that happening are slim.

WCF addresses this issue with a practical solution. The queuing channel within WCF offers the concept of integration channels, which should be used to communicate with the legacy applications that use MSMQ. The integration channel for queues in WCF continues to use the classic MSMQ messaging formats and is implemented via the MsmqIntegrationBinding binding.

Behind the scenes, the MSMQ message is mapped out to a WCF message, and once this has been achieved, it invokes the WCF service. Alternatively, when a WCF application sends out a message, the reverse occurs. The properties of the WCF message are mapped back to those available in the legacy MSMQ message format, thus enabling the legacy application to consume the message.

The next section discusses these two scenarios in greater detail.

Integrating a WCF Client with an MSMQ Receiver

Leveraging existing investments in applications is a scenario that you will witness fairly often. Typically you will find that your key business processes are on opposite sides of the queue, and typically one of them will not be a WCF application.

In this scenario, the WCF client will hand the message to the integration channel, which will convert it to the MSMQ message format. Then the queue manager will store it in its local store. When the receiver MSMQ application becomes available, it will hand the message over to the queue manager for the receiver application, and the message will be consumed, as shown in Figure 8–7.

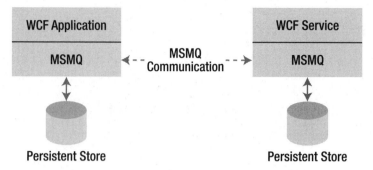

Figure 8–7. Integrating with an MSMQ application

We will now look at how you can integrate your WCF application with a legacy application using the MSMQ integration channel. Here are the steps (assuming you already have the message-receiving service up and running):

1. First, create an interface that defines the service contract for the WCF service that will send queued messages to the MSMQ receiver, as shown in Listing 8–10.

Listing 8–10. MSMQ Receiver Interface

```
[ServiceContract]
interface ITradeService
{
    [OperationContract(IsOneWay = true)]
    void SubmitPurchaseOrder(MsmqMessage<BuyTrade> msg);
}
```

2. Second, create a configuration that specifies the use of the IntegrationBinding binding, as shown in Listing 8–11.

Listing 8–11. IntegrationBinding Configuration

```
<?xml version="1.0" encoding="utf-8" ?>
<configuration xmlns="http://schemas.microsoft.com/.NetConfiguration/v2.0">
    <system.serviceModel>

    <client>

        <endpoint  name="TradeServiceLegacy"
                address="msmq.formatname:DIRECT=OS:.\private$\LegacyQueue"
                binding="msmqIntegrationBinding"
                bindingConfiguration="TradeServiceBinding"
                contract="QuickReturns.ITradeService">
        </endpoint>

    </client>

    <bindings>

        <msmqIntegrationBinding>
            <binding name="TradeServiceBinding" >
```

```
            <security mode="None" />
         </binding>
      </msmqIntegrationBinding>

   </bindings>
  </system.serviceModel>
</configuration>
```

You can now perform a buy or a sell in a transacted manner using MSMQ. And that's it. It's quite easy to integrate an MSMQ application with a WCF application. Now that you've accomplished this, you'll see how you can integrate an MSMQ client with a WCF application.

Integrating an MSMQ Client with a WCF Service

This scenario is commonly encountered when legacy applications need to interact with newer, more up-to-date applications. Traditionally this has been a nightmare scenario.

Legacy applications seldom have the flexibility to be integrated with newer technologies. In a business scenario, when critical processes reside in two different technologies, this can mean a great deal of frustration. However, if your legacy application uses MSMQ for messaging, then you can rectify this situation easily with WCF. The sender can still continue sending messages as it always has, and no change is required to the client application. WCF can easily integrate and communicate with the legacy system.

The msmqIntegrationBinding binding also allows you to integrate with MSMQ clients fairly easily. Here's how you can accomplish this:

1. Create an interface that defines the service contract for the WCF service that will receive queued messages from an MSMQ client, as shown in Listing 8–12.

Listing 8–12. msmqIntegrationBinding

```
// Define a service contract
 [ServiceContract(Namespace = "http://QuickReturns")]
 [KnownType(typeof(SomeOrder))]
public interface ITradeProcessor
{
    [OperationContract(IsOneWay = true, Action = "*")]
    void SubmitSomeOrder(MsmqMessage<SomeOrder> msg);
}
```

2. Next, implement the IOrderProcessor interface, and apply the ServiceBehavior attribute, as shown here:

```
// Service class that implements the service contract
// Added code to write output to the console window
public class TradeProcessorService : ITradeProcessor

{
    [OperationBehavior(TransactionScopeRequired = true,
            TransactionAutoComplete = true)]
    public void SubmitSomeOrder(MsmqMessage<SomeOrder> somemsg)
    {
        SomeOrder so = (SomeOrder)somemsg.Body;
                    }
}
```

3. Next, create the configuration to use the integration binding, as shown in Listing 8–13.

Listing 8–13. Configuration for the Integration Binding

```
<?xml version="1.0" encoding="utf-8" ?>
<configuration >

  <appSettings>
    <!-- use appSetting to configure MSMQ queue name -->
    <add key="orderQueueName" value=".\private$\ReceiveOrders" />
  </appSettings>
  <system.serviceModel>
    <services>
      <service
        name="QuickReturns.LegacyReceive" >
        <endpoint address="msmq.formatname:DIRECT=OS:.\private$\ReceiveOrders"
                           binding="msmqIntegrationBinding"
              bindingConfiguration="OrderProcessorBinding"
                  contract="QuickReturnsLegacyReceive">
        </endpoint>
      </service>
    </services>

    <bindings>
      <msmqIntegrationBinding>
        <binding name="OrderProcessorBinding" >
          <security mode="None" />
        </binding>
      </msmqIntegrationBinding>
    </bindings>
  </system.serviceModel>
</configuration>
```

Here, you've defined the service endpoints and let the application know which method to bind the application to. And you've told it where the endpoint is actually located.

4. You will now create the service host, in this case using a console-based executable, as shown in Listing 8–14.

Listing 8–14. Creating the Service Host

```
// Host the service within this EXE console application
public static void Main()
{
// Get MSMQ queue name from app settings in configuration
    string queueName = ConfigurationManager.AppSettings["LegacyQueue"];


// Create the transacted MSMQ queue if necessary
    if (!MessageQueue.Exists(queueName))
        MessageQueue.Create(queueName, true);
```

```
using (ServiceHost serviceHost = new ServiceHost(typeof(TradeService)))
{
    serviceHost.Open();

// The service can now be accessed
    Console.WriteLine("The service is ready.");
    Console.WriteLine("Press <ENTER> to terminate service.");
    Console.ReadLine();

// Close the ServiceHostBase to shut down the service
    serviceHost.Close();
    }
}
```

5. Start the host, and you are good to receive and process messages from an MSMQ client.

As you have seen, using queues with WCF is fairly easy. There is not a lot of complexity or code required to integrate legacy applications using the integration channel with WCF.

Some Pointers on Using MSMQ

As discussed, MSMQ offers you the ability to provide a durable store for your messages and an easy way to integrate with other non-WCF applications that use MSMQ, but you should keep in mind a few pitfalls and pointers when using MSMQ:

- The durability of the messages depends on the durability of the queue. MSMQ queues have a property called Durable. When this property is set to true, every message received on the queue will be written to disk until processed. If this property is set to false, keep in mind that if the machine hosting the queue fails, all messages in the queue will be lost. By default, it is set to true. While leaving this property at its default setting will cause some performance overhead, it's not recommended that you change it, since that would mean that end-to-end reliability could no longer be guaranteed. Of course, both the client and server ends need to have durability enabled to provide the reliability that you want.

- Disabling the DLQ is not recommended. If you are developing for MSMQ 4.0 or later, it is recommended that you configure one DLQ per application and use the poison message–handling capabilities. For more information, refer to the MSMQ guide on MSDN.

- In a web farm scenario, be aware that MSMQ 3.0 is not able to perform remote transacted reads. This is a limitation of MSMQ, not WCF.

Use the ReceiveContext API to lock the message in the queue and prevent other services or service instances from processing it.

Summary

This chapter covered the following:

- Why you need reliable messaging

- How to use the reliable messaging options offered by WCF

- How to implement reliable messaging using reliable sessions

- What queuing channels are available in WCF

- How to use the MSMQ transport channel

- How to use the integration channel

- How to integrate with an MSMQ receiver application

- How to integrate your application with an MSMQ client

We recommend the Vista SDK and WCF documentation for further information about this topic. Please dive into the code listings that implement reliable messaging within the .NET Framework also. You'll find the API-level implementation of the subject discussed there, as well as guidance on best practices.

In Chapter 9, you will learn about support for transactions in WCF and how to implement transactions. Transactions are important in business dealings. Executing a set of processes as a transaction can ensure reliability and consistency of data.

CHAPTER 9

■ ■ ■

Using Transactions in WCF

Transactions are fundamental to applications for ensuring consistent data behavior, and also for ensuring the implementation of atomic, consistent, independent, and durable (ACID) behavior in an application. In the QuickReturns Ltd. application, ACID behavior means that when you make a trade, it is absolute. It will either be complete in its entirety or it will be rolled back, leaving no room for ambiguity. Without transactions, you could not be sure that the trade was indeed conducted, and you would have no means of verifying the validity without ambiguity. Having a transactional system ensures that trades are consistently applied and final.

You also need to ensure that the systems being built provide recoverability. This means that when a service or machine fails and comes back online, its data is still available.

Scalability is another area where transactions are critical, since it clearly earmarks the point at which resources are requested and released at the end of the transaction. Transactions enable you to avoid deadlocks, whereby two or more threads try to acquire the same resources and cause the application to hang. Typically, deadlocks are resolved by making one of the threads release its resources. Transactions are critical with regard to deadlocks—they ensure safe system state and that any data that any unapplied data is rolled back successfully.

Finally, transactions are important for preserving data integrity. When you perform the same query to your persistent data store, you want to receive the same result each time, and transactions allow you to do this.

WCF provides rich support for transactions, and this chapter will look at that support in detail. Specifically, we will cover the following topics:

- The need for transactions

- The types of transactions in WCF

- How to define transactions in WCF

- How to use transactions with queues

■**Note** This chapter builds on the concepts introduced in Chapter 8. Be sure you're familiar with those concepts before moving forward, since they really do go hand in hand with the concepts in this chapter.

What's a Transaction?

Broadly speaking, a transaction is a mechanism for ensuring that several operations succeed or fail as an atomic unit. In other words, it ensures that all operations succeed or all operations fail in the event that even one of the constituent components of the transaction encounters an error. Broadly speaking, transactions enforce the ACID rule popularized in database programming. WCF provides a simple, centralized way to support transactions within your applications. Prior to WCF, although there were mechanisms to support transactions (`Begin Transaction...End Transaction` in Visual Basic, for example), achieving a single, standard means of support nondatabase transactions was not trivial. A transaction enables you to carry out a set of operations as a single execution unit whereby you achieve reliable results.

In the QuickReturns Ltd. scenario, you conduct trades on the stock exchange; not knowing for sure whether a trade was successful could have disastrous results. Using the transaction mechanism, you achieve the following results:

Atomicity: This ensures that the trades go through the system as single unit or abort as a single unit.

Consistency: This guarantees that any transaction the database performs will take it from one consistent state to another. All orders that are part of a single transaction work with the correct attributes (buy/sell, associated quantities/prices), and that behavior is repeated identically.

Isolation: This ensures that each transaction is independent and isolated from other transactions occurring in the system; the transactions don't have any impact on each other's behavior. In the trade system, multiple users will often use the system to trade at the same time. The isolation of the transactions ensures that the trades conducted by individual users (and even trades from a single user occurring at the same time) are distinct and separate from each other.

Durability: As the name suggests, this ensures that all data is committed to a nonvolatile resource, such as a database, XML file, or flat file. The data of the transaction must remain available even after the transaction has long since completed. In our example, durability is provided via a record of the trades that have taken place. You can check when a particular trade was conducted and have the data available to you whenever you want it.

WCF implements the WS-Atomic protocol to enable transaction support. This enables you to build transactions that can interact with multiple endpoints inside WCF and with third-party systems, such as web services developed in Java.

A transaction has three essential components that interact, as shown in Figure 9–1: the application, the persistent store, and the transaction manager.

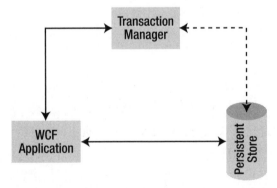

Figure 9–1. Participants in a transaction

■**Note** Looking again at QuickReturns Ltd. from a business perspective, you might need transactions that span multiple business activities. For example, you might put in a sell order and then want to buy oil futures at a predefined price. Should you be unable to get your oil futures at the desired price, you might want to hold off on the sale itself. This scenario is referred to as a *compensating transaction*, whereby all discrete components of the flow are treated as a single transaction. Compensating transactions offer looser coupling than the atomic transaction protocol, with the trade-off that compensating transactions are inherently more difficult to code and maintain. WCF does not provide support for compensating transactions out of the box. Should you need a compensating transaction, you would need to implement the code yourself, using a complementary product such as Windows Workflow Foundation (WF), or using Microsoft Distributed Transaction Coordinator (MS DTC). For more information about MS DTC, refer to http://msdn.microsoft.com/en-us/library/ms684146(v=vs.85).aspx.

The application initiates a transaction, which can take place over any of the supported protocols, and the transaction is committed to a persistent store (e.g., a SQL Server or Oracle database, or even a flat file). The coordination between the application and the persistent store (also sometimes referred to as the *resource manager*) is handled by the *transaction manager*. The role of the transaction manager is to enlist all parties in the transaction, preparing them for the transaction. This means ensuring that they are available and ready to participate in the transaction.

Two example of transaction managers are MS DTC and the Lightweight Transaction Manager (LTM). The LTM is implemented by System.Transactions and provides an extremely fast means for transaction management for volatile data within the application domain.

Figure 9–2 displays the transaction stack in .NET 3.0, including the Kernel Transaction Manager (KTM), which is available in Windows Server 2008. (See the "Kernel Transaction Coordinator" sidebar for more information.)

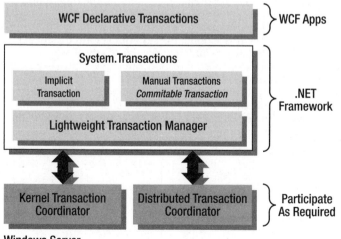

Figure 9–2. Transactions in .NET

KERNEL TRANSACTION MANAGER

The KTM is a feature of Windows Server 2008 that allows you to make transactions available as a kernel object rather than a user object. The advantage of the KTM is that it allows you to access system objects such as the file system or files via transactions. You can leverage this in conjunction with WCF applications that need to read from files and write to files—for example, to provide transactional support.

It is important to keep in mind that the KTM is not part of WCF, but rather the Windows Server 2008 family. You can find more information about the KTM and its usage at http://msdn.microsoft.com/library/ default.asp?url=/library/en-us/KTM/fs/transaction_managers.asp.

Understanding the Types of Transactions in WCF

Implementing reliable messaging comes with multiple challenges. You could broadly categorize these challenges into communication issues and processing issues. More often than not, these are interrelated challenges that are nontrivial in nature to solve.

In WCF, transactions are implemented in System.ServiceModel, which enables you to easily configure timeouts, activation (just-in-time), and the behavior of the transaction in terms of functionality, contracts, and flow. The System.Transactions namespace allows you to implement your own transactions, and you can use the System.Transactions namespace's TransactionScope class to use the implicit model of transactions within WCF.

The transactions themselves internally use a mechanism called *two-phase commit*. The two-phase commit protocol lets all the nodes involved in a distributed transaction participate in an atomic manner. During the course of the two-phase commit transaction protocol, the state of the transaction transitions multiple times. The two-phase commit protocol has three stages: active, phase 1, and phase 2. In the active stage, the transaction is created. The superior resource manager (the resource manager of the creator) enlists the other resource managers, who become active in the transaction. In phase 1, the creator issues the commit command for the transaction, and the enlisted resource managers respond about whether they are prepared to commit. If the managers are prepared to commit, the transaction will move to phase 2. Otherwise, it will abort.

In phase 2, the superior resource manager will write a durable entry to an internal log, and then issue the commit to the enlisted resource managers. Once this is done, the superior resource manager will begin sending the commit to the enlisted resource managers and, irrespective of any errors (network, resource unavailability, etc.), will continue until all enlisted resource managers have been sent a commit message. Then the superior resource manager will wait for the confirmation of the commit from the enlisted resource managers, for an error message, or until a timeout occurs. Should all enlisted resource managers respond positively about the commit, the superior resource manager will erase the log entry, and the transaction will end. In the event of an error, the transaction will abort. Internally, the System.Transactions namespace utilizes the two-phase commit protocol. Figure 9–3 explains this graphically.

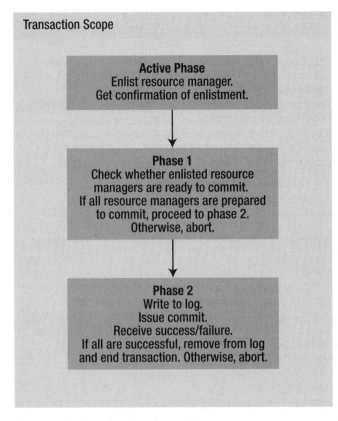

Figure 9–3. The two-phase commit transaction

So, in the QuickReturns Ltd. scenario, when the client invokes the trade, it will utilize its resource manager to enlist the trade service's resource manager. Then, in phase 1 of the two-phase commit, it will get its confirmation to participate in the transaction once the data has been marshaled to the trade service resource manager. Then, in the second phase, the data will be committed and the transaction completed.

You can also use the MS DTC to implement transactions that span multiple Windows (XP/2003 or later) infrastructures. In the scenario where MS DTC is utilized to provide transactions, each of the machines and applications that participate within the transaction has its own local resource managers that cooperatively manage transactions that span multiple systems. *Distributed* transactions are in essence transactions that update data across two or more systems as a single unit. Distributed transactions are difficult to implement in the absence of MS DTC, since the application's resource manager must detect and recover from a variety of failure scenarios, including those involving network infrastructure, local availability of resources in a distributed environment, and state management across multiple machines. We'll dive into the problem space of distributed transactions in the next section. For further details about MS DTC in the context of WCF, please refer to the "MS DTC and WCF" sidebar.

MS DTC AND WCF

MS DTC is designed to support transactions that span multiple Windows systems. Each of the machines participating in the transaction has local transaction managers that are enlisted by MS DTC for the transaction, and the initiating manager handles the coordination between the local managers on the remote systems. The transaction is executed as a single atomic transaction whereby MS DTC will commit to all participating machines in a single unit or roll back the transactions across all the participating machines. MS DTC transactions utilize the OLE transaction–compliant resource managers and explicitly control the duration and the scope of the transaction; they can be invoked from any application written in C or C++. You can interface with these applications through the interop interfaces in WCF, which we'll discuss in greater detail in Chapter 10.

For further details about MS DTC programming, please refer to the DTC Programmer's Reference at `http://msdn.microsoft.com/library/default.asp?url=/library/en-us/cossdk/html/c0f7d3dd-4da1-45df-8516-d0d2ec1b0ca6.asp`.

Defining Transactions in WCF

WCF supports the WS-Atomic transaction protocol. Transactions in WCF are defined with the `System.ServiceModel` namespace and feature three main components. These are the `ServiceBehavior` attribute, the `OperationBehavior` attribute, and the `TransactionFlow` attribute. We will look at each of these in a little more depth and examine what these achieve individually in the transaction in the following sections. You'll learn about their implications prior to jumping into the how-tos of implementing them.

Using the TransactionFlow Attribute

The `TransactionFlow` attribute specifies whether the service can be related to the external interactions, and the level at which the incoming transaction is accepted. The available options of the `TransactionFlow` attribute are `Allowed`, `NotAllowed`, and `Mandatory`. You set this in `App.config`, which essentially passes information about the transaction to the service, and will either slow down or speed up the transaction rate depending upon the network conditions. Transaction flow is determined by the bindings and by default is disabled. Unless you explicitly utilize it, it will not be enabled, as shown in Listing 9–1. The listing enables the transaction flow for the `ITradeService` interface.

Listing 9–1. Enabling Transaction Flow

```
<!-- binding configuration - configures WSHttp binding
     for Transactions sessions -->
<bindings>
    <wsHttpBinding>
        <binding name="ITradeService" transactionFlow="true">
            <reliableSession enabled="false" />
        </binding>
    </wsHttpBinding>
</bindings>
<behaviors>
    <serviceBehaviors>
```

```
            <behavior name="MyServiceTypeBehaviors" >
                <!-- Add the following element to your service
                        behavior configuration. -->
                <serviceMetadata httpGetEnabled="true"/>
                <serviceDebug httpHelpPageEnabled="true"
                        includeExceptionDetailInFaults="false"/>
            </behavior>
        </serviceBehaviors>
</behaviors>
```

Using the ServiceBehavior and OperationBehavior Attributes

The ServiceBehavior attribute defines the behavior of the contract and the attributes of the transaction. In essence, it specifies how the transaction will behave under circumstances such as a failure in the network. It also specifies whether resources should be released when a transaction completes, and it ensures concurrency in the transaction. The attributes of the ServiceBehavior attribute include the following:

TransactionAutoCompleteOnSessionClose: This specifies whether outstanding transactions are completed when the session closes, and by default is false. For instance, if in the QuickReturns Ltd. example you were to shut the trading service down, this would affect how the incoming sessions would behave. The default setting ensures that if an error occurs (when the service is shut down or unavailable, or when there is a network error), the transaction will abort and roll back to its original state. You can also set this to true, in which case the incoming session will degrade gracefully. In other words, it will shut down in a controlled fashion, instead of just crashing. Additionally, any uncompleted transactions will be successfully completed—but only from the perspective of the client. This can potentially lead to an inconsistent state, since the trade service will not be available, even though the client will think that the transactions completed correctly.

ReleaseServiceInstanceOnTransactionComplete: This specifies whether the underlying service instance is released when a transaction completes. The default value for this property is true. This means each instance will create a new transaction scope. Releasing the service instance is an internal action taken by the service, and has no impact on sessions and/or instances established by clients. The transaction scope is the entire process of enlisting the various parties in a communication, exchanging the data, and then terminating the connection once the exchange of the data is complete. In the QuickReturns Ltd. example, the transaction scope would establish the client connectivity to the trade service and then pass the actual trade messages. Then, once the service received the data, it would terminate the specific connection created for the transaction.

Within the ReleaseServiceInstanceOnTransactionComplete attribute, you have four primary ways of completing transactions:

- An operation with TransactionAutoComplete set to true returns control to the initiator of the transaction.

- A service calls SetTransactionComplete.

- A client closes a session associated with an active transaction that is still executing, or a network error occurs; in either of these scenarios, the result is a rollback if TransactionAutoComplete is set to false.

- The transaction aborts for any given reason.

- All of the above can be set quite easily in the OperationBehavior attribute, as defined in Listing 9–2.

Listing 9–2. Setting the OperationBehavior Attribute

```
[OperationBehavior(TransactionScopeRequired=true,TransactionAutoComplete=true)]
void ITradeService.AddTrade(Trade trade)
```

The TransactionIsolationLevel property deals with how the data is to be versioned (i.e., the isolation level to be applied). If TransactionScopeRequired is set to true and no transaction flows, then the TransactionIsolationLevel property takes one of two IsolationLevel values: ReadCommited, for which only nonvolatile data can be read, or ReadUnCommited, for which volatile data can be read. If this property is left blank, it will default to Unspecified. This means that the method will accept any isolation level for a transaction that flows into it, and will use Serializable (in which each transaction is completely separate from all other transactions) when you create a new transaction. Should you decide to change the default value on the calling application, keep in mind that it must match the local values for the transaction to succeed. A mismatch in the values will cause the transaction to fail.

The TransactionTimeout property, just as the name suggests, sets the time period within which a new transaction created by the service must complete. If this time is reached and the transaction has not completed, it aborts. The TimeSpan set in this property is used as the TransactionScope timeout for any operations that have TransactionScopeRequired set to true, and that have established a new transaction. Although it is important to give your transactions adequate time to complete, setting this value too high or too low will have a serious impact on the performance of the application. Listing 9–3 shows how to implement the transaction isolation level, which in this case is set to ReadCommited.

Listing 9–3. Setting the Transaction Isolation Level

```
ServiceBehavior(TransactionIsolationLevel=
        System.Transactions.IsolationLevel.ReadCommited)]
    public class TradeService : ITradeService
```

The OperationBehavior attribute, as the name suggests, helps you configure the behavior of the transaction. By default this is set to false, which means that if a transaction scope has not been defined, then the operation will occur outside the scope of the transaction.

Let's put this into context: in the previous chapter, we did not transactions or define the OperationBehavior attribute in the code. So, even though the trade service was receiving messages reliably from the client application, there really was no guarantee that the data was actually persisted correctly. This is a scary scenario.

However, keep in mind that even when the OperationBehavior attribute is set to false and you do want a transaction scope, the attribute is derived from the calling application. So, what would happen if you defined a TransactionScope on the client but not on the service? In this case, the transaction scope of the client would be utilized to create a transaction scope on the service, even though none was defined for the service. This is a boon for developers, who can now really decouple their application from the implementation of the service.

Now that we've gone through the dense and somewhat difficult theory of transactions and their attributes, we'll look at how to add transaction support to a WCF application.

■**Note** We will continue to build upon the concepts covered in Chapter 8, since reliable messaging and transactions really do go hand in hand. As mentioned, you need both reliable messaging and transactions to achieve reliable and durable results for your solution.

Defining Transactions in QuickReturns Ltd.

You'll now begin to modify the QuickReturns Ltd. application to use transactions. Open the
Chapter09\ReliableMessaging\QuickReturnsTransactional solution.

This exercise assumes that you are going to sell a stock and log the sale in a database. The two deals
will be committed in a single transaction. You'll begin by modifying the client.

■**Note** The TradeServiceDB database used in this example uses SQL Server Express, which is freely downloadable
from http://msdn.microsoft.com/vstudio/express/sql/download/default.aspx. You must have this
installed for the example to work. Install SQL Server Express by downloading the setup file and running it. It is
recommended that once the download begins, you select the Run option when prompted. Once the download
completes, this will automatically launch the installation. It is recommended that you accept the default settings
during the installation process. You can find complete details of the installation and additional components at the
previously mentioned link. Also, keep in mind that if you have installed Visual Studio in a non-Express edition, SQL
Server Express is installed by default. Please check your local installation to see whether SQL Server Express is
already installed as part of your Visual Studio installation.

Begin by adding a reference to System.Transactions in the QuickReturns Ltd. solution. Open
program.cs in the client application of TradeService, and modify it to look like the code in Listing 9–4.
You begin with adding support for the transactions by referencing System.Transactions. Thereafter, you
add a transaction endpoint to allow the client application to utilize transactions.

Listing 9–4. Modifying the Client program.cs File for Transactions

```
using System;
using System.ServiceModel;
using System.Transactions;

namespace QuickReturns
{
    // The service contract is defined in generatedClient.cs,
    //     generated from the service by the svcutil tool

    // Client implementation code
    class Client
    {
        static void Main()
        {
            // Create a client using either wsat or oletx
            //     endpoint configurations
            TradeServiceClient client = new TradeServiceClient(
                "WSAtomicTransaction_endpoint");

            // In the event you decide to use the Ole transaction
            //     endpoint, uncomment the line below and comment the line above
```

```
    // TradeServiceClient client = new
        TradeServiceClient("OleTransactions_endpoint");

    // Start a transaction scope
    using (TransactionScope tx =
                new TransactionScope(TransactionScopeOption.RequiresNew))
    {
        Console.WriteLine("Starting transaction");

        // Call the Add service operation
        // - generatedClient will flow the required active transaction
        int qty;
        int price;
        int result;


        // Call the CalcValue service operation
        // - generatedClient will not flow the active transaction
        qty = 100;
        price = 15;
        result = client.CalcValue(qty, price);
        Console.WriteLine("  Sold ACN Quantity {0},
            For$ {1} With a Total Value of ${2}",
            qty, price, result);

                        // Complete the transaction scope
        Console.WriteLine("  Completing transaction");
        tx.Complete();
    }

    Console.WriteLine("Transaction Committed");

    // Closing the client gracefully closes the
    //      connection and cleans up resources
    client.Close();

    Console.WriteLine("Press <ENTER> to terminate client.");
    Console.ReadLine();
        }
    }
}
```

Notice that the transaction scope is defined, which encapsulates the operations you want to handle in a single transaction.

You'll now modify the App.config file on the client project to reflect the usage of transactions, as shown in Listing 9–5. What you are doing here is enabling the transaction flow attribute.

Listing 9–5. Modifying the Client App.config File

```
<system.serviceModel>
    <client>
        <endpoint name="TradeServiceConfiguration"
          address="http://localhost:8000/TradeService"
        binding="wsHttpBinding "
        bindingConfiguration="ReliableHttpBinding"
        contract="Client.ITradeService,Client"/>
    </client>
    <bindings>
        <wsHttpBinding>
            <binding name="ReliableHttpBinding" transactionFlow="true">
                <reliableSession enabled="true" ordered ="true"/>
            </binding>
        </wsHttpBinding>
    </bindings>
</system.serviceModel>
```

Now that this is done, modify the ITradeService interface in the client project. This will then reflect the changes that you will be making to ITradeService later. Listing 9–6 shows the changes.

Listing 9–6. Modifying the Client ITradeService

```
<configuration>
  <system.serviceModel>
    <bindings>
      <netTcpBinding>
        <binding name="transactionalOleTransactionsTcpBinding"
                 transactionFlow="true"
                 transactionProtocol="OleTransactions" />
      </netTcpBinding>
      <wsHttpBinding>
        <binding name="transactionalWsatHttpBinding"
                 transactionFlow="true" />
      </wsHttpBinding>
    </bindings>
    <client>
      <endpoint
        address="http://localhost:8000/QuickReturns/TradeService"
        binding="wsHttpBinding"
        bindingConfiguration="transactionalWsatHttpBinding"
        contract="ITradeService"
        name="WSAtomicTransaction_endpoint">

        <!--The username and the domain over here will have to be replaced
        by the identity under which the service will be running-->
        <!--identity>
            <userPrincipalName value="username@domain" />
        </identity-->
      </endpoint>
      <endpoint
```

```
        address="net.tcp://localhost:8008/QuickReturns/TradeService"
        binding="netTcpBinding"
        bindingConfiguration="transactionalOleTransactionsTcpBinding"
        contract="ITradeService"
        name="OleTransactions_endpoint">
        <!--The username and the domain over here will have to be replaced
        by the identity under which the service will be running -->
          <!--identity>
                <userPrincipalName value="username@domain" />
          </identity-->
      </endpoint>
    </client>
  </system.serviceModel>
</configuration>
```

Now that you have accomplished this, you can enhance the trade service to accomplish your goals. Next, you'll modify ITradeService in the QuickReturns Ltd. trade service in the same manner as you did for the client. Please refer to Listing 9–7 for details.

Listing 9–7. Modifying ITradeService in the QuickReturns Ltd. Trade Service

```
using System;
using System.ServiceModel;
using System.Transactions;
using System.Configuration;
using System.Data.SqlClient;
using System.Globalization;

namespace QuickReturns
{
    // Define a service contract
    [ServiceContract(Namespace = "QuickReturns")]
    public interface ITradeService
    {
        [OperationContract]
        [TransactionFlow(TransactionFlowOption.Mandatory)]
        int CalculateTradeValue(int qty, int price);

    }
```

Once you have included the references to System.Transactions and in particular Sys.Data.SqlClient, you will have the basis for supporting transactions and the logging database. Next you'll set the transaction isolation level for the trade service, as shown in Listing 9–8.

Listing 9–8. Setting the Transaction Isolation Level

```
// Service class that implements the service contract
 [ServiceBehavior(TransactionIsolationLevel =
        System.Transactions.IsolationLevel.Serializable)]
```

Now you'll set the transaction scope, which will encapsulate the operations you want to occur within the transaction, as shown in Listing 9–9.

Listing 9–9. *Setting the Transaction Scope*

```
public class TradeService : ITradeService
{

    [OperationBehavior(TransactionScopeRequired = true)]

    public int CalculateTradeValue(int qty, int price)
    {
        RecordToLog(String.Format(CultureInfo.CurrentCulture,
         "Recording  CAN Trade Value {0} with price {1}",
         qty,price ));
        return qty * price;
    }

    private static void RecordToLog(string recordText)
    {
        // Record the operations performed
        if (ConfigurationManager.AppSettings["usingSql"] == "true")
        {
            using (SqlConnection conn = new
            SqlConnection(ConfigurationManager.AppSettings
            ["connectionString"]))
            {
                conn.Open();
                // You are now going to log our trade to the log table
                //       by actually inserting the data into the table
                SqlCommand cmdLog = new SqlCommand(
                    "INSERT into Log (Entry) Values (@Entry)",
                    conn);
                cmdLog.Parameters.AddWithValue("@Entry", recordText);
                cmdLog.ExecuteNonQuery();
                cmdLog.Dispose();

                Console.WriteLine("  Logging Trade to database:
                  {0}", recordText);

                conn.Close();
            }
        }
        else
            Console.WriteLine("  Noting row: {0}", recordText);
    }
}
```

Next, you can modify the App.config file for the service host to ensure that all transactions are passed on to the QuickReturns Ltd. trade service. The console-based service host does not require any modifications, since the host service itself does not change. You will be calculating the trade value and returning this to the client, as well as logging the trade into the TradeService database. This is a simple database with a log table, which has an identity field and the log field. Both the transactions occur within a transaction scope and will fail or succeed as a single unit, as shown in Listing 9–10.

Listing 9–10. Modifying the Host App.config File

```
<?xml version="1.0" encoding="utf-8" ?>
<configuration>
  <appSettings>
    <!-- Sets connect to a database -->
    <add key="usingSql" value="true" />
    <!-- Sets the database connection string -->
    <add key="connectionString" value="DataSource=.\SQLEXPRESS;
          AttachDbFilename=
          |DataDirectory|\TradeServiceDb.mdf;Integrated Security=
          True;User Instance=True" />
</appSettings>
```

Now that you have established the database connectivity for the logging, you can modify the <Service> attributes. In Listing 9–11, you will be configuring the bindings of the service to use the WS-Atomic transaction protocol.

Listing 9–11. Setting the WSAtomicTransaction Binding Configuration in App.config

```
<system.serviceModel>
  <services>
    <service
        name="QuickReturns.TradeService"
        behaviorConfiguration="TradeServiceBehavior">

      <host>
        <baseAddresses>
          <add baseAddress="http://localhost:8000/QuickReturns/tradeservice" />
          <add baseAddress="net.tcp://localhost:8080/QuickReturns/tradeservice" />
        </baseAddresses>
      </host>

      <!-- specify wsHttpBinding with the WSAtomicTransactional
            binding configuration -->
      <endpoint address=""
              binding="wsHttpBinding"
              bindingConfiguration="transactionalWsatHttpBinding"
              contract="QuickReturns.ITradeService"
              name="WSAtomicTransaction_endpoint" />

      <!-- specify netTcpBinding and an OleTransactions
            transactional binding configuration since that is
            what WCF uses internally-->
      <endpoint address=""
              binding="netTcpBinding"
              bindingConfiguration="transactionalOleTransactionsTcpBinding"
              contract="QuickReturns.ITradeService"
              name="OleTransactions_endpoint" />

        <!-- specify the Metadata Exchange -->
      <endpoint address="mex"
```

```
            binding="mexHttpBinding"
            contract="IMetadataExchange"
            name="mex_endpoint"/>
  </service>
</services>
```

As shown in Listing 9–12, you will continue to modify App.config so that it utilizes the transactionFlow and sets it to true.

Listing 9–12. Configuring Transaction Flow

```
<!-- binding configuration - configures transaction flow  -->
<bindings>
  <netTcpBinding>
    <binding name="transactionalOleTransactionsTcpBinding
         " transactionFlow="true"  transactionProtocol=
         "OleTransactions"/>
  </netTcpBinding>

  <wsHttpBinding>
    <binding name="transactionalWsatHttpBinding" transactionFlow="true" />
  </wsHttpBinding>
</bindings>

<!--For debugging purposes -->
<behaviors>
  <serviceBehaviors>
    <behavior name="TradeServiceBehavior" >
      <serviceMetadata httpGetEnabled="true" />
      <serviceDebug includeExceptionDetailInFaults="false" />
    </behavior>
  </serviceBehaviors>
</behaviors>

</system.serviceModel>
</configuration>
```

Finally, you need to enable support for WS-Atomic transactions in WCF. To do this, first open the .NET Framework command prompt. At the command prompt, simply run xws_reg –wsat+ and press Enter. This completes the configuration of the transaction support for QuickReturns Ltd.

You can also register WsatUI.dll using regasm.exe to provide the Microsoft Management Console snap-in for WSAT configuration. Navigate to Control Panel ➤ Administrative Tools ➤ Component Services, and select Properties from My Computer, as shown in Figure 9–4.

To register WsatUI.dll, you need to run regasm.exe /codebase WsatUI.dll at the command prompt. You can then configure the parameters of the WS-Atomic transaction protocol from the user interface, as illustrated in Figure 9–5.

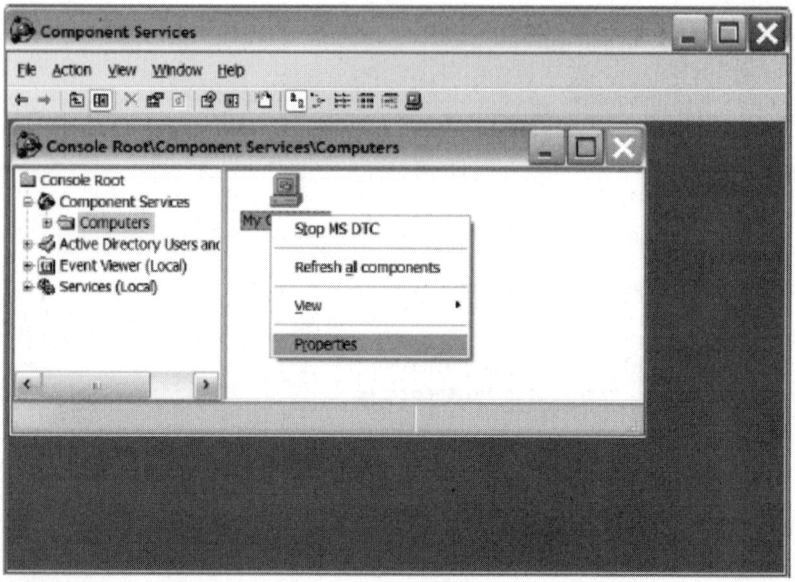

Figure 9–4. Selecting the properties for My Computer in Component Services

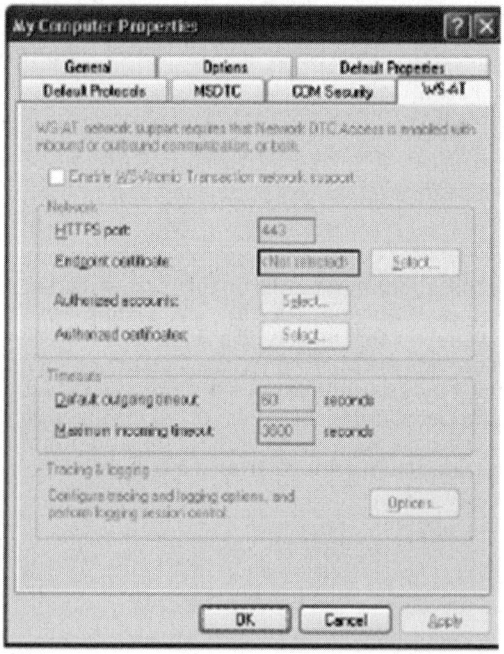

Figure 9–5. The WsatUI.dll user interface

When you run the application, you'll see the trades sent by the client in the TradeAuditService window, along with the committed trades.

Now that you've seen how to configure the application to use transactions in conjunction with reliable messaging, you'll learn how to make your queues utilize transactions easily.

Working with Transactions and Queues

In Chapter 8 you saw that MSMQ plays an important part in WCF and offers you a great deal of advantages in terms of reliability in scenarios that require integration with legacy applications, as well as scenarios where you require guaranteed delivery.

It is important to note that the queuing and dequeuing of messages between a client and the queue is implicitly transactional. In other words, the transfer of a message to and from a queue is transactional in nature; either the entire message will be placed on the queue or none of it will. This is fine for scenarios that require one-way messaging only. However, what if you require a series of operations under the sponsorship of a single transaction scope?

The scenario where you require multiple operations to occur as a single transaction in the context of MSMQ is often referred to as a *sessiongram*, while the single, one-way operation is referred to as a *datagram*. In using sessiongram scenarios, you are aiming for a group of operations to occur within the scope of a single transaction *exactly once and in order*.

■**Note** In reality, a transaction using message queues requires two transactions. The first transaction occurs between the application and the queue, and the second occurs between the queue and the receiver. If an error occurs in either one of these transactions, the transaction will abort. However, note that the messages sent under the transaction are discarded, while messages received by the queue remain in the queue until they are retried at a later time. Transactions using queues provide a level of isolation, inherent reliability, and security. However, for version 1.0 of WCF, they are not interoperable with heterogeneous systems that do not use MSMQ. Technically, you can use IBM MQSeries through the interop mechanism to handle transaction using queues with WCF, which we'll cover in Chapters 10 and 13.

WCF makes programming MSMQ transaction scenarios very simple with regard to how you configure the audit service and the client parts of your application.

Examine QueueMessagingClient shown in Listing 9–13. The example shows the support for transactions and how to set a transaction scope.

Listing 9–13. QuickReturns Ltd. QueueMessagingClient

```
using System;
using System.Transactions;

namespace QuickReturns
{
    class Client
    {
        public static void Main()
        {
```

```
// Create a proxy for the client
using (TradeServiceClient proxy = new TradeServiceClient())
{
    // Create a transaction scope. This is the only line of
    //    code required to enable transactions in WCF using MSMQ
    using (TransactionScope scope = new
        TransactionScope(TransactionScopeOption.Required))
    {
        proxy.DoTrade("MSFT", "IBM", 60);
        Console.WriteLine("Beginning Transaction 1....");
        Console.WriteLine("Selling 1000 stocks of ACN and Buying IBM ");
        Console.WriteLine("Ending Transaction 1....");
        Console.WriteLine("");
        // Mark the beginning of the second transaction
        Console.WriteLine("Beginning Transaction 2....");
        proxy.DoTrade("ACN", "ABN", 100);
        Console.WriteLine("Selling 100 stocks of ABN and Buying ACN ");
        Console.WriteLine("Beginning Transaction 2....");

        // Complete the transaction
        scope.Complete();
    }

}

Console.WriteLine();
Console.WriteLine("Press <ENTER> to terminate client.");
Console.ReadLine();
    }
  }
}
```

MSMQ operations are by default one-way only, and to enable transactions on the service, you would require either a duplex or a request-response contract. In the current scenario, this is not possible. If you run your client only, you will see the console application shown in Figure 9–6. At this point, the messages have been put on the queue successfully, and you can rest assured that the queue will deliver the messages to the trade service when it does become available.

Even though the service is not running, the queue is able to pick up the messages and store these for when the service becomes available. You must keep in mind that the reliable and durable storage provided is in fact a feature of MSMQ, not WCF. The WS-ReliableMessaging standard does not make any assertion regarding message durability. This means that should the machine crash, any existing messages would be lost. However, MSMQ as a technology is independent of WCF, and provides you with a transport that is both reliable and durable. Messages that have been persisted to the queue survive machine reboots and are lost only in the event of a catastrophic hardware failure. In the current scenario, you can benefit from this feature when the client passes on the messages to MSMQ and the trade service is not available. To simulate a failure scenario, you could reboot the machine and then start TradeService, and the messages would be delivered successfully. MSMQ also provides you with the means of decoupling the transport from the application. By doing this, MSMQ can open up a whole new world of scenarios for integration. An application at the end of the queue may or may not be a WCF application or even a Windows-based application. The only requirement is that it is able to communicate with MSMQ. This decoupling of the transport from the application and the availability of a durable store for the application provide you the tools to build highly resilient enterprise applications without having to write code, since the Windows platform provides you with the functionality out of the box.

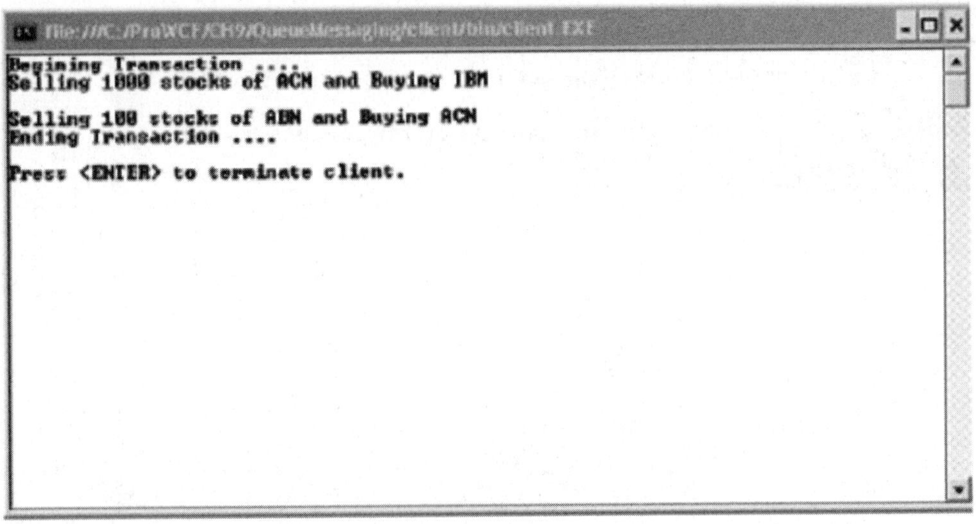

Figure 9–6. The client placing messages on the queue

■**Note** WCF provides support for integrating with MSMQ out of the box. However, queues are possible without MSMQ, and you can even write your own queue providers. Technically, it is possible to interact with your queue provider if it provides an API that WCF understands. However, this is extremely difficult to accomplish. Please refer to http://msdn.microsoft.com/library/default.asp?url=/library/en-us/msmq/html/ff917e87-05d5-478f-9430-0f560675ece1.asp for further details about the MSMQ provider. To get started with building custom queue providers, refer to Web Service Message Queue (WSMQ). WSMQ is an open source initiative to provide a web service–based message queue, and will help you get started in writing your own queues.

When you start an instance of the trade service, the messages are passed on to the service by the queue, as shown in Figure 9–7.

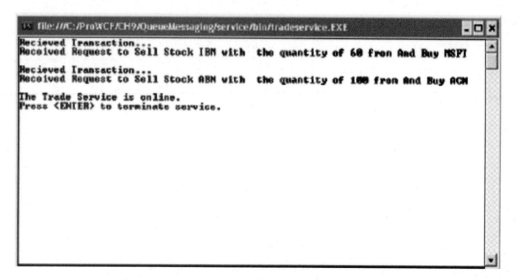

Figure 9–7. Transactions received by the trade service

A rule of thumb when using transactions with queues is that you should set the ExactlyOnce property of the binding to true if you are using transacted queues and to false if using nontransacted queues. However, be aware that setting this to false can degrade reliability, and you should evaluate this on a case-by-case basis.

A WORD ABOUT DEAD LETTER AND POISON QUEUES

In Chapter 8 you learned about the dead letter queues (DLQs) and poison queue functionality. It is possible to use the functionality provided by a poison queue to ensure that your transactions are retried multiple times at set intervals, rather than having fail after one attempt. This feature is available in Windows Server 2008 and later, and adds to the powerful arsenal of tools available to you.

A message will generally become poisoned if the queue has tried to deliver it to the receiver but the number of retries has been exceeded. Although this can happen because of network outages and service unavailability, among other reasons, you can configure the message to be retried after a set amount of time has elapsed, and you can configure the number of times the queue should retry. Once this number has been exceeded, the message will be placed in the DLQ.

The DLQ is configurable on a per-system or per-application basis in Windows Server 2008 and later. In versions of Windows Server prior to Windows Server 2008, there is only one DLQ per system. Consequently, if multiple applications or parts of an application are using MSMQ, then all the messages that have exceeded their retry or timeout parameters will end up in this queue. Processing the messages from the DLQ then becomes a challenge, especially if you have discrete destinations based on message types. For example, if you take the QuickReturns Ltd. application, in an MSMQ scenario you might have trade messages, as well as messages related to the trader's accounts. You would need to write discrete code to interrogate the messages and route these to their appropriate destinations when building systems not based on MSMQ 4.0 or later.

The ability to configure per-application DLQs in Windows Server 2008 means that you can then have one DLQ for the trade service and another for the account service. Doing this will allow you to provide greater levels of resilience in your application. We recommend that you study these features as they become available in MSMQ 4.0 on Windows Server 2008, and utilize the functionality available to you to increase the reliability of your applications.

Summary

In this chapter, you learned about the following:

- The need for transactions to solve issues involving deadlocks, and ensuring repeatability and recoverability

- How transactions are supported by WCF with the WS-Atomic transaction protocol

- How to use transactions with your services and sessions using the various behavior attributes provided by WCF, including ServiceBehavior and OperationBehavior

- How to use the MSMQ transport channel with transactions by incorporating support for transactions into your application

Transactions are critical to your applications, and you must look at the requirements for transactions in conjunction with the scope of reliable messaging, since these go hand in hand. It is safe to say that building an enterprise application without transactional support is a recipe for failure.

Looking ahead to Chapter 10, you will learn about how to integrate with legacy COM+ applications. The topics that will be covered include integration of COM+ with WCF, how to run COM+ services within WCF, and typed and early-bound contracts with COM.

CHAPTER 10

■ ■ ■

Integrating with COM+

This chapter is about working with the past. That past is based upon component technology created by Microsoft for providing a desktop-oriented protocol for reusing application logic. That technology expanded into a distributed technology that helped better position Microsoft in the enterprise sphere and compete with other existing technologies.

Not without faults, numerous applications were developed based upon this component technology, and many enterprises made large investments in it. To avoid the problems associated with introducing new technology that would force businesses to scrap their original Microsoft-based investments, Microsoft and the WCF team worked hard to provide an evolutionary, as opposed to revolutionary, approach for bridging the technological divide.

Introduced in 1993, the Component Object Model (COM) was the basis for many emerging technologies from Microsoft, including Object Linking and Embedding (OLE), ActiveX, and Distributed COM (DCOM). COM was initially introduced to compete with Common Object Request Broker Architecture (CORBA), a language-independent and cross-platform distributed system technology. COM+, introduced in 1998, was more of ancillary technology that worked with COM, but did not replace it. Key features of COM+ are transactional components, queued components, role-based security, and object pooling. COM+ 1.5 added features such as application pooling, SOAP services, services without components, and some other features.[1]

Today, COM+ 1.5 is a core part of the Windows platform. Even with the .NET Base Class Library (BCL), COM interoperability still occurs. *Runtime callable wrappers (RCWs)* are used throughout the .NET BCL—one prime example of an Runtime Callable Wrapper in the .NET Framework is the web browser control, which is a managed wrapper for the web browser's ActiveX control. Additionally, serviced components use COM+ transactions.

Why Integrate with COM+?

Although the future of the Windows platform seems to be a managed world, COM+ will still be around. COM exists in the core Windows platform,[2] but more importantly, it also exists in the billions of lines of code that independent software developers have written to produce solutions. A great number of solutions have been built on COM+ by enterprises that have also spent billions of their dollars. So, clearly WCF needs to work with legacy implementations in order to justify an investment in extending existing applications.

Few applications built today are completely standalone. In fact, the terms *application* and *solution* need a little definition. Generally, an *application* represents a standalone, deployable set of components,

---

[1] You can learn more about these features in the article "What's new in COM+ 1.5," available on MSDN at `http://msdn.microsoft.com/library/en-us/cossdk/html/e7073ba5-6b19-4d94-8cc0-b4e16bb44afd.asp`.

[2] In addition to the Win32 API that has gone legacy, but still exists and matures.

functionality, and so on. A *solution*, however, represents a combination of applications coupled together (either tightly or loosely) to address numerous business-processing requirements.

So today, we need to build solutions. These solutions will most likely require integration with existing data and processes that exist in legacy technology, and some of that technology will be COM+. It's also important to understand that existing COM+ applications aren't going to be thrown away you rewritten in .NET and WCF. As you build new .NET-based applications with services to be shared, we will often need a way to provide legacy COM+ applications to call your services. Fortunately, the WCF team has provided the core tools to facilitate both sides of the interoperability needs.

This chapter will walk you through how to consume COM+ application services from WCF clients. Additionally, you'll look at how legacy applications can use applications that expose WCF services built on .NET.

Running a COM+ Application As a WCF Service

Let's take a look at a scenario involving a hypothetical position-tracking system (or custody system) for QuickReturns Ltd. called OldHorse (see Figure 10–1). OldHorse was built in the late 1990s using Visual Basic 6. Since other groups within QuickReturns Ltd. leverage OldHorse, the OldHorse development team provided COM interfaces allowing client applications to interoperate with OldHorse using COM+.

When an asset manager makes a trade, the trade information needs to be posted to the custody system. Additionally, as you'll see later, the custody system needs to check with the asset manager's system for pricing and pending trade information.

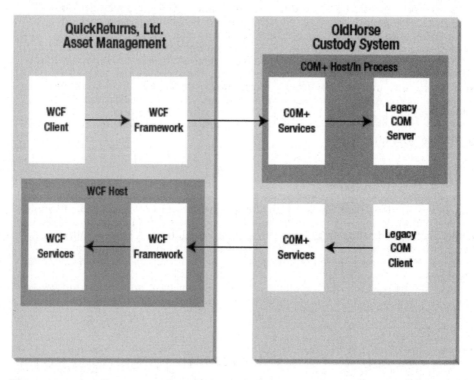

Figure 10–1. QuickReturns Ltd.'s OldHorse system

Visual Basic 6 COM+ Component Sample Setup

The example will use a simple Visual Basic 6 COM (ActiveX DLL) component that exposes two interfaces. The complete solution is contained in the chapter sample code's `Visual Basic 6 Project` folder. The following code snippets listings 10–1 and 2 are just the method signatures representing the Visual Basic 6 COM interface. This example is meant as an illustration of a Visual Basic 6 component and should not be viewed as a Visual Basic 6 best practice.

When looking at Visual Basic 6 COM components, you'll soon notice some issues related to how the WCF interfaces leverage type library information in regard to COM+ application components. Visual Basic 6 COM packs both the component logic and the type library information inside the COM DLL; this adds some attributes that prevent some interfaces from being initially wrapped in WCF COM+ integration.

Prior to working through this example, set up a virtual directory in IIS called `VB6ComSample` that is set for ASP.NET 2.0 and has anonymous access enabled.

The `PositionManagement` interface shown in Listing 10–1 provides a set of simple methods that allow the retrieval of the position for a given ticker, in addition to a method for updating the persisted quantity associated with a ticker.[3] One element that is not shown is a constructor. COM+ objects don't offer a constructor. They can provide information in other ways, such as with an initialization method. Visual Basic 6 and COM offer several ways of providing static configuration information, such as COM+ initialization strings on the configured component; however, that requires implementing `IObjectConstructString` in Visual Basic 6 and using the `ConstructionEnable` attribute in .NET. For the sake of simplicity in this example, we're just showing method interfaces. The ability to provide a connection string on object construction is something that could be provided through COM+ initialization.

Listing 10–1. PositionManagement.cls

```
'Simple interface that allows a nominal change in the quantity of a position
'ticker: Ticker symbol of security
'quantity: Amount (+/-) to shift existing position
'Throws an error if quantity is not sufficient to support the change (overdrawn)
Public Function UpdatePosition(ByVal Ticker As String, _
        ByVal Quantity As Long) As Long
...
Public Function GetQuantity(ByVal Ticker As String) As Long
...
```

The second component is the `Position` component. This class is largely a data class with read/write properties. In addition, it has two methods; one provides retrieval of a specific position for a ticker, and the other returns a concrete `Position` object for a specific ticker. Listing 10–2 shows the abbreviated class (the full class can be found in the chapter code, in `\OldHorsePositionTracking\VB6\PositionManagement`).

Listing 10–2. Visual Basic 6 Position Class: Position.cls

```
Public Property Let Quantity(ByVal vData As Long)
...
Public Property Get Quantity() As Long
...
```

---

[3] Note that these are simplified interfaces for example purposes only and do not represent a proper interface definition for a fully functional custody system.

```
Public Property Let Ticker(ByVal vData As String)
...
Public Property Get Ticker() As String
...
Public Function GetQuantity(ByVal Ticker As String) As Long
...
Public Function GetPosition(ByVal Ticker As String) As Position
...
```

The PositionManagement class is configured in Visual Basic 6 to be an MTS component with a Required transaction setting. This setting is reflected in the generated WCF service inside the configuration file and is handled automatically by the COM+ Integration wizard, which makes a call to the ComSvcConfig.exe utility. This allows flow from a WCF client to your COM+ component, ultimately being managed by the Microsoft Distributed Transaction Coordinator (MSDTC).

Once the project is built to an ActiveX DLL, it is ready to be installed and configured as a COM+ application. Follow these steps to create the OldHorse COM+ application for a Visual Basic 6 COM component:[4]

1. From Administrative Tools, launch Component Services. (You can also get to this Microsoft Management Console (MMC) via the dcomcnfg.exe command.) Expand the Component Services node until you find the computer you want to configure for your COM+ application. In this example, it's the local machine, or My Computer. Select the COM+ Applications object in the console, right-click, and choose New Application, as shown in Figure 10–2.

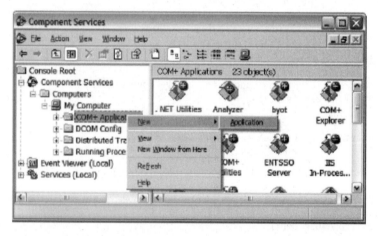

Figure 10–2. Creating a new COM+ application

2. At this point you're presented with the COM+ Application Install wizard. Click through the first page of the wizard. On the second page, click the "Create an empty application" button, as shown in Figure 10–3.

---

[4] We won't go into too much depth about how to create Visual Basic 6 COM+ applications. Note that these steps for COM+ applications can be developed through the COM Administration type library. However, .NET offers the RegSvcs.exe utility, which provides a simple command-line interface for this.

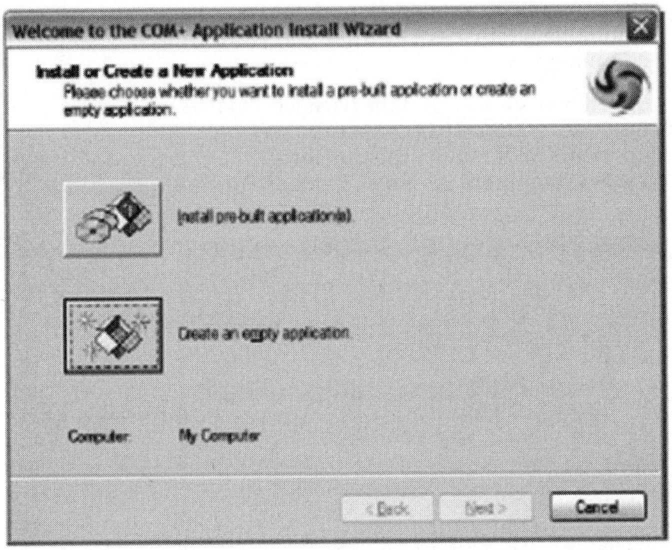

Figure 10–3. Creating an empty COM+ application

3. On the next page of the wizard, enter the name of your application, and ensure you select "Library application" as the activation type (see Figure 10–4).

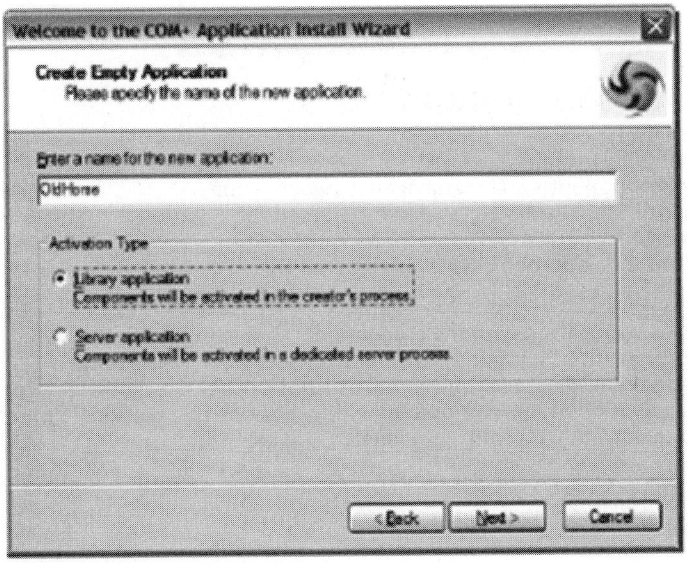

Figure 10–4. OldHorse library activation

4. Click through to the last page of the wizard. At this point, you should now have a COM+ application defined in Component Services. However, this is an empty package and has no associated components.

5. The next step is to add your compiled ActiveX DLL into the package. Do that by first selecting the Components tree from within the OldHorse COM+ application. Right-click the Components folder under the OldHorse application, and then choose New ➤ Component, as shown in Figure 10–5.

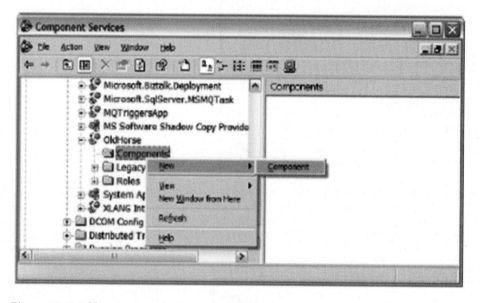

Figure 10–5. Adding a new component to the OldHorse application

6. This opens the COM+ Component Installation wizard. Click Next in the wizard, and then choose Install New Component(s). Then navigate to where your Visual Basic 6 COM component's DLL resides (if you have extracted the samples, it is located in the directory \OldHorsePositionTracking\VB6\ PositionManagement\bin). Choose it, and then click Next until the wizard is dismissed.

At this point you should have a COM+ application with the components shown in Figure 10–6. First, you'll see two components, each with a single interface listed—the name given by the Visual Basic 6 framework. Second, in the right pane, notice the Required transaction attribute. (Click the detail view to see this pane.) This attribute forces the activation of this component within a COM+ transaction—either a new transaction or an inherited transactional context from the caller.

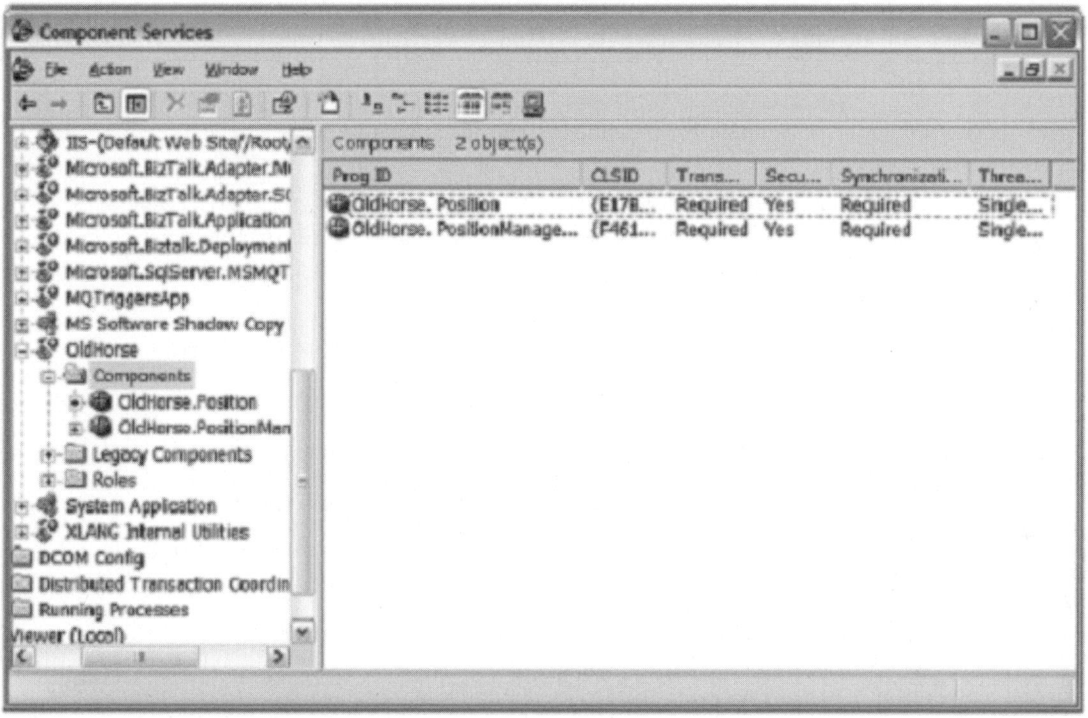

Figure 10–6. Configured OldHorse COM+ application

COM+ Application WCF Service Wrapper

Once a COM+ application is configured, you're ready to leverage WCF's utilities for creating the necessary resources for calling a COM+ component from a WCF client. The primary utility for this is the ComSvcConfig.exe utility. This is a command-line utility that is installed with the .NET runtime (versions 3.0 and later). Additionally, the SvcConfigEditor.exe utility provides a graphical interface with some additional features that help hide the complexities of the command-line ComSvcConfig.exe utility. You should get used to the SvcConfigEditor.exe utility, as it facilitates the composition of proper configuration files for WCF with configuration-time validation of many elements.

Using the SvcConfigEditor.exe Utility

Before you proceed, it's important to understand some caveats related to COM+ interoperability with WCF. There are restrictions as to what COM+ interfaces can be exposed as web services through the COM+ integration layer. The interfaces that are restricted are listed in the SDK, but some of them are as follows:

Interfaces that pass object references as parameters: This violates a core tenet of SOA, in that passing a reference across a service boundary is expensive.

Interfaces that pass types that are not compatible with the .NET Framework COM interop conversions: This is a general incompatibility issue for types that won't serialize between the interoperability layers.

Interfaces for applications that have application pooling enabled when hosted by COM+: This causes problems with multiple listeners on the same URI moniker, because there will be more than one application pool attempting to reserve the service endpoint address.

Interfaces from managed components that have not been added to the GAC: This is a general limitation of how COM+ hosts configured managed components. There are other means of using COM+ from managed applications (e.g., services without components[5]), but they are not supported with WCF COM+ integration.

The first item mentioned here is important because given that one of the core tenets of SOA is that boundaries are explicit, it would be expensive to share an interface pointer across the service boundary. Also, given that the default WCF service behavior `InstanceContext` mode is `PerCall`, this is something your SOA implementation should consider.

In addition to the previously listed limitations, you'll soon see some limitations with Visual Basic 6 components, specifically with regard to how they're implemented.

At this point, you're ready to create a WCF interoperability layer around your COM+ components. Start by launching the `SvcConfigEditor.exe` utility, which is located in the Microsoft SDK's `Bin` directory. The easiest way of executing WCF Service Configutation edtor is to launch the CMD shell shortcut from your Start menu under the Microsoft Windows SDK program group or from within the Visual Studio 2010 Tools menu as WCF Service Configuration Editor.

Start with no configuration file, and have the utility generate the necessary parts; this will allow you to call the OldHorse component from a WCF client.

From the menu bar of `SvcConfigEditor.exe`, select File ➤ Integrate ➤ COM+ Application. At this point you should see a listing of all the COM+ applications, including OldHorse, that are present on the local machine, as shown in Figure 10–7.

Next, expand the `OldHorse.PositionManagement` node until you can see the list of interfaces (which will have only one item in it), select the _PositionManagement interface, and click Next. At this point, you should see the page shown in Figure 10–8.

---

[5] Services without components were introduced with COM+ 1.5. See `http://msdn2.microsoft.com/en-us/library/ms172373.aspx`.

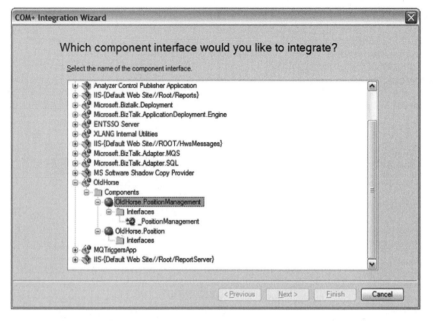

Figure 10–7. *COM+ Integration wizard*

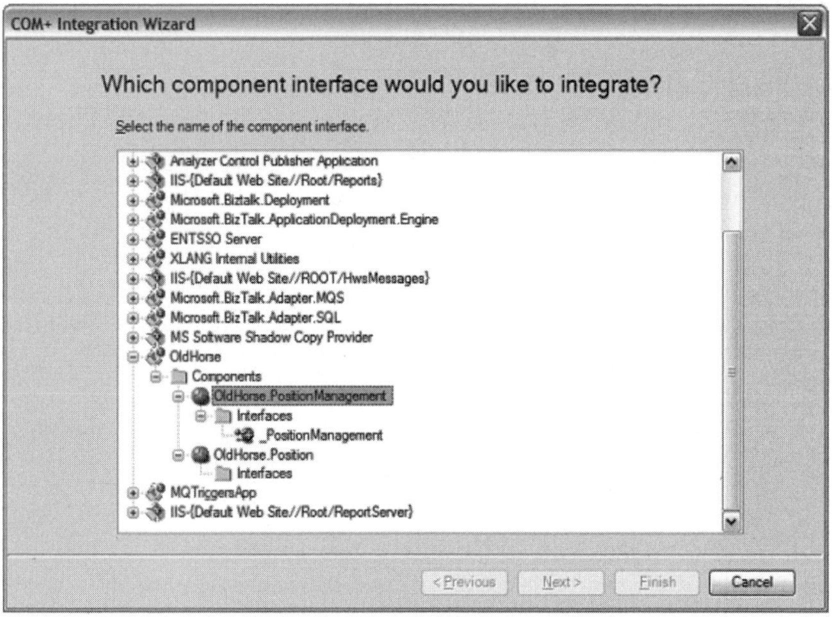

Figure 10–8. *_PositionManagement interface*

Click Next. You will be presented with the hosting mode options. Choose the web hosting in-process mode, which allows per-message activation and hosting within the IIS/WAS worker process. The other hosting options are not available for library-activated (in-process) applications, and are enabled when the activation type is Server Activated (out of process). Ensure that the "Add MEX endpoint" option is enabled. This allows clients to leverage WS-MetadataExchange (WS-MEX) to query the interface for contract and service information.

The next page of the wizard lists the IIS virtual directories on the local machine. Make sure you choose an IIS virtual directory that is configured for .NET 2.0 or above. For this example, we've preconfigured a virtual directory called /localhost/VB6ComSample (see Figure 10–9) that is configured for ASP.NET 2.0.

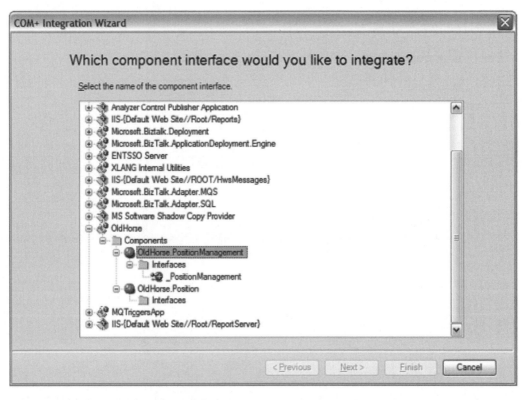

Figure 10–9. Choosing an IIS virtual directory

At this point, click Next, and you'll be presented with the summary of options shown in Figure 10–10.

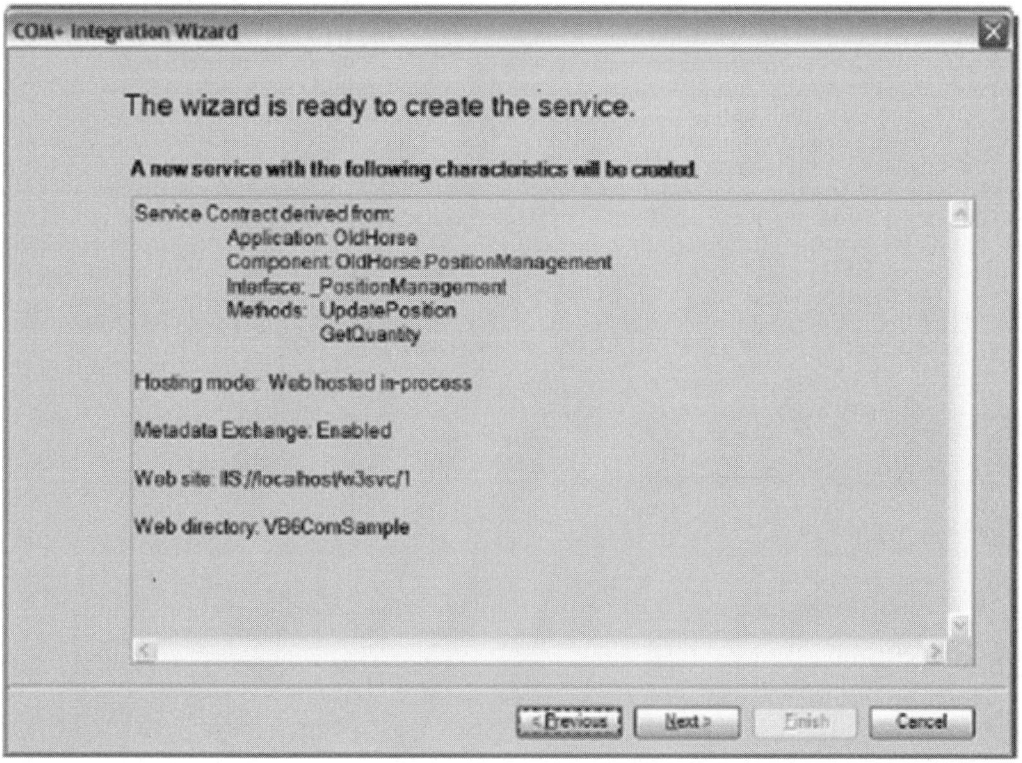

Figure 10–10. COM+ integration summary page

Click Next again, and SvcConfigEditor.exe will make a call to the ComSvcConfig.exe utility with the appropriate command-line options. This generates two files in the virtual directory. If the SvcConfigEditor.exe utility cannot find the ComSvcConfig.exe utility, you'll be presented with a message box asking you to specify where it is located.[6]

The two resources that are generated provide the WCF wrapper service resource file and a web.config file. The WCF service file is generated with the COM ProgID as the file name. For this example, the component OldHorse.PositionManagement generates the file OldHorse.PositionManagement.svc. The contents of that file appear in Listing 10–3.

Listing 10–3. OldHorse.PositionManagement.svc

```
<%@ServiceHost .ServiceModel.ComIntegration.
WasHostedComPlusFactory" WasHostedComP12Service=
"{f4612210-b755-4e17-87db-f82d9751d582},
{d3a08ae7-1857-409d-97aa-d86c0b366f5f}" %>
```

---

[6] The ComSvcConfig.exe utility is located at %SystemRoot%\Microsoft.NET\Framework\v3.0\Windows Communication Foundation.

The SVC file contains a single line that points to the service factory that will provide the COM+ integration: WasHostedComPlusFactory. The second parameter, WasHostedComP12Service, provides two initialization parameters for the factory class. The first is the GUID for the COM interface as specified by the type library for the COM component. If you leverage a tool such as OleView (which comes with the Windows SDK), view the type library for OldHorse, and dump the Interface Definition Language(IDL), you'll see that the supplied GUID matches the Universal Unique Identifier(UUID) of the implementation class, which is PositionManagement.

The second parameter represents the COM+ application ID, which you can make visible by choosing the properties of the COM+ application from the Component Services management console. So, the combination of the application ID and the CLSID (ProgID reference from COM) is a direct pointer that allows the WCF COM+ integration runtime to locate, instantiate, and service the WCF client call.

If you check the properties of the OldHorse.PositionManagement component from within Component Services, you'll see that the CLSID GUID and application GUID both match the generated GUIDs in the OldHorse.PositionManagement.svc file, as shown in Figure 10–11.

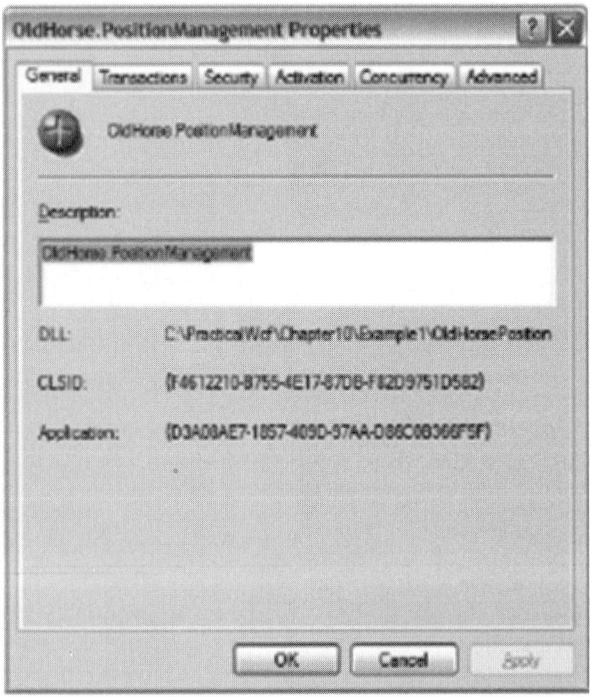

Figure 10–11. OldHorse.PositionManagement properties

Using the ComSvcConfig.exe Utility

You can also use the standalone ComSvcConfig.exe utility to generate the required resource's COM+ application integration. The primary difference is that it doesn't provide the up-front validation that the SvcConfigEditor.exe utility does for validating supported COM interfaces prior to generation. Instead, it provides that information as error messages at runtime.

Using the same COM+ application as an example, the following command generates the required resources for wrapping your COM+ application's `PositionManagement` interface in a WCF service and hosting it inside IIS/WAS (all on a single line).

```
ComSvcConfig.exe /install /application:OldHorse
/contract:OldHorse.PositionManagement,_PositionManagement
/hosting:was /webdirectory:VB6ComSample /mex
```

In addition to the /install option listed here, there are two additional primary actions: /list and /uninstall. The /list option enumerates what WCF COM+ integration services currently exist on the local machine. The /uninstall option removes the application .svc file in addition to updating the web.config (or application configuration) file, removing all references to the identified application and interface.

Client Proxy Generation

At this point, you're ready to create the client proxy for your WCF COM+ integration, using either the SvcUtil.exe utility or the Visual Studio 2010 Add Service Reference add-in, as described in Chapter 5. Before proceeding, ensure that the IIS web site that you will be using has anonymous access enabled (accessed through the Directory Security tab in the IIS Virtual Directory properties). A completed solution appears in the sample code in the \VB6ComClient directory.

In this section, you'll create a simple console application. Start Visual Studio 2010 and create a new Windows console project. Once you have done this, right-click the project (or select the Project menu) and choose Add Service Reference. You can find detailed steps for generating service proxies in Chapter 4. The URI to specify for the Add Service Reference dialog box looks like Figure 10–12.

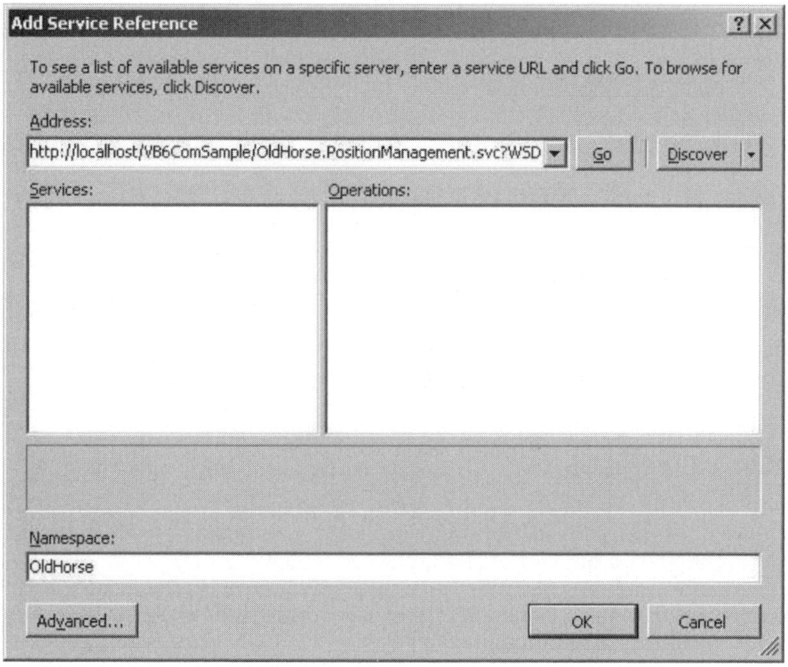

Figure 10–12. Adding a service reference to a COM+ WCF wrapper

Once you've generated the service reference, you can now provide the client code. Inside the Main method, the example code looks like Listing 10–4, which shows the completed client project's program.cs class file.

As shown in Listing 10–4, you simply instantiate a proxy type using the default constructor (which reads address, binding, and contract information from the configuration file). Using the _PositionManagementClient object (which was automatically generated from SvcUtil.exe), you then make a call to the methods exposed on the interface.

Listing 10–4. WCF COM+ Integration Client

```
namespace VB6ComClient
{
    class Program
    {
        static void Main( string[] args )
        {
            OldHorse._PositionManagementClient proxy =
                new VB6ComClient.OldHorse._PositionManagementClient();


            int q = proxy.GetQuantity( "MSFT" );
            Console.WriteLine( "We have " + q + " of MSFT" );
            q = proxy.UpdatePosition( "MSFT", 100 );
            Console.WriteLine( "We now have " + q + " of MSFT" );
            proxy.Close();
            proxy = null;
            Console.WriteLine("Press return to end..." );
            Console.ReadLine();

        }
    }
}
```

Consuming the PositionManagement interface from a WCF client is done just like with any other WCF-generated proxy type. In this model, the call is handed from the client over HTTP. It is then received by the IIS/Http.sys listener framework, and finally passed on to the WCF framework inside the WasHostedComPlusFactory type. The WCF framework does a runtime lookup of the COM+ information, instantiates the Visual Basic 6 COM component, and services the call.

Given the default service InstanceContext behavior is PerCall, the WCF COM+ integration framework will service each call with a new PositionManagement object. So, if you require server-side state, you must modify the service behavior. Review Chapters 3 and 6 for details about service behavior.

Visual Basic 6 COM+ Hiding Interfaces

During the generation of the WCF COM+ integration components for your OldHorse Visual Basic 6 ActiveX DLL, the Position component, while visible on the component selection page (as shown in Figure 10–7 earlier in the chapter), offered no visible interfaces for use with the WCF COM+ integration. This is because Visual Basic 6 generates hidden interfaces for the type library information that is bundled with the COM DLL for nonprimitive types. Generally, when using other COM+ languages, specifically C/C++, generating the type library information (a critical aspect of COM+ programming) is done using IDL and compiled into a type library that is then used by the implementation programmer to ensure adherence to the *contract*. Any interfaces that have hidden types as parameters or return values are not available in the WCF COM+ integration framework.

So, if you have an investment in Visual Basic 6 COM+ components, you may need to consider alternate methods of generation of type library information. Please see the sidebar "Visual Basic 6 COM and Contract-First Programming" for more details.

VISUAL BASIC 6 COM AND CONTRACT-FIRST PROGRAMMING

When COM was introduced, it provided a capable component architecture that permitted developers to leverage binary compatibility and reuse components across solutions. With this came the complexity of COM (reference tracking especially) and the language of COM itself. A core component of COM definitions are buried inside the type library for each COM component. C/C++ programmers are used to seeing IDL, which describes the COM interfaces of implementation components.

Visual Basic programmers are generally not accustomed to working with IDL. This is because Visual Basic 6 hides the inner workings of COM. However, it is possible to take a contract-first approach in working with Visual Basic 6 and COM.

For the OldHorse Visual Basic 6 COM implementation, the reason the WCF COM+ Integration wizard ignores the Position interface is because of the GetPosition method, which returns a Position object. Visual Basic 6 hides the internally generated _Position (note the underscore) interface from consumers of the type library; therefore, it's not possible to create a type of _Position by a caller—generally that's up to the COM component.

Using OleView.exe (which comes with the Windows SDK), if you dump the IDL and inspect the _Position interface, you can see that it's marked with a hidden attribute (see Listing 10–5).

Listing 10–5. OldHorse Visual Basic 6 COM Position IDL

```
  [
odl,
uuid(7E22753A-CD1B-4620-A952-E3CDFD456431),
version(1.0),
hidden,
dual,
nonextensible,
oleautomation
]
interface _Position : IDispatch {
    [id(0x68030001), propput] HRESULT Quantity([in] long );
    [id(0x68030001), propget] HRESULT Quantity([out, retval] long* );
    [id(0x68030000), propput] HRESULT Ticker([in] BSTR );
    [id(0x68030000), propget] HRESULT Ticker([out, retval] BSTR* );
    [id(0x60030002)] HRESULT GetQuantity(
                    [in] BSTR Ticker,
                    [out, retval] long* );
    [id(0x60030003)] HRESULT GetPosition(
                    [in] BSTR Ticker,
                    [out, retval] _Position** );
};
```

USING OLEVIEW.EXE

OleView.exe is a COM/OLE viewer utility that helps you view COM interfaces and type libraries registered on a machine.

To view the OldHorse type library information, open OleView.exe, and then navigate to the Type Libraries folder. In that folder you should see the OldHorse (Ver 1.0) type library registration. Initially, in the right pane you'll see the type library information as stored in the registry under the HKCR\TypeLib\{GUID}, where the GUID is the type library's UUID.

At this point, to view the IDL, double-click the entry OldHorse (Ver 1.0) in the left pane; this opens another window showing you the detailed interface information in the left pane, along with the IDL in the right pane.

```
[
  uuid(E17BC5E8-0378-4775-88DE-BADB73C57F03),
  version(1.0)
]
coclass Position {
    [default] interface _Position;
};
```

Through the IDL you can see why the WCF COM+ Integration wizard did not display this interface, and how you use interface names when you are using the ComSvcConfig.exe utility. You don't actually use the class names as declared inside the Visual Basic 6 class files; you use the generated interface names that Visual Basic 6 provides (prefixed with an underscore).

So again, if you require access to the Position object through the WCF service boundary, a couple of workarounds are available to you:

- You can remediate Visual Basic 6 to leverage contract-first COM+ development (see the preceding sidebar "Visual Basic 6 COM and Contract-First Programming").

- You can provide a .NET wrapper that interacts directly with Visual Basic 6 COM components and exposes .NET types on the service boundary.

.NET Enterprise Services and COM+ Components

For another example, we've included a simple .NET 2.0 class library that represents the OldHorse2 COM+ application, but is written in .NET 2.0 using Enterprise Services and serviced components. This solution file is located in the Chapter 10 project files, at OldHorsePositionTracking\DotNet\OldHorse2Sln.

Before you step through this example, set up a virtual directory inside IIS called DotNetComSample. Make sure that it's configured as ASP.NET 2.0 and has anonymous access enabled. The script CreateVirtualDirs.bat will create the IIS virtual directories and set the .NET runtime to 2.0 for the sites.

The solution also contains a couple of batch files (reg.bat and unreg.bat) that handle the GAC installation and COM+ application configuration. These batch files use the GacUtil.exe utility and the RegSvcs.exe utility, which handle GAC and COM+ registration. As listed in the SDK requirements, a .NET component that is also a serviced component (COM+) must be registered in the GAC, which requires that it to have a strong name.

The implementation of OldHorse2 is identical to the Visual Basic 6 COM example, except it uses attributes from the Enterprise Services namespaces. Additionally, the Guid attribute is applied to ensure that you leverage a consistent CLSID and APPID, instead of relying on the framework to regenerate each time.

Listing 10–6 shows the PositionManagement class for the OldHorse2 project. The code provides the Visual Basic 6 version of the sample interface, along with Transaction attributes and AutoComplete attributes for transaction management.

Listing 10–6. *OldHorse2 PositionManagement.cs*

```
using System;
using System.EnterpriseServices;
using System.Runtime.InteropServices;

namespace OldHorse2
{
    [Guid( "3B26F4CA-E839-4ab6-86D4-AADB0A8AADA5" )]
    public interface IPositionManagement
    {
        long UpdatePosition( string ticker, long quantity );
        long GetQuantity( string ticker );
    }

    [Guid( "08F01AD6-F3EB-4f41-A73A-270AA942881A" )]
    [Transaction(TransactionOption.Required)]
    public class PositionManagement : ServicedComponent, IPositionManagement
    {
        public PositionManagement() {}

        #region IPositionManagement Members

        [AutoComplete]
        public long UpdatePosition( string ticker, long quantity )
        {
            IPosition pos = new Position();
            pos = pos.GetPosition( ticker );
            pos.Quantity += quantity;
            return pos.Quantity;
        }


        [AutoComplete]
        public long GetQuantity( string ticker )
        {
            IPosition pos = new Position();
            pos = pos.GetPosition( ticker );
            return pos.Quantity;
        }

        #endregion
    }
}
```

As you can see in the code in Listing 10–6, interface IPositionManagement implemented by the class PositionManagement, which also inherits from ServicedComponent. Additionally, the class has the TransactionOption.Required setting, with each method having the AutoComplete attribute from Enterprise Services. This will ensure that each instance and call through the PositionManagement type takes place within a COM+ transaction.

In the same project, we've also defined the Position class. Listing 10–7 shows its contents. Notice that we've followed the same approach of providing a specific interface and corresponding implementation class.

Listing 10–7. OldHorse2 Position.cs File

```
using System;
using System.Runtime.InteropServices;
using System.EnterpriseServices;

namespace OldHorse2
{
    [Guid( "D428B97A-13C8-4591-8AC3-5E8622A8C8BE" )]
    public interface IPosition
    {
        long Quantity
        { get; set; }

        string Ticker
        { get; set; }

        long GetQuantity( string ticker );
        IPosition GetPosition( string ticker );
    }


    [Guid( "02FD3A3B-CFCE-4298-8766-438C596002B4" )]
    public class Position : ServicedComponent, IPosition
    {
        ...
        #region IPosition Members
        public long Quantity
        ...
        public string Ticker
        ...
        public long GetQuantity( string ticker )
        ...
        public IPosition GetPosition( string ticker )
        ...
    }
}
```

Once the project is compiled to a managed assembly, it's necessary to register it in the GAC using the GacUtil.exe utility that comes with the .NET 2.0 Framework. The command to register it is as follows:

```
gacutil /i bin\debug\OldHorse2.dll
```

Once it's registered in the GAC, you can then install it in COM+. .NET offers a useful command-line utility that does all the work for you. The following command creates the COM+ application along with registering the .NET assembly's components:

```
regsvcs bin\debug\OldHorse2.dll
```

You can provide the assembly with Enterprise Services types that control the COM+ registration, as shown in Listing 10–8. In this way, you don't have to build the application first and install the components through the wizard. If you want execute the same functionality outside of .NET or for non-.NET components, you can leverage the COM+ administrative interfaces for controlling COM+ applications.

Listing 10–8. OldHorse2 Assembly Attributes for COM+

```
[assembly: ComVisible( true )]
[assembly: Guid( "c41f4ee8-3475-47b6-b381-5e7774e4287d" )]
[assembly: ApplicationName("OldHorse2")]
[assembly: ApplicationActivation(ActivationOption.Library)]
[assembly: ApplicationAccessControl(false)]
```

These commands are best executed from the Windows SDK command (located in the Tools folder) or the Visual Studio 2010 command prompt (select Start ➤ All Programs). Additionally, the commands are contained in the batch files previously mentioned. Once registered, you should see the OldHorse2 application in Component Services, as shown in Figure 10–13.

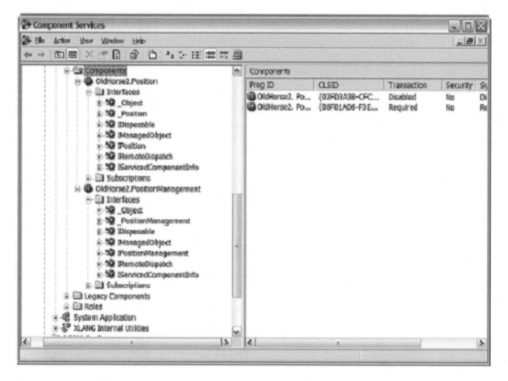

Figure 10–13. OldHorse2 .NET COM+ registration

Now, using OleView.exe (from the Windows SDK), refer to the IDL that is generated by the .NET Framework. The full IDL files are in the Chapter 10 code, in the \OldHorsePositionTracking directory. Listing 10–9 shows the IDL listing.

Listing 10–9. OldHorse2 .NET IDL

```
[
  odl,
  uuid(D428B97A-13C8-4591-8AC3-5E8622A8C8BE),
  version(1.0),
  dual,
  oleautomation,
  custom(0F21F359-AB84-41E8-9A78-36D110E6D2F9, OldHorse2.IPosition)

]
interface IPosition : IDispatch {
...


[
  odl,
  uuid(3B26F4CA-E839-4AB6-86D4-AADB0A8AADA5),
  version(1.0),
  dual,
  oleautomation,
  custom(0F21F359-AB84-41E8-9A78-36D110E6D2F9, OldHorse2.IPositionManagement)

]
interface IPositionManagement : IDispatch {
...
```

The code has been abbreviated here, but you can see that neither of the declared interfaces (IPosition and IpositionManagement) have the hidden attribute. Therefore, you should have a different User experience when you run the WCF COM+ Integration wizard, as shown in Figure 10–14.

Start the SvcConfigEditor.exe utility and access the COM+ integration feature. You should now see the OldHorse2 application along with the IPosition and IPositionManagement interfaces.

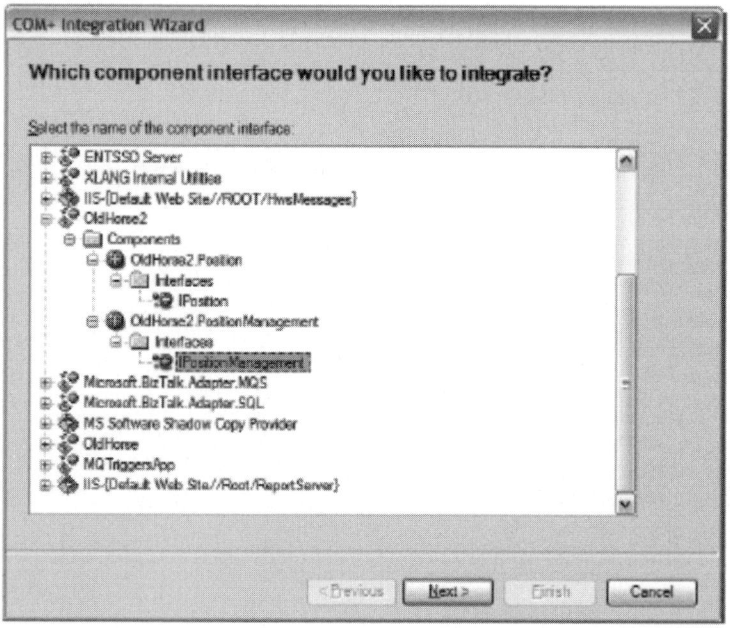

Figure 10–14. OldHorse2 WCF COM+ Integration wizard

Select the IPositionManagement interface, and click Next. You should now see that both methods appear (see Figure 10–15).

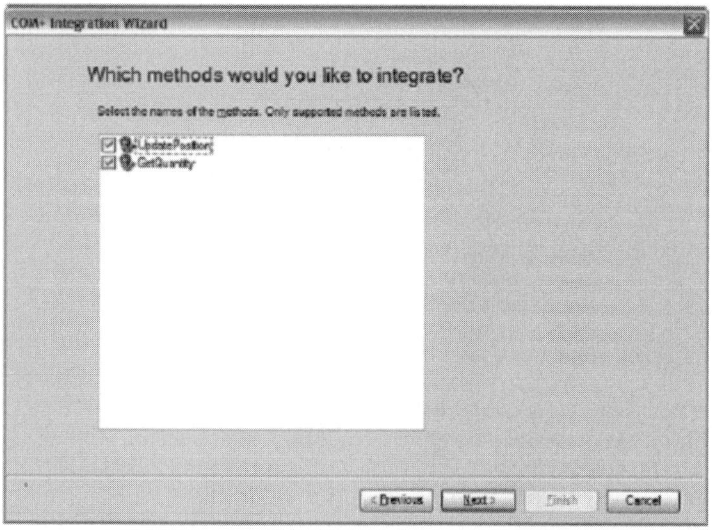

Figure 10–15. OldHorse2.PositionManagement interface methods

Click Next twice, and then click Finish. At this point you'll have two resources generated in the virtual directory root—a web.config file and a service host file called OldHorse2.PositionManagement.svc.

Client Proxy Generation

Once again, create a Visual Studio 2010 console application, and choose Add Service Reference to add to the project using the URI shown in Figure 10–16.

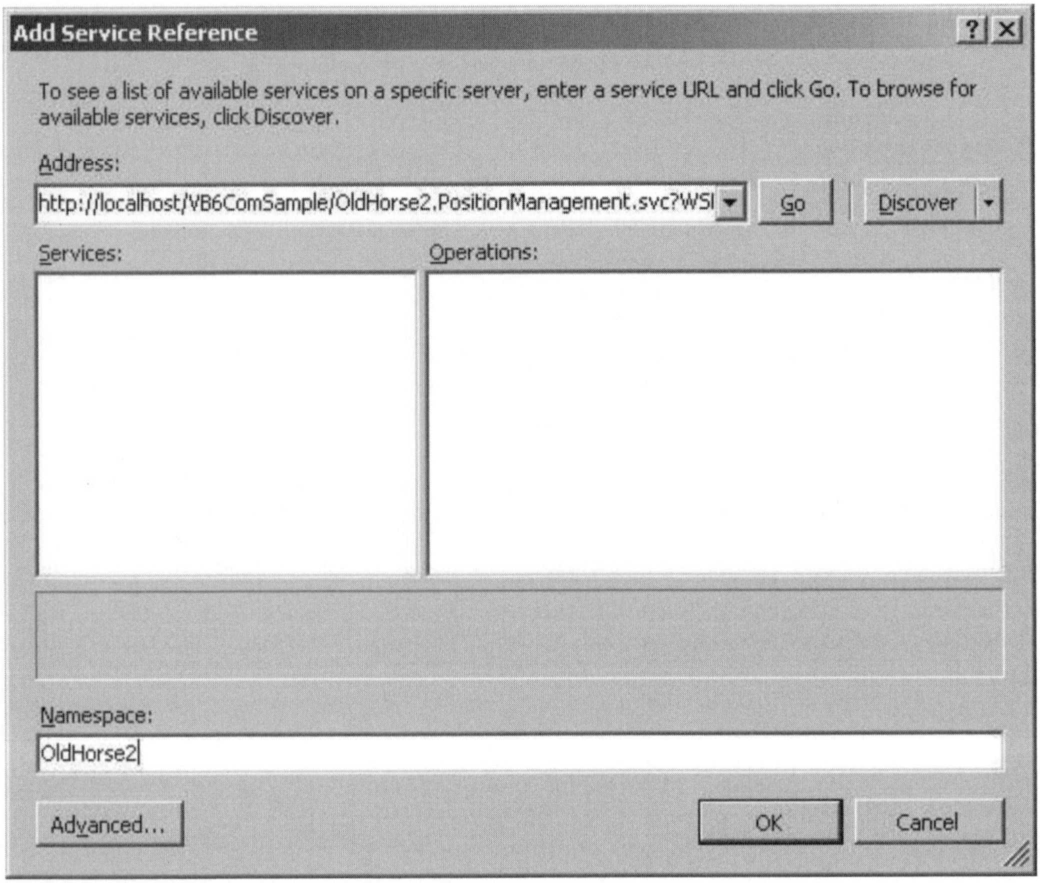

Figure 10–16. Adding a service reference to the project

In the completed solution, Listing 10–10 shows the code that performs the same call that the Visual Basic 6 COM client performed. The only difference is that the type name is no longer prefixed with an underscore. This is because when authoring components in .NET, you have control over the interface names, whereas in Visual Basic 6 it's left up to the Visual Basic 6 framework, hidden from normal levels of control. Other than that, there's no discernable difference from the consumer side, as shown in Listing 10–10.

Listing 10–10. OldHorse2 Position Management Client

```
namespace DotNetComClient
{
    class Program
    {
        static void Main( string[] args )
        {

            OldHorse2.PositionManagementClient();
            OldHorse2.PositionManagementClient proxy =
                new OldHorse2.PositionManagementClient();
            long q = proxy.GetQuantity("MSFT");
            Console.WriteLine( "We have " + q + " of MSFT" );
            q = proxy.UpdatePosition( "MSFT", 100 );
            Console.WriteLine( "We now have " + q + " of MSFT" );
            proxy.Close();
            proxy = null;
            Console.WriteLine( "Press return to end..." );
            Console.ReadLine();

        }
    }
}
```

Consuming WCF Services from COM+

Up to now, we've focused on solutions that need to leverage existing legacy application logic that is hosted in COM+. We've focused primarily on Visual Basic 6 and its distinct ability to hide some things that you need control over in order to fully leverage and reuse your application logic.

This section approaches the problem scenario from the perspective that these legacy solutions are not stagnant. In fact, it has been estimated that nearly 90 percent of IT budgets are focused on maintaining and extending existing solutions—many of those built on Visual Basic 6 and other legacy technologies.[7]

So, those applications aren't going away. In fact, they will most likely need to be extended to support new functionality or change the way they interface with other applications.

For the examples in this chapter, you'll look at how you can make a WCF service look like a COM+ component. This allows your legacy clients that understand COM+ to work with your new .NET 3.0–based applications that expose service endpoints. Note that both the .NET 3.0 and .NET 2.0 runtimes are required when calling from any client. This is a requirement because the dynamic invocation framework is leveraged in process by the client process.

---

[7] Len Erlikh. "Leveraging Legacy System Dollars for E-Business." (IEEE) IT Pro, May/June 2000. See also
http://doi.ieeecomputersociety.org/10.1109/6294.846201 and
http://www.cs.jyu.fi/~koskinen/smcosts.htm.

QuickReturns Ltd. Quote Service

The QuickReturns Ltd. system, built on .NET , provides a quote service using WCF. All parts of the QuickReturns Ltd. application leverage this service. Some of the OldHorse custody systems, however, require the ability to reuse this application logic, and they use WCF COM integration capabilities. The new QuickReturns Ltd. quote service is hosted in ASP.NET and IIS, and exposes its services using WCF.

Let's discuss how you can leverage runtime registration of the COM interface through the use of the WSDL and MEX service monikers.

Typed Contract Service Moniker

We'll provide a quick walkthrough for the first scenario: consuming a WCF service from COM clients. This example will provide both an automation client (VBScript) and an early binding client (Visual Basic 6). The Visual Studio 2010 solution file QuickReturnsQuotes.sln contains the web site and proxy projects.

The first part of the solution is the QuickReturnsQuotes WCF service, which is hosted in IIS and ASP.NET. If you haven't already run the setup script, to set up this virtual directory in IIS, run the batch file CreateVirtualDirs.bat. IIS must be installed along with .NET 2.0 and the .NET 3.0 runtime components.

Open the solution file QuickReturnsQuotes.sln. The solution file contains two projects. The first is the web site that was just mapped using the scripts mentioned previously. If the project doesn't load, there's a problem with the script on your machine, and you'll have to map the site manually and reload the project. Ensure that you have IIS and .NET 2.0 installed, and ASP.NET registered with IIS (use the aspnet_regiis.exe command in the Framework folder).

The second project represents the proxy that when compiled, with a strong name, will be registered both in the GAC and as a COM interface using the RegSvcs.exe utility that's part of the .NET 2.0 Framework.

This project has several extra member files along with both prebuild and postbuild event command lines:

makeProxy.bat: This is the batch file that calls SvcUtil.exe to generate the proxy stub source files; this file is part of the project prebuild steps.

reg.bat: This is the batch file that registers the assembly in the GAC and for COM interoperability; this file is part of the project postbuild steps.

unreg.bat: This is the batch file that will remove the assembly from the GAC and from COM interoperability.

■**Note** For the build steps and these batch files to work, Visual Studio 2010 must be installed in the default path. If you chose a different path or haven't installed Visual Studio 2010, you need to update the path to the utilities as required.

If you build the solution and all is successful, then you should have a GAC-installed assembly registered for COM interoperability and ready for use by COM clients. To verify, you can open Windows Explorer to the C:\Windows\Assembly path and see the assembly TypedServiceProxy listed, as shown in Figure 10–17.

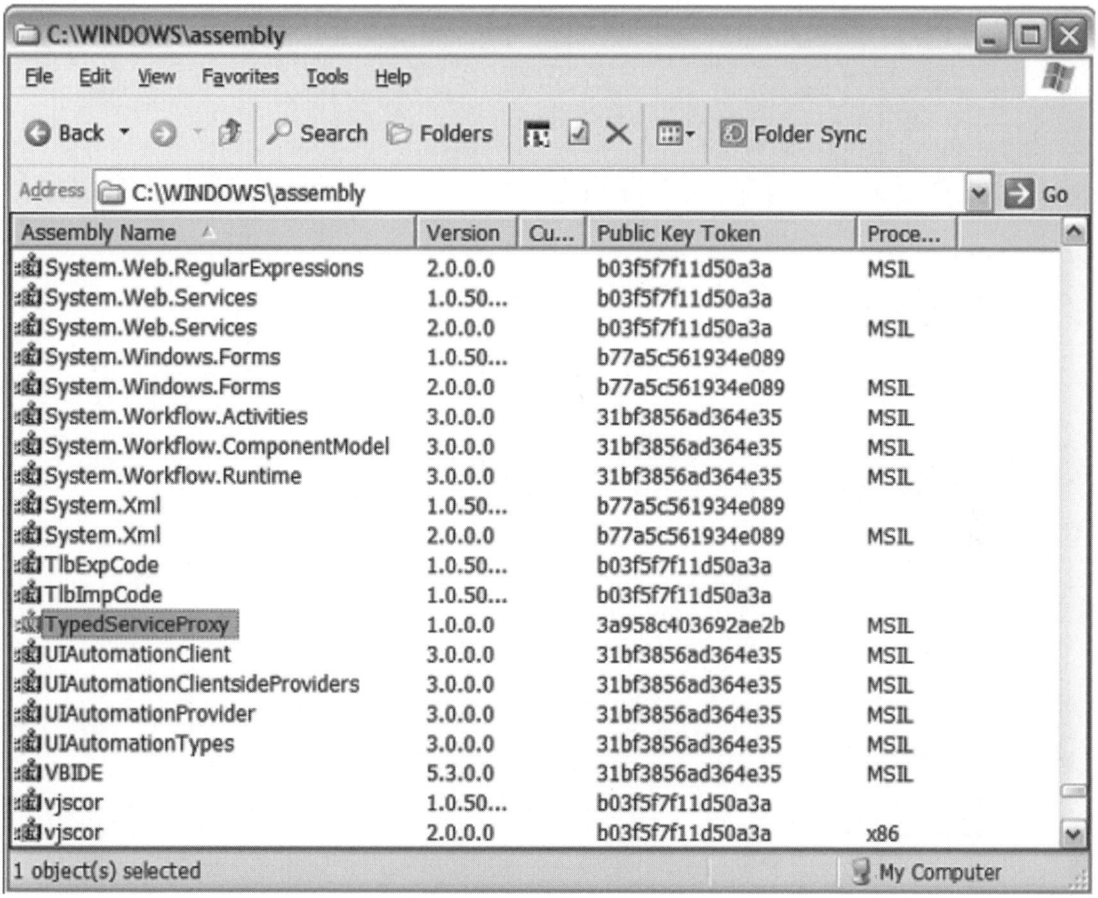

Figure 10–17. QuickReturns Ltd. WCF proxy in the GAC

■**Note** If you haven't modified any of the project Guid attributes, then the next two steps are not required for this project to work. Next steps would be a normal step in your solutions to validate the correct interface GUIDs.

The next steps are to both verify the registration for COM and retrieve the interface ID that is stored in the registry. The best tool for this is OleView.exe, which comes with the Windows SDK. Start OleView.exe and open the top-level node labeled Type Libraries. Scroll down until you find TypedServiceProxy, as shown in Figure 10–18.

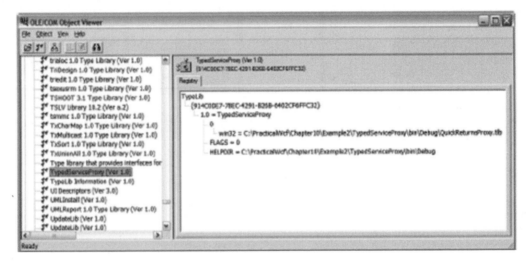

Figure 10–18. TypedServiceProxy registered in COM

Next, you need to retrieve the interface ID (the GUID) for the IQuoteService interface. The OleView.exe utility can view the IDL for any COM registered classes. Double-click the item TypedServiceProxy in the list to open the ITypeLib viewer, as shown in Figure 10–19.

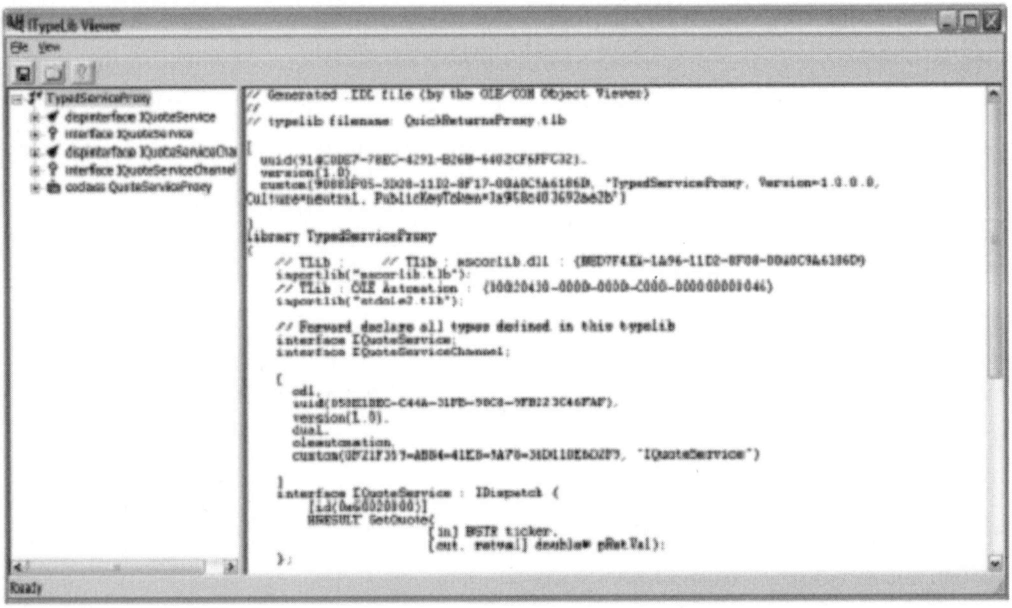

Figure 10–19. ITypeLib viewer for TypedServiceProxy

In the right pane of the viewer, find the IDL definition for the IQuoteService interface (which inherits from IDispatch, implying that it supports automation as well as early-bind COM clients). Now, just above the definition is a list of IDL attributes for this interface. We're looking for the universally unique identifier (UUID) just above it. For this component, its value is 058E1BEC-C44A-31FB-98C8-9FB223C46FAF.

Inside the TypedServiceProxy project file, you'll see a VBScript file that illustrates how to call from an automation client. Since this is an early-bound client, it requires the interface ID to be part of the service moniker construction string for the GetObject call. The call flows into the quote service through COM and then through the WCF framework to the quote service .NET assembly hosted in IIS/ASP.NET.

Listing 10–11 is the source file for QuickReturnsScriptClient.vbs; note the wrap on some lines.

Listing 10–11. QuickReturnsScriptClient.vbs Automation Client

```
Option Explicit
Dim quoteProxy, moniker, result
moniker = "service:address=http://localhost/QuickReturnsQuotes/service.svc,
    binding=wsHttpBinding"
moniker = moniker + ", contract={058E1BEC-C44A-31FB-98C8-9FB223C46FAF}"
'... cut comments

Set quoteProxy = GetObject(moniker)
result = quoteProxy.GetQuote("MSFT")
WScript.Echo "MSFT's price is " + CStr(result)
```

The moniker string value used for the GetObject COM call provides the address endpoint URI in addition to the binding type, which is wsHttpBinding because we're hosting in IIS. The final parameter of the moniker is the contract type. Using this GUID, the WCF framework looks up the type library information to obtain the COM interface and instantiates the proxy on the client side. The proxy in turn leverages the .NET Framework 3.0 to construct a channel and message for the request through the service boundary. This is all done "automagically" by the WCF components, which must be installed on the client tier as well.

Typed Contract: Early Bound

Visual Basic 6 can use *early binding*, which allows the lookup and discovery of the interfaces in your COM component at design time. So, at runtime, the COM client expects that the UUID of your interface is registered (via type library registration). The type library that needs to be registered and referenced is part of the reg.bat batch file in the TypedServiceProxy project—QuickReturnsProxy.tlb. COM interfaces are to be considered immutable. If they change, then the underlying IDL will change. Therefore, any changes to your interfaces in the base WCF service class will require a regeneration of the proxy and a regeneration of the type library for use by clients.

■**Note** If you open the Visual Basic 6 project, you may need to reset the project references back to TypedServiceProxy on your machine. Project Refernces are accessible from Project ➤ References from within the Visual Basic 6 IDE.

If you look at the Visual Basic 6 TypedServiceVbClient project, you can see that the project should have a reference to the TypedServiceProxy type library. In the button click event handler, you can now make references directly to the types inside the COM interface (see Listing 10–12; please note the line wrap).

Listing 10–12. Early-Bound Visual Basic 6 Client

```
Private Sub Command1_Click()
    Dim obj As TypedServiceProxy.QuoteServiceClient
    Dim moniker, Ticker As String
    Dim price As Double

    moniker = "service:address=http://localhost/QuickReturnsQuotes/
service.svc, binding=wsHttpBinding"
    On Error GoTo ErrHandler

    Ticker = UCase(Trim(txtTicker.Text))
    Set obj = GetObject(moniker)
    price = obj.GetQuote(Ticker)
    MsgBox "Price is " & CStr(price)
    Exit Sub

ErrHandler:
    MsgBox Err.Number & " : " & Err.Description & " : " & Err.Source
End Sub
```

The obj object is declared to be of the interface proxy type. The moniker is then set to include only the address and the binding type. Since you're using just the default settings for the wsHttpBinding, you aren't required to supply a bindingConfiguration value. If you needed to override any of the default settings for the binding, you could supply an application configuration file with the name file.exe.config and place it in the program directory of the client. For this example, the file name would be TypedServiceVbClient.exe.config.

You then use the COM GetObject statement, which makes a call through the COM framework into the Service Control Manager (SCM; affectionately pronounced *scum*), activating the COM registered WCF proxy type. Then, as each method is called on the activated instance, the WCF framework is responsible for both transforming and marshaling the call from COM into the WCF framework and ultimately across the service boundary to the service class.

Dynamic Discovery

There are scenarios where registering the COM type library is not feasible. An example is with Microsoft Excel spreadsheets that require dynamic discovery and invocation through COM locally to WCF services. For these, the WCF framework and COM integration provide a dynamic model, or what's known as *late binding*.

What the WCF framework provides is the runtime construction of a proxy and COM interface for the COM client at object construction time. By first querying the service metadata, after being provided some initialization parameters, the WCF framework generates both a WCF proxy and a COM callable wrapper that the COM client interfaces with. You currently have two choices for the service monikers: WS-MEX and WSDL. Given that this is a nontyped model, it is callable only by clients that support automation (IDispatch), such as VBScript, Visual Basic 6, and Excel.

Metadata Exchange Contract Service Moniker

WCF supports the WS-MEX protocol, which provides the discovery of services in addition to policy and schema information. (See Chapter 4 for more information.) The WCF COM integration framework uses this to dynamically derive the service endpoint interfaces along with binding and service behavior.

There's an additional VBScript file: QuickReturnsScriptClientMex.vbs. Listing 10–13 shows its contents (note the line wrap).

Listing 10–13. *QuickReturns Ltd. Script Using the Mex Service Moniker*

```
Option Explicit
Dim quoteProxy, moniker, result

moniker="service:mexAddress=http://localhost/QuickReturnsQuotes/service.svc/mex, "
moniker=moniker + "address=http://localhost/QuickReturnsQuotes/service.svc,"
moniker=moniker + "contract=IQuoteService, "
moniker=moniker + "contractNamespace=http://PracticalWcf/QuoteService, "
moniker=moniker + "binding=WSHttpBinding_IQuoteService, "
moniker=moniker + "bindingNamespace=http://tempuri.org/"

Set quoteProxy = GetObject(moniker)
result = quoteProxy.GetQuote("MSFT")
WScript.Echo "MSFT's price is " + CStr(result) WSDL Contract Service Moniker
```

In the code in Listing 10–13, you don't have a local configuration file or a strongly typed object (in COM or .NET). You must supply the discovery information to the GetObject call. One part of the code is the URI for where the MEX metadata is found. The others are the URI of the service endpoint, binding, and contract information that will be mapped into the MEX response.

The contract and contractNamespace come directly from the metadata binding information inside the <wsdl:binding> element from the metadata. Both of them must match what the MEX response contains; otherwise, you'll receive a contract-mismatch error. For this sample, this represents the <wsdl:binding> element that is visible if you request the WSDL for the service using the following URI:

```
http://localhost/QuickReturnsQuotes/service.svc?wsdl
```

WSDL Contract Service Moniker

Similar to how WCF works with the WS-MEX protocol to dynamically derive the COM and WCF interfaces and types, the service moniker can also work with a WSDL contract. Listing 10–14, contained in the file QuickReturnsScriptClientWsdl.vbs, illustrates how to make a call using the service moniker for WSDL.

Listing 10–14. *QuickReturns Ltd. Script Using the WSDL Service Moniker*

```
Option Explicit
Dim quoteProxy, wsdl, moniker, result

wsdl = GetWsdlFromUrl ("http://localhost/QuickReturnsQuotes/service.svc?wsdl" )
moniker="service:wsdl=" & wsdl & ", "
moniker=moniker + "address=http://localhost/QuickReturnsQuotes/service.svc,"
moniker=moniker + "contract=IQuoteService, "
moniker=moniker + "contractNamespace=http://tempuri.org/, "
moniker=moniker + "binding=WSHttpBinding_IQuoteService, "
```

```
moniker=moniker + "bindingNamespace=http://tempuri.org/"
Set quoteProxy = GetObject(moniker)

result = quoteProxy.GetQuote("MSFT")
WScript.Echo "MSFT's price is " + CStr(result)

Function GetWsdlFromUrl( strUrl )
    Dim WinHttpReq, resp
    Set WinHttpReq = CreateObject("WinHttp.WinHttpRequest.5")
    resp = WinHttpReq.Open("GET", strUrl, False)
    WinHttpReq.Send()
    GetWsdlFromUrl = WinHttpReq.ResponseText
End Function
```

■**Note** For the previous dynamic HTTP request for the WSDL to work, the correct version of the WinHttp service's component needs to be referenced by the CreateObject call. On some installations, this may be WinHttp.WinHttpRequest.5.1. Please see http://msdn.microsoft.com/library/en-us/winhttp/http/winhttp_start_page.asp for more information.

The first statement after the variable declarations makes a call to the included function that invokes GetWsdlFromUrl. This VBScript function just makes an HTTP get call to the URI to retrieve the HTTP response, which for that URI is the WSDL document for the service interface.

The moniker initialization string is then composed of the WSDL response along with the remaining service moniker attributes. The WSDL string is an XML response that fully describes the IQuoteService interface exposed at the endpoint address. It's the same XML you would see if you opened the URL http://localhost/QuickReturnsQuotes/service.svc?wsdl directly from a browser.

Again, using the dynamic service moniker, the COM interface makes a call into the WCF framework to dynamically construct the types necessary to make a round-trip request into the WCF service that is hosted in IIS—all without the COM client knowing the underlying workings of WCF (other than the moniker construction). What the dynamic generation provides is the generation of a fully configured proxy that matches the service endpoints' advertised metadata, including policy, security, and contract information.

We'll briefly summarize the high-level steps to consuming a WCF service as a COM interface leveraging a typed contract service moniker:

1. Generate a proxy using the WCF SvcUtil.exe utility.

2. Create a project/solution in Visual Studio 2010 that contains the generated proxy class file.[8]

3. Add the attribute ComVisible to the solution; you can add this to the AssemblyInfo.cs file.

4. Provide a strong name for the assembly; this is optional but allows loading to the GAC to ensure a single version is loaded.

---

[8] This is not required, but it makes things easier.

5. Register the assembly for COM using the `RegAsm` tool.

6. Install the assembly in the GAC; this is optional but ensures that a single version is loaded.

7. Create an application configuration file for your client executable; for example, if the client is called `OldHorseClient.exe`, then the configuration file is `OldHorseClient.exe.config`. This is the standard .NET configuration file-naming requirement.

8. Use the `GetObject` statement in your COM environment (Visual Basic 6, scripting, and so on) with the service moniker to instantiate the WCF service interface.

Security Credentials with IChannelCredentials

In any modern IT infrastructure, security is paramount for interoperability among applications in a distributed solution. In our example, there are clear requirements for securing our services. The examples so far haven't demonstrated any way of securing our services, whether exposed to legacy COM+ clients or wrapping COM+ services with the WCF services.

Chapter 7 discussed WCF security in detail, and covered both the declarative and programmatic means for securing services. Fortunately, the COM+ interoperability tier of WCF leverages the same base framework for supplying both transport and message security.

For the final steps in the COM+ integration, we'll discuss how to secure the WCF service that you are consuming from late-bound COM+ clients. A few additional steps are required to configure the IIS instance that hosts the QuickReturnsQuotesSecure web site. Again, we've supplied a script, `CreateVirtualDirs.bat`, that configures IIS and sets the ASP.NET runtime to .NET 2.0, which is required for running .NET 3.0 services.

The first modification is to the service's `web.config` file. Here you add the necessary security configuration elements to enable both transport-level and message-level security. Make the modification to the binding element that is associated with the endpoint, as shown in Listing 10–15.

ENABLING SSL ON IIS

Using transport security requires SSL; consequently, you need to enable the web site to use SSL, which requires the presence of a server certificate. To install a test certificate, you can use the IIS 6 Resource Kit (`SelfSSL.exe`).[9] Simply execute the following command:

```
selfssl /t
```

This installs a server certificate for use by IIS and places it on the Trusted Certificate list. WCF by default validates the certificate if you trust the issuer, so for this example, it will fail without the /t switch.

---

[9] You can download the IIS 6 Resource Kit from the following URL:
`http://www.microsoft.com/downloads/details.aspx?FamilyID=56fc92ee-a71a-4c73-b628-ade629c89499&DisplayLang=en`.

Listing 10–15. Security-Enabled web.config

```
<bindings>
  <wsHttpBinding>
    <binding name="Binding1">
    <security mode="TransportWithMessageCredential">
      <message clientCredentialType="UserName" />
    </security>
    </binding>
  </wsHttpBinding>
</bindings>
```

For this solution we're using wsHttpBinding. To add transport and message security, you add the security element and set the mode to TransportWithMessageCredential. This mode provides both an SSL-based channel and message-encoded authentication. Additionally, for the message element, you inform the WCF framework that you require UserName authentication. This informs WCF that the client will embed a username and password into the message, and will pass over SSL.

The solution includes the TypedServiceProxySecure project class library, which contains a set of batch files that dynamically generate the proxy file, and provides both GAC installation and COM+ registration. These steps of executing the batch files are in the prebuild and postbuild steps associated with the project.

Once you've configured your service to support the security model required, you can update the late-bound VBScript client to make a call matching the security requirements of the service.

If you take the late-bound VBScript file QuickReturnsScriptClientMex.vbs and run it without specifying any credentials, an exception raised to the client indicating that the username has not been provided, so you need to specify it in ClientCredentials.

Fortunately, COM+ integration makes that easy from the COM+ client. You just need to make a call to set the credentials on the channel. Listing 10–16 shows the updated VBScript that supports username and password authentication (notice the line wrap).

Listing 10–16. Late-Bound VBScript with Security

```
Option Explicit
Dim quoteProxy, moniker, result

moniker="service:mexAddress=http://xpshawnci/QuickReturnsQuotesSecure/"
moniker=moniker + "service.svc/mex, "
moniker=moniker + "address=https://xpshawnci/QuickReturnsQuotesSecure/service.svc, "
moniker=moniker + "contract=IQuoteService, "
moniker=moniker + "contractNamespace=http://tempuri.org/, "
moniker=moniker + "binding=WSHttpBinding_IQuoteService, "
moniker=moniker + "bindingNamespace=http://tempuri.org/"

Set quoteProxy = GetObject(moniker)
quoteProxy.ChannelCredentials.SetUserNameCredential "xpshawnci\soauser", "p@ssw0rd"

result = quoteProxy.GetQuote("MSFT")
WScript.Echo "MSFT's price is " + CStr(result)
```

The only modification we need to make is adding the call, as shown in bold. Here we make a call to the ChannelCredentials.SetUserNameCredential method, passing in the username and password of the principal. The WCF framework then generates a security token that is put into the message. On the receiving side, the server validates that token. If we supply an invalid username or password, the late-bound client will receive an error stating that the security token could not be validated.

Internally, the SetUserNameCredential call creates a new ClientCredential object, sets the username and password, and adds it to an internal collection of security credentials that are associated with the channel.

Other methods of supplying credentials are part of the IChannelCredentials interface, implemented by the System.ServiceModel.ComIntegration.ChannelCredentials type. The IChannelCredentials interface supports other credential types, such as Windows credentials (SetWindowsCredentials), certificate-based credentials (SetClientCertificateFromStore, SetClientCertificateFromStoreByName), and SetIssueToken credentials (for use with security token service [STS] services).

Summary

This chapter focused on interoperability with COM, both from a consumer and service perspective. Although you might be lucky enough to forget the past, WCF hasn't left it all in the dust. The WCF framework provides a strong extensible starting point to help in the evolutionary model of moving solutions into the SOA age.

The next chapter focuses on working with data in and around WCF. All services have data associated with them in some form. With WCF and SOA in general, careful consideration is required to understand not only the "how to implement the service" but also the implication of what happens to data as it crosses the explicit service boundaries.

CHAPTER 11

■ ■ ■

Working with Data

Data is the most important part of an application. Almost every application needs to operate on data—whether it's creating, consuming, or processing data. Without data, almost all applications would be useless. You can use many patterns when designing applications to work with data. In the early days of client-server applications, a favorite approach was the *n*-tier approach, where the application was divided into *n* tiers (the most common division was three tiers). In the three-tier approach, the first tier is the presentation tier, which handles all the presentation of the application (the UI), and is essentially what the user interacts with. The next tier is the business layer, which contains all the business rules to which the application needs to adhere. The last tier is the data layer, which performs the create, read, update, and delete (CRUD) functionality. The data layer usually connects to the required back-end data sources using one of many well-known mechanisms, such as OLE DB or ODBC.

In the SOA world, however, data is transferred in the form of a *message* over the wire. You can think of the WCF as a messaging infrastructure because it can receive, process, and dispatch messages. In addition, it can also construct messages and dispatch and deliver them to a desired location. Often, the messages are represented as objects in memory and need to be converted to an appropriate format so they can be transmitted across the wire. The process of converting them is called *serialization*, and is explained in the "XML Serialization" section of this chapter. Similarly, on the other end of the wire, the process of converting the message to an object that can be represented in memory is called *deserialization*. This chapter introduces the concepts of data contracts in addition to the basics of serialization.

After completing this chapter, you will have the following knowledge:

- You'll know why you need serialization.

- You'll understand the serialization options available in WCF.

- You'll understand best practices for data connectivity.

Understanding the Data Transfer Architecture

At the heart of the message capabilities of WCF is the Message class. The WCF architecture and runtime are essentially two pillars—the channel stack and the service framework—and the Message class is the bridge between the two. On the send side, the first pillar (the channel stack) converts a Message instance with some specified action to the act of either sending or receiving data. On the receiving side the channel stack is responsible for the reverse—converting an action into some specific message.

Although there is no restriction on using the Message class and channel stack *directly*, it is not usually recommended because it is fairly expensive (time-wise) and complex. Also, there are runtime issues such as lack of metadata support, lack of strongly typed proxies, and so on. To overcome these restrictions, WCF has the second pillar: the service framework, which provides a relatively easy programming model for working with Message objects. This framework maps .NET types and services via service contracts and sends messages to operations that are .NET methods marked with the

OperationContract attribute. The framework converts the incoming Message instances into the parameters on the server side. On the client side, it does the opposite and converts the return types to the outgoing Message instance.

Although the Message class is the most fundamental concept of WCF, it is usually not interacted with directly. You should use one of the other WCF service model constructs (such as data contracts, discussed later in the "Introducing Data Contracts" section), message contracts, and operation contracts (introduced in Chapter 3) to describe the incoming and outgoing messages. You should use Message only when working with some advanced scenarios. We'll discuss all the aforementioned Message classes and WCF constructs a little later in this chapter, in the "Introducing Message Contracts" section.

Regardless of which construct you use when message contents are described using message contracts or parameters, the message contents need to be serialized to convert these between the .NET type and the relevant SOAP or binary representation. But before examining the options available in WCF, you need to understand the available serialization options and the advantages and challenges of each of them.

Exploring the Serialization Options in WCF

Serialization is the process of converting the state of an object into a format that can be either persisted to disk or transmitted over the wire. On the flip side, deserialization is the process of converting an incoming stream, which is either read from disk or read over the wire to an object in memory. Collectively, these allow data to be stored and transmitted with relative ease.

This is all good, but why serialize in the first place? Serialization is a key aspect of any distributed technology, and .NET is no exception. For example, in an ASP.NET application, you can use serialization to save the session state to the configured medium (i.e., memory, state server, or database). One of the main problems that serialization solves for you is *interoperability* with other systems and platforms. Serialization is not a new concept, but it is an important one because without serialization, it would be difficult to support interoperability between various platforms. Since XML serialization converts the object or data structure at hand to an architecture-independent format, you do not encounter issues with different programming languages, operating systems, or hardware (e.g., issues with memory layout, byte ordering, or different platforms representing data structures differently).

The .NET Framework features two options for serializing objects: binary and XML serialization. The primary difference is that binary serialization allows you to maintain type fidelity, whereas XML serialization does not. *Type fidelity* allows for preserving the complete state of an object, including any private members of the object. However, by default, XML serialization will serialize only the public fields and properties of the object. If, for example, you need to pass an object by value across either machine or domain boundaries, then you need to use binary serialization. You can use binary serialization only when the runtimes and platforms on both ends of the stream are the same; this is because the platforms know how the type is represented internally in memory. If this is not the case, then the object will not be able to deserialize on the other end. XML serialization, as the name suggests, uses XML, and as a result is a better choice for sharing data across different platforms or the Internet.

In .NET, by default only primitive types (such as integers) are serializable, and there is no need for any additional steps to serialize these primitive types. Since the .NET runtime has no knowledge of complex types, these are not serialized by default; the .NET runtime needs more information about how these types should be serialized. Because each operation in a WCF service needs to either consume or generate data that is transmitted over the wire, in WCF it is important that every type is correctly serialized.

■**Note** The ability to serialize an object can be enabled only when writing the code; in other words, serialization is a design-time feature. If this is not enabled at design time for an object, then that object cannot support serialization at runtime. The ability to serialize an object cannot be switched on at runtime in an ad hoc manner. Also note that *serializing* and *deserializing* are sometimes also known as *hydrating* and *dehydrating*.

WCF (being part of .NET 3.0 and later) not only supports the serialization options available in .NET, but also adds a few new ones. A data contract is the default serializing option among the following available options:

- Serializable attribute/ISerializable interface

- Data contracts

- XML serialization

- Message contracts

- Message class

Introducing Data Contracts

Data contracts are the "agreement" between a service and its consumer. At an abstract level, the contract defines how the data will be exchanged between the two, and also defines what data is returned for each type (i.e., serialized to XML). For a service and its consumer to communicate, they do not necessarily have to share the same types; they need only share the data contracts. The default serialize engine in WCF is the data contract serializer, which is implemented as the DataContractSerializer class and is the recommended way to go for WCF. All .NET primitive types can be serialized without any other requirement. However, new complex types need to have an associated data contract defined before they can be serialized.

Data contracts are defined by applying the DataContract attribute to the type, and can be applied to classes, structs, and enums. Just as each operation in a service needs to be decorated with the OperationContract attribute, every data member (fields, property, event, etc.) in the data contract needs to be decorated with the DataMember attribute. This indicates to the data contract serializer that this member needs to be serialized.

■**Note** Unlike binary serialization, which automatically includes all public and private members in a class, and XML serialization, which automatically includes public members in a class, a data contract is designed with an *opt-in* model. This means that members of a class that are not explicitly marked with the DataMember attribute are not automatically serialized, regardless of their accessibility levels, and hence are *not* included in the data contract.

Some of the important aspects of data contracts and their implications in the WCF runtime are as follows:

- Member accessibility levels (private, public, internal, etc.) do not affect the data contract. Members that are private in one context could end up being accessed publicly elsewhere after serialization.

- Static fields cannot be included in the data contract. As a result, if a DataMember attribute is applied to a static field, it will be ignored.

- All data members for a data contract need to be serialized and deserialized for the data contract to be valid.

- Every property should have get and set accessors. This is important because the properties get and set are used during the serialization and deserialization processes.

- There is no special process for generic types; they are treated the same as nongeneric types.

- The WCF runtime takes care of defining the underlying SOAP message and the serialization of the data. As long as the data types are serializable, WCF will handle the underlying message exchange.

For example, in the QuickReturns Ltd. trading application, look at the stock quote of a particular company. Figure 11–1 shows the data entities that this quote will include—Change, price-to-earnings ratio (PERatio), average volume (AvgVol), LastTrade, and so on.

As discussed earlier, to make this class into a serializable type to allow you to transmit this data to other applications that may or may not be based on WCF, you need to apply the DataContract and DataMember attributes, as shown in Listing 11–1. Although this structure consists of mostly primitive data types, which can be serialized, you still need to explicitly mark them as part of the data contract so the runtime is aware of which members constitute the data members.

Figure 11–1. QuickReturnStockQuote class

Listing 11–1. *QuickReturnStockQuote Data Contract*

```
[DataContract]
public class QuickReturnStockQuote
{
    [DataMember]
    internal string Symbol;

    [DataMember]
    internal string CompanyName;

    [DataMember]
    internal decimal LastTrade;

    [DataMember]
    internal decimal Change;

    [DataMember]
    internal decimal PreviousClose;


    [DataMember]
    internal decimal AvgVol;

    [DataMember]
    internal double MarketCap;

    [DataMember]
    internal decimal PERatio;

    [DataMember]
    internal decimal EPS;

    [DataMember]
    internal decimal FiftyTwoWeekHigh;

    [DataMember]
    internal decimal FiftyTwoWeekLow;
}
```

Data Contract Names

Sometimes, even though a consumer and a service might not share the same *type*, they can still pass data between each other as long as the data contracts are *equivalent* on both sides. This equivalence is based on a combination of the data contract, the data member names, and their order. This data contract and these data member names follow a few simple rules that you can use to map the different types in situations where they differ on either end. These rules are as follows:

- The *fully qualified* data contract name consists of both the namespace and a name.

- Data members have only names (no namespaces).

- Namespaces, data contracts, and member names are case sensitive.

The default namespace for a data contract is in the form of a URI, which can be either absolute or relative. By default, the namespace is the same as the CLR namespace for that type, and maps to `http://schemas.datacontract.org/2004/07/Clr.Namespace` (where `Clr.Namespace` is the correct CLR namespace). If required, you can change the default namespace in two ways. First, you can change the `Namespace` property of the `DataContract` attribute. Second, you can apply the `ContractNamespace` attribute to the relevant module or assembly.

A data contract's default name is the name for that type. You can use the `Name` property of the `DataContract` attribute to override the default name. Similar to the data contract, the default name for a data member is the name of that member (field or property). You can use the `Name` property on the `DataMember` attribute to override that default. Listing 11–2 shows an updated version of the data contract from Listing 11–1 with the default names overridden.

Listing 11–2. QuickReturnStockQuote Data Contract with Names Specified

```
[DataContract]
public class QuickReturnStockQuote
{
    [DataMember(Name = "TickerSymbol")]
    internal string Symbol;

    [DataMember]
    internal string CompanyName;

    [DataMember]
    internal decimal LastTrade;

    [DataMember]
    internal decimal Change;

    [DataMember]
    internal decimal PreviousClose;

    [DataMember(Name = "AverageVolume")]
    internal decimal AvgVol;

    [DataMember(Name = "MarketCapital")]
    internal double MarketCap;

    [DataMember(Name = "PriceEarningRatio")]
    internal decimal PERatio;

    [DataMember(Name = "EarningsPerShare")]
    internal decimal EPS;

    [DataMember(Name = "52WkHigh")]
    internal decimal FiftyTwoWeekHigh;

    [DataMember(Name = "52WkLow")]
    internal decimal FiftyTwoWeekLow;
}
```

Data Contract Equivalence

As stated earlier, the client and service do not have to have the same type to be able to exchange data. However, the data contracts of both the types need to present on both ends to be *equivalent*. In other words, they need to have the same namespace and names. Also, every data member on one side needs to have an equivalent on the other end.

■**Note** In cases where both the sides have the same types but different data contracts (when they're not equivalent), the data contracts should not be given the same name and namespace. Doing so can lead to unexpected runtime exceptions.

If a data contract inherits from another data contract, then that data contract is treated as one data contract that includes all the types from the base. Also, in accordance with the rules of object-oriented programming (OOP), when passing data contracts, a base class cannot be sent when the expected data contract is from a derived class. On the flip side, a data contract from the derived class can be sent when expecting data from the derived class, but only if the receiving endpoint is aware of the derived type via the KnownType attribute. This attribute can be applied only to data contracts; it can't be applied at the data member level (this is discussed later in this chapter, in the "Introducing Data Contracts" section). As an example, the data contract for the MyStockQuote type shown in Listing 11–3 is the same as the one in Listing 11–2.

Listing 11–3. MyStockQuote Data Contract

```
[DataContract(Name="QuickReturnStockQuote")]
public class MyStockQuote
{
    internal string TickerSymbol;
    [DataMember(Name="CompanyName")]
    internal string Name;
    [DataMember]
    internal decimal LastTrade;
    [DataMember]
    internal decimal Change;
    [DataMember]
    internal decimal PreviousClose;
    [DataMember(Name = "AverageVolume")]
    internal decimal Volume;
    [DataMember(Name = "MarketCapital")]
    internal double MktCap;
    internal decimal PriceEarningRatio;
    [DataMember(Name = "EarningsPerShare")]
    internal decimal EPerS;
    [DataMember(Name = "52WkHigh")]
    internal decimal WeekHigh52;

    [DataMember(Name = "52WkLow")]
    internal decimal WeekLow52;
}
```

Another factor that affects the data equivalence is the order of members. Data contracts must have members in the same order. By default, the order is alphabetical; however, you can change this using the Order property of the DataMember attribute. The sequence of elements is as follows:

- The first in order is the data member of the base types if there is an inheritance hierarchy for the current data member type.

- Next are the data members of the current type (in alphabetical order) that *do not* have the Order property set in the DataMember attribute.

- Last are the data members that do have the Order property set in the DataMember attribute; if more than one is set to the same Order property, then they appear alphabetically.

For example, the code in Listing 11–4 produces the same data equivalence as in previous examples.

Listing 11–4. Coordinate Data Contract Equivalence

```
[DataContract(Name = "QuickReturnStockQuote")]
public class MyStock1
{
    // Order is alphabetical (CompanyName, LastTrade, TickerSymbol)

    [DataMember]
    internal string CompanyName;

    [DataMember]
    internal decimal LastTrade;

    [DataMember]
    internal string TickerSymbol;
}

[DataContract(Name = "QuickReturnStockQuote")]
public class MyStock2
{
    // Even though the TickerSymbol and LastTrade member orders have changed
    // the order is alphabetical (CompanyName, LastTrade, TickerSymbol)
    // and is equivalent to the preceding code


    [DataMember]
    internal string CompanyName;

    [DataMember]
    internal string TickerSymbol;

    [DataMember]
    internal decimal LastTrade;
}

[DataContract(Name = "QuickReturnStockQuote")]
public class MyStock3
{
    // Order is according to the Order property (CompanyName, LastTrade,
```

```
    // TickerSymbol), equivalent to the preceding code

    [DataMember(Order=1)]
    internal string CompanyName;

    [DataMember(Order=3)]
    internal string TickerSymbol;

    [DataMember(Order=2)]
    internal decimal LastTrade;
}
// This class will be used by MyStock4 later
[DataContract(Name = "QuickReturnStockQuote")]
public class MyStockBase
{
    [DataMember]
    internal string TickerSymbol;

    [DataMember]
    internal string CompanyName;
}

[DataContract(Name = "QuickReturnStockQuote")]
public class MyStock4 : MyStockBase
{
    // Order is alphabetical (CompanyName, LastTrade, TickerSymbol)
    // and includes all the data types from the current class and
    // the base class

    [DataMember]
    internal decimal LastTrade;
}
```

■**Note** Primitive types (and certain other types, such as DateTime and XmlElement) are treated as primitive because they are always known to the .NET runtime. As a result, you do not need to add them via the KnownType attribute. The only exception to this is when using arrays of primitive types.

Sometimes both the endpoints involved will not be aware of the types, and this warrants the use of the KnownType attribute. These situations are as follows:

- When the data type sent is inherited from the type that is expected.

- When the type sent is declared as an interface, as opposed to a concrete implementation such as a class, structure, or enumeration. Since you cannot know in advance what type implements that interface, the KnownType attribute is required.

- When the declared type that is being sent is declared to be of the type Object. Because every type inherits from Object, the type cannot be known in advance.

Some of the types, even though declared, might not fall into one of the previous three situations. For example, a HashTable internally stores the actual object using the Object type. Listing 11–5 shows an example of how you can use the KnownType attribute when using a HashTable. The class QuickReturnPortfolio implements a HashTable, and because of the KnownType attribute, the runtime is aware that only the types QuickReturnStock and QuickReturnBond are stored in the HashTable.

Listing 11–5. Data Contract Using the KnownType Attribute

```
[DataContract]
public class QuickReturnStock { }

[DataContract]
public class QuickReturnBond { }

[DataContract]
[KnownType(typeof(QuickReturnStock))]
[KnownType(typeof(QuickReturnPortfolio))]
public class QuickReturnPortfolio
{
    [DataMember]
    System.Collections.Hashtable thePortfolio;
}
```

Though the KnownType attribute has been generally used in WCF 3.x to support inheritance and polymorphism, it does not have any mechanism to work dynamically. This means you have to know ahead of time what types you want to register as known types. Also, in the preceding listing, QuickReturnStock and QuickReturnBond have been identified at design time. What if you want to resolve the type to be serialized at runtime, not design time? In WCF 3.x, there is no straightforward way to override the mapping algorithm used by DataContractSerializer. If you pass types other than those in KnownTypes(for belowexception, "QuickReturnAccount " was passed"), then you will get following exception:

```
Unhandled Exception: System.Runtime.Serialization.SerializationException: Type
'Serialization.QuickReturnAccount with data contract name
'QuickReturnAccount:http://schemas.datacontract.org/2004/07/Serialization' is not expected.
Consider using a DataContractResolver or add any types not known statically to the list of
known types - for example, by using the KnownTypeAttribute attribute or by adding them to
the list of known types passed to DataContractSerializer
```

As mentioned in the preceding exception message, you need to either add the type to the list of known types passed to DataContractSerializer or use DataContractResolver. .NET 4.0 ships with the DataContractResolver class, which can be used to implement a custom callback mechanism to serialize known types and then resolve them on deserialization. This provides an opportunity for developers to pass types at runtime. Developers can implement the callback mechanism by inheriting from the DataContractResolver class. This class resides in the System.Runtime.Serialization namespace. In order to use the DataContractResolver class, you needs to inherit from this class and override its two methods, TryResolveType and ResolveName. To do this, perform the following steps:

1. Create a new class that inherits from the DataContractResolver class, as follows:

```
class MyDataContractResolver : DataContractResolver
{

}
```

2. Override the `TryResolveType` and `ResolveName` methods. `TryResolveType` is called on serialization to map a type into the name and namespace used to define the `xsi:type`, while `ResolveName` is called on deserialization to map the `xsi:type` name and namespace back into a type. The `TryResolveType` method returns a Boolean indicating whether the resolver is able to resolve the type that was passed in, and two `XmlDictionaryStrings`, which will be used to write the resolved name and namespace on the wire. `ResolveName` also takes a declared type and a known type resolver, but it works the opposite way. It takes two strings that represent the name and namespace, and returns a type. The following is the code to override the methods:

```
public override Type ResolveName(string typeName, string typeNamespace,
    Type declaredType, DataContractResolver knownTypeResolver)
{
    ... // Implement your mapping
}
// Used at serialization
// Maps any type to a new xsi:type representation
public override bool TryResolveType(Type type, Type declaredType,
    DataContractResolver knownTypeResolver, out XmlDictionaryString typeName,
    out XmlDictionaryString typeNamespace)
{
    ... // Implement your mapping
}
```

3. Register your custom `DataContractResolver`. This can be done in a variety of ways:

   - The easiest way is to create a DataContract serializer and pass `DataContractResolver` as a parameter. When you use this `DataContractSerializer` instance to serialize/deserialize objects, your custom `DataContractResolver` will be called to perform the custom type resolution.

   - You can plug it into `DataContractSerializer`'s `ReadObject` and `WriteObject` methods.

   - You can plug it into WCF by setting it on the `DataContractSerializerOperationBehavior`.

Based on your requirements, you can choose any of the preceding three options to register your custom `DataContractResolver`. One of the classic implementations of the `DataContractResolver` class is the `ProxyDataContractResolver`, which also ships with .NET 4.0. By default, `DataContractSerializer` cannot serialize or deserialize POCO (plain-old CLR object) proxies as POCO entities. `ProxyDataContractResolver` helps in mapping proxy types to POCO types.

Data Contract Versioning

Change is a fact of life, and in a service-oriented world you do not have the luxury of assuming that everyone will change their implementation as your solution evolves. Some consumers will still be using the old version of the contract; therefore, you need to be able to support them by versioning data contracts.

Broadly speaking, data contract changes fall into two categories: nonbreaking and breaking. *Nonbreaking* changes occur when a consumer is able to communicate with a service using a newer version of a data contract, and vice versa. *Breaking* changes, on the other hand, do not allow this communication without changes to the consumer as well. Any change to a type that does not affect how an item is serialized and deserialized on the other end is a nonbreaking change. Listing 11–6 shows two versions of a class called QuickReturnQuote. Although the underlying type has changed between the two versions, the data contract is still the same because the Name property will be applied to the changing member to mask the internal name change.

Listing 11–6. Coordinating Data Contract Equivalence

```
// Version 1 of the QuickReturnQuote class
[DataContract]
public class QuickReturnQuote
{
    [DataMember(Name = "TickerSymbol")]
    internal string Symbol;

    [DataMember]
    internal decimal LastTrade;

    [DataMember]
    internal decimal Change;
}

// Version 2 of the QuickReturnQuote class
[DataContract]
public class QuickReturnQuote
{
    [DataMember]
    internal string TickerSymbol;

    [DataMember(Name="LastTrade")]
    internal decimal Value;

    [DataMember]
    internal decimal Change;
}
```

Table 11–1 summarizes the options available when changing a data contract, and the impact that change has on the consumers, if any.

Table 11–1. *Data Contract Change and Its Impact*

Change	Impact of Change
Changing name or namespace	Breaking
Changing order of data members	Breaking
Renaming data members	Breaking
Changing data contract	Breaking
Adding data members	Nonbreaking (in most cases)
Removing data members	Nonbreaking (in most cases)

Changing contracts is a tricky situation no matter how careful you are. You can change contracts in many ways—by adding, removing, or modifying—and you can cause many issues on both ends of the wire. These can range from obvious issues where an exception is thrown, to more complex ones where the data may lack integrity and not make sense. Figure 11–2 shows a versioning decision tree that you can use to predict the effects of any changes applied to the data contracts. The versioning decisions are depicted with diamonds, and the actions based on those decisions are represented as rectangles. The arrows represent the direction of the flow. The dark-gray actions represent nonbreaking changes, and light-gray ones show breaking changes.

Let's take an example service and walk through the flowchart. When you need to modify your existing service and can do so by adding a new service, then the easiest way is to use *service contract inheritance*. This new type will point to a new endpoint, which only the new consumers of this service will be aware of; the existing consumers will continue using the existing published version of the service. However, if this is not an option, then changing the data contract may be difficult. If you need to add more data, the easiest option is to add new *optional* data members (as shown in Figure 11–2).

If adding new members is not an option and you need to change the service operation and its corresponding data contract, then, as shown in the decision tree, it is best to implement a new version of the data contract (depicted as "v.Next") within a new namespace, and also have it point to a new endpoint. It is recommended that you incorporate a version number in the namespace. At this point, if you choose, you can deprecate the old endpoint. However, this action of deprecating constitutes a breaking change. If you are only deleting a service operation, you can keep the same data contract and just implement the v.Next version of the service and namespace pointing to a new endpoint.

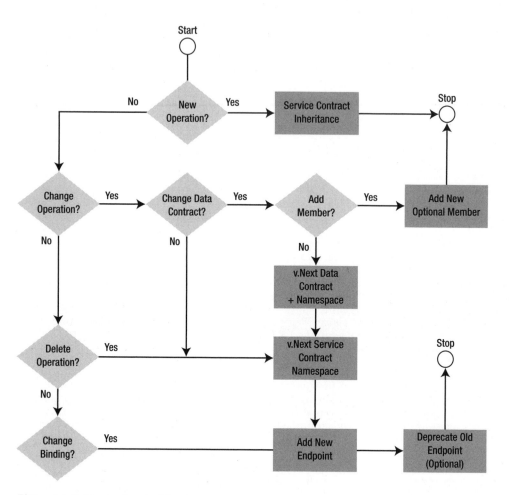

Figure 11–2. *Versioning decision tree*

Round-Tripping

As you have seen so far, versioning data contracts is fairly straightforward, and for the most part a data contract can evolve with the service in a nonbreaking fashion. However, there is one particular case in which the type cannot be evolved: *round-tripping*. Round-tripping occurs when, for a data contract, data passes from a new version to an old version and back to a new version. Since round-tripping guarantees that no data is lost, enabling it makes the type forward-compatible with any changes supported by data contract versioning in the future.

To allow a type to take part in round-tripping, you need to implement the IExtensibleDataObject interface. This interface contains the ExtensionData property, which is used to store any data from future versions of the data contract that might not be known to the current version. When the WCF runtime comes across any data that is not part of the original contract, that data is stored in this property and persisted. This property is essentially a property bag for the data, and is not processed in any other fashion.

One caveat to using the round-tripping feature is that sometimes it may cause the WCF runtime to produce schema-invalid messages. Round-tripping should be disabled when strict schema compliance is a requirement, such as if a future version of a data contract adds new members. When serialized, these new members are stored in the ExtensionData property. Now, when this new data contract is serialized the next time, the ExtensionData property will be serialized, instead of the content of that ExtensionData property (i.e., the new members). This will result in a message with a schema in which the new members are not present.

If at some point in the future you want to remove support for unknown members and switch off round-tripping (e.g., if you have a new requirement for strict schema compliance), you can do so quite easily. You can disable round-tripping by setting the IgnoreExtensionDataObject property in the ServiceBehavior attribute to true. Listing 11–7 shows how you can apply this at the service level. The Main class implements a service defined by the interface IQuickReturnTraderChat.

Listing 11–7. Ignoring ExtensionDataObject at the Service Level

```
[ServiceBehavior(InstanceContextMode =
      InstanceContextMode.Single,
      IgnoreExtensionDataObject=true)]
public partial class Main : Form, IQuickReturnTraderChat
{
    // Code removed for clarity
}
```

If you want to implement certain behaviors at the operation level, as opposed to the service level, then use the OperationBehavior attribute instead of the ServiceBehavior attribute. However, the OperationBehavior attribute supports only a subset of the features of the ServiceBehavior attribute.

■**Note** The ServiceBehavior attribute specifies the internal execution behavior of a specific service and applies at the service-wide level, affecting all the operations within that service. You can use this attribute to enable most common features (concurrency, exception details, shutting down an automation session, transaction behavior, etc.), which otherwise would need to be manually implemented.

XML Serialization

As you have seen so far, the default way to serialize data types is with the data contract serializer, which is implemented via the DataContractSerializer class. However, WCF also supports XmlSerializer. Although XmlSerializer supports fewer types than DataContractSerializer, it provides better control over the resulting XML, and also supports more of the XSD standard. The following are some scenarios in which XmlSerializer is a better option than DataContractSerializer:

- If you are migrating an application from ASP.NET web services to WCF and want to reuse existing types instead of data contracts

- When more control over XML is required for it to adhere to some schema

- When services need to follow legacy SOAP encoding standards

You also need to be aware of the underlying differences between the two platforms. While DataContractSerializer expects every member that needs to be serialized to be decorated with the

DataMember attribute, XmlSerializer serializes any public member. If you are not careful, this can lead to situations where data you were not expecting to be serialized is exposed, which can cause security and information disclosure issues.

■**Note** The two serialization options (DataContractSerializer and XmlSerializer) serialize the same type to XML differently, which makes their interchange usage difficult, because you might get runtime exceptions or behavior that's not expected.

To use XmlSerializer instead of DataContractSerializer, just apply the XmlSerializerFormat attribute to the *service*. Listing 11–8 shows the QuickReturnStockQuote example discussed earlier in the chapter, implementing XmlSerializer. Note that in addition to the required attribute, the accessibility of the class members has changed to public. This is because, as stated earlier, only public members will be serialized by XmlSerializer.

Listing 11–8. QuickReturnStockQuote Using XmlSerializer

```
[DataContract]
[XmlSerializerFormat]
public class QuickReturnStockQuote
{
    [DataMember(Name = "TickerSymbol")]
    public string Symbol;

    [DataMember]
    public string CompanyName;

    [DataMember]
    public decimal LastTrade;

    // Abbreviated for clarity
}
```

You should be aware of the following rules when using XmlSerializer:

- The XmlSerializer attribute, when being used on methods or parameters, can be used only when the class is a typed message. This cannot be applied directly to a service operation's parameters or its return values. Don't worry if you don't understand what a typed message or a MessageContract attribute is at this point; both are covered later in the "Introducing Message Contracts" section of this chapter.

- This attribute takes precedence when applied to a typed message member when that message member has conflicting properties set. For example, the ElementName property on XmlSerializer overrides the Name property on the MessageContract attribute.

- The SoapInclude and XmlInclude attributes (which are used to recognize a type when serializing or deserializing with SOAP) are not supported. Instead, you must use the KnownType attribute.

- When performing SOAP encoding, XmlSerializer does not support the MessageHeaderArray attribute, which is used to customize part of the SOAP header element.

Security

When switching from DataContractSerializer to XmlSerializer, you need to take into account some security changes. Unlike DataContractSerializer, XmlSerializer needs write access to the temp folder of the machine. And theoretically, another process could overwrite the temp assemblies that XmlSerializer created with other assemblies containing malicious code. Since XmlSerializer supports the loading of pregenerated serialized assemblies, it is recommended that you sign the WCF solution that uses XmlSerializer. If the solution is unsigned, then the possibility exists for a malicious program to place an assembly with the same name as the pregenerated assembly in the application folder or GAC, and load it.

■**Note** We have been primarily discussing XML serialization so far, but, as mentioned earlier, .NET also supports binary serialization. This allows an object in memory to be converted into a stream of bytes, which—in addition to persisting to disk—allows you to marshal by value. *Marshalling by value* occurs when objects are passed between application domains via parameters or return values. The objects need the flexibility to be serialized in order to do that. Binary serialization, although it is efficient and produces compact code, works only with the .NET platform and is not portable across platforms.

Introducing Message Contracts

When using data contracts, your concentration is usually on the data structure and the serialization aspects of that structure—not so much on the SOAP message, which carries the payload between the service and the consumer. In other words, you're focusing on the data contracts that control the format of the SOAP message. However, if you are in a situation where you want an equal amount of control over the structure and the content of the message because of operational reasons, then you need to use message contracts as opposed to data contracts. When using message contracts, you can use a *data type* as either the parameter to a service call or the return value from a call. It is this data type that is precisely serialized to the SOAP message, defining the precise schema for the message. Another way to put it is that a message contract is nothing but a mapping for a data type and the SOAP envelope that is created.

Applying the MessageContract attribute to a type defines its message contract. Those type members that need to be part of the SOAP header need to have the MessageHeader attribute applied, and those that will be part of the SOAP body need to have the MessageBodyMember attribute applied. You can apply both the MessageHeader attribute and the MessageBodyMember attribute to all members of a type, irrespective of their accessibility levels.

As with data contracts, you can use the Name and Namespace properties on the MessageHeader and MessageBodyMember attributes. If the namespace has not changed, the default is the namespace of the service contract. Listing 11–9 shows the earlier example of QuickReturnStockQuote (from Listing 11–2), but this time a message contract is implemented instead of a data contract. This allows you to precisely control the schema of the message when QuickReturnStockQuote is the data type.

Listing 11–9. QuickReturnStockQuote Implementing a Message Contract

```
[MessageContract]
public class QuickReturnStockQuote
{
    [MessageHeader(Name="TickerSymbol")]
    internal string Symbol;

    [MessageHeader]
    internal string CompanyName;

    [MessageBodyMember]
    internal decimal LastTrade;

    [MessageBodyMember]
    internal decimal Change;

    [MessageBodyMember]
    internal decimal PreviousClose;

    [MessageBodyMember(Name = "AverageVolume")]
    internal decimal AvgVol;

    [MessageBodyMember(Name = "MarketCapital")]
    internal double MarketCap;

    [MessageBodyMember(Name = "PriceEarningRatio")]
    internal decimal PERatio;

    [MessageBodyMember(Name = "EarningsPerShare")]
    internal decimal EPS;

    [MessageBodyMember(Name = "52WkHigh")]
    internal decimal FiftyTwoWeekHigh;

    [MessageBodyMember(Name = "52WkLow")]
    internal decimal FiftyTwoWeekLow;
}
```

Listing 11–10 shows the SOAP representation of QuickReturnStockQuote.

Listing 11–10. SOAP Message Representation of QuickReturnStockQuote

```
<soap:Envelope>
    <soap:Header>
        <TickerSymbol>MSFT</TickerSymbol>
        <CompanyName>Microsoft</CompanyName>
    </soap:Header>
    <soap:Body>
        <LastTrade>29.24</LastTrade>
        <Change>0.02</Change>
        <PreviousClose>29.17</PreviousClose>
        <AverageVolume>59.31</AverageVolume>
        <MarketCapital>287.44</MarketCapital>
```

```
            <PriceEarningRatio>24.37</PriceEarningRatio>
            <EarningsPerShare>1.20</EarningsPerShare>
            <_52WkHigh>29.40</_52WkHigh>
            <_52WkLow>21.45</_52WkLow>
        </soap:Body>
</soap:Envelope>
```

Fine-Tuning SOAP

As stated earlier, a message contract is all about fine-tuning the various aspects of a SOAP envelope, empowering you to integrate with other platforms. This section will discuss your options for customizing the SOAP envelope, and we'll cover other SOAP aspects such as SOAP wrappers, element order, SOAP actions, and SOAP header attributes.

You can control the wrapping of the SOAP body parts. The default behavior is to have the body parts in a wrapper element when serialized. You should not wrap more than one body part at a time, because this is not compliant with WS-I Basic Profile (version 1.1). The only situation where you would do this is when you need to achieve interoperability with another system that expects this format. You can control the name and the namespace of the wrapper element by setting the WrapperName and WrapperNamespace properties in the MessageContract attribute.

The default order of elements is alphabetical; however, both the MessageHeader and MessageBodyMember attributes support the Order property, which can be used to set the specific ordering of elements, just as in a data contract. The only difference between the two concerns inheritance—unlike a data contract, in a message contract the base type's members are not sorted before the child type's members.

If you need to implement a SOAP action, then you need to define it with the service operation of the service contract through the OperationContract attribute. To specify the SOAP action, you need to set the Action and ReplyAction properties on the OperationContract attribute when defining the service operation. The SOAP specification allows the three attributes listed in Table 11–2 in the header. By default, these header attributes are not emitted, but they can be set via the Actor, MustUnderstand, and Relay properties on the MessageHeader attribute, respectively. Note that if the MustUnderstand property is set to true and you have a new version of the message contract, then you will get an exception at runtime because there is an extra header in the SOAP message that is "not understood."

Table 11–2. *Valid SOAP Header Attributes*

Value	Description
Actor (version 1.1)/Role (version 1.2)	Specifies the header's target URI
MustUnderstand	Specifies whether the node processing the header must understand it.
Relay	Specifies whether the header can be relayed downstream to other nodes

At times, a service might be required to support legacy XML. This is especially true in integration and interop situations where the platforms might differ between the consumer and the service. If required, you can enable legacy XML encoding by setting the Use property on the XmlSerializerFormat attribute to Encoded, as shown in Listing 11–11. However, this is not recommended for two reasons. First, arrays are not supported, and second, object references are preserved within the message body.

Listing 11–11. QuickReturnStockQuote Using Legacy SOAP Encoding

```
[XmlSerializerFormat(Use=OperationFormatUse.Encoded)]
public class QuickReturnStockQuote
{
    [DataMember(Name = "TickerSymbol")]
    public string Symbol;

    [DataMember]
    public string CompanyName;

    [DataMember]
    public decimal LastTrade;

    // Abbreviated for clarity
}
```

The only time a message type can inherit from another type is when the base type also has a message contract. Also, when inheriting, the message headers are a collection of all the headers in the inheritance hierarchy. Similarly, all the body parts are also consolidated in the inheritance hierarchy; they're ordered first by the Order property specified in the MessageBodyMember attribute (if any) and then alphabetically. If the same name for either the header or the body part is repeated in the inheritance hierarchy, then the member that is lowest in the hierarchy is used to store the information.

■**Note** If required, the WCF runtime allows you to use your own serializer by inheriting the XmlObjectSerializer class and overriding the WriteStartObject, WriteObjectContent, and WriteEndObject members.

You also need to consider legacy XML support. If there is a requirement by your service to produce WSDL for interop scenarios, you need to be careful. WSDL and message contract support is tricky because WSDL supports only a subset of the message contract features. As a result, when generating WSDL, the features from a message contract will not get reflected, because of the lack of this support. You should consider these points when working with WSDL:

- WSDL does not have the notion of an array of headers, and will show only one header, as opposed to the array.

- Similar to the previous point, protection-level information is not fully supported and may be missing.

- The class name of the message contract type will be the message type generated in the WSDL.

- If many operations in a service contract use the same message contract across those operations, then the WSDL that is generated for that service contract will contain multiple message types even though at the end of the day they are the same type. These multiple messages are made unique in the WSDL by appending a numeral at the end, such as 2, 3, and so on. As a result, the message types created when importing such WSDL are identical except for their names.

Security

You have three options for making a message secure when using message contracts. Depending on which you choose, different parts of a SOAP message are digitally signed and encrypted. The options you have are to secure the entire SOAP message, to secure only the header of the SOAP message, and to secure only the body of the SOAP message (i.e., the payload). To enable the option you choose, set the ProtectionLevel property on either the MessageHeader attribute or the MessageBodyMember attribute. Although for each header the protection level is determined individually, the body's security level is determined collectively, with the highest level being applied across all body parts. For these security options to work, the bindings and behaviors need to be set up correctly (e.g., attempting to sign without providing the correct credentials); otherwise, you will get an exception. Table 11–3 summarizes the possible values of the ProtectionLevel property.

Table 11–3. ProtectionLevel Property Values

Value	Description
None	No encryption or digital signature (this is the default option)
Sign	Digital signature only
EncyrptAndSign	Both digitally signs and encrypts

Performance

Since each message header and body part is serialized independently, the same namespace will be repeatedly declared for each. It is recommended you consolidate these multiple headers and body parts into a single header or body part to reduce the size of the message on the wire and improve performance. For example, you can rewrite the original code from Listing 11–8 (showing QuickReturnStockQuote implemented as a message contract) as shown in Listing 11–12.

Listing 11–12. QuickReturnStockQuote Implemented for Optimal Performance

```
[MessageContract]
public class QuickReturnStockQuote
{
    [MessageHeader(Name="TickerSymbol")]
    internal string Symbol;

    [MessageHeader]
    internal string CompanyName;

    [MessageBodyMember]
    internal StockDetails StockInformation;
}

[DataContract]
public class StockDetails {
    [DataMember]
    internal decimal LastTrade;
```

```
    [DataMember]
    internal decimal Change;

    [DataMember]
    internal decimal PreviousClose;

    [DataMember(Name = "AverageVolume")]
    internal decimal AvgVol;

    [DataMember(Name = "MarketCapital")]
    internal double MarketCap;

    [DataMember(Name = "PriceEarningRatio")]
    internal decimal PERatio;

    [DataMember(Name = "EarningsPerShare")]
    internal decimal EPS;

    [DataMember(Name = "52WkHigh")]
    internal decimal FiftyTwoWeekHigh;

    [DataMember(Name = "52WkLow")]
    internal decimal FiftyTwoWeekLow;
}
```

Using the Message Class

Up until now, you have been looking at the various serialization techniques and data transfer architectures available as part of WCF. In looking at data transfers, it is important to understand the core foundation of WCF—the Message class.

As stated earlier, the Message class is one of the two pillars of WCF, and serves as a general-purpose container of data for all communication between a service and the consumers of that service. However, you should use it only in a few specific scenarios. For example, you should use it if you need either an alternative way of handling an incoming message or an alternative way of creating the outgoing message (say, saving the message to disk). The Message class is closely aligned with the SOAP protocol and contains a header and body. The Message class is defined in the System.ServiceModel.Channels namespace, and you create a simple message by calling the CreateMessage static method on the factory. Listing 11–13 shows a sample operation contract using Message.

Listing 11–13. Message Class in Operations

```
[ServiceContract()]
public interface IQuickReturnStock
{
    [OperationContract]
    System.ServiceModel.Channels.Message GetCurrentTicker();

    [OperationContract]
    void SetTickerSymbol(System.ServiceModel.Channels.Message data);
}
```

When you use the Message class in an operation, you should be aware of the following rules:

- The operation cannot have any out or ref parameters.

- You cannot have more than one input parameter, and that input parameter can be only of type Message.

- The return type can be only Message or void.

Listing 11–14 shows an example of creating a simple message using an object. At the simplest level, the CreateMessage overloaded method takes objects and uses the default data contract serializer for serialization. There is also an overloaded version of CreateMessage, which takes XmlObjectSerializer as the serializer instead of using the default.

Listing 11–14. *Creating Messages from Objects*

```
public class MyMessageService : IQuickReturnStock
{
    private Message IQuickReturnStock.GetCurrentTicker()
    {
        QuickReturnStockMessage stock = new QuickReturnStockMessage();
        stock.ticker = "MSFT";
        stock.companyName = "Microsoft Inc";
        MessageVersion ver =
            OperationContext.Current.IncomingMessageVersion();
        return Message.CreateMessage(ver,"GetDataResponse",stock);
    }

    // Abbreviated for clarity
}

[DataContract]
public class QuickReturnStockMessage
{
    [DataMember] public string ticker;
    [DataMember] public string companyName;
}
```

Similar to how the message in Listing 11–14 was created using objects, you can create a message using XML readers instead. A few scenarios where this would make more sense than using objects would be when reading from a file system, using an XmlDictionaryWriter object, and creating fault messages (using the CreateFault method).

When writing messages, you'll primarily use three different methods. First is the WriteBodyContents method, which writes the body contents of the message to a given XML writer. Second is the WriteBody method, which writes the body content as well, but also encloses the appropriate wrapper elements (such as <soap:body>). Third is the WriteMessage method, which writes out the entire message, including the wrapping SOAP envelope and headers. Note that if SOAP is turned off, all three methods produce the same result: writing out the message body contents.

When reading messages, the primary way to do so is via the GetReaderAtBodyContents method, which returns an XmlDictionaryReader object. Alternatively, if you require a type-safe way to access the message, then use the GetBody method, which allows access to the message body as a typed object. In addition, the Message class has properties such as Headers, Properties, Version, IsFault, IsEmpty, and so on, which represent access to other parts of the message, such as the header and properties.

Filtering

WCF has a filtering mechanism, which you can use to examine parts of messages, match them, and then make some operational decision at runtime. This filtering mechanism is implemented as a set of classes, and is designed to be fast, with each filter implemented specifically for a certain kind of message matching. The filtering takes place after a message has been received, and sits in the stack while the message is being dispatched to the relevant application. At this level, the filtering system can interact with all other WCF subsystems (routing, security, event handling, etc.). As an example, if there is a queue, then a message can be moved to the front of the queue for processing, based on its priority.

Filtering is typically used when you need to route messages to different modules within a system depending their content. Two of the more common scenarios for this are *routing* and *demultiplexing*. In the first scenario, the listener running at an endpoint filters for a specific action, and only the matching action gets to the endpoint. In the demultiplexing scenario, various listeners are on the wire, and only those with the filtered endpoint address reach the intended endpoint.

Filters

Internally, the filtering mechanism consists of a filter and a filter table. The filters implemented via the abstract MessageFilter class make a Boolean decision based on the configured conditions. These filters are used in a filter table instead of being tested individually, and each filter has an associated table with the filter data. The filter table implements the IMessageFilterTable interface, and is created by calling the generic CreateFilterTable<FilterData> method on the abstract MessageFilter class. The Match method on the MessageFilter class determines whether an incoming message satisfies a particular filter.

This method returns true if a match is found based on the specified criteria. Once a filter is created, the criteria used cannot be changed, because there is no implementation in the filter to detect this change. The only way to work around this is to delete the existing filter and create a new one with the updated criteria. Out of the box, WCF has a few concrete implementations of the abstract MessageFilter class, as shown in Table 11–4.

Table 11–4. Concrete MessageFilter Implementations in WCF

Classes	Description
XPathMessageFilter	Uses an XPath expression to specify the criteria
MatchAllMessageFilter	Matches all messages
MatchNoneMessageFilter	Matches none of the messages
ActionMessageFilter	Tests whether the message action matches a given set of actions
EndpointAddressMessageFilter	Tests whether the message is valid for a given addresses
PrefixEndpointAddressMessageFilter	Similar to EndpointAddressMessageFilter, except matches a prefix of the URI

Filter Tables

Internally, the filter table is similar to a `HashTable`, and is a key/value pair where the filter is the key and some metadata as the value. This metadata can contain any relevant information needed, such as the type of the filter data or the actions to take for a matching message. Filter tables have methods that return both single matching and multiple matching records. Note that these records are not ordered in any sequence. The `MessageFilterTable` class is the most generic implementation of the `IMessageFilter` interface in WCF, and can store any type of filter.

You can assign filter priorities using a number; the higher the number, the higher priority the filter has. You can assign the same priority to more than one type of filter at the same time. The same filter type can have more than one priority at the same time as well. You can match these filters in a top-down fashion, starting with the highest-priority filter. Once a matching filter is found at a certain priority, the WCF runtime will not examine any filters of that type with a lower priority.

■**Note** If you want, you can also send attachments with WCF using Direct Internet Message Encapsulation (DIME). If you want to be WSE compliant, then you should use DIME's successor, Message Transmission Optimization Mechanism (MTOM). For more details, refer to Chapter 13.

Best Practices for Versioning

Versioning, in the context of data contracts, is all about schema validation, You need to version the changes to this schema. Versioning for data contracts can be divided into two groups: one that requires schema validation and one that does not. The group in which schema validation is required is quite rare in today's enterprise environment, and many systems can handle the fact that certain elements are extra and not defined in a schema.

Versioning with Schema Validation

Data contracts should be considered *immutable* when schema validation is required both ways (i.e., new to old and vice versa). You should create a new data contract whenever a new version is required, because this will generate a new schema. This new data contract should also incorporate the relevant name, namespace, and updated service type information. In most cases, changes to data contracts in these circumstances need to be rippled across to every layer in the solution. This means that if a data contract is part of another data contract, and if the child data contract is updated even though the parent is not, then the parent data contract will need to be versioned as well.

It is quite common in a heterogeneous environment that you won't have control over the incoming messages, though you'll usually have some degree of control over the outgoing messages. If there is a requirement that the generated messages (i.e., the outgoing messages) need to *strictly comply* with a schema, then you need to turn off the round-tripping feature. In round-tripping, the original incoming message (which you have no control over) will have extra information that does not comply with your schema. This extra information is stored and then returned with the outgoing message. When this happens, the outgoing message won't be compliant with you schema. As mentioned earlier, you have two options for switching off round-tripping. One option is not to implement `IExtensibleDataObject`, and the second is to set the `IngoreExtensionDataObject` property to `true` on the `ServiceBehavior` attribute.

Versioning without Schema Validation

When schema validation is not required, the guidelines for versioning are as follows:

- Type inheritance should not be used to version data contracts; instead, either create a new type or change the data contract on an existing type.

- Always implement the IExtensibleDataObject interface to support round-tripping.

- Do not change the name or namespace for the data contract, because the versions for that data contract evolve. If the underlying type changes, then make appropriate changes to keep the data contract the same; for example, by using the Name property.

- Similar to the data contract point earlier, do not change any names or namespaces for the data members. If the underlying data member (field, property, event, etc.) changes, preserve the data member by using the Name property. Also, changing either the type or the order of any of the data member is not allowed, because in most cases doing so will also cause the data contract to change.

- When there is a new version containing new data members, these rules should always be followed:

  - For the new member, the IsRequired property should be set to false (the default value).

  - A callback method using the OnDeserializing attribute should be provided in cases where a default value of null or zero for a data member is not acceptable. This should provide the default value that will be acceptable by the data member.

  - In the old version of the data contract, the Order property should not be set. Any new members added in subsequent versions should have their Order property set to that version. For example, version 2 of the data contract should have the Order property set to 2, version 3 to 3, and so on. With regard to order, all newly added members should placed be *after* the existing members; you can use the Order property to handle this.

- Data members should not be removed, even if the IsRequired property is set to false.

- The IsRequired property cannot be changed between versions.

- The EmitDefaultValue property cannot be changed for the required data members between versions.

- When creating a new version, do not create a branched version hierarchy.

- Enumerations are just like any other data members, and the same practices for reordering, adding, removing, and so on apply as stated previously.

Putting It All Together: Quote Client Sample Application

We have introduced many different concepts in this chapter. In the following sections, we will show how to create a sample application that illustrates the concepts that we have discussed. This sample consists of a service and a client. The service, called QuickReturnQuoteService, is quite straightforward and exposes two operations: GetPortfolio and GetQuote. The data contract for the service is exposed via a class called StockQuote. The first operation, GetPortfolio, accepts an array of stock tickers, which makes up the portfolio and returns an array of type StockQuote, which contains the details of each of the stocks in the portfolio. Similarly, GetQuote accepts one ticker and returns the type StockQuote.

Creating the Service

As mentioned, the service is quite simple and exposes the interface called IQuickReturnQuoteService. Listing 11–15 shows this interface. The service also has two endpoints—one is over HTTP and the other is a MEX endpoint. In this example, the service resides in a folder called wcf, which is part of inetpub and is located at C:\inetpub\wwwroot\wcf.

Listing 11–15. IQuickReturnQuoteService Interface

```
[ServiceContract]
public interface IQuickReturnQuoteService
{
    [OperationContract]
    StockQuote[] GetPortfolio(string[] portfolioTickers);

    [OperationContract]
    StockQuote GetQuote(string ticker);
}
```

The QuoteService class shown in Listing 11–16 is the concrete implementation for the IQuickReturnQuoteService interface for the service.

Listing 11–16. QuoteService Concrete Implementation

```
public class QuoteService : IQuickReturnQuoteService
{
    public StockQuote[] GetPortfolio(string[] portfolioTickers)
    {

        ArrayList tickers = new ArrayList();

        foreach (string stockTicker in portfolioTickers)
        {
            StockQuote stockQuote = new StockQuote(stockTicker);
            tickers.Add(stockQuote);
        }

        return (StockQuote[])tickers.ToArray(typeof(StockQuote));
    }

    public StockQuote GetQuote(string ticker)
    {
        StockQuote quote = new StockQuote(ticker);
```

```
        return quote;
    }
}
```

You can access the two endpoints exposed by the service via the `http://localhost/wcf/`
`QuickReturnQuoteService.svc` and `http://localhost/wcf/QuickReturnQuoteService.svc/mex` URLs.
Listings 11–17 and 11–18 show the `.svc` and `web.config` files. Note that for a production system, it is
recommended that you switch off the debug options; these are enabled only for development purposes.

Listing 11–17. QuickReturnQuoteService.svc File

```
<%@ServiceHost language=c# Debug="true" Service="QuickReturn.QuoteService" %>
```

Listing 11–18. web.config

```xml
<?xml version="1.0"?>
<configuration>
    <system.serviceModel>
        <services>
            <service name="QuickReturn.QuoteService"
                behaviorConfiguration="QuoteServiceBehavior">
                <endpoint  address=""
                    binding="wsHttpBinding"
                    contract="QuickReturn.IQuickReturnQuoteService"
                />
                <endpoint  address="mex"
                    binding="mexHttpBinding"
                    contract="IMetadataExchange"
                />
            </service>
        </services>

        <behaviors>
            <serviceBehaviors>
                <behavior name="QuoteServiceBehavior">
                    <serviceMetadata httpGetEnabled="true"/>
                    <serviceDebug
                        includeExceptionDetailInFaults="true"/>
                </behavior>
            </serviceBehaviors>
        </behaviors>
    </system.serviceModel>
</configuration>
```

The data contract is implemented via the `StockQuote` class, as shown in Listing 11–19. To show some
of the versioning concepts, we have two versions of the data contract. Version 1 is simple and consists of
just three data members: `LastTrade`, `CompanyName`, and `TickerSymbol`. Version 2, which is shown in Listing
11–19, adds data members. Since we are not hooking into a stock exchange, to simulate this feed the
constructor takes a few ticker symbols and randomly generates a number from 10 to 100 for the stock
price. Note that we have abbreviated Listing 11–19 for clarity.

Listing 11–19. Version 2 of the StockQuote Data Contract

```
[DataContract]
public class StockQuote
{
    // Constructor - simulates the changes when connected to an exchange
    public StockQuote(string ticker)
    {
        Random rnd = new Random();
        int deltaTrade = rnd.Next(100);

        switch (ticker)
        {
            case "MSFT":
                symbol = ticker;
                companyName = "Microsoft";
                lastTrade = 35.0M + deltaTrade;
                break;
            case "IBM":
                symbol = ticker;
                companyName = "IBM";
                lastTrade = 34.0M + deltaTrade;
                break;
            case "INTU":
                symbol = ticker;
                companyName = "Intuit";
                lastTrade = 33.0M + deltaTrade;
                break;
            case "GOOG":
                symbol = ticker;
                companyName = "Google";
                lastTrade = 32.0M + deltaTrade;
                break;
        }
    }

    private string symbol;
    [DataMember(Name = "TickerSymbol")]
    public string Symbol  { ... }

    private string companyName;
    [DataMember]
    public string CompanyName { ... }

    private decimal lastTrade;
    [DataMember]
    public decimal LastTrade { ... }

    private decimal change;
    [DataMember]
    public decimal Change { ... }

    private decimal previousClose;
    [DataMember]
```

```
    public decimal PreviousClose { ... }

    private decimal avgVol;
    [DataMember(Name = "AverageVolume")]
    public decimal AvgVol { ... }

    private double marketCap;
    [DataMember(Name = "MarketCapital")]
    public double MarketCap { ... }

    private decimal peRatio;
    [DataMember(Name = "PriceEarningRatio")]
    public decimal PERatio { ... }

    private decimal eps;
    [DataMember(Name = "EarningsPerShare")]
    public decimal EPS { ... }

    private decimal fiftyTwoWeekHigh;
    [DataMember(Name = "52WkHigh")]
    public decimal FiftyTwoWeekHigh { ... }

    private decimal fiftyTwoWeekLow;
    [DataMember(Name = "52WkLow")]
    public decimal FiftyTwoWeekLow { ... }
}
```

Creating the Client

The client is a simple Windows form application that contains a DataGridView. There are two buttons: one for invoking the GetPortfolio and the other for invoking the GetQuote operations on the service. The data contract returned by the service is bound to this DataGridView. The client consumes both versions of the service, simulating a real-world situation where some consumers of the service would be using the newer version while others might still be using the old one. This simulation can be done in two ways. The first is to create two different client projects, and the second is to create two different proxies. For this example, we chose the second way. We generated two proxies for the service, one in a code file called QuoteService1.cs and the other in QuoteService2.cs. QuoteService1.cs is used for version 1 of the service and QuoteService2.cs is used for version 2. If you download the sample application for this book, you can include *only* one of these files in the solution at any time.

We used the SvcUtil.exe tool to generate both the proxy and the service configuration for the service. The service configuration is saved in the App.config file for the client. Listing 11–20 shows the command line to use the SvcUtil.exe tool. Note that this assumes the service lives at http://localhost/wcf.

Listing 11–20. Command Line to Generate the Service Proxy

```
svcutil /language:c# /config:App.config
        http://localhost/wcf/QuickReturnQuoteService.svc?wsdl
```

Listing 11–21 shows the App.config file that is automatically created by the SvcUtil.exe tool. Note that this tool adds many of the defaults, such as service timeouts, buffer pool sizes, and so on. Depending on your operational requirements in a production environment, you might want to either handcraft these settings or modify the configuration file that the SvcUtil.exe tool generates.

Listing 11–21. App.config Generated by SvcUtil.exe

```xml
<?xml version="1.0" encoding="utf-8"?>
<configuration>
    <system.serviceModel>
        <bindings>
            <wsHttpBinding>
                <binding name="WSHttpBinding_IQuickReturnQuoteService"
                         closeTimeout="00:01:00"
                    openTimeout="00:01:00" receiveTimeout="00:10:00"
                         sendTimeout="00:01:00"
                    bypassProxyOnLocal="false" transactionFlow="false"
                         hostNameComparisonMode="StrongWildcard"
                    maxBufferPoolSize="524288" maxReceivedMessageSize="65536"
                    messageEncoding="Text" textEncoding="utf-8"
                         useDefaultWebProxy="true"
                    allowCookies="false">
                    <readerQuotas maxDepth="32" maxStringContentLength=
                        "8192" maxArrayLength="16384"
                        maxBytesPerRead="4096"
                        maxNameTableCharCount="16384" />
                    <reliableSession ordered="true" inactivityTimeout=
                        "00:10:00"
                        enabled="false" />
                    <security mode="Message">
                        <transport clientCredentialType="Windows"
                            proxyCredentialType="None"
                            realm="" />
                        <message clientCredentialType="Windows"
                            negotiateServiceCredential="true"
                             algorithmSuite="Default"
                             establishSecurityContext="true" />
                    </security>
                </binding>
            </wsHttpBinding>
        </bindings>
        <client>
            <endpoint address="http://localhost/wcf/
                    QuickReturnQuoteService.svc"
                binding="wsHttpBinding"
                    bindingConfiguration=
                    "WSHttpBinding_IQuickReturnQuoteService"
                contract="IQuickReturnQuoteService"
                    name="WSHttpBinding_IQuickReturnQuoteService">
                <identity>
                    <servicePrincipalName value=
                        "host/AmitBahree-PC " />
                </identity>
            </endpoint>
        </client>
    </system.serviceModel>
</configuration>
```

The code for the client where the service is invoked is fairly straightforward, as shown in Listing 11–22. Because you do not have any persistence storage, the tickers are hard-coded and the service is then invoked. The result from the service is bound to the data grid on the form.

Listing 11–22. Calling the Service and Binding the Data Contract to the Grid

```
private void buttonGetPortfolio_Click(object sender, EventArgs e)
{
    this.Cursor = Cursors.WaitCursor;

    // We hard-code an array of a few stocks that we want the service
    // to return. In the real world, this would be retrieved
    // from some persistent store
    string[] stocks = { "INTU", "MSFT", "GOOG", "IBM" };

    // Invoke the service
    StockQuote[] portfolio = theService.GetPortfolio(stocks);

    // Bind the data contract returned by the service to the grid
    BindData(ref dataGridView, portfolio);
}

private void BindData(ref DataGridView dataGrid, object data)
{
    BindingSource bindingSource = new BindingSource();
    bindingSource.DataSource = data;

    dataGrid.DataSource = bindingSource;
    dataGrid.Columns["ExtensionData"].Visible = false;
}
```

As stated earlier, the client consumes two versions of the service. When you talk to the simpler version of the service (version 1), you can see the result for both the GetPortfolio and GetStock operations (shown in Figures 11–3 and 11–4, respectively). Only three elements are known by the client—LastTrade, CompanyName, and TickerSymbol. To implement this old version, include the QuoteService1.cs file in the solution.

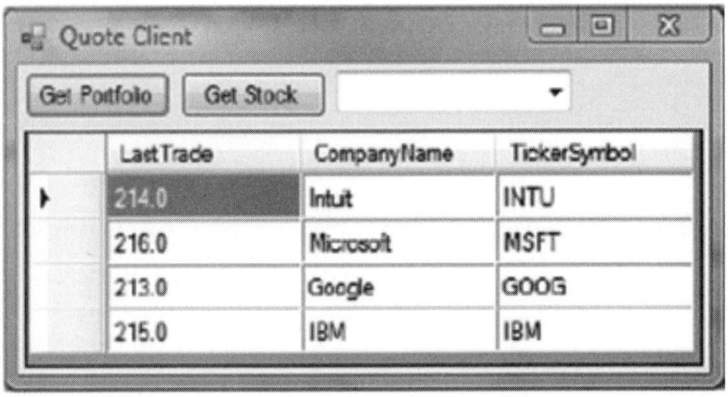

Figure 11–3. Sample portfolio using version 1 of the service

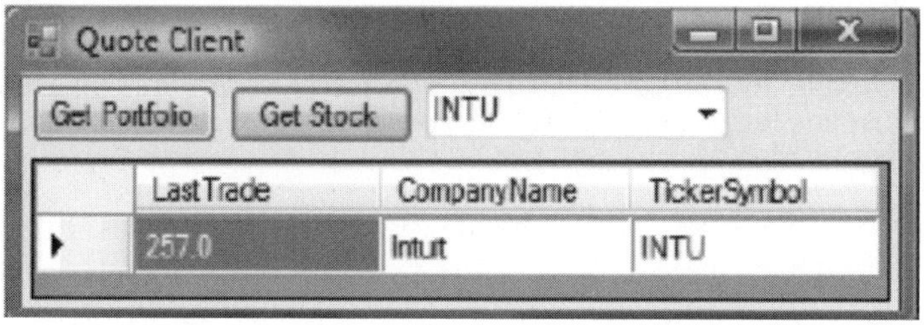

Figure 11–4. Sample quote using version 1 of the service

If the client is aware of the updated service and wants to consume version 2, then there are more data members returned by each of the operations (see Figures 11–5 and 11–6). To implement this new version, include the QuoteService2.cs file in the solution instead of QuoteService1.cs.

Also note that no elements on the service end have changed in the sample—only the client elements have been changed to simulate a client that either consumes the old version or the new version of the service.

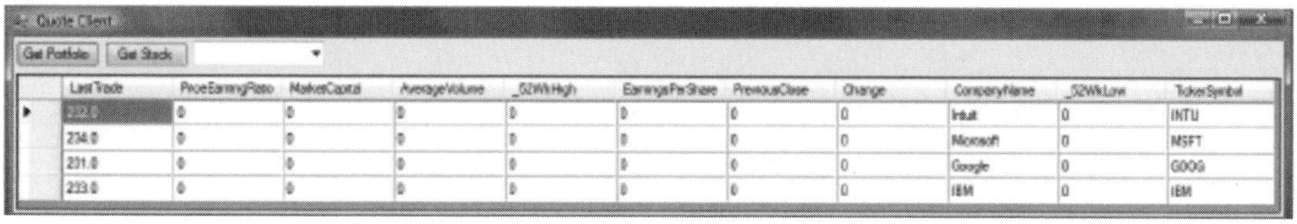

Figure 11–5. Sample portfolio using version 2 of the service

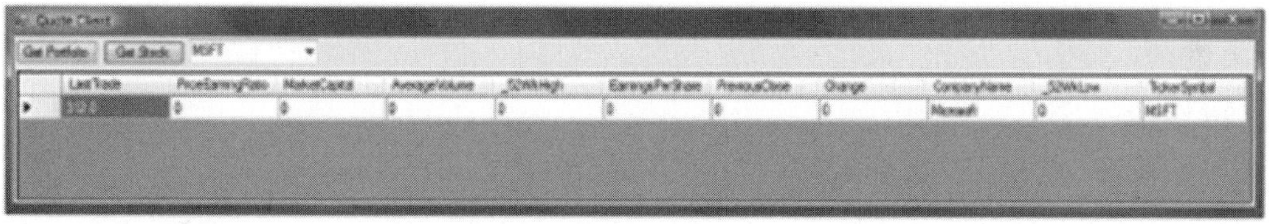

Figure 11–6. Sample quote using version 2 of the service

Summary

In conclusion, for any data to be passed to or from a service, it first needs to be serialized. Although both .NET and ASP.NET in general support serialization, WCF truly extends this concept and makes it easy to implement. Of the various options you examined, data contracts (the default) provide one of the most flexible serialization engines, designed with change and versioning in mind. The WCF runtime flexibility allows you to switch to legacy support when required.

The ability to map your business components to data members in a natural OOP paradigm is a powerful feature. This makes the development, testing, and maintenance of data contracts, along with versioning, more intuitive.

This chapter also discussed the powerful ability to filter messages based on one or more criteria, allowing you to support scenarios that would have previously required a lot of effort.

Today's needs demand application components that are available across the organization. The need for collaboration, online or offline, is a mandate for all companies. The next chapter will cover the aspects of developing peer-to-peer computing with WCF.

CHAPTER 12

■■■

Developing Peer-to-Peer Applications with WCF

In this chapter, we will dive into the core concepts of peer-to-peer (P2P) computing. We will cover what P2P means, the advantages that it brings, and the challenges that you'll face when working with it. We will also cover what a typical development environment looks like when writing P2P applications. We will explore some of the options provided by Microsoft in enabling P2P, both in the context of WCF and in Windows in general.

Introducing P2P Computing

Peer-to-peer is a term that has gained a lot of popularity in recent times. Today, organizations and businesses increasingly depend on collaboration between individuals and groups to perform essential tasks. P2P computing essentially comprises a set of networked computers that rely on the computing power and bandwidth of the individual computers on the network. This is different from the traditional approach of relying on a smaller number of more powerful server computers on the network. A computer connected to a P2P network is called a *node* or *peer*. The nodes in a P2P network are usually connected on an ad hoc basis, and the real power in a P2P network lies in these nodes. The peers are responsible for uploading and downloading data among each other without the need for a server. Two types of P2P networks exist:

- Pure P2P networks

- Hybrid P2P networks

A pure P2P network has no concept of a client or a server; it has only nodes, which act in the capacity of both a server and a client as needed. A hybrid P2P network, on the other hand, has a central server that keeps track of the various peers on the network. This server only responds to requests from the peers for information; it does not store any data. The peers are responsible for hosting the information. For example, in a file-sharing P2P application, the files are stored by the peer, and the server is aware only of what files are stored by what peer.

In the real world, pure P2P solutions that implement only peering protocols and do not rely on the concept of clients and servers are rare. Most P2P solutions rely on some nonpeer elements in the solution (e.g., Domain Name Systems [DNSs], which are used to translate computer hostnames to IP addresses). Some of the P2P solutions also have the notion of a *superpeer*, where other peers are connected to this superpeer in a starlike fashion. Over time, these superpeers can also be used as local servers. The networks in P2P applications are also called *meshes* (or sometimes *mesh networks*), as they are akin to a wire mesh. Each node in a mesh at a minimum has bidirectional communication capabilities with its neighbors. A *cloud* is a mesh network with a specific address scope. These scopes are closely related to IPv6 scopes, and the peers in a cloud are those that can communicate within the same IPv6 scope.

Why Use P2P?

Usually, the nodes, or peers, in a P2P network are ordinary computers that most people use in their day-to-day life at home or work. Often these computers are on a home Internet connection (such as dial-up or broadband), and on average most of them are available only for a relatively short period of time in a day. Setting up a P2P network is relatively easy—you do not need to have a technical background in computer science or be an ubergeek. As a result, P2P is popular and has a wide adoption rate among all categories of users.

One of the guiding principles for P2P solutions is that all nodes provide resources to the group (processing power, bandwidth, storage, etc.). Therefore, when the overall demand increases with the addition of more nodes, so does the capacity. This is significantly different from a traditional client-server model, where adding more clients would slow everyone because more clients are competing for the same set of resources on the server. In addition, the distributed, ad hoc nature of the P2P network increases the resilience of the overall system by eliminating single points of failures by distributing data over multiple peers. Because of this, data can be shared effectively, and a network can be scaled up at a relatively low cost. By its nature, a P2P solution allows support for ad hoc and disconnected networks.

■**Note** Although most users have come across P2P applications that are used for sharing files—possibly using the likes of Gnutella, Kazaa, Napster, BitTorent, and so on—P2P applications are used across many other domains and industries, including telephony and video, gaming, data replication, anonymity, instant messaging, and distributed computing, and so on.

Broadly speaking, P2P solutions can fall into one of the following domains:

Real-time communication: P2P enables services such as serverless instant messaging and real-time game play. You can use instant messaging with voice and video today, but most implementations require the use of a server to function. If you are in an isolated network environment (such as those defined by many enterprises), then you would not be able to use most instant messaging solutions; but with serverless instant messaging, you can overcome these boundaries. Similar to instant messaging solutions, real-time gaming networks are more aligned toward enthusiastic gamers, allowing them to go head to head with other gamers. However, if you are not a hard-core gamer or if you want to set up an ad hoc game that can communicate in a variety of networking situations, without P2P networking this would be a significant challenge in today's environment.

Collaboration: P2P allows you to share files, workspaces, and experiences with others. Users can create ad hoc workspaces that can be populated with content and tools to be used for solving a common goal. These can also provide collaborative functionality, such as in message boards; sharing files becomes just another aspect of this workspace. A P2P network allows people to share files in an easy and user-friendly way. Sharing your experiences with others in near real-time is a new opportunity using P2P networks. With the wide availability of wireless networks, it is becoming easier for people to share their day-to-day experiences in real time One example of collaborative P2P system is Groove. Groove (which is part of Microsoft Office 2007 and later) allows team to work in a secure environment in a virtual office or workspace without considering team members be physically in the same office or even country. This allows them to share and synchronize files, manage projects, host discussion threads, schedule meetings, share text in real time, and so on.

Content distribution: P2P allows for the easy distribution of content. This content could be software updates, text, audio, video, and so on. If you want to distribute a large amount of audio and video today, you need a lot of bandwidth to handle the volume. But when using a P2P, only a small number of peers need to get the data from the centralized servers, and can propagate the content on the mesh to the next closest peer who wants it. Similarly with this kind of system, product updates within an organization can be propagated quickly to everyone. Many of the open source and Linux implementations also use this model to distribute their builds.

Distributed processing: P2P computing allows you to distribute computing tasks among various peers on the network and aggregate the results later. A large task can be broken into small chunks that each peer can handle. Once each peer is finished with their task, they send the results to a central aggregation point. A peer can be configured to process these tasks only when it is idle, which frees up the machine's resources for other purposes. One of the pioneers of distributed procession was the University of California's SETI@home project. The SETI@home project (http://en.wikipedia.org/wiki/SETI@home) brought this concept to the general public by sparking off contests between peers to see who could process more data in a given period of time.

The Challenges of P2P

There are a variety of challenges that P2P network faces s. Some of these challenges are technical, and include things like build complexity and how to achieve universal connectivity. There are also legal challenges, which largely involve copyright and intellectual property issues (e.g., the sharing of music or movies). P2P networks, like most networks, can also be open to attacks. P2P networks are particularly prone to poison, polluting, defection, and denial of service attacks.

■**Note** *Poison attacks* are attacks where the contents are different from the description of that content. *Polluting attacks* are those where invalid chunks are added to an otherwise valid file. *Defection attacks* are those where users or software use a network without contributing resources to it.

P2P faces many other challenges as well. Currently, there are no standards defined, which means interoperability between different P2P meshes is something that is difficult to achieve. Firewalls are becoming increasingly sophisticated, and although a P2P network can be based purely on IP, there are still many symmetric NAT firewalls out there. This might give the impression that these NATed addresses will cause the P2P mesh to not reach all endpoints. However, this rarely causes any issues and for the majority of the solutions is not a concern. Management and diagnostics are still issues, however. Because of the nondeterministic flow in a network, trying to diagnose a bug, for example, becomes a daunting task. Also, applying something like a distributed policy to a P2P network can present a challenge. For example, many enterprises do not have control over diagnostics because of not being able to apply a distributed policy and In many situations, this is not acceptable to apply a distributed policy because of various regulatory, legal, and compliance requirements. This also makes it difficult to isolate and locate individual users who can cause security concerns (again because of the lack of user accountability).

On the legal front, media coverage has given the perception that all P2P is illegal and bad, and anonymous P2P networks that allow for easy content sharing don't help the cause. While various organizations are fighting battles in the courts over file sharing, the end user is often left confused with regard to its legality. This is partly because laws are different from country to country, and there is a lot of gray area and interpretation. For example, RIAA has gone after a few thousand users in the United States and is also looking to target some in the United Kingdom and other countries. At the same time, certain countries, such as France, have legalized P2P (and later changed the local laws without absolute clarification). All this has led to a blurred distinction between what is legal and what is not.

■**Note** The discussion of the legal issues surrounding P2P are intentionally vague in this section, since local laws change often, and it is impossible to cover all scenarios. The important thing to remember is that the legal issues have nothing to do with P2P technology itself, but with the way the technology is being used.

P2P Development Life Cycle

When developing and deploying P2P applications, you face three primary issues: how to achieve end-to-end connectivity; how to provide a common foundation consisting of various state data, identity management, and so on, for peers to use when exchanging state; and how to deploy and scale the solution in a secure manner. Each of these is an important piece of the puzzle to enable the P2P solution to work.

End-to-end connectivity: Because of the loose and disparate nature of a mesh, from a development and debugging perspective, ensuring that the various peers can seamlessly connect to each other is a challenge. Further complicating is the fact that the peers connecting to the mesh might be using one or more communication technologies.

Common foundation: This is the "administrative" functionality that every P2P application needs in order to manage the various peers on the mesh. This includes identity management, contact management, node discovery, node naming, secure session management, multipeer communication, and so on.

Secure and scalable deployment: This is the ability to build on protocols specifically engineered for large-scale deployment, and it provides built-in security.

How Are Nodes Identified?

On a mesh, each node needs to be identified by a unique ID, usually called a *peer ID* or *mesh ID*. To resolve these peer IDs to their corresponding Internet addresses, the Peer Name Resolution Protocol (PNRP) is used (instead of DNS). Each peer node can have its own peer ID, irrespective of the node's type (computer, user, group, device, service, etc.). This list of IDs is distributed among the peers using a multilevel cache and referral system that allows name resolution to scale to billions of IDs while requiring minimal resources on each node.

An *endpoint* is defined as a combination of a peer ID, port number, and communication protocol. Using an endpoint, data can be sent between nodes in two ways. One of these is for a peer to directly send the data to another peer. The other is for a peer to send the data to all the other peers on the same mesh; this is also known as *flooding*. A flooded message could arrive at the same peer multiple times via different routes on the mesh.

Installing the Windows P2P Networking Stack

The Windows P2P networking stack is not installed on Windows XP by default. If you are running Windows XP with SP2, then perform the following steps to install the P2P networking stack:

1. Click Start ➤ Control Panel ➤ Add/Remove Programs.

2. Click Add/Remove Windows Components.

3. In Components, click Networking Services, and then select Details.

4. Select the Peer-to-Peer check box, and then select OK.

5. Click Next, and follow the instructions on the screen.

If you are running Windows XP with SP1, then you need to install the Windows Advanced Networking Pack for Windows XP, which is a free download available at
`http://www.microsoft.com/downloads/en/details.aspx?FamilyId=E88CC382-8CE6-4739-97C0-1A52A6F005E4&displaylang=en`.

If you are running Windows Vista or later, then this is already installed; however, you might have to enable the firewall exceptions. To do so, follow these steps:

1. Click Start ➤ Control Panel ➤ Security.

2. Under Windows Firewall, select Allow a Program Through Windows Firewall.

3. Click the Exceptions tab.

4. Check Windows Peer to Peer Collaboration Foundation.

5. Click OK.

Windows P2P Networking

Microsoft introduced the Windows P2P networking stack as a developer platform in Windows XP SP1. This stack is not installed by default; to install it on Windows XP (with SP2), you need to select the Peer-to-Peer option as part of the networking services within the Windows components that are available via the Add/Remove Programs option in the Control Panel. If you have only Windows XP SP1, then you need to install the Advanced Networking Pack to get the P2P networking stack.

Figure 12–1 shows the architecture for P2P networking as defined by Microsoft. The significant components that make up this stack are graphing, grouping, Name Service Provider (NSP), PNRP, and Identity Manager. It is worth pointing out that this stack is *unmanaged code* with only a subset of the functionality exposed via WCF.

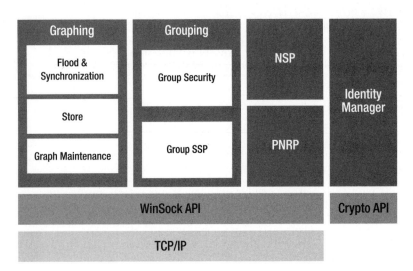

Figure 12–1. Windows PNRP, graphing, grouping, and identity manager networking architecture

Identity Management

P2P solutions usually do not use DNS because of the transient nature of the mesh. In theory, using dynamic DNS is an option, but in actuality few DNS servers on the Internet support this. This raises an interesting question about how to resolve peer names to their network addresses (including ports, protocols, and so on). To allow this, Windows P2P networking uses PNRP. Some of the key attributes of PNRP that make it ideal for resolving names are as follows:

> *Name resolution is distributed and serverless*: Each peer on the mesh caches a portion of the list of names on the mesh and further refers to other peers. Although this is not a true serverless environment, because there is a root node that is used to initiate the process, this node is not used for name resolutions.

> *IDs are used, not names*: IDs identify peers instead of names. Since IDs are numbers, there are no language or locale issues.

> *Multiple IDs can be used*: Since every service on the mesh can have its own identifier, the same node might end up having more than one ID.

> *A large number of IDs can be scaled to*: Because the list of IDs can grow to a large number, a multilevel cache and referral system that does not require significant resources is implemented between the peers.

Peer Names

Peer names can be registered either as secured or as unsecured. Unsecured names are recommended for use in private networks only, because the names are strings and can easily be spoofed. However, secured names need to be registered, and are protected with a certificate and digital signature.

A PNRP ID is 256 bits long; the high-order 128 bits are a hash of the peer name assigned to the endpoint, and the lower 128 bits are an autogenerated number used for service location. The format for the peer name is *Authority.Classifier*. When using a secured network, the *authority* is a secure hash (using the Secure Hash Algorithm [SHA]) of the public key of the peer name in hex. When using an unsecured network, the authority is the single character 0 (zero). The *classifier* is a Unicode string up to 150 characters long that identifies the application. The autogenerated number, used by the lower 128 bits, uniquely identifies different instances using the classifier participating in the same mesh. The combination of a 256-bit mesh ID and the service location allow multiple PNRP IDs to be registered from a single computer.

PNRP Name Resolution

When a peer wants to resolve the peer name, it constructs the peer ID as discussed earlier and tries to find that entry in its cache for the ID. If a match is found, then it sends a PNRP request message to the peer and waits for a response. This approach ensures that the target peer node, with which another peer is trying to communicate, is active in the cloud. If no match is found, then an iterative process is used with the target peer that informs the sender of the peer that is the closest match to the ID that is trying to be resolved. It is up to the original sender at this stage to send the same request to the matching peer as the one to which it was pointing. If the new peer that the sender is pointing to isn't the correct one either, then that in turn will return the next closest matching peer to the sender, and so on.

When a PNRP request message is forwarded, both the nodes that are forwarded to and the responses received are cached. This prevents the possibility of an endless loop. The name records have built-in security because of the public/private key pair. NSP is a mechanism by which you can access an arbitrary name provider; in the Windows P2P network stack, this provider interface is PNRP.

Graphing

A *graph* is a collection of peer nodes where one node may communicate with another using the neighbor's peer connections. A peer graph is built on the concept of flooding, which makes it possible to send data to all peers connected to that specific graph. To be able to handle changes in this data, the flooding protocol sends these changes in data to all the peers. This is achieved by associating each peer with a unique GUID that has an increasing version number or sequence number, and is further qualified by an age or a status. A synchronous process in a graph ensures that peers have the same set of data. The graphs themselves are insecure, and the P2P stack's architecture provides pluggable modules that provide security. These modules can define various aspects both at the connection and message level, including authentication, confidentiality, and integrity.

Grouping

Grouping is nothing but a combination of graphing, PNRP, and the peer grouping *security provider* from Microsoft. This security provider provides management of the credentials of the members that are part of the group and supports the secure publication of records. Every group is identified by a unique ID that is used by peers on the network for identification. For groups, the PNRP secure names are used as IDs. Every peer has a set of two credentials—the first of which is to prove ownership to a peer's identity, a unique peer name, and credentials. The second set of credentials proves that a peer is a member of a group. For secure groups, participation is restricted to a known set of peers. Information is spread through the groups using records. A *record* consists of many pieces of information, including the peer's validity, data for record validity when challenged, a time stamp for validation, and the actual payload containing the record information. Security is a combination of the following:

- Peer name
- Group membership certificates

- Roles
- Secure publishing
- Security policies
- Secure connections

How Does a P2P Mesh Work?

As stated earlier, a mesh network is nothing but a P2P network, and is responsible for routing data between nodes. A mesh network also allows for continuous connection, and if there are any blocked paths, they can be reconfigured in a leaping manner, from peer to peer, until a connection is established. This property makes them *self-healing*, allowing them to continue to operate even when a peer drops out. All peers in a mesh propagate the same mesh name, which gives new peers joining the mesh visibility into other nodes that are on the mesh. Figure 12–2 shows a sample mesh network with multiple peers connected.

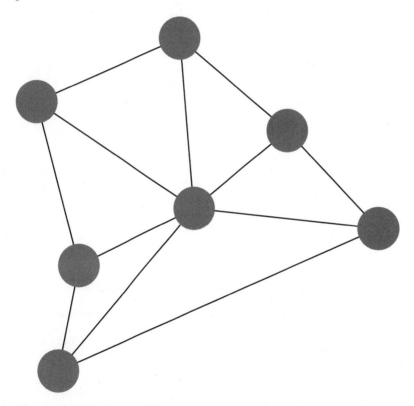

Figure 12–2. Mesh network

Types of Mesh Networks

Broadly speaking, two types of mesh networks are available: groupings and peer channels, and each has its own service model. Grouping is primarily used by the Data Replication service, and is available in Windows XP (with SP2). With grouping, the various peers in the mesh exchange messages by replicating records containing the data. Peer channel, on the other hand, is primarily a message-based service and is available in WCF. The peers in the mesh share data by building *synchronous* services. Both meshes have built-in security; grouping is implemented via a password and grouped certificates that are managed by the mesh. Peer channel security is also implemented via a password (to join the mesh), as well as individual certificates that are managed directly by the applications in the mesh. Both types of meshes support PNRP for node discovery; however, only peer channel supports a developer-supplied model such as a web service. While a grouping mesh implementation is unmanaged and accessed via the Win32 API library, the peer channel is part of WCF, which is managed code.

The connection types between the peers in a mesh can also be of two topology types: full or partial. In *full topology*, each peer is connected to every other peer on the mesh. In *partial topology*, a peer is connected only to a handful of other peers—most likely those with which it exchanges the most data and has affinity. The example in Figure 12–2 shows a mesh with a partial topology. It is rare to come across a full topology mesh because it is not practical to operate in that mode. If there are n nodes in a full topology mesh, then each node is connected to $n - 1$ nodes at the same time. In other words, if there are 1,000 nodes in a mesh, each of the 1,000 nodes has a connection open to 999 other nodes at the same time. This would lead to a situation where the mesh would soon start running out of resources as more nodes joined the network.

Types of P2P applications

Three types of P2P applications exist:

- One-to-one

- One-to-many

- Many-to-many

Figure 12–3 shows the normal flow of a P2P application. When one peer in a mesh wants to communicate with another, the steps are to find the other peer, send an invitation, and create a session between the two.

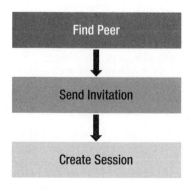

Figure 12–3. P2P application flow

Let's examine each of the previous steps in a little more detail:

Find peer: Essentially, to "talk" to some other peer, the first thing you need to do is find it. There are two ways to go about this. The first is to find other peers on the LAN you are part of. The other is to find peers or peer-groups using PNRP. If you are finding other peers on the LAN, you should use the People Near Me feature and integrate that into your application. People Near Me uses WS-Discovery to find users who are signed in. People Near Me is out of the scope of this book, but at a high level it is collaboration with people located nearby. There are many requirements for this to work, including people discovery, application discovery, metadata discovery, security, and invitation. PNRP, on the other hand, is a serverless name resolution that can be either on the local network or over the Internet.

Send invitation: Invitations are sent in real time, and can go to People Near Me or peers over the Internet, via either a user message or some application data, such as a mesh name or endpoint. A listener at the other end detects this incoming invitation request and launches the appropriate application.

Join mesh: The last step to establish a session is to specify the name and credentials (if applicable) of the mesh that one you are is intending to join.

Figure 12–4 shows the scenario where you have peers that are part of a mesh and are trying to communicate with each other.

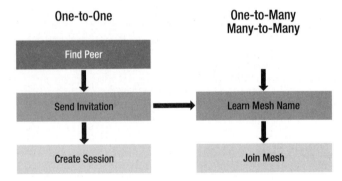

Figure 12–4. *P2P one-to-many application flow*

What Is Peer Channel?

The P2P networking stack that we have been discussing so far is unmanaged code, and a developer needs to use C++ to use it to its full potential. This stack is part of Windows XP, and has improved as part of Windows Vista and later. Microsoft also has a managed code implementation for a subset of the functionality that is exposed by the P2P networking stack, called *peer channel*; it is part of WCF. Since peer channel is a managed stack, you can use any .NET language, which makes implementing P2P applications easier and more productive than using unmanaged code.

A typical channel in WCF has two participants—a client and a server—but a peer channel can have any number of participants. A message that is sent by one participant will be received by all other participants on the channel. However, certain mechanisms in peer channel allow you to send a message to only part of the mesh, instead of the whole mesh. To resolve the addresses of a node in a peer channel mesh, you can use either PNRP or a custom resolver. When a node is resolved, that target node can either accept or decline the connection. If the connection is accepted by the target node, it sends it a welcome message that among other things will contain the list of other nodes that are part of the mesh.

If the connection is refused, then the existing node will send the prospective node a refusal message containing the reason and a list of the addresses of the other nodes in the mesh.

In WCF, a node that will be part of a mesh is defined via the `PeerNode` class in your application. The endpoint address for that node is defined via the `PeerNodeAddress` class (which internally implements the `EndpointAddress` class). The number of neighbors of each node dictates the overall structure of a peer channel mesh that is actively maintained, resulting in an evenly distributed mesh. For example, consider a node that tries to maintain between two to seven connections to its neighbors in a mesh. Although an ideal state for the node is to have three connections, it will accept up to seven. Once the node has reached that threshold, it will start refusing any new connections. If a node loses all its neighbors, it will enter a maintenance cycle, in which it tries to acquire new neighbors to get to its optimum state of three connections.

■**Note** You cannot change or configure either the thresholds or the underlying mesh, because the peer channel owns and maintains these.

The peer channel also tries to improve efficiency by limiting communication within the mesh by keeping repetitive messages passed to a minimum. When a node sends a message to the mesh, it sends it to the neighbors to which it is connected. These neighbors in turn inspect the message and then forward it to their neighbors, but they do not forward it to the neighbor from whom they got the message to start. In addition, a connection to a neighbor might be terminated if it keeps trying to resend a message that has been processed previously. Internally, each node keeps an idempotent local cache of the WS-Addressing message ID and the ID of the neighbor that delivered that message. This allows for an optimized mesh network that does not waste resources with repeating data.

A node can send messages to a subset of the mesh by assigning a hop count to the message. A *hop count* keeps a count of the number of nodes to which a message has been forwarded. This count is expressed as an integer within the message header and is decremented with each hop until it reaches a value of zero, after which message is not forwarded.

QuickReturnTraderChat Sample

To get a better understanding of how everything comes together using the peer channel, let's start with a simple application called `QuickReturnTraderChat`. We have a few traders spread across a stock exchange who need the ability to chat with each other. The exchange, being a secure environment, does not allow any access to IM clients, and the traders want to use `QuickReturnTraderChat` to talk to each other. This application allows more than one trader to broadcast a message to the other traders, similar to an IRC channel. You will first look at the nonsecure version of this sample and then later update that to make it secure so no one else can eavesdrop on the conversation.

The application is simple, and is implemented as a Windows application containing one form. For clarity, we will omit the Windows form boilerplate code so you can concentrate on the peer channel aspects. You can always get the latest version of the complete source code from this book's web site.

Message Interface

A peer channel service contract is just a WCF service contract with the requirement that the `OperationContract` attribute is set up as one-way, as shown in Listing 12–1. The interface is called

IQuickReturnTraderChat and has only one operation, called Say, which accepts two parameters: user and message.

Listing 12–1. IQuickReturnTraderChat Service Contract

```
[ServiceContract()]
public interface IQuickReturnTraderChat
{
    [OperationContract(IsOneWay = true)]
    void Say(string user, string message);
}
```

Service Configuration

Listing 12–2 shows the service side of the configuration. This application listens at the net.p2p//QuickReturnTraderChat address. Being a P2P application, the binding is set to netPeerTcpBinding, and the contract for the endpoint is set to QuickReturnTraderChat.IQuickReturnTraderChat, which follows the *Namespace.Interface* format. The binding configuration is intentionally kept separate (shown later in Listing 12–3).

Listing 12–2. Service Configuration

```
<service name="QuickReturnTraderChat.Main">
    <host>
        <baseAddresses>
            <add baseAddress="net.p2p://QuickReturnTraderChat"/>
        </baseAddresses>
    </host>

    <endpoint
        name="QuickTraderChat"
        address=""
        binding="netPeerTcpBinding"
        bindingConfiguration="BindingUnsecure"
        contract="QuickReturnTraderChat.IQuickReturnTraderChat"
    />
</service>
```

Binding Configuration File

As stated earlier, a P2P application's binding is set to netPeerTcpBinding and the resolver mode to Pnrp (see Listing 12–3). Since this application is not secure, we switch off the security mode by setting this to None.

Listing 12–3. Binding Configuration

```
<bindings>
    <netPeerTcpBinding>
        <binding  name="BindingUnsecure">
            <security mode="None"/>
            <resolver mode="Pnrp"/>
        </binding>
```

```
          </netPeerTcpBinding>
      </bindings>
```

Main Application

The main application, as shown in Figure 12–5, consists of a Windows form that has two text boxes, one for the message being sent (called textBoxMessage) and the other to show the conversation (called textBoxChat). The form also contains one Send button (called buttonSend).

Figure 12–5. QuickReturnTraderChat application

The class implementing the Windows form is called Main and is implemented as shown in Listing 12–4. This form inherits from the .NET Form class and also implements the IQuickReturnTraderChat interface that was defined earlier. Since this is a WCF service, the class is decorated with the ServiceBehavior attribute and the InstanceContextMode, which controls when a new service object should be created. In our case, we want this to behave as a singleton; as a result, the InstanceContextMode is set to Single.

Listing 12–4. Service Host Class Definition

```
[ServiceBehavior(InstanceContextMode = InstanceContextMode.Single)]
public partial class Main : Form, IQuickReturnTraderChat
{
}
```

As shown in Listing 12–5, the Main class implements two methods, StartService and StopService, which start and stop the service host, respectively. The Main class also has a few member variables, which expose the Channel, ServiceHost, and ChannelFactory.

Listing 12–5. Service Host Implementation

```
IQuickReturnTraderChat channel;
ServiceHost host = null;
ChannelFactory<IQuickReturnTraderChat> channelFactory = null;
string userID = string.Empty();
private void StartService()
{
    // Instantiate new ServiceHost
    host = new ServiceHost(this);

    //Open ServiceHost
    host.Open();

    // Create a ChannelFactory and load the configuration setting
    channelFactory = new ChannelFactory<IQuickReturnTraderChat>
                                    ("QuickTraderChatEndpoint");
    channel = channelFactory.CreateChannel();

    // Lets others know that someone new has joined
    channel.Say("Admin", "*** New User " + userID + " Joined ****" +
                                        Environment.NewLine);
}
private void StopService()
{
    if (host != null)
    {
        channel.Say("Admin", "*** User " + userID + " Leaving ****" +
                                        Environment.NewLine);

        if (host.State != CommunicationState.Closed)
        {
            channelFactory.Close();
            host.Close();
        }
    }
}
```

IQuickReturnTraderChat Implementation (Receiver)

Both the service side and the receiver side implementation are in the same class. Listing 12–6 shows the configuration for the receiver, which is quite similar to the sender configuration and uses the same binding.

Listing 12–6. Receiver Configuration

```
<client>
    <endpoint
        name="QuickTraderChatEndpoint"
        address="net.p2p://QuickReturnTraderChat"
        binding="netPeerTcpBinding"
        bindingConfiguration="BindingUnsecure"
        contract="QuickReturnTraderChat.IQuickReturnTraderChat"
</client>
```

The receiver here is fairly simple; all it does is echo the message to the chat text box on the Windows form, as shown in Listing 12–7.

Listing 12–7. Receiver Implementation

```
void IQuickReturnTraderChat.Say(string user, string message)
{
    textBoxChat.Text += user + " says: " + message;
}
```

Invoking the Service

The service is invoked in the click event of the Send button, as shown in Listing 12–8. The second line is where you invoke the service. As you might recall, the channel is of type IQuickReturnTraderChat and is defined in the Main class (shown in earlier in Listing 12–4).

Listing 12–8. Service Invocation

```
private void buttonSend_Click(object sender, EventArgs e)
{
    string temp = textBoxMessage.Text + Environment.NewLine;

    // Invoke the service
    channel.Say(userID, temp);

    textBoxMessage.Clear();
}
```

As you can see, creating a P2P application with WCF is fairly trivial, and you do not need to do anything with the Windows P2P networking stack. Although we have kept the QuickReturnTraderChat application fairly simple to show you how to implement a P2P application, if you need to perform some more advanced tasks, such as cloud management or detecting and repairing network splits, then you will need to use the P2P networking stack and C++. At the time of writing, Microsoft does not have any .NET wrappers for the P2P stack, and you would need to interop to unmanaged code.

P2P Security

Security in a P2P network is an interesting challenge. When securing a P2P network, there are two points of interest from an application point of view. First, only authorized users should get on the network. Second, the message you receive should originate from a known and trusted source, and the message itself should not have been tampered with during transmission. The first scenario is relatively simple to achieve: when a new application or user logs onto the mesh, they are challenged to authenticate before they are allowed to join the mesh. The second aspect is a little more difficult because you are not directly connected to another peer in the mesh. However, with WCF this is relatively straightforward because the PeerSecuritySettings class is exposed via the Security property part of the NetPeerTcpBinding class.

So, how does it all come together with WCF? For OutputChannels, which reside on the sender, each message that is sent is signed using a certificate, and all messages, before being sent to an application, are validated for this credential. The certificate that is needed is provided via the PeerCredential.Certificate property. The validation stated earlier can be implemented via an instance of the X509CertificateValidator class, which is provided as part of PeerCredential.MessageSenderAuthentication. When the message arrives on the other end, peer channel ensures the validity of the message before forwarding it up the chain to the application.

Peer Channel Security

As mentioned earlier, you specify the security settings for peer channel using the Security property, which is available on NetPeerTcpBinding. This property operates like any other standard binding in WCF. You can apply four types of security at this level, and they are exposed via the Mode property; the underlying class is in the PeerSecuritySettings class. These four options for security are as follows:

None: No security is required.

Transport: No message security is implemented; only neighbor-to-neighbor security is required.

Message: Only message authentication is required when communicating over an open channel.

TransportWithMessageCredential: This is essentially a combination of Transport and Message, defined previously. This would require that the message be secure and that authentication be required over secure neighbor-to-neighbor channels.

■**Note** If security is enabled on the binding and is set to Message or TransportWithMessageCredential, then all messages that pass on both the outbound and inbound need to be secured using X.509Certificate.

Peer channel provides two ways to authenticate two peers, which are configured using the PeerTransportSecurityElement.CredentialType property: either via Password or Certificate. When CredentialType set to Password, then every peer needs a password to connect. The owner of the mesh is responsible for setting the password initially, and communicating the password to peers who you want to allow to join the mesh. On the other hand, when this is set to Certificate, then authentication is based on X509Certificate.

When an application initiates a peer channel instance, an instance of the peer channel transport manager is started. The transport manager resolves the endpoint address of the requested peers and the mesh. PNRP acts as the default resolver for this; however, you can choose to implement a custom resolver as well. Once the address is resolved, the transport manager initiates a connection request to each of the peers.

Password-Based Authentication

When using password-based authentication, the steps to initiate a connection are the same as CredentialType with value as Password with the transport manager. The main difference is that when a peer initiates a connection request, the link between the two peers is over a SSL connection. Also, as the first step after initiating a connection between the two peers, the initiator peer will send a custom handshake message that authenticates the password. If the responder peer is satisfied with this, it will accept the connection and send a similar response to the originating peer. If the initiator peer is satisfied with this, the connection is established; if not, the connection is abandoned. This aforementioned handshake needs to contain some metadata for it to function. First, the certificate with the secure connection can be established, and second the password for the handshake can be established. The class PeerCredential is exposed as the Peer property on the ChannelFactory.Credentials property. This is demonstrated in the secure version of the chat sample that was discussed earlier in this chapter. This secure version is called QuickReturnSecureTraderChat; you'll see it a little later in the "QuickReturnSecureTraderChat Sample" section.

Certificate-Based Authentication

When using the certificate-based authentication mode, the application has more control over the authentication process as compared to the WCF runtime. There is no custom handshake involved; instead, the transport manager, after receiving the certificate, passes it on to the application to authenticate. To get certificate-based authentication, the application needs to provide a couple of certificates. The first certificate establishes the SSL connection and the identity between the peers, and the second certificate provides a concrete implementation by the application for the X509CertificateValidator abstract class. (This is also demonstrated in the secure version of the chat sample a little later in the chapter.)

Message Security

If you are interested in securing the message itself to ensure that it has not been tampered with during transmission, then you need to use the Message security option. Effectively, when this is requested, the peer channel on every outbound message includes a signature, and the peer channel on every inbound message validates the signature. The signature is validated against the same certificate (without the specific private keys, of course). The signatures added to the message are compatible with all the peers on the mesh.

■**Note** Peer channel can verify signatures that are specific to the application because it provides a "hook" that allows you to participate in its signature verification routine. This hook is in a concrete implementation of the abstract X509CertificateValidator class. This allows you to have any criteria for the pass or fail validation.

QuickReturnSecureTraderChat Sample

The QuickReturnSecureTraderChat application essentially is the same as the QuickReturnTraderChat sample discussed earlier in the chapter, with the exception that this one uses security. For the sake of simplicity, we have implemented this as a separate solution. In the real world, you would probably read the security information via a configuration setting, and based on that, either enable or disable the security options.

You can set security, as discussed earlier, using either a password or an X.509 certificate. For this sample, we will use a password, but you will see how easy it is to change this to use a certificate.

Service Configuration

Listing 12–9 shows the service side of the configuration, which is similar to the service configuration used in the earlier example. Although the address and the namespace have been updated, the real configuration change is the use of a different binding, configured by the bindingConfiguration parameter.

Listing 12–9. Service Configuration

```
<service name="QuickReturnSecureTraderChat.Main">
    <host>
        <baseAddresses>
            <add baseAddress="net.p2p://QuickReturnSecureTraderChat"/>
        </baseAddresses>
    </host>

    <endpoint
        name="QuickTraderChatSecurePasswordEndPoint"
        address=""
        binding="netPeerTcpBinding"
        bindingConfiguration="BindingSecurePassword"
        contract="QuickReturnSecureTraderChat.IQuickReturnTraderChat"
        />
</service>
```

Binding Configuration

The updated binding configuration used by both the host and the client in this example is called BindingSecurePassword. The main difference between this and the previous example is the addition of the security details, as shown in Listing 12–10. As you can see, the security mode is set to Transport and the type to Password.

Listing 12–10. Secure Binding Configuration

```
<binding  name="BindingSecurePassword">
    <security mode="Transport">
        <transport credentialType="Password"/>
    </security>

    <resolver mode="Pnrp"/>
</binding>
```

Main Application

The main application is the same as the one shown previously in Figure 12–5. The only difference between this and the earlier example is the addition of a new member variable to hold the password, which is read from the App.config file.

Note It is not recommended to save the password in App.config in clear text, because that would allow anyone to read it. It is recommended to save the password in an encrypted storage or accept the password from the user at runtime. To hold the password in memory, use the SecureString class, which was introduced in .NET 2.0.

Listing 12–11 shows the updated member variable list used by the solution. The channel is of the type IQuickReturnTraderChat, which as you know is the contract implemented by the service. The members host and channelFactory are the service host and the channel factory, respectively. And the two string variables store the user and password that are read from the App.config file using ConfigurationManager.AppSettings in the constructor for the Main class.

Listing 12–11. Member Variable List

```
IQuickReturnTraderChat channel;
ServiceHost host = null;
ChannelFactory<IQuickReturnTraderChat> channelFactory = null;
string userID = "";
string password = null;
```

The StartService method in the Main class has been updated slightly, as shown in Listing 12–12. This now uses a different endpoint configuration file and sets the password for both the host and the channel. The StopService method remains the same as earlier, and is not listed again here. As you can see in the listing, the password for both the host and the ChannelFactory is set via the Credentials.Peer.MeshPassword property. The binding configuration has been updated, and is read from QuickTraderChatSecurePasswordEndPoint.

Listing 12–12. Service Host Implementation

```
private void StartService()
{
    // Instantiate new ServiceHost
    host = new ServiceHost(this);

    // Set the password
    host.Credentials.Peer.MeshPassword = password;

    // Open ServiceHost
    host.Open();

    // Create a ChannelFactory and load the configuration setting
    channelFactory = new ChannelFactory<IQuickReturnTraderChat>
                        ("QuickTraderChatSecurePasswordEndPoint");

    // Set the password for the ChannelFactory
```

```
channelFactory.Credentials.Peer.MeshPassword = password;

// Create the Channel
channel = channelFactory.CreateChannel();

// Lets others know that someone new has joined
channel.Say("Admin", "*** New User " + userID +
                    " Joined ****" + Environment.NewLine);
}
```

One interesting security behavior is that if you have a set of peers listening on the same endpoint but with different passwords, then they will be isolated from each other. For example, say you have four users, called User1, User2, User3, and User4. Say User1 and User2 are chatting, and are connected to the mesh using password1. If User3 and User4 start chatting with another password (say, password2), then even though all four users are on the mesh and listening on the same endpoint, the messages between User1 and User2 cannot be seen by Users3 and User4, and vice versa.

■**Tip** To use an X.509 certificate instead of a password to secure a mesh, set the transport `credentialType` in the binding to `Certificate`, and set the `Credentials.Peer.Certificate` property to the certificate on both the host and the client.

Working with NetShell

NetShell, also known as `netsh`, is an indispensable command-line utility for both administrators and developers. Although `netsh` is primarily aimed at administrators because it allows them to administer network services, it is equally useful to a developer. To start `netsh`, open a command prompt and type **netsh**.

■**Note** On Windows XP, NetShell is available only when you have P2P networking installed. Although NetShell is installed by default on Windows Vista and later, on these operating systems you need to allow NetShell as an exception in the firewall for it to work.

The commands in `netsh` work with the concept of a *context* that determines the networking aspect within which you want to operate, and accumulates various possible commands in that context. In most situations, you would switch to some context for the specific operation in which you are interested. Contexts can have subcontexts, which in turn can have further subcontexts, forming a tree-like hierarchy. Figure 12–6 shows how we switch the context to P2P ▼❏ PNRP ▼❏ Cloud.

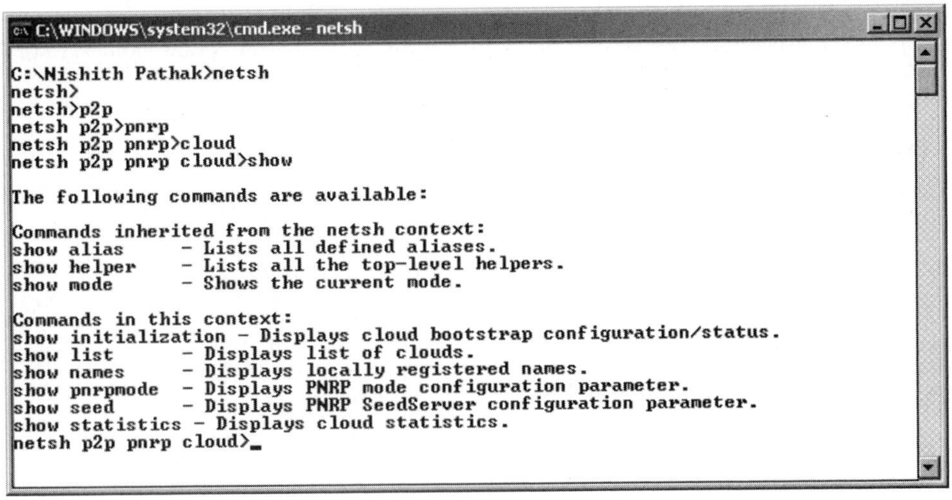

```
C:\WINDOWS\system32\cmd.exe - netsh                                    _ □ ×

C:\Nishith Pathak>netsh
netsh>
netsh>p2p
netsh p2p>pnrp
netsh p2p pnrp>cloud
netsh p2p pnrp cloud>show

The following commands are available:

Commands inherited from the netsh context:
show alias      - Lists all defined aliases.
show helper     - Lists all the top-level helpers.
show mode       - Shows the current mode.

Commands in this context:
show initialization - Displays cloud bootstrap configuration/status.
show list        - Displays list of clouds.
show names       - Displays locally registered names.
show pnrpmode    - Displays PNRP mode configuration parameter.
show seed        - Displays PNRP SeedServer configuration parameter.
show statistics  - Displays cloud statistics.
netsh p2p pnrp cloud>_
```

Figure 12–6. netsh context

The commands you enter in netsh factor into the context in which you are working. For example, the command show entered (as shown in Figure 12–6) within a PNRP network, and shows the commands for that context. You can switch from one context to another at any time.

Listing Clouds

If you want to see the clouds to which you are currently connected, then you can use the show list command, as shown in Figure 12–7. In this example, there are two clouds, one of which is currently synchronizing.

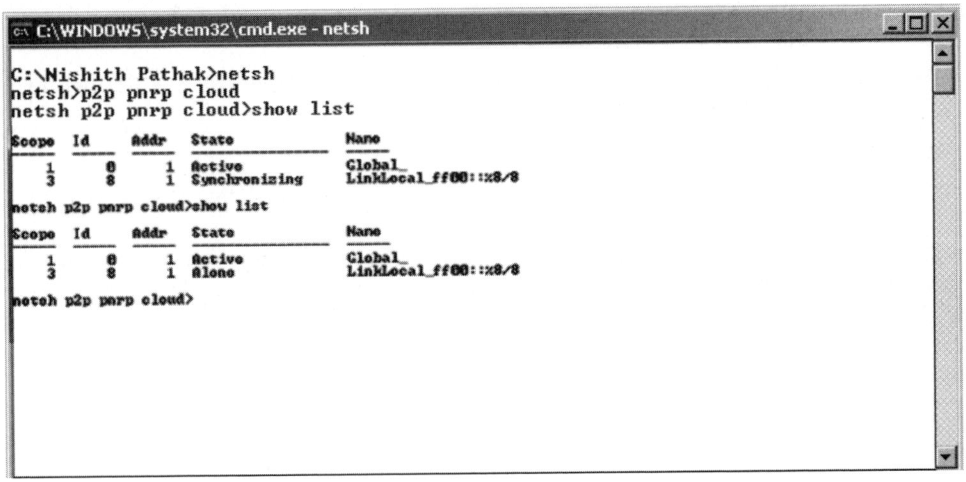

```
C:\WINDOWS\system32\cmd.exe - netsh                                    _ □ ×

C:\Nishith Pathak>netsh
netsh>p2p pnrp cloud
netsh p2p pnrp cloud>show list

Scope   Id    Addr   State           Name
-----   --    ----   -----           ----
  1      0      1    Active          Global_
  3      8      1    Synchronizing   LinkLocal_ff00::x8/8

netsh p2p pnrp cloud>show list

Scope   Id    Addr   State           Name
-----   --    ----   -----           ----
  1      0      1    Active          Global_
  3      8      1    Alone           LinkLocal_ff00::x8/8

netsh p2p pnrp cloud>
```

Figure 12–7. Listing clouds

To see the configuration and status of the cloud, you can use the show initialization command (or the short form, show init). If a computer is connected to the Internet, then it is part of the global cloud, called Global_. If a cloud is connected to one or two LANs, then individual clouds are available for each network adapter (or link). In Listing 12–13, there are two clouds: Global_ and LinkLocal_ff00::%8/8.

Listing 12–13. Cloud Listing

```
Scope  Id     Addr   State             Name
-----  -----  -----  ----------------  -----
    1      0      1  Active            Global_
Synchronize server:        pnrpv2.ipv6.microsoft.com;pnrpv21.ipv6.microsoft.com
Use Server:                Used
Use SSDP:                  No addresses
Use Persisted cache:       No addresses
Cloud Configured Mode:        Auto
Cloud Operational Mode:       Full Participant


Scope  Id     Addr   State             Name
-----  -----  -----  ----------------  -----
    3      8      1  Alone             LinkLocal_ff00::%8/8

Synchronize server:
Use Server:                Disabled
Use SSDP:                  No addresses
Use Persisted cache:       No addresses
Cloud Configured Mode:        Auto
Cloud Operational Mode:       Full Participant
```

Scope, as the name suggests, represents the scope of the cloud, and essentially shows the PNRPCLOUDINFO data structure that is part of the P2P SDK. The following list defines each of the columns in the previous data:

Scope: This is the scope of the cloud, and can be one of the four values shown in Table 12–1 (in the next section).

Id: This represents the unique identifier for that cloud.

State: This represents the state of the cloud, and is represented by the PNRP_CLOUD_STATE structure in the SDK. This can be one of the seven values shown in Table 12–2 (in the next section).

Synchronize Server: This represents the seed server used.

Use Server: If a caching server was used to load the current state of the cloud, then this displays the DNS name of that server.

Use SSDP: Simple Service Discovery Protocol (SSDP) is the protocol used to locate nearby nodes. You can use this to identify neighboring nodes if a seed server is not available.

Use Persisted cache: This represents any previous cached entries loaded.

Cloud Scopes

The scope of a cloud can be one of the four values shown in Table 12–1.

Table 12–1. Cloud Scope Values

Value	Description
0	The cloud can be in any scope (represented by PNRP_SCOPE_ANY).
1	The cloud is in global scope (represented by PNRP _GLOBAL_ SCOPE).
2	The cloud is in site-local scope (represented by PNRP_SITE_LOCAL_SCOPE).
3	The cloud is in link local scope (represented by PNRP_LINK_LOCAL_SCOPE).

The state of a cloud can be one of the seven values shown in Table 12–2.

Table 12–2. Cloud State Values

Value	Description
Virtual	The cloud is not yet initialized.
Synchronizing	The cloud is in the process of being initialized but is not active yet.
Active	The cloud is active.
Dead	The cloud has lost its connection to the network but was initialized.
Active	The cloud is active.
Disabled	The cloud is disabled in the registry.
No Net	The cloud has lost its connection to the network but was active.
Alone	The cloud is in standalone mode.

Listing Peers in a Cloud

To see the locally registered nodes in a cloud, use the command show names in netsh. In Listing 12–14, shows two peers connected to the cloud, identified by P2P Name. Note that the exact list of peers you see will of course be different from the ones shown here. If you have the QuickReturnTraderChat application running from earlier in the chapter, then you should see that.

Listing 12–14. Peer Listing

```
P2P Name:        0.quickreturntraderchat
Identity:        2460f44f457b670116f55709f3e6324dd12ad70e.PnrpProtocolV2
Comment:         a?????????
PNRP ID:         cf284a913c76d8289f16c4fefbe18b7a.5bcca4c6a1090f379d15b0f12fc89b08
State:           OK
IP Addresses:    192.168.1.73:11989 tcp
                 [2001:0000:4136:e37a:2847:1735:a83d:dc55]:11989 tcp

P2P Name:        0.78873591048
Identity:        2460f44f457b670116f55709f3e6324dd12ad70e.PnrpProtocolV2
Comment:         Local Machine Id
PNRP ID:         ad1d55aa343d35df9d118343e3c3de09.7700660055004400f956
ced74b6beb3cState:        OK
```

The following list defines each of the columns in the previous data:

P2P Name: This is the name of the peer connected to the cloud. The first peer in Listing 12–14, called 0.quickreturntraderchat, is the QuickReturnTraderChat application discussed earlier in the chapter.

Identity: As the name suggests, this represents the identities. Note that the identities of both peers are the same. This is because these peers are unsecured and the default identity is used for them.

PNRP ID: This represents the corresponding 256-bit PNRP ID.

IP Addresses: This represents the endpoints (including the ports) associated with this peer.

Cloud Statistics

To see the cloud statistics, enter the command show statistics (the abbreviated show stat will also work) in netsh. This will display the statistics for all the active clouds. For example, Listing 12–15 lists statistics for the global cloud; most of the entries are self-explanatory. The IP Addresses column is a list of the addresses used to connect to the cloud.

Listing 12–15. Statistics

```
IP Addresses:              [2001:0000:4136:e37a:2847:1735:a83d:dc55]:3540

Number of cache entries:        34
Estimated cloud size:           142
Number of registered names:     3
Throttled resolves:             0
Throttled solicits:             0
Throttled floods:               0
Throttled repairs:              0
```

There are more commands within the cloud context; we discussed only the most important ones to give you a basic understanding. We encourage you to use the documentation and SDK to explore other commands in netsh.

Working with Peers

To switch to the peer context from within PNRP, just type **peer** in netsh. The peer context, as the name suggests, allows you to work with peers and gives you the ability to add, delete, and enumerate entries, among other things. We will not be covering all the commands—just a couple of the more interesting ones. As you know, before one peer can talk to another, it needs to resolve that peer. To do this with netsh, you use the resolve command—passing it the peer name. In this example, if you try to resolve the peer 0.quickreturntraderchat, you get the result shown in Listing 12–16.

Listing 12–16. Peer Resolution

```
netsh p2p pnrp peer>resolve 0.quickreturntraderchat
Resolve started...
Found:
        Comment:    aD????????
        Addresses:  [fe80:0000:0000:0000:79ae:4fe7:e034:eac7]%8:28365
        Extended payload (binary):
        Comment:    aD????????
        Addresses:  [fe80:0000:0000:0000:79ae:4fe7:e034:eac7]%8:28136
        Extended payload (binary):
        Comment:    aD????????
        Addresses:  169.254.2.2:28365
                    192.168.1.73:28365
                    [2001:0000:4136:e37a:2847:1735:a83d:dc55]%0:28365
        Extended payload (binary):
```

We have two instances of QuickReturnTraderChat running, which you can see in the previous example. We also have two network cards, one of which is connected to the Internet and the other of which is on an internal network. The first network adapter (which is connected to the Internet connection) has the IP address 192.168.1.73 (which is of course NATed), and the other has the address 169.254.2.2. Both are listening on port 28365.

Another command of interest is traceroute, which resolves a peer with path tracing. If the name is registered, then the result is quite similar to the resolve command used earlier, as shown in Listing 12–17.

Listing 12–17. Known Peer Traceroute

```
netsh p2p pnrp peer>traceroute 0.quickreturntraderchat Global_
Resolve started...
Found:
        Addresses:  169.254.2.2:28365 tcp
                    192.168.1.73:28365 tcp
                    [2001:0000:4136:e37a:2847:1735:a83d:dc55]%0:28365
tcp
        Extended payload (string):
        Extended payload (binary):
Resolve Path:
[2001:0000:4136:e37a:2847:1735:a83d:dc55]:3540, (0), (0)
        Accepted
[2001:0000:4136:e37a:2847:1735:a83d:dc55]:3540, (0), (0)
        Accepted Final Inquire
```

However, if the peer is not registered, then you see more interesting behavior, as shown in Listing 12–18. Note that an invalid name (0.quickreturntraderchatwedontkow) was provided to mimic this behavior. Also, the listing has been abbreviated for clarity. The exact number of hops would vary on the size of your cloud.

Listing 12–18. Unknown Peer Traceroute

```
netsh p2p pnrp peer>traceroute 0.quickreturntraderchatwedontkow Global_
Resolve started...
Not Found.
Resolve Path:
[2001:0000:4136:e37a:2847:1735:a83d:dc55]:3540, (0), (0)
        Accepted
[2001:0000:4136:e37e:140b:26c5:affa:3034]:3540, (8), (31)
        Rejected (Dead end)

[2001:0000:4136:e37e:244b:1e65:abdb:f294]:3540, (7), (140)
        Rejected (Dead end)
[2001:0000:4136:e37e:1c75:1b9a:bef2:f5a3]:3540, (4), (312)
        Accepted Suspicious
[2001:0000:4136:e37e:0c31:07f8:5351:cf06]:3540, (4), (2000)
        Rejected (Unreachable)
[2001:0000:4136:e37e:1c75:1b9a:bef2:f5a3]:3540, (4), (125)
        Rejected (Dead end)
[2001:0000:4136:e37a:384f:1905:bde1:91be]:3540, (4), (297)
        Rejected (Dead end)
[2001:0000:4136:e378:1cb4:2170:a795:ebd9]:3540, (3), (78)
        Rejected (Dead end)
 [2001:0000:4136:e37a:0c25:34ef:e7ef:9e09]:3540, (2), (203)
        Accepted
```

SOA with P2P

As stated earlier, one of the biggest challenges with the SOA approach is knowing how to deploy services. For example, when designing a solution, should you take the more traditional *n*-tier approach with a middle tier, should the services be implemented in a more distributed approach where each service is a completely independent entity on the network, or should the approach be somewhere between those two extremes? Although SOA does not impose any technologies, platforms, or protocols, traditionally we treat the various entities involved (the service provider, consumer, service broker, etc.) as separate from each other. A better approach would be to treat these roles as different aspects of the services, as opposed to explicit boundaries.

Instead of implementing a service on a server, if that service is implemented in every node of a network (such as a P2P network), then you can shift the server requirements (availability, scalability, etc.) from relying on one particular server to being a function of the entire network. Hence, as the number of services on the network increase, the capabilities of the network increase proportionally, thus overall making it more scalable and robust. Also, unlike a traditional approach, in the P2P world, there is nothing to deploy other than the peer itself.

This is not to underestimate the challenges that the services in a P2P environment face in an enterprise where there will be a disparate set of technologies and products on numerous runtimes. These will require different authentication and authorization approaches, and in many cases it would not be practical, because every service must also carry the weight of the network functionality that a peer provides in a P2P implementation. Also, disparate technologies make it difficult to standardize operation requirements such as reliability and management. Lastly, P2P implementations would cause significant overhead for an enterprise's development team, since they would have to ensure that every service peer could deal with the process, reliability, and management every time a new service was built.

If an enterprise can use a single runtime environment that provides a standardized implementation and uses a common set of libraries such as WCF, that will help eliminate many of these challenges. The caveat is that all the services need to adhere to this standard. Another option is to be more creative and implement "smart" networking intermediaries that will take ownership over areas of control such as security, reliability, operational management, and so on, when delegated by the services. This would free the service endpoints to consume and provide services.

Effectively, we are trying to combine the best of how a centralized and a decentralized system would work. It is quite clear that there are many synergies between an SOA implementation and a P2P implementation. Today, SOA implementations have concentrated a lot on web services, which in turn rely heavily on the central computing paradigm. Similarly, most P2P implementations today have concentrated more on their resilient paradigm. In the future, we'll likely see a combination, in which both peer and the web services rely on a common set for service description and invocation (probably based on WSDL and SOAP). Figure 12–8 shows a high-level view of this convergence of web- and peer-based service orientation.

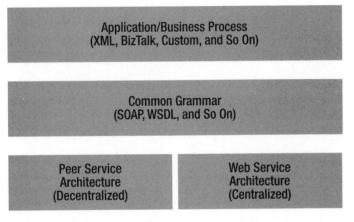

Figure 12–8. *Combined web and peer service orientation*

FUTURE DIRECTION

The future of P2P will be interesting, and the trend may be toward the convergence of grid and P2P computing. Today these two technology stacks might seem quite different, but there is a lot of overlap between the two.

Some of the problems of P2P are peer discovery and topology formation, effective resource utilization, and standardization of APIs and interfaces. Some of the enhancements that Microsoft is working on for P2P networking increase the mesh capabilities to provide support services such as replicated data, distributed agreements, and voting. Another fundamental shift in P2P networking is the ability to guarantee the loss of data. Today, P2P algorithms by design are built around the idea that data loss is a fact of life and partial failure is acceptable. However, the algorithms are being enhanced to support better real-time integration with Quality of Service (QoS) guarantees. QoS will help bandwidth-intensive applications such as Voice over IP (VOIP) or media streaming. There are also enhancements to add support for subgroups and routing controls within those.

Summary

To summarize, P2P is about devices communicating directly with each other without going through a centralized server. Every node in a P2P network needs to carry the responsibility of both a server and a client, although centralized servers that help nodes find other nodes are quite common in P2P scenarios. (These are usually lightweight servers that don't participate in the communication between the nodes). Successful P2P implementations (e.g., instant messaging and file sharing) that include thousands to millions of peers have proved that P2P networks are quite reliable and secure.

In this chapter, you learned how building P2P solutions with WCF and peer channel is relatively simple. While powerful, it's easy to implement, debug, and deploy, which will enable further adoption by both developers and users.

The next chapter will introduce interoperability with other SOA implementations and will cover some of the challenges of using J2EE, MTOM, and WS-ReliableMessaging in a cross-platform implementation.

Implementing SOA Interoperability

How do you achieve the "connected systems" ideology that facilitates intelligent, standalone systems communicating with each other using a universal language? Is it practical to assume that one technology will dominate the market? Would that technology promote its proprietary standard as the default communication model? This is highly unlikely and defeats the core principles of SOA. We need to ask how services on heterogeneous platforms will communicate with each other, what interoperability options are available to an enterprise, and how will WCF communicate with these non-Microsoft SOA offerings.

The objective of this chapter is to educate you about non-Microsoft SOA offerings and illustrate how they achieve interoperability. We'll focus primarily on what products are available and where they stand in comparison to implementing solid interoperable stacks. We will not be able to dive into deep technical issues with each alternative SOA implementation. This chapter will merely introduce non-Microsoft offerings to increase your awareness. We will also discuss some practical issues regarding the interoperability of binary data, existing and emerging standards, and other competing technologies.

We'll conclude the chapter by discussing some of the key standards in the WS-* specifications that provide a solid enterprise-ready stack. These standards provide the foundation for why WS-* and SOA are so critical for the future of integrated architectures in the enterprise. These standards will assist solution architects in identifying the critical success factors needed for investing in these technologies. We will specifically address Message Transmission Optimization Mechanism (MTOM) and WS-ReliableMessaging, as well as their vendor implementations. We will begin by discussing the interoperability options available in Java.

Achieving Java/J2EE Interoperability

It is safe to assume that most enterprises use multiple software platforms, and their stakeholders have made significant investments in existing solutions based on COM, COM+, and other non-Microsoft technologies.

The WCF team has provided a comprehensive integration model for working alongside, around, and within existing COM+ solutions. In Chapter 10, we focused on how WCF can work with existing COM+ applications from both a client and a service. This chapter focuses on interoperability capabilities and issues with regard to non-Microsoft technologies, including Java/J2EE.

The tack for cross-platform interoperability is to work primarily with the standards as published by industry-supported and industry-controlled committees. However, each vendor has the tendency to implement its "interpretation" of the standards. To achieve a neutral perspective, the WCF team generated many compatibility tests for a subset of the different vendor implementations. In addition to performing internal testing, Microsoft created the WCF Interoperability Plug-Fest program (http://www.mssoapinterop.org/ilab) to work with stack vendors to achieve greater compliance and compatibility.

One of the more notable participants in the Plug-Fest program was Sun(now brought by Oracle). The Sun web services team worked alongside the WCF team on several occasions, and publicly released an open source framework focused primarily on interoperability with WCF. Started as Project Tango (see `http://weblogs.java.net/blog/haroldcarr/archive/2006/02/an_overview_of_1.html`) it has evolved into Web Services Interoperability Technology (WSIT), which is available today in open source form (see `http://en.wikipedia.org/wiki/Web_Services_Interoperability_Technology` . The main capabilities and standards provided in WSIT are as follows:

- Bootstrapping communication (WS-MetadataExchange, WS Transfer and WS-Policy)

- Securing communication (WS-SecurityPolicy, WS-SecureConversation, WS-Security, and WS-Trust)

- Optimizing communication (MTOM and WS-SecureConversation)

- Enabling reliability (WS-ReliableMessaging and WS-RMPolicy)

- Enabling atomic transactions (WS-Coordination and WS-AtomicTransactions)

Another major participant in the WCF/.NET interoperability process is the Axis project from the Apache Software Foundation (`http://ws.apache.org/axis2`). It's a major participant in that the WCF team has worked with Axis on its own, ensuring WCF compliance with the WS-* standards by leveraging Axis. Additionally, the Axis team reported that it too has done interoperability testing for the Axis2 1.0 release from May 2006. With the growing popularity of REST-based services, Axis has recently started support on RESTful-based services with Axis2 version 1.4.

Non-Microsoft SOA Platforms

We'll now focus on a few key vendors that have openly supported and worked with .NET interoperability issues. Table 13–1 lists the leading vendors and their support of the WS-* standards within their products.[1]

Table 13–1. Vendor Implementation of WS- Standards*

Vendor/Product	MTOM?	WS-Security?	WS-ReliableMessaging?
Microsoft	Yes	Yes	Yes
IBM	Yes	Yes	Yes
BEA	Yes	Yes	Yes
Sun	Yes	Yes	No
Apache	Yes	Yes	Yes
Tibco	No	Yes	No
gSOAP	Yes	Yes	No

---

[1] Apache is listed as a vendor even though it is an open source foundation supported by community members.

Interoprability with WS-I Basic Profile

In the beginning stages of the industry's implementation of the web standards, people recognized that many of the stacks were built upon an inconsistent foundation of technologies. Some vendors had chosen different versions of WSDL or SOAP for their implementation. So, achieving interoperability among different implementations was a substantial challenge. In many instances, it was impossible without a significant amount of custom coding. The amount of coding required made most enterprises favor in-house development over vendor implementations when interoperability was required.

The early vendor SOA frameworks did not conform to common open standards (in other words, they were vendor-specific). This was mostly because of both customer and market demands. However, this was a major obstacle for achieving true interoperability between multiple vendors.

The major industry participants combined resources, forming the Web Services Interoperability (WS-I) Organization (`www.ws-i.org`) to facilitate and move web service standards forward in a non-proprietary and open manner. WS-I consists of a mix of products, services, and most importantly, user corporations—the primary focus of why we as solution architects exist. Currently, approximately 90 organizations—including major industry titans like Microsoft, IBM, Novell, and Oracle—are participating, with nearly 30 percent comprised of user corporations. We'll now discuss core components of the WS-I Basic Profile in the next section.

Core Components

In April 2004, WS-I released first version of Basic Profile, commonly known as Basic Profile 1.0. Since then, WS-I has been actively contributing to baselining the web standards for interoperability. The latest version is Basic Profile 2.0, which was published in November 2010 (`http://ws-i.org/profiles/BasicProfile-2.0-2010-11-09.html`). This set of specifications laid the groundwork for vendors and customers to begin from a sound base. The specification represents the first generation of interoperable web service specifications. The importance of the Basic Profile cannot be underestimated. With its initial release, many product companies and open source groups recognized that the market will no longer tolerate standalone proprietary interoperability stacks.

The Basic Profile 2.0 specification is built upon a consistent set of foundation specifications:

- SOAP 1.2

- WSDL 1.1

- UDDI 2.0

- XML 1.0 (second edition)

- XML Schema Part 1: Structures

- XML Schema Part 2: Datatypes

- RFC 2246: The Transport Layer Security Protocol Version 1.0

- RFC 2459: Internet X.509 Public Key Infrastructure Certificate and CRL Profile

- RFC 2616: HyperText Transfer Protocol 1.1

- RFC 2818: HTTP over TLS

- RFC 2965: HTTP State Management Mechanism

- The Secure Sockets Layer Protocol Version 3.0

Given the agreement among the participants, interoperability at the basic level was now a greater possibility. In November 2010, the WS-I committee updated the Basic Profile to version 2.0, which included some updates and corrections to published errata.

It is important to understand that interoperability is not a guarantee that vendors will adhere to specifications. Other key deliverables from WS-I apart from profiles includes sample applications and Testing tools. One of the notable releases of WS-I are sample applications that demonstrate interoperability among web service applications, developed using multiple platforms/languages and programming tools. Given the complex nature of the WS-* specifications, small variations in how each framework interprets the specifications generally lead to incompatibilities. This is why Microsoft has worked with other vendors to validate WCF with its major competitors. We'll now discuss the Basic Profile implementation by Microsoft, starting with ASP.NET.

ASP.NET Support of Basic Profile

Since ASP.NET 1.0/1.1 was a shipping product prior to the official specification release (it was still a draft in 2002), it didn't offer official support for Basic Profile 1.0; however, it was possible by following simple guidelines(`http://www.ws-i.org/Profiles/BasicProfile-1.1.html`) to implement it. With ASP.NET 2.0, you enable support for Basic Profile 1.1 by applying the `WebServiceBinding` attribute to your service class, as shown in Listing 13–1.

Listing 13–1. Enabling Basic Profile in ASP.NET 2.0

```
[WebService(Namespace = "http://tempuri.org/")]
[WebServiceBinding(ConformsTo = WsiProfiles.BasicProfile1_1)]
public class WebService : System.Web.Services.WebService {...}
```

Microsoft Web Service Extensions

During the evolution of web services, Microsoft provided an add-on framework to the core .NET runtime (both 1.1 and 2.0) in support of the evolving web service standards. With .NET 1.1 Microsoft released version 1.0 and 2.0 of Web Services Enhancements (WSE). With the release of .NET 2.0, Microsoft updated WSE to version 3.0.

WSE 2.0 offered no direct evidence that it would produce services that were guaranteed to be Basic Profile compliant. ASP.NET 3.0, however, added the `WebServiceBinding` attribute, which allowed it to conform to Basic Profile 1.1, WSE 3.0 inherited that capability from WSE 2,0 and enables you to build secure webservice quickly and easilyAdditionally, the Microsoft Patterns and Practices team published a reference application (http://msdn.microsoft.com/library/en-us/dnsvcinter/html/WSI-BP_MSDN_LandingPage.asp) demonstrating how to build services that conform to WS-I Basic Profile, along with an implementation guidance document. (You can find the Microsoft WS-I Basic Security Profile sample application at `http://msdn.microsoft.com/en-us/library/ff650138.aspx`.)

WCF Basic Profile Support

WCF enables WS-I Basic Profile 1.1 through the `BasicHttpBinding` class. So, with WCF, writing base-level interoperable services that conform to WS-I Basic Profile is as easy as leveraging the `BasicHttpBinding` class through code, as shown in Listing 13–2.

Listing 13–2. Applying Basic Profile in Code

```
Uri baseAddress = new Uri( "http://localhost:8080/MyService" );
// Instantiate new ServiceHost
myServiceHost = new ServiceHost( typeof( MyService ), baseAddress );
// The following for programmatic addition of Basic Profile 1.2
BasicHttpBinding binding = new BasicHttpBinding();
myServiceHost.AddServiceEndpoint(
    typeof( IMyInterface,
    binding,
    baseAddress);
```

In Listing 13–2, we added the BasicHttpBinding instance to the ServiceHost instance's endpoints. Again, the power of WCF is that you can also enable the capability for Basic Profile 1.1 support declaratively through configuration, as shown in Listing 13–3.

Listing 13–3. Applying Basic Profile Through Configuration

```
<bindings>
    <basicHttpBinding>
        <binding name="WebServiceSoap"
        ...
        </binding>
</bindings>
```

Using the declarative, configuration-driven model allows the distinct abstraction of both the service and the client of the service (given that both sides are WCF-based) from the transport and the messy details of the available bindings. Abstraction is critical to the WCF programming model, and is what sets the tools and framework apart from competing stacks such as Axis2. Although other stacks provide tools and a configuration-driven approach, the WCF/Visual Studio combination enables rapid application development without requiring you to learn additional object models or implementation patterns.

As the WS-* specifications advance requirements for greater control over security, reliable messaging, and atomic transactions, WCF allows, when using the declarative model, direct support without your having to recode the service or client implementation. So, with the declarative method, you can update the application configuration file as shown in Listing 13–4.

Listing 13–4. Applying WSHttpBinding in Configuration

```
<bindings>
    <wsHttpBinding>
        <binding name="... "
        ...
        </binding>
    </wsHttpBinding>
</bindings>
```

Through the wsHttpBinding configuration element, you can now support additional levels of reliability and security for internal and external services for enterprise solutions.

Implementing Basic Profile ensures you of seamless integration with other services from non-Microsoft platforms. However, one of the most common issues of transferring information is sending attachments to another non-Microsoft platform. This is a necessity today, as substantial binary files, graphics files, and product files (such as Acrobat PDF files) are often exchanged between multiple platforms. How do you send these binary data over WCF services? What mechanisms are available in WCF to achieve this?

Sending Binary Data Over Web Services

When you look at most types of services, they utilize short, succinct messages that contain primarily text. The common one-way and two-way message exchange patterns simply pass a few parameters. WCF, along with most web service frameworks, has been optimized for these patterns.

However, since the inception of messaging technologies (e.g., MQSeries, WebSphere MQ, and other message-oriented middleware), solutions have required the transfer of large objects and binary data between tiers. In the past, large objects were sent out of band, often using FTP with PGP or other convoluted solutions. Existing systems leverage data formats that are usable across platforms in their existing forms. Image data (GIF, JPEG, and TIF) is an example of this type of data. Also, the prevalence of PDF files is another example of a data format that transgresses platforms easily.

Base64 Encoding

One method that can be leveraged for sending binary attachment is embedding the binary data as a Base64-encoded stream. This is a simple method, which is directly supported by the xs:base64Binary XML schema type. However, it has some significant drawbacks. The first is the additional overhead with the encoding/decoding of the binary data, which adds processing cost. The other potentially more significant issue is that the Base64 algorithm can increase the payload size by approximately 33 percent.[2]

Although Base64 method is effective for sending binary data, the overall issues related to size can impact the performance of services. Given that the web service response is generally buffered prior to transmission, large objects will consume memory resources in addition to the CPU overhead of encoding. Also, direct embedding of the binary resource inside the XML document impacts the performance of XML parsers, which are now required to buffer or read past the embedded data in order to obtain other elements and values.

SOAP with Attachments (SwA)

An alternative to embedding binary data inside the XML document was published(www.ietf.org/rfc/rfc2045.txt) in December 2000. This specification was built upon the Multipurpose Internet Mail Extensions (MIME) specifications. A similar specification, WS-Attachments, follows the same pattern, leveraging MIME at its core. Both, as you'll soon see, have been superseded and have minimal industry support.

MIME provides a way to transfer the binary data alongside the core SOAP response inside a MIME message. Listing 13–5 shows a stub of a MIME message.

Listing 13–5. MIME Message Sample

```
MIME-Version: 1.0
Content-Type: Multipart/Related; boundary=MIME_boundary; type=text/xml;
      start="<claim061400a.xml@claiming-it.com>"
Content-Description: This is the optional message description.

--MIME_boundary
Content-Type: text/xml; charset=UTF-8
Content-Transfer-Encoding: 8bit
Content-ID: <claim061400a.xml@claiming-it.com>
```

---

[2] You can find scenarios, patterns, and implementation guidance for WSE 3.0 at http://msdn.microsoft.com/en-us/library/ff650778.aspx

```
<?xml version='1.0' ?>
<SOAP-ENV:Envelope
xmlns:SOAP-ENV="http://schemas.xmlsoap.org/soap/envelope/">
<SOAP-ENV:Body>
..
<theSignedForm href="cid:claim061400a.tiff@claiming-it.com"/>
..
</SOAP-ENV:Body>
</SOAP-ENV:Envelope>

--MIME_boundary
Content-Type: image/tiff
Content-Transfer-Encoding: binary
Content-ID: <claim061400a.tiff@claiming-it.com>

...binary TIFF image...
--MIME_boundary--
```

The section in bold is the body of the SOAP response. This contains an element called theSignedForm with a relative reference of cid:.... The cid reference represents the Content-ID that is present within the MIME message. SwA provides a way to optimize access to the XML body without forcing parsers and readers to consume the binary data until absolutely necessary.

SwA has several issues. One primary issue is that the URI reference outside the SOAP body bypasses any message-level security. To alleviate this, it's necessary to provide transport-level encryption or security, such as SSL or S/MIME. However, these URI references could be outside the MIME message itself and not be required to be relative to the current message which mandates the need of transport level security.

Direct Internet Message Encapsulation (DIME)

When Microsoft shipped WSE 1.0 for .NET 1.1, it provided a method(MIME) for passing attachments in a SOAP message but outside the SOAP envelope. As a result of its presence as an attachment with SOAP message, it falls outside the capabilities of SOAP security and consequently requires transmission or transport-level security such as SSL. While only Microsoft submitted it to the Internet Engineering Task Force, both IBM and Microsoft authored it. Because of a variety of reasons, it didn't gain industry backing.

Direct Internet Message Encapsulation (DIME) on the other hand uses simpler message format and is more efficient and faster than DIME. DIME uses the best features of MIME to support in the webservice word. DIME leveraged fixed fied size..This works well for Windows and most Unix variants, but requires additional overhead on platforms that don't conform to the same sequencing methods. DIME also supported chunking of a message (splitting a message over multiple DIME records).

The WSE 2.0 programming model requires developers to manipulate the SOAP response by adding attachments programmatically. Listing 13–6 is a snippet of WSE 2.0 code that adds the file attachment, along with its content type (image/jpeg), directly to the SOAP response.

Listing 13–6. Using DIME in WSE 2.0

```
[WebMethod]
public void GetFile(string fileName)
{
    SoapContext respContext = ResponseSoapContext.Current;
```

```
    DimeAttachment dimeAttach = new DimeAttachment("image/jpeg",
        TypeFormat.MediaType, fileName);
    respContext.Attachments.Add(dimeAttach);
}
```

As shown in Listing 13–6, the implementation details are not abstracted from the service implementation. The service developer is now forced to understand the implications and requirements of transferring binary or large objects through the service tier. A more natural method would be just to return the binary data as a stream or an array of bytes.

Microsoft realized the transitional status of DIME, and when WSE 3.0 (for .NET 2.0) was released, Microsoft terminated the support of DIME. The technology that replaced it is called Message Transmission Optimization Mechanism (MTOM). Listing 13–7 is a similar interface but implemented with MTOM support as part of WSE 3.0.

Listing 13–7. Using MTOM in WSE 3.0

```
[WebMethod]
public byte[] GetFile(string fileName)
{
    byte[] response;
    String filePath = AppDomain.CurrentDomain.BaseDirectory +
        @"App_Data\" + fileName;
    response = File.ReadAllBytes(filePath);
    return response;
}
```

As you'll soon see, the transition from the WSE 3.0 implementation of MTOM to the WCF implementation of MTOM was nearly seamless, given the more natural way of implementing service interfaces without implementation-dependant details. Also, WSE 3.0 MTOM is wire-level compatible with WCF's initial release.

MTOM

With the limitations of the attachment-oriented approaches, industry participants developed MTOM, a new specification that alleviated many of the issues of past specifications while ensuring compatibility with the emerging WS-* standards. Along with MTOM, XML-binary Optimization Packaging (XOP) is managed by the WCF encoding class MtomMessageEncodingBindingElement. You can control message encoding by setting the messageEncoding attribute on the binding with either Text or Binary. Listing 13–8 is an example of an application configuration that establishes through the declarative model that MTOM encoding should be used.

Listing 13–8. Using MTOM Through Configuration

```
<system.serviceModel>
    <services>
      <service name="MtomSvc.MtomSample">
        <endpoint binding="wsHttpBinding"
              contract="MtomSvc.IMtomSample"
              bindingConfiguration="MyBinding"/>
      </service>
    </services>
    <bindings>
      <wsHttpBinding>
```

```
        <binding name="MyBinding" messageEncoding="Mtom" />
      </wsHttpBinding>
    </bindings>
</system.serviceModel>
```

In the configuration file shown in Listing 13–8, we've applied the Mtom value to the messageEncoding attribute for the default settings of wsHttpBinding. This tells the WCF framework that it should apply MTOM (with XOP) to the messages during normal channel processing, inside the WSHttpBinding instance. The content optimization is based upon how the XOP implementation is applied within WSHttpBinding by using the internal class System.ServiceModel.Channels.MtomMessageEncoder. The series of MIME message consisting of a SOAP request and for the final response from the server a binary stream (marked as Content-Type: application/octet-stream) traverses across the wire, on the chosen transport.

In the Chapter 13 sample code, MtomTest provides a WCF client and server using configuration, and WSHttpBinding does its message exchange, leveraging the MTOM capabilities of WCF. The sample code contains a single service method that returns an array of bytes, as shown in Listing 13–9.

Listing 13–9. WCF GetFile Service Contract

```
namespace MtomSvc
{
    [ServiceContract()]
    public interface IMtomSample
    {
        [OperationContract(
            ProtectionLevel=System.Net.Security.ProtectionLevel.None)]
        byte[] GetFile( string fileName );
    }

    public class MtomSample : IMtomSample
    {
        public byte[] GetFile( string fileName )
        {
            byte[] result = File.ReadAllBytes(
                Path.Combine(
                    AppDomain.CurrentDomain.BaseDirectory, fileName) );

            return result;
        }
    }
}
```

Here, we've used the same method signature as in the WSE 3 example in Listing 13–7, which leveraged MTOM, and we've defined an interface and provided an implementation in a concrete class. We've also applied an OperationContract property of ProtectionLevel.None to the operation so that the only protection is authentication (the alternatives being Sign and EncryptAndSign).

■**Tip** Check the requirements for running the samples on the MSDN site at http://windowssdk.msdn.microsoft.com/en-us/library/ms751525.aspx. Many of the samples from the SDK, including this book's code, have certain requirements for security and when running in workgroup mode.

The service class just reads the file name passed on the request into an array of bytes, and then returns that to the caller. The MtomTest client application displays the results in a text box or, for the image request, converts it into an image and updates the Image control.

You'll now look at what occurs during the request and reply from the client. Figure 13–1 illustrates the calling sequence from client to server over the life of the request. This will illustrate the initial key exchange (and subsequent token generation) between the client and services. This will also illustrate how the token is utilized to invoke a GetFile command at the service.

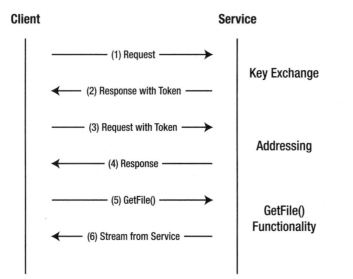

Figure 13–1. MTOM message exchange

The MtomTest sample directory contains several logs, along with a series of text files taken from the MIME parts of the requests. Those text files are labeled 1.txt through 6.txt—they match Figure 13–1, with each odd-numbered file representing the request coming from the client, and each even-numbered file representing the response from the server.

The first two request-reply pairs represent the key exchange as part of the WS-Security implementation within WCF. This is primarily for establishing a token exchange that will be used later for message signing. The third and fourth requests illustrate the token being used to inquire about endpoints. This objective of this call is to illustrate how the token is utilized by the client to communicate with the server. The following code snippet illustrates the binary token that is used to pass on credentials to the service:

```
<s:Body>
<t:RequestSecurityTokenResponse Context="uuid-af1f0d7a-6fd7-4c06-9ce0-
7a5acb18669f-2" xmlns:t="http://schemas.xmlsoap.org/ws/2005/02/trust"
xmlns:u="http://docs.oasis-open.org/wss/2004/01/oasis-200401-
wss-wssecurity-utility-1.0.xsd">
<t:BinaryExchange ValueType="http://schemas.microsoft.com/net/2004/07/
secext/WS-SPNego">TlRMTVNTUAADAAAAGAAYAHgAAAAYABgAkAAAA
BAAEABIAAAAEAAQAF
gAAAAQABAAaAAAABAAEACoAAAANYKY4gUBKAoAAAAPQwBMAFcAQw
BGAFgAUAAxAGMAaQBjAG8AcgBpAGEAcwBDAEwAAVwBDAEYAWABQAD
EA5OLHzcQEcZYAAAAAAAAAAAAAAAAAAAsz6BrLvbKI9JA2UWtQEQolh
```

```
SFoU9HXfUOvvvDPQuWoNlKxIgckKTwQ==
</t:BinaryExchange>
</t:RequestSecurityTokenResponse>
</s:Body>
```

The fifth request is the actual SOAP request, and uses an action of
`http://tempuri.org/IMtomSample/GetFile`. The body of the SOAP request contains an unencrypted
request value inside the SOAP body:

```
<fileName>LogoText.JPG</fileName>
```

If you look at the file `6.txt`, you'll see a MIME message consisting of two parts. The first part is the
SOAP envelope representing the `GetFileResponse` message, as shown in Listing 13–10. Inside that
element is an `xop:Include` element that points to the second part of the MIME message.

Listing 13–10. GetFileResult with XOP Reference

```
<GetFileResult>
    <xop:Include
     href="cid:http%3A%2F%2Ftempuri.org%2F1%2F632858870617208016"
     xmlns:xop="http://www.w3.org/2004/08/xop/include"/>
</GetFileResult>
```

The second part of the MIME message is the raw binary stream as read initially from the file system
into the byte[]. If you look in the file `6.txt`, you can see the MIME content header for the binary stream,
as shown in Listing 13–11.

Listing 13–11. Binary Content Part of the MIME Message

```
--uuid:c336b34f-7c2b-4ca6-9534-141723adcf4c+id=9
Content-ID: <http://tempuri.org/1/632858870617208016>
Content-Transfer-Encoding: binary
Content-Type: application/octet-stream

ÿØÿà JFIF ` ` ÿÛ C \\ \          (binary data)
```

The `Content-ID` in this part of the MIME message is not HTML encoded, while in the SOAP response
part (Listing 13–10) it is. The other aspect is that the encoding type is `binary` and marked as an `octet-
stream`. What follows the customary set of two Carriage Return/Line Feed(CR/LF - 0x0D, 0x0A) is the raw
binary data directly from the byte[]. The content length matches the original file size (you can examine
this with the ethereal logs) without any compression or modification.

The exchange used in Listing 13–10 doesn't apply any message level security to either the request or
the reply. If you update the `OperationContract` attribute's `ProtectionLevel` property to `EncryptAndSign`,
you get message-level encryption on both the SOAP envelope and the binary data that is contained in
the second part of the MIME message. The capture results with `EncryptAndSign` for the final response are
contained in the file 6-WithEncryptAndSign.txt.

MTOM Industry Acceptance

The W3C published the MTOM specification in January 2005. Since that time, several other key vendors
have signed on to ship products that contain support for MTOM. Microsoft was one of the first to
support it, beginning with Visual Studio 2005 and WSE 3.0. Microsoft continues that support up through
WCF in .NET 4.0.

At the time of this writing, many of the non-Microsoft frameworks have indicated an intention to support MTOM in future versions of their application server software or have shipped early adopter code.

If you look at the Java technology stack, some competing technologies provide the foundation for web services. As a result, how you enable MTOM support in the Java environment varies according to the choice you make with regard to the primary application server and development tools.

Sun's Tango project, along with its NetBeans tools and frameworks, provides a similar model to Microsoft's. Both provide a metadata-driven approach and tools to abstract and simplify developing web services based upon the emerging standards.

Apache's Axis2 Support of MTOM

You'll now look at how Axis2 1.0 provides support for MTOM. Axis2 1.0 was released as an early adopter version in May 2006.[3] The Axis2 project was a major rewrite from the initial Axis web services project. Axis2 leverages a pipeline handler model for message handling (similar to Axis) with an extensibility model that allows both the community and enterprises to extend Axis2.

The Axis2 project has more of a code generation model with the use of tools to facilitate developing web services. Additionally, Axis2 uses the Axis Object Model Element (AXIOM `OMElement`), that becomes the primary message that is passed through the participants in a distributed architecture. The Axis2 project also has an Eclipse plug-in(`http://ws.apache.org/axis2`) wizard for helping generate code either from WSDL or Java classes .(`www.eclipse.org`).

So, using the `MtomTest` sample, you can first generate the WSDL using the `SvcUtil.exe` utility provided by WCF via the following command line (after starting the `WCFHost` project):

```
svcutil /t:metadata http://localhost:8080/ FileService
```

This creates three output files, representing the base WSDL with the two imports. Using this WSDL, you can now create the Java classes for consuming the `MtomTest` web service, as shown in Figure 13–2.

---

[3] You can find MTOM and XOP at `www.w3.org/TR/soap12-mtom` and `www.w3.org/TR/xop10`, respectively.

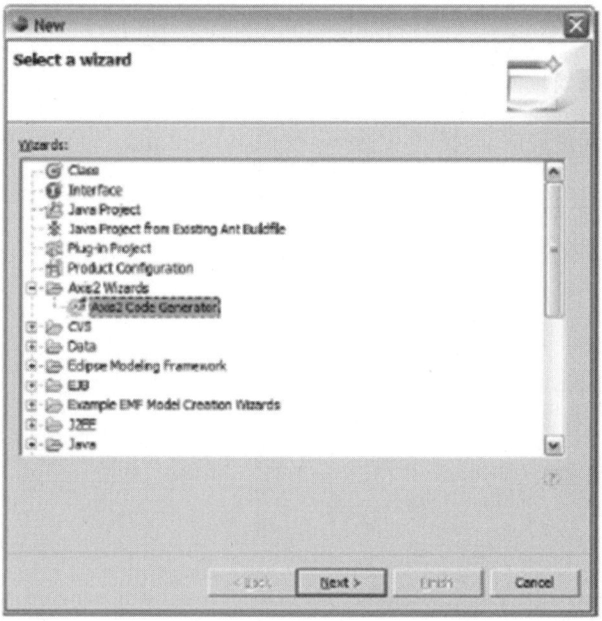

Figure 13–2. Accessing the Axis2 Code Generator from Eclipse

The wizard lists the Axis2 Code Generator (accessible from the New menu option). We won't cover the capabilities of the Code Generator in too much detail. The next step is to choose either to generate a Java class from a WSDL or to generate a Java class to a WSDL. We will choose to generate a WSDL to a Java class (using the "Generate Java source code from a WSDL file" option), as shown in Figure 13–3.

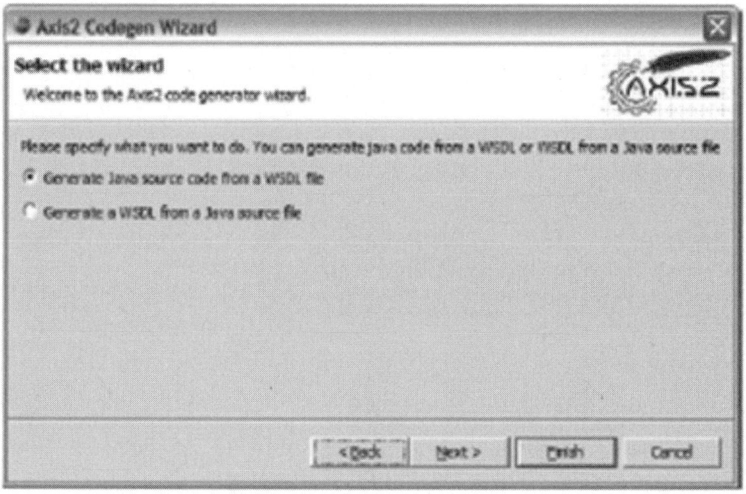

Figure 13–3. Generating Java code from WSDL

Click Next, and you will then be prompted to choose the input WSDL file. This will be the file you created using the SvcUtil.exe utility. Then click Next again, and you will see the choices for code generation, as shown in Figure 13–4.

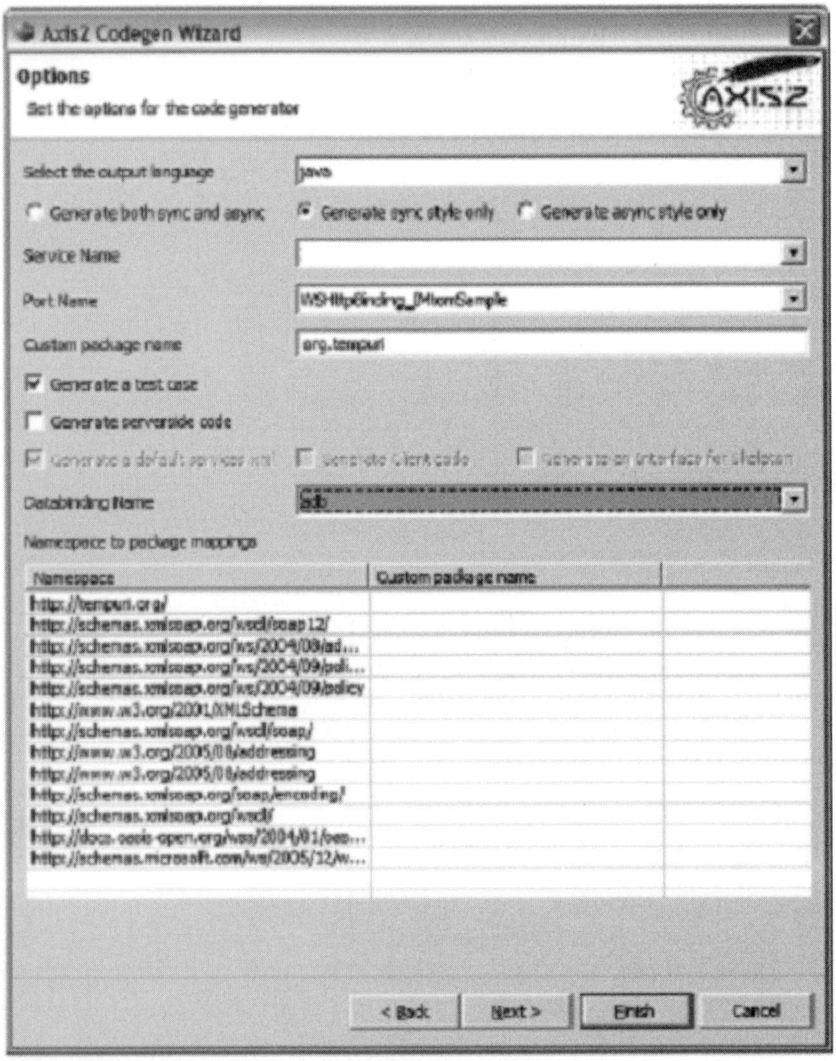

Figure 13–4. Axis2 code generation options

Enter the service name in the Service Name box. For this example, we'll just generate the client-side proxy along with a test case class that will demonstrate the calling paradigm provided by the Axis2 framework. We've just enabled synchronous calling and the generation of a test case.

The next page of the wizard asks for the output directory. Make sure you don't click the Finish button yet. You must first specify a directory; otherwise the wizard will complete without an error, but won't produce any results. We've included the generated code as part of the chapter sample code; it's in the `MtomTest\Java` directory, and the WSDL used is in the `MtomTest\Wsdl` directory. Note that the WSDL2Java-generated class is called `FileServiceTest`.

Listing 13–12 shows the test case–generated code from the WSDL2Java wizard.

Listing 13–12. Axis2 WSDL2Java-Generated Code

```
public class FileServiceTest extends junit.framework.TestCase {
    public void testGetFile() throws java.lang.Exception {
        org.tempuri. FileServiceStubstub = new org.tempuri.FileServiceStub ();
        org.apache.axiom.om.OMElement param4 =
                    (org.apache.axiom.om.OMElement)
                        getTestObject(org.apache.axiom.om.OMElement.class);

        // todo Fill in the param4 here
        assertNotNull(stub.GetFile(param4));
    }

    // Create an OMElement and provide it as the test object
    public org.apache.axiom.om.OMElement getTestObject(java.lang.Object dummy) {
      org.apache.axiom.om.OMFactory factory =
            org.apache.axiom.om.OMAbstractFactory.getOMFactory();
      org.apache.axiom.om.OMNamespace defNamespace =
            factory.createOMNamespace("", null);

      return org.apache.axiom.om.OMAbstractFactory.getOMFactory()
            .createOMElement("test", defNamespace);
    }
}
```

As you can see in the code, the most important thing to note is navigating the `OMElement`, which is a hierarchical object model representing an XML InfoSet(http://ws.apache.org/axis2/tools/1_0/eclipse/wsdl2java-plugin.html).

Compare the coding approach presented by Axis2 and AXIOM to that presented by WCF. The .NET Framework provides methods to develop against a strongly typed object model representation of XML data, as well as through hierarchical navigation using XML technologies. Microsoft provides tools to make the serialization and representation of XML data more seamless using a user-friendly integrated development environment (Visual Studio. The result is that you can do more with less coding, leaving the intricacies of working with XML to the framework.

Sun Microsystems's Support of MTOM

Sun, the creator of Java, has worked with Microsoft on WCF interoperability testing, as mentioned previously. The WSIT project, as of this writing, is in early adaptor form and is source code (http://ws.apache.org/axis2/1_0/OMTutorial.html#OM) only. However, given the marketing from Sun's team and the demonstration since e JavaOne 2006 conference, it is clear that Sun is committed to a viable and working framework.

WSIT relies on two foundational Java technologies: JAX-WS(https://wsit.dev.java.net) and JAXB(http://jax-ws.dev.java.net). The combination of these technologies provides a similar development experience to the WCF model. Both rely on attributes and metadata for web service definition, and they provide a strongly typed development experience that increases developer productivity.

Sun's NetBeans project, which is an open source stepchild of the Java community, provides a development environment that additionally removes the need for developers to hand-code new APIs or understand navigating an object graph. The NetBeans WSIT module,(http://jaxb.dev.java.net) as shown in Figure 13–5, hides the intricacies of the framework requirements.

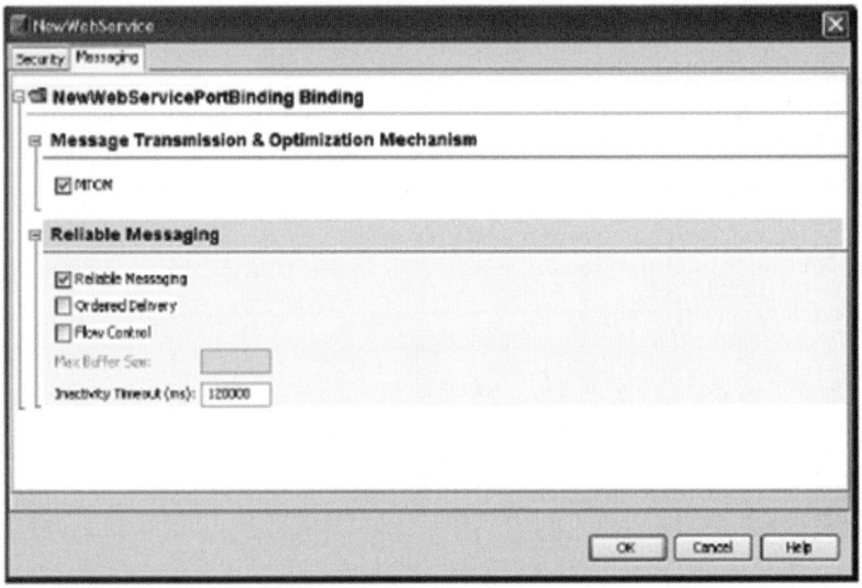

Figure 13–5. NetBeans WSIT module

Before moving on, we'll make a few important observations regarding the state of the Java community and the vendor support of a consistent approach to working with web services and the emerging standards: JBoss, acquired by Red Hat in 2006, has stated that it will no longer work with the Axis project and will proceed with the development of its own SOAP stack(http://websvc.netbeans.org/wsit) JBoss has started supporting the MTOM specification(http://wiki.jboss.org/wiki/Wiki.jsp?page=WebServiceStacks). Till now, we discussed various options available to transfer binary data between Microsoft and non-Microsoft SOA offerings. We'll now discuss how WS-ReliableMessaging is used in non-Microsoft SOA offerings.

Using WS-ReliableMessaging

Solutions need to be reliable. If a system is either unavailable or loses requests for processing, the users of that system will eventually demand explanations. For example, if you're buying a book on Amazon and you get through the order process, think you've purchased the book, and then wait weeks for its pending arrival, how many times do you think you'll shop at Amazon again before investigating alternative services?

The situation is even worse if you're booking a trade that could be worth a considerable amount of money and the message to the clearance system gets lost. If you have a trader who just purchased 100,000 shares of Microsoft stock, what happens if that ticket never makes it to the back-office system?

Since the inception of web services, their attraction to loosely coupled platform interoperability has been amazing. Web services represent a neutral technology that no one vendor owns or controls at the expense of competitors and clients. Vendors can't hold clients to a single platform. However, web services have one significant drawback that we view as critical for their further acceptance in the enterprise. This limitation has held back web services as the enabling glue for tying applications together in a loosely coupled manner. That limitation is reliability.

The foundation of web services, for many implementations, has traditionally been HTTP. SOAP over HTTP is generally considered the default mechanism for web services. However, HTTP doesn't guarantee reliability when dealing with duplication, ordering, or system outages.

The WS-ReliableMessaging specification was created to address the needs of reliability for solutions that span applications across heterogeneous platforms. With WS-ReliableMessaging, it is possible to interact across applications in a reliable manner, but not in a durable one.

The WS-ReliableMessaging specification addresses reliability from within a session, or more specifically, a service exchange between a client and a server. What WS-ReliableMessaging provides is a guarantee through delivery assurance that a message sent is received. That leaves the implementation, not the WS-ReliableMessaging specification, to fulfill the delivery assurance or raise a SOAP fault.

The key delivery assurances that can be provided by each WS-ReliableMessaging implementation are as follows:

AtMostOnce: Messages are delivered without duplication, but lost messages are not handled.

AtLeastOnce: Messages are delivered once or more. If delivery fails, a fault is raised.

ExactlyOnce: Message are delivered only once. If delivery fails, a fault is raised.

InOrder: Messages are delivered in the order in which they're sent. Duplication and dropped messages are not addressed.

■**Note** The current WCF implementation supports ExactlyOnce, and the InOrder capability is optional. You can enable it by applying the reliableSession element in configuration or in code for a custom binding or on a binding that supports reliable sessions (such as WSHttp, WSDual, or NetTcp).

System availability and durability of sent messages are not part of the WS-ReliableMessaging specification, and they're not currently supported in WCF(http://specs.xmlsoap.org/ws/2005/02/rm). One suggestion for how to approach the durability and system availability aspects is to leverage MSMQ in conjunction with reliable sessions; but this doesn't address the cross-platform issues. However, these issues can be addressed by using gateway technologies such as Host Integration Server (HIS) or other MSMQ-to-MQSeries bridges. But again, the limitations on the stack from each vendor on each side of the channel come into play. So, unless you have an extensible stack and you're prepared to develop customized bindings on the receiving end, the current shipping limitation is WCF in conjunction with MSMQ.

Network availability is addressed by dealing with timeouts on acknowledgments. Inactivity timeout settings, when exceeded without acknowledgment, will result in failure. Therefore, if a session is interrupted by an unreliable network connection, the WCF stack and any WS-ReliableMessaging implementations that support AtLeastOnce or ExactlyOne will raise a fault.

WS-ReliableMessaging Example

We'll now look at the WsReliableMessaging sample that's part of the Chapter 13 downloadable samples. Using the MTOM sample as a base, we've modified the bindings to indicate that we require reliable sessions on the service interface. Using the WCF Service Configuration Editor (SvcConfigEditor.exe) that's part of the Windows SDK (select Tools ➤ WCF SvcConfigEditor in Visual Studio), you can modify the App.config file for the WcfHost application in the sample, as shown in Figure 13–6.

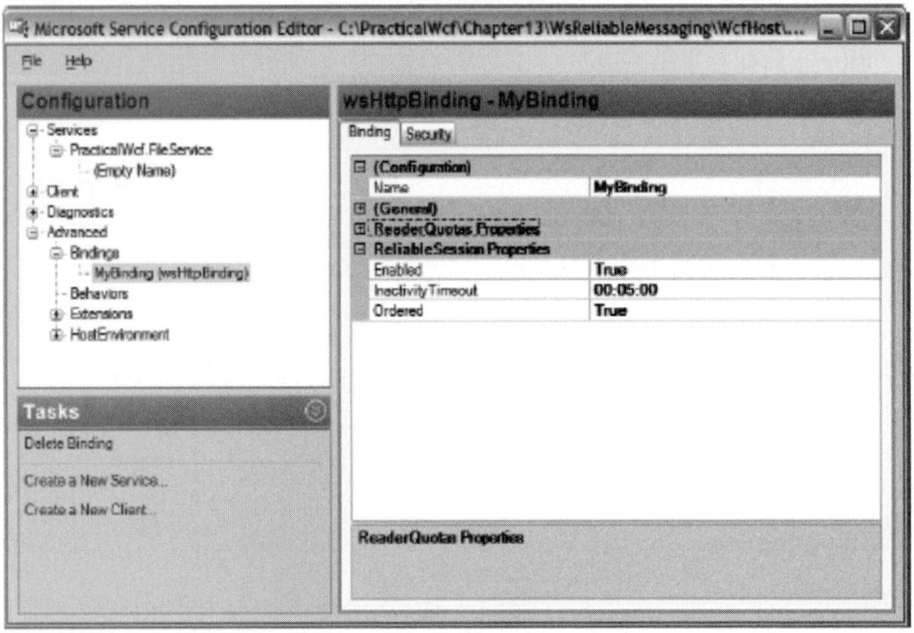

Figure 13–6. Enabling WS-ReliableMessaging on WcfHost

This configuration translates to the application configuration file shown in Listing 13–13.

Listing 13–13. WS-ReliableMessaging Enabled via Configuration

```
<system.serviceModel>
  <services>
    <service name="PracticalWcf.FileService">
      <endpoint
        binding="wsHttpBinding"
        bindingConfiguration="MyBinding"
        contract="PracticalWcf.IFileService" />
    </service>
  </services>
  <bindings>
    <wsHttpBinding>
      <binding
        name="MyBinding"
        messageEncoding="Mtom">
        <reliableSession
          inactivityTimeout="00:05:00"
          enabled="true" />
        <security>
          <message
```

```
            clientCredentialType="Windows"
            negotiateServiceCredential="true"
            establishSecurityContext="true" />
        </security>
      </binding>
    </wsHttpBinding>
  </bindings>
</system.serviceModel>
```

RELIABLE MESSAGING AND WS-SECURITY

The WS-ReliableMessaging specification "strongly recommends" securing reliable scenarios. The following is part of section 5 of the specification located at http://specs.xmlsoap.org/ws/2005/02/rm/ws-reliablemessaging.pdf:

> *It is strongly recommended that the communication between services be secured using the mechanisms described in WS-Security. In order to properly secure messages, the body and all relevant headers need to be included in the signature.*

The specification goes on to clarify the suggestion based upon sequencing, and in the end to alleviate message replay concerns. Given the strong suggestions from the committee and the significant IBM representation on the committee as part of the WCF geeks, it's no surprise that the requirement exists with WCF.

The reliableSession element shown in Listing 13–13 enables WS-ReliableMessaging on all the service interface interactions that leverage WSHttpBinding. Note that the establishSecurityContext attribute is set to true (the default) for the binding. At this time, WCF requires a combination of WS-Security with reliable sessions. If you set the establishSecurityContext attribute to false, when starting the host you will receive a System.InvalidOperation exception with the message "{"Cannot establish reliable session without secure conversation. Enable secure conversation."}."

In keeping with the WCF core ability to support both a declarative and a programmatic-driven implementation, it is also possible via code to enable reliable sessions, as shown in Listing 13–14.

Listing 13–14. WS-ReliableMessaging Using Code

```
WSHttpBinding binding =
    new WSHttpBinding( SecurityMode.Message, true );

myServiceHost.AddServiceEndpoint(
    typeof( IFileService),
    binding,
    baseAddress);
```

The code in Listing 13–14 uses the WSHttpBinding constructor override, which accepts a SecurityMode value, along with a Boolean value that enables reliable sessions on the binding. An alternate override is to specify a configuration name, which allows a combination programmatic-driven and configuration-driven approach to development.

If you examine the HTTP traffic for the service exchange, you should see an overall increase (doubling) in request-reply traffic between the client and server for the same service interface call. What is happening is that with each request, additional acknowledgment messages are indicating success on each message. These additional messages are the delivery assurance mechanisms that are part of WS-ReliableMessaging. An example of one of these messages is the Ack.txt. file contained in the \Capture directory. This message contains a CreateSequenceResponse, which is sent as a reply to an initial CreateSequence initiation that establishes the reliable session. The full Ethereal capture is present in the file wsrm.log in the \Capture directory. You can find full details of the exchange of messages in section 2.4 of the WS-ReliableMessaging specification.

Platform Support of WS-ReliableMessaging

Industry and platform support of WS-ReliableMessaging is a critical aspect of overall web service adoption in the enterprise. Prior to web services, applications were coupled using varied means, with some being file based and many using queued messaging technologies such as MQSeries or Tibco. Most of the time, the coupling was tighter than ideal.

As web services became more prevalent, the desire to connect systems both within an enterprise and outside the firewall has been a critical success factor in a technology's overall adoption.With WS-ReliableMessaging, you now have a means, theoretically, to connect these heterogeneous systems using orthogonal approaches that aren't incompatible on the wire. Now, when dealing with varied application architects and organizations, you can converse in a language that is consistent across implementations. You can discuss the web service contract and not the details of how you plan to converse. You can publish your metadata on your services or consume the metadata of the partners you need to interact with, all using a common language.

The differences between each implementation, however, are stark at the time of this writing. IBM, for example, has supported use of WS-ReliableMessaging in its 6.1 release of WebSphere Application Server,..Since then IBM is constrantly working in the area of WS-ReliableMessaging. At the time of writing, IBM developed a Java API for XML-Based Web Services (JAX-**WS**) provider or requester application, and configure a policy set to configure WS-ReliableMessaging(for more info, refer https://publib.boulder.ibm.com/infocenter/wasinfo/v7r0/ index.jsp?topic=/com.ibm.websphere.express.doc/info/exp/ae/twbs_wsrm_ep.html). Since 2009, JBoss (now part of Red Hat) has provided support for reliable messaging (http://community.jboss.org/wiki/JBossWS WSRe liableMessaging). Also, BEA Systems' WebLogic application server 10.0 include an implementation of WS-ReliableMessaging (http://download.oracle.com/docs /cd/E13222_01 /wls/essex/TechPreview /pdf/ reliable_messaging.pdf). The two most notable implementations are the Sun Tango/WSIT project, as previously mentioned, and Axis2. The teams for both projects, along with the WCF teams, are working on platform interoperability tests to ensure that at shipping time (or close to it) there will be viable frameworks that support interoperability with WCF.

Summary

One of the key objectives of SOA is to obtain interoperability between heterogeneous platforms. WCF achieves this objective by implementing common standards that are endorsed by competitive vendors. IBM, Sun, BEA, and Tibco products comply with WCF by implementing WSIT standards. These are available today as open source offerings. WCF also complies with Basic Profile so that it's compatible with the early web service offerings.

Some of these WSIT standards include bootstrapping communication (WS-MetaDataExchange), securing communication (WS-SecurityPolicy, WS-Security, and WS-Trust), optimizing communication (MTOM and WS-SecureConversation), enabling reliability (WS-ReliableMessaging), and enabling atomic transactions (WS-Coordination and WS-AtomicTransactions). MTOM also helps developers transfer binary attachments from one platform to another (e.g., from Microsoft WCF to Apache Axis2). WS-ReliableMessaging implemented by WCF offers guaranteed delivery, similar to traditional Tibco or MQSeries offerings. In summary, WCF offers a wide variety of interoperability options for integrating with non-Microsoft platforms through these various WS-* standards.

APPENDIX

■ ■ ■

QuickReturns Ltd.

QuickReturns Ltd. is the sample company we use throughout this book to explain the concepts of the WCF. This appendix contains the high-level architecture that we have created.

The following is a simplified model of an equity trading market and its participants. We have combined some of the roles in order to simplify the perspective. This model is not meant to replicate a real interorganizational structure; it's just a basic representation for demonstration purposes.

The following are the primary participants, along with a general description of what services they provide or expect from other participants:

Asset manager: This is an individual providing portfolio management and issuing trades to buy or sell stock through a market. Asset managers make decisions about what specific securities to buy or sell in order to establish a portfolio that meets their client's needs.

Market maker: This is an individual providing execution and market-making activities on a set of stocks listed on an exchange. Market makers provide orderly market monitoring by maintaining two-sided displayed quotes, ensuring the quote is not inverted in the spread. They provide liquidity needs for investors. They clear and settle transactions through a depository.

Exchange: This is an entity that provides an organized forum for market makers to publish market prices on listed securities. The exchange provides execution services and systems that match, capture, record, and track security transactions among market participants.

Depository/securities processing system: This is an entity that keeps track of open positions for all market participants on the listed securities. Generally, each participant would have their own securities-processing system or subscribe to a corresponding service from another participant. However, for this example, the model is simplified, and the depository provides all the necessary needs.

Market Overview

Figure A–1 shows an overview of how the example stock-trading market works

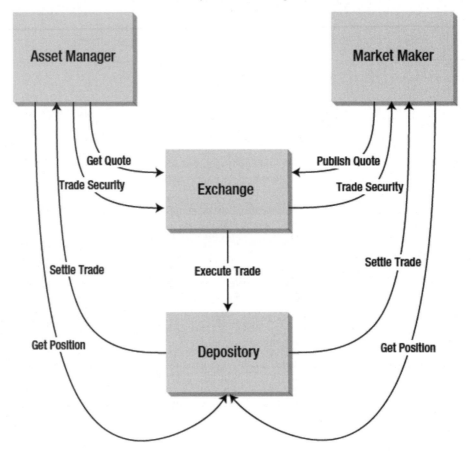

Figure A–1. *Market overview*

Service and Collaboration

The following sections list each entity, along with the primary service it publishes and the primary consumers of that service (in parentheses).

Asset Manager

The following are the specifics of the asset manager.

Settle Trade (Depository)

This is where a participant is notified by the depository that a trade has been settled; this includes the settlement details.

```
public void SettleTrade ( Settlement settlement );
```

Market Maker

The following are the specifics of the market maker.

Trade Security (Exchange)

This is where a participant is notified that another participant has "hit" either a bid or an asking price on a listed security based upon the published quote.

```
public Execution TradeSecurity ( Trade trade );
```

Settle Trade (Depository)

This is where a participant is notified by the depository that a trade has been settled; this includes the settlement details.

```
public void SettleTrade ( Settlement settlement );
```

Exchange

The following are the specifics of the exchange.

Publish Quote (Market Maker)

This is the process where a market maker announces what their bid is and asks for a particular security.

```
public void PublishQuote ( Quote quote );
```

Get Quote (Asset Manager)

This is where an exchange provides the announced bid. We use this to inquire about the listed securities by the participants.

```
public Quote GetQuote ( String ticker );
```

Trade Security (Asset Manager)

This is where a participant chooses to buy or sell, based upon an asking or bid quote, respectively, as published on the exchange.

```
public Execution TradeSecurity ( Trade trade );
```

Depository

The following are the specifics of the depository.

Execute Trade (Exchange)

This is when a trade occurs on an exchange, and the depository is notified in order to update appropriate positions (both cash and security) and provide notification to the respective participants through settlement reporting.

```
public void ExecuteTrade ( Execution execution );
```

Get Position (Asset Manager, Market Maker)

This is where a participant requests the position on either a security or a cash . Positions can be reported in either positive (long) or negative (short) numbers; fractional shares are not allowed.

```
public Position GetPosition ( String ticker );
```

Data Contracts

The following are the data contracts in the application.

Quote

A quote represents what the market is for a given listed security. Table A–1 shows the quote data contract.

Table A–1. Quote Data Contract

Field	Format	Description
Ticker	String	Primary exchange security identifier
Bid	Decimal	The price at which the publisher is willing to buy the security
Ask	Decimal	The price at which the publisher is willing to sell the security
Publisher	String	Identifier of the publisher
UpdateTime	DateTime	Update time in GMT for the published quote

Trade

A trade represents a commitment to buy or sell a set quantity of shares for a specific listed security by a specific publisher. Table A–2 shows the trade data contract.

Table A–2. Trade Data Contract

Field	Format	Description
Ticker	String	Primary exchange security identifier
Type	Character	*B* or *S* for *Buy* or *Sell*
Publisher	String	Identifier of publisher
Participant	String	Identifier of participant
Quoted Price	Decimal	Price from original quote corresponding to either the bid price or the asking price when the trade is a sell or buy type, respectively
Quantity	Integer	Quantity of shares as part of the trade
TradeTime	DateTime	Time stamp in GMT of when the trade was requested using the exchange's clock as the master

Execution

An execution represents a committed exchange of a security among market participants at a set price and quantity. An execution is generally provided as a result of a trade and to the depository for position tracking. Table A–3 shows the execution data contract.

Table A–3. Execution Data Contract

Field	Format	Description
Trade	Trade type	The corresponding trade
Settlement Date	DateTime	The expected settlement date

Settlement

A settlement represents the final update, cash, and position at settlement time (T+1 in our model) on an executed trade between market participants. Table A–4 shows the settlement data contract.

Table A–4. Settlement Data Contract

Field	Format	Description
Execution	Execution type	The corresponding execution type
Status	Enum	Indicator of settlement status: Cleared, Failed, DK (do not know)

Position

A position represents a long or short (+/−) quantity that is registered in a specific market participant's account at the depository. Positions are impacted by execution reports. Table A–5 shows the position data contract.

Table A–5. Position Data Contract

Field	Format	Description
Ticker	String	Primary exchange security identifier
Participant	String	Identifier of participant
Quantity	Integer	Quantity of shares on an account for the market participant
Unsettled Quantity	Integer	Summary quantity of any unsettled trades
Unsettled Trades	Integer	List of unsettled trades encapsulated in execution type array

Index

■ X, Y, Z

You Need the Companion eBook

Your purchase of this book entitles you to buy the companion PDF-version eBook for only $10. Take the weightless companion with you anywhere.

We believe this Apress title will prove so indispensable that you'll want to carry it with you everywhere, which is why we are offering the companion eBook (in PDF format) for $10 to customers who purchase this book now. Convenient and fully searchable, the PDF version of any content-rich, page-heavy Apress book makes a valuable addition to your programming library. You can easily find and copy code—or perform examples by quickly toggling between instructions and the application. Even simultaneously tackling a donut, diet soda, and complex code becomes simplified with hands-free eBooks!

Once you purchase your book, getting the $10 companion eBook is simple:

❶ Visit **www.apress.com/promo/tendollars/**.

❷ Complete a basic registration form to receive a randomly generated question about this title.

❸ Answer the question correctly in 60 seconds, and you will receive a promotional code to redeem for the $10.00 eBook.

eBookshop

Apress®
THE EXPERT'S VOICE™

233 Spring Street, New York, NY 10013

Offer valid through 8/11.